budgetbooks

BROADWAY SONGS

EASY PIANO

ISBN 0-634-08066-0

7777 W. BLUEMOUND RD. P.O. BOX 13819 MILWAUKEE, WI 53213

For all works contained herein:
Unauthorized copying, arranging, adapting, recording or public performance is an infringement of copyright.
Infringers are liable under the law.

Visit Hal Leonard Online at
www.halleonard.com

CONTENTS

4	All Good Gifts *Godspell*	78	Gus: The Theatre Cat *Cats*
8	All the Things You Are *Very Warm for May*	82	Guys and Dolls *Guys and Dolls*
14	Alone at the Drive-In Movie *Grease*	90	I Ain't Down Yet *The Unsinkable Molly Brown*
18	Along Came Bialy *The Producers*	94	I Don't Know How to Love Him *Jesus Christ Superstar*
24	And All That Jazz *Chicago*	85	I Dreamed a Dream *Les Misérables*
28	Any Dream Will Do *Joseph and the Amazing Technicolor® Dreamcoat*	98	I Enjoy Being a Girl *Flower Drum Song*
32	Anything You Can Do *Annie Get Your Gun*	102	I Have Dreamed *The King and I*
36	As Long As He Needs Me *Oliver!*	106	I Will Never Leave You *Side Show*
11	Baubles, Bangles and Beads *Kismet*	112	I've Grown Accustomed to Her Face *My Fair Lady*
38	Being Alive *Company*	115	If He Walked into My Life *Mame*
42	The Best of Times *La Cage Aux Folles*	118	If I Can't Love Her *Beauty and the Beast: The Broadway Musical*
50	Cabaret *Cabaret*	126	The Impossible Dream (The Quest) *Man of La Mancha*
60	A Cock-Eyed Optimist *South Pacific*	130	Kansas City *Oklahoma!*
64	Consider Yourself *Oliver!*	134	Leaning on a Lamp Post *Me and My Girl*
45	Everything's Coming Up Roses *Gypsy*	142	Love Changes Everything *Aspects of Love*
68	Falling in Love with Love *The Boys from Syracuse*	139	Love, Look Away *Flower Drum Song*
74	Footloose *Footloose*	148	Mama, I'm a Big Girl Now *Hairspray*
71	Getting to Know You *The King and I*	155	Mame *Mame*

158	Maybe This Time *Cabaret*	231	Sun and Moon *Miss Saigon*
162	Memory *Cats*	236	The Surrey with the Fringe on Top *Oklahoma!*
166	Movin' Out (Anthony's Song) *Movin' Out*	244	The Sweetest Sounds *No Strings*
170	My Cup Runneth Over *I Do! I Do!*	241	Ten Cents a Dance *Simple Simon*
178	No Other Love *Me and Juliet*	248	There's a Small Hotel *On Your Toes*
173	Oklahoma *Oklahoma!*	252	There's No Business Like Show Business *Annie Get Your Gun*
182	Ol' Man River *Show Boat*	256	This Is the Moment *Jekyll & Hyde*
186	On Broadway *Smokey Joe's Cafe*	260	Thoroughly Modern Millie *Thoroughly Modern Millie*
188	One *A Chorus Line*	264	Till There Was You *The Music Man*
194	People *Funny Girl*	266	Turn Back, O Man *Godspell*
202	The Rain in Spain *My Fair Lady*	272	Who Will Love Me As I Am? *Side Show*
197	River in the Rain *Big River*	277	Wish You Were Here *Wish You Were Here*
206	So in Love *Kiss Me, Kate*	280	With a Song in My Heart *Spring Is Here*
214	Some Enchanted Evening *South Pacific*	286	With One Look *Sunset Boulevard*
218	Someone Like You *Jekyll & Hyde*	292	Without You *Rent*
211	The Sound of Music *The Sound of Music*	283	You'll Never Walk Alone *Carousel*
222	Stayin' Alive *Saturday Night Fever*	298	Younger Than Springtime *South Pacific*
226	Summer Nights *Grease*		

ALL GOOD GIFTS
from the Musical GODSPELL

Words and Music by
STEPHEN SCHWARTZ

Copyright © 1971 by Range Road Music Inc., Quartet Music, Inc. and New Cadenza Music Corporation
Copyright Renewed
International Copyright Secured All Rights Reserved
Used by Permission

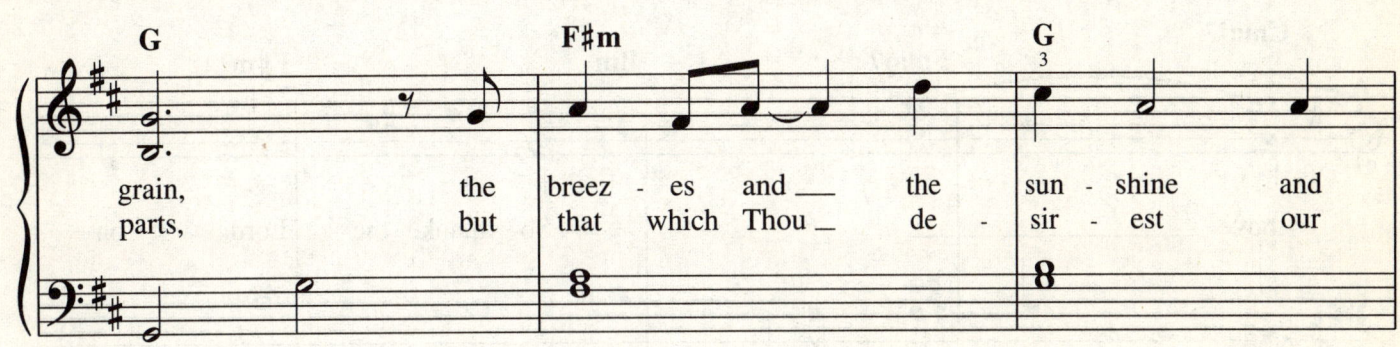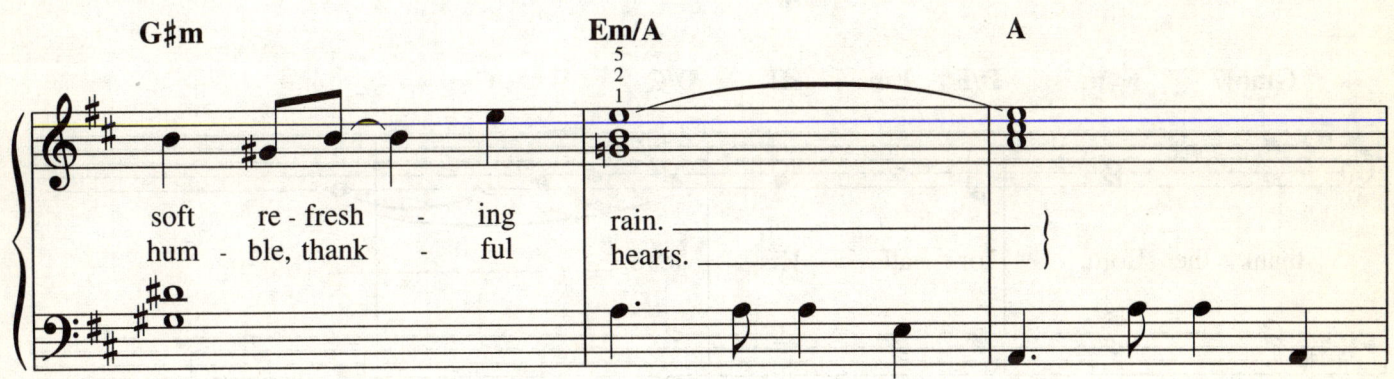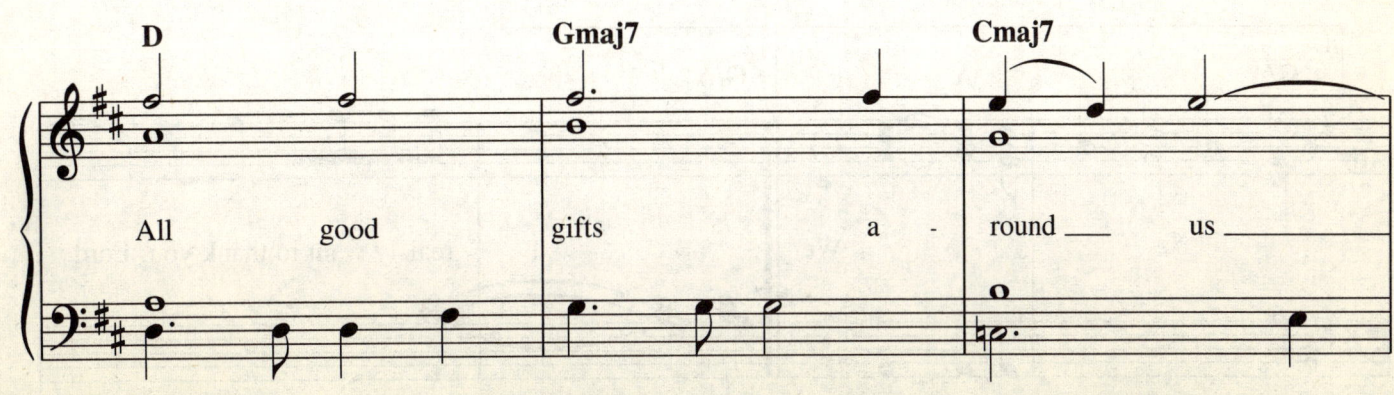

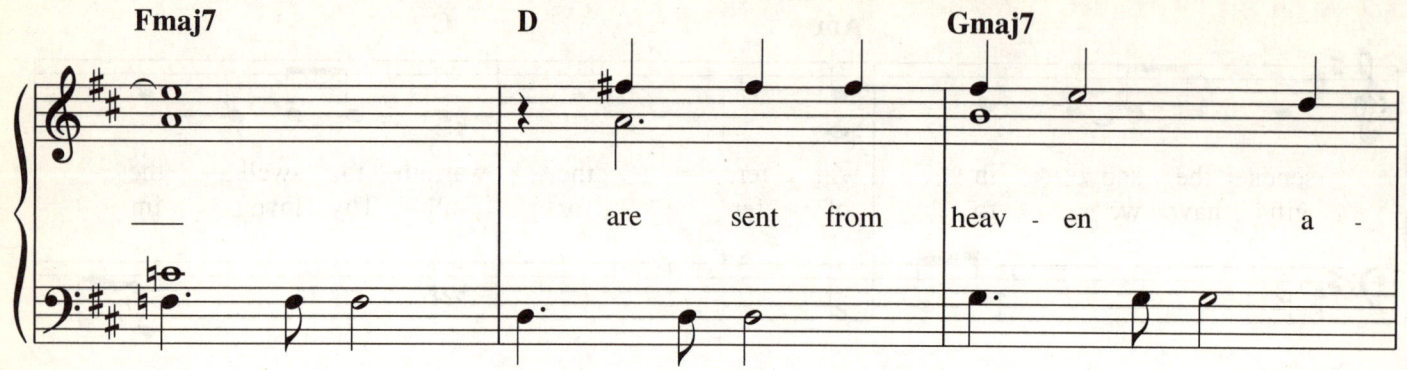

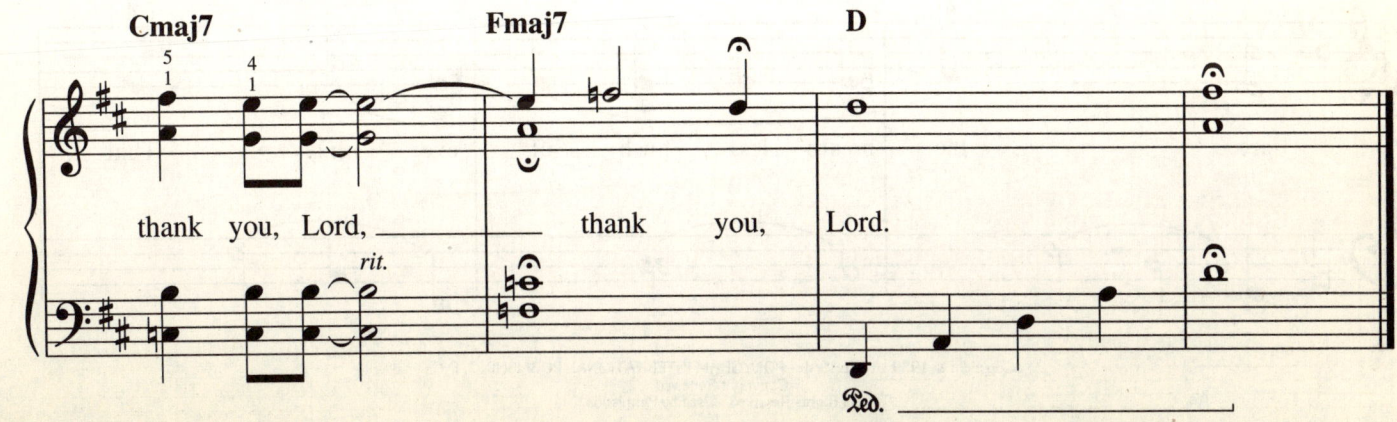

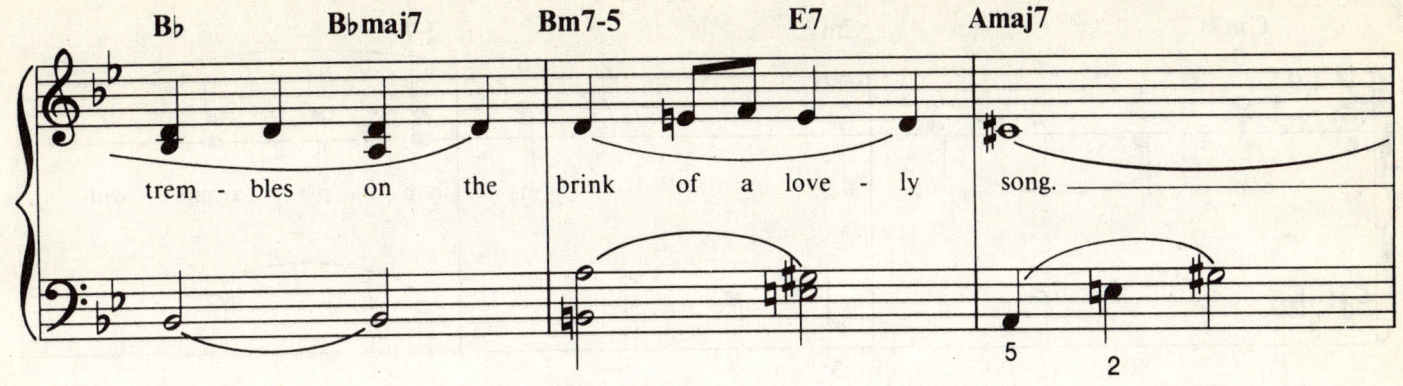
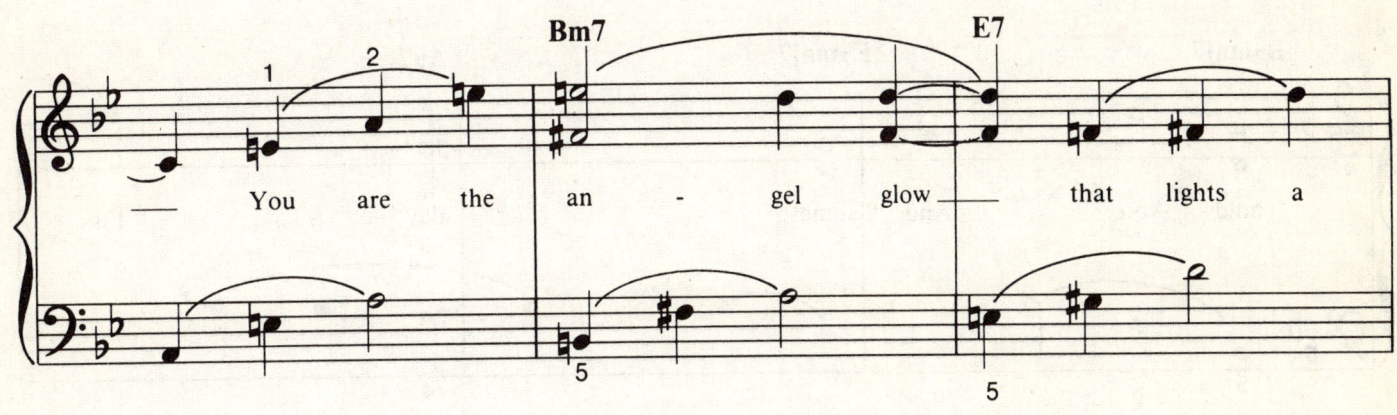

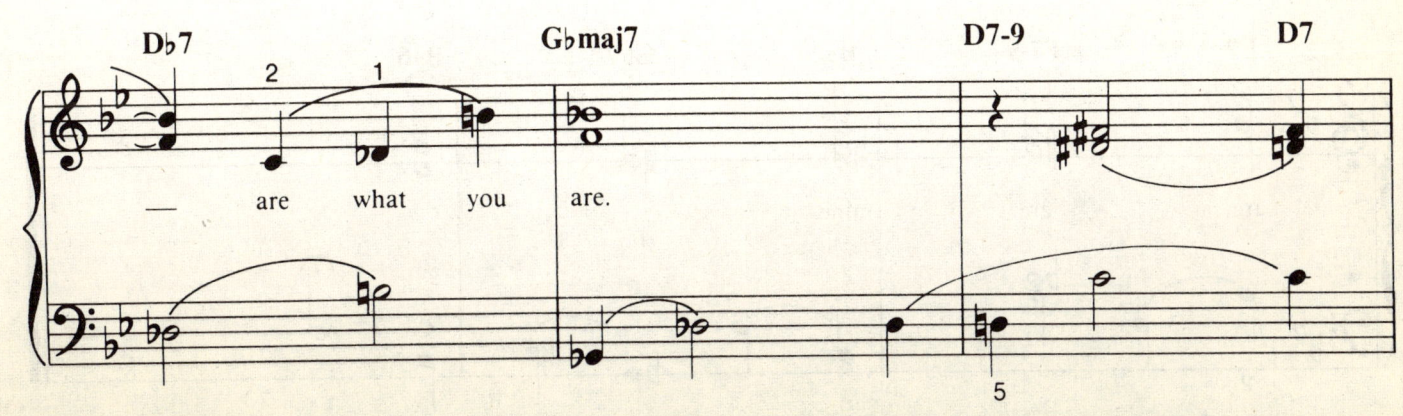

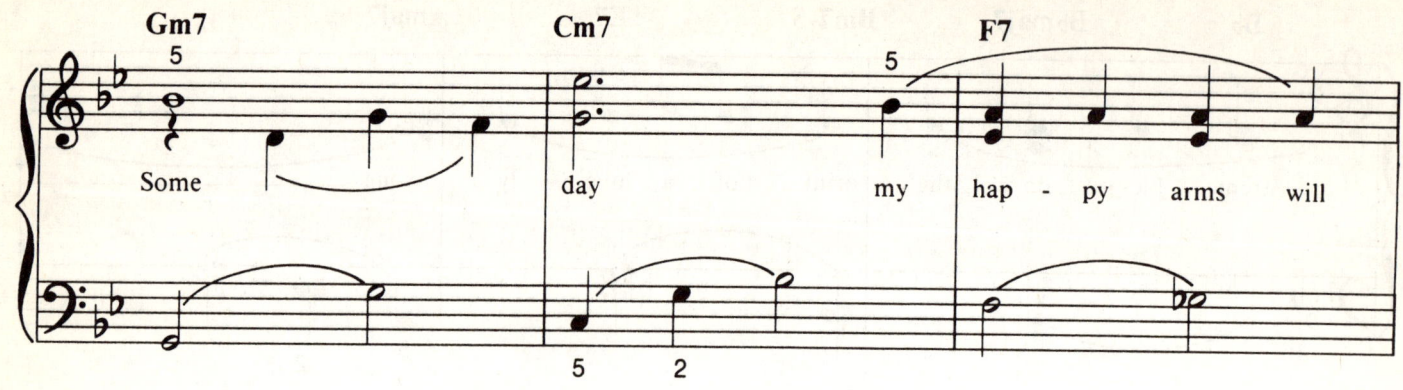
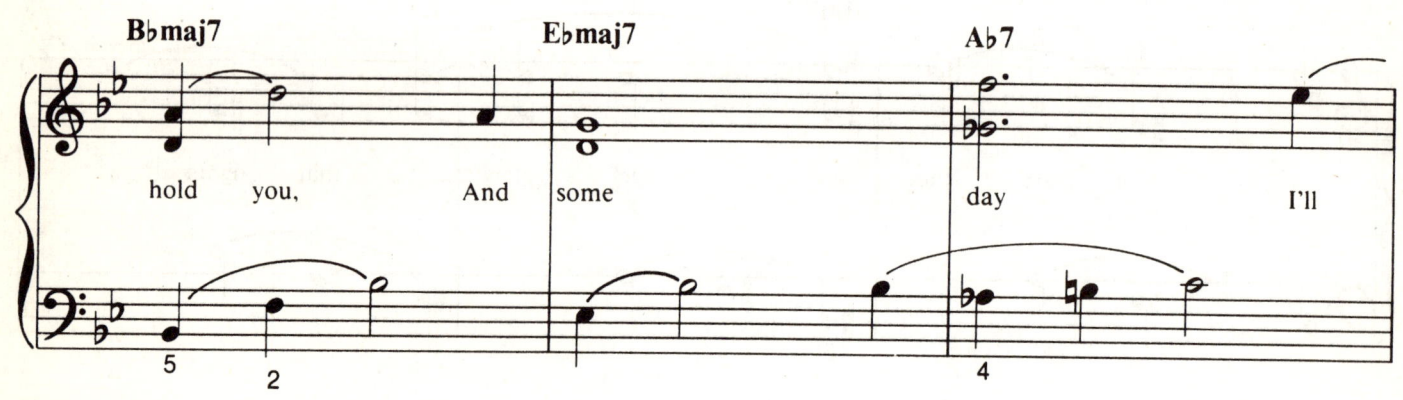
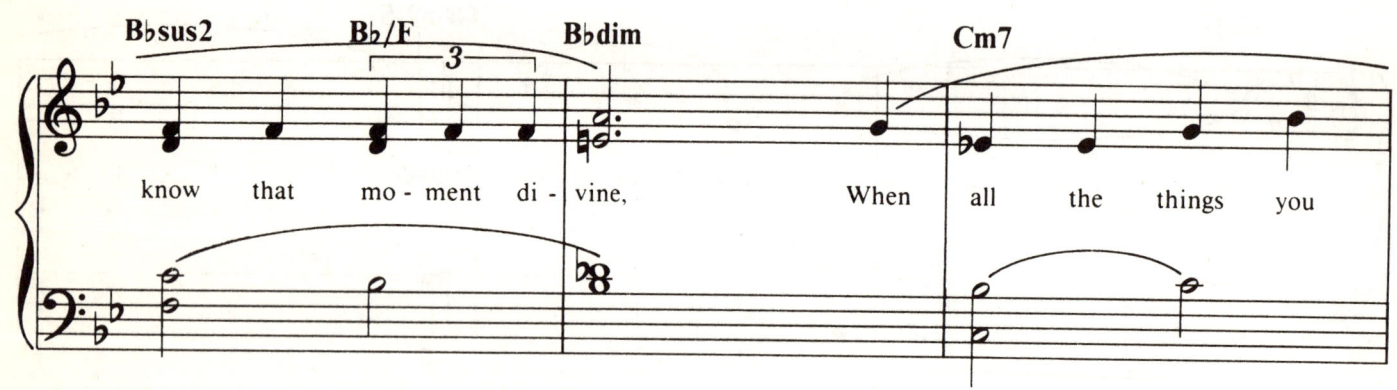

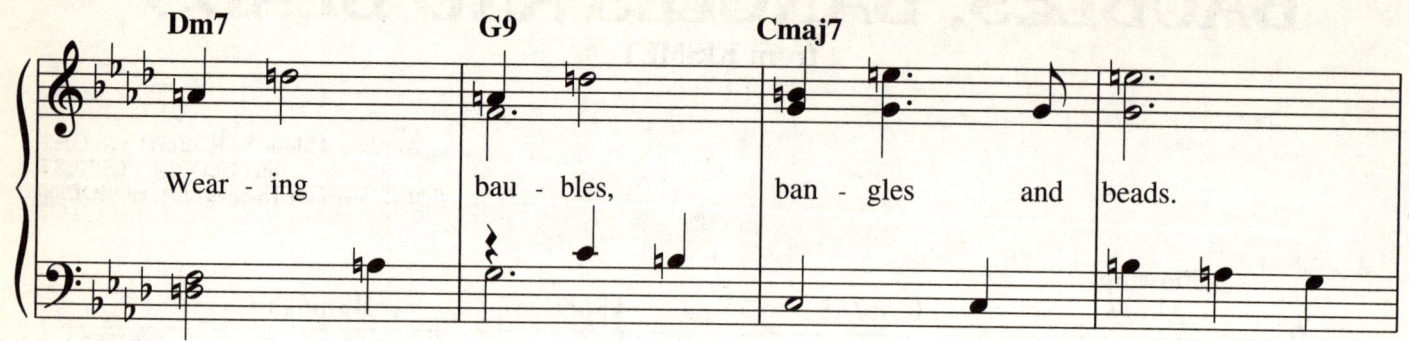
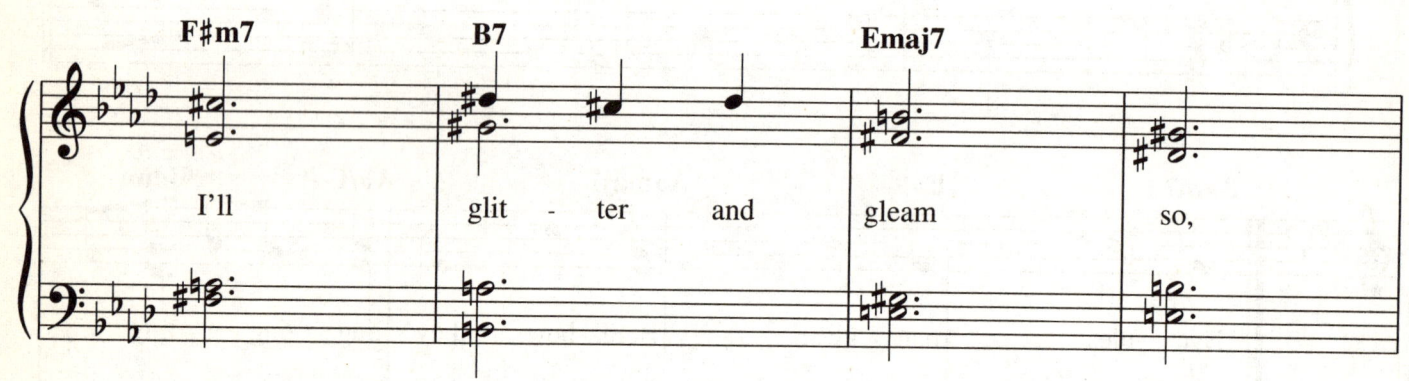
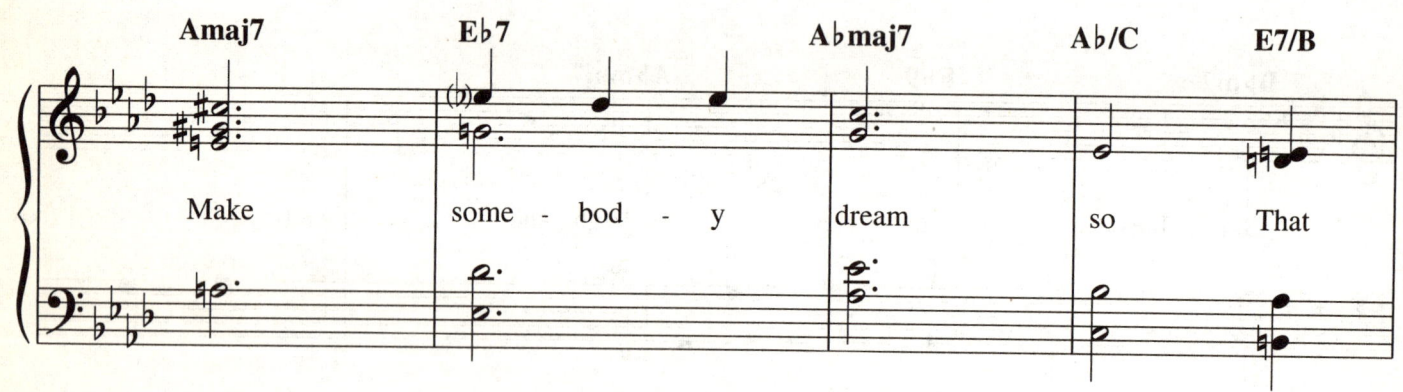
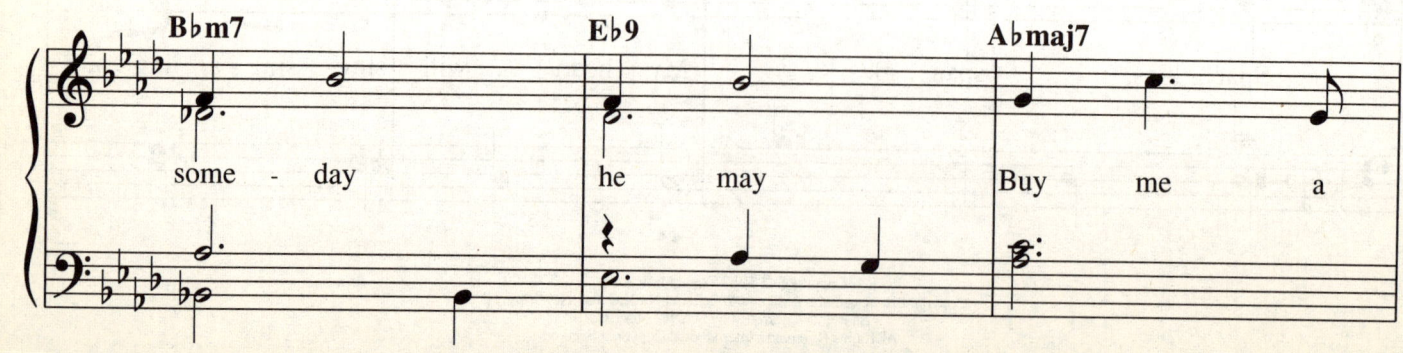

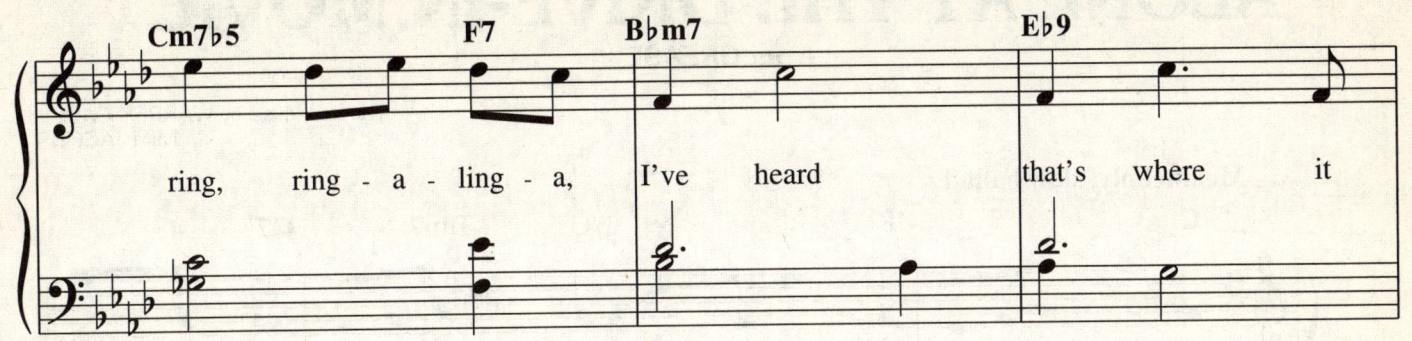

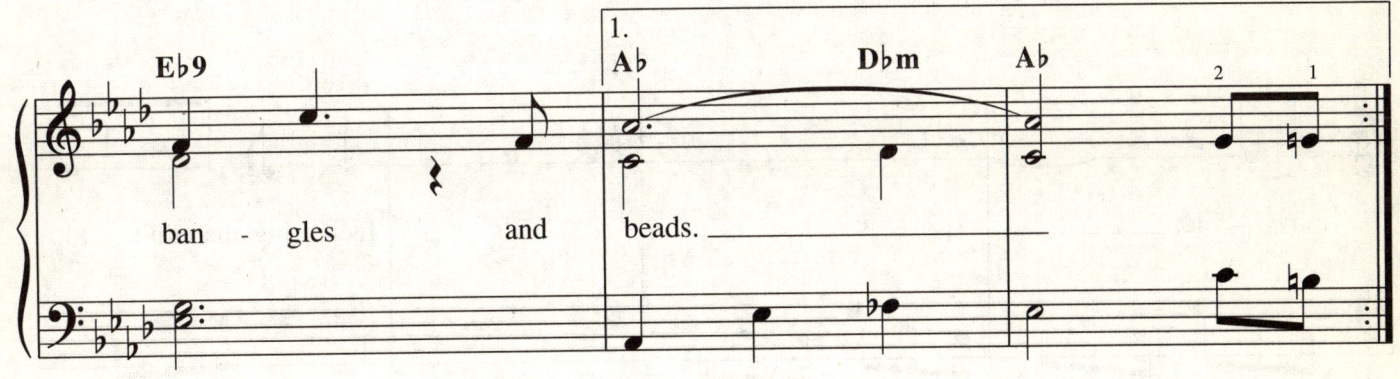

ALONE AT THE DRIVE-IN MOVIE

from GREASE

Lyric and Music by WARREN CASEY
and JIM JACOBS

© 1971, 1972 WARREN CASEY and JIM JACOBS
© Renewed 1999, 2000 JIM JACOBS and THE ESTATE OF WARREN CASEY
All Rights Administered by EDWIN H. MORRIS & COMPANY, A Division of MPL Music Publishing, Inc.
All Rights Reserved

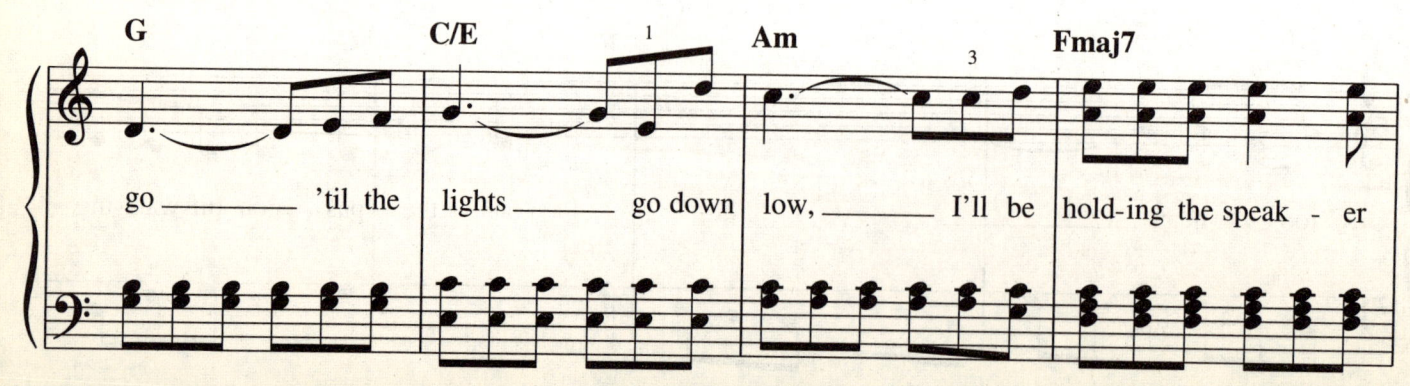

ALONG CAME BIALY
from THE PRODUCERS

Music and Lyrics by
MEL BROOKS

Copyright © 2000 Mel Brooks Music (BMI)
All Rights Reserved   Used by Permission

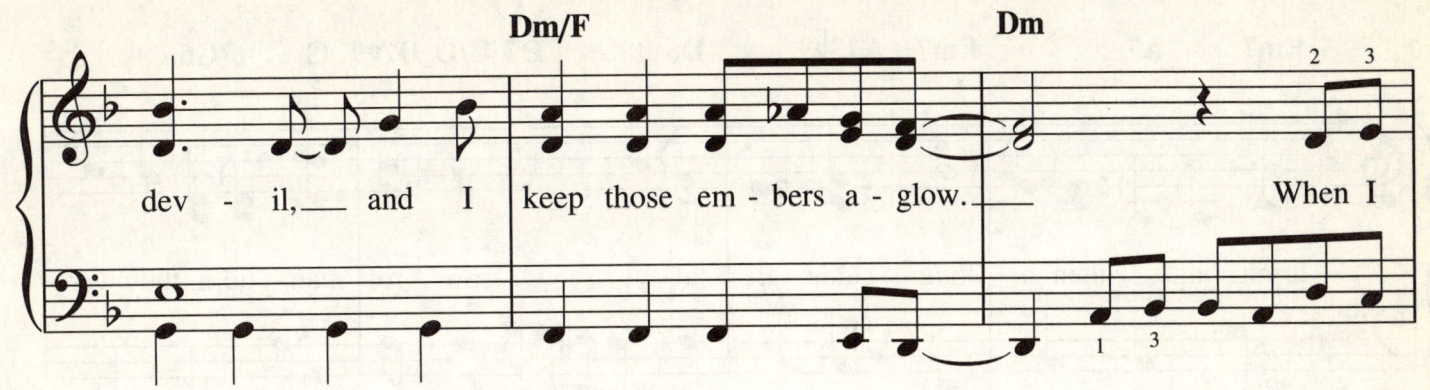
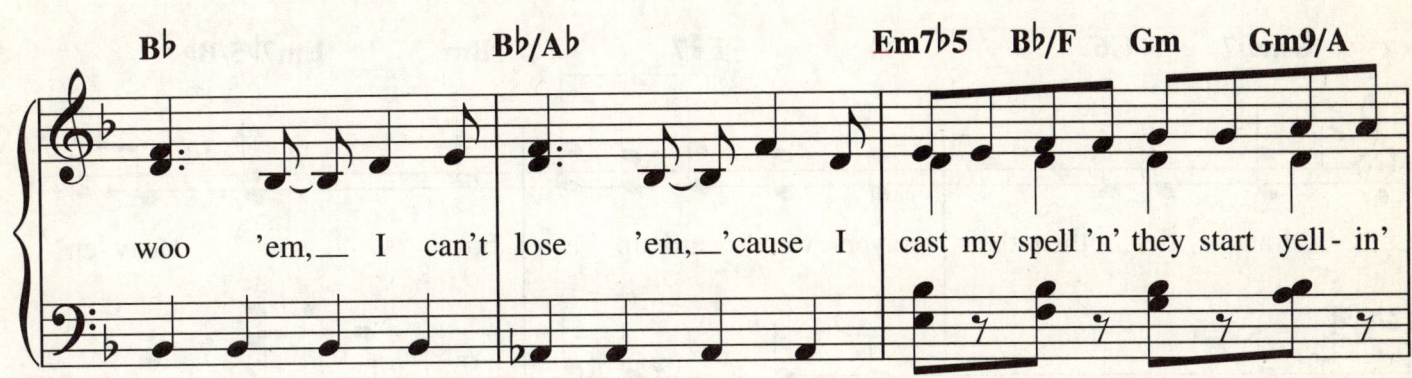

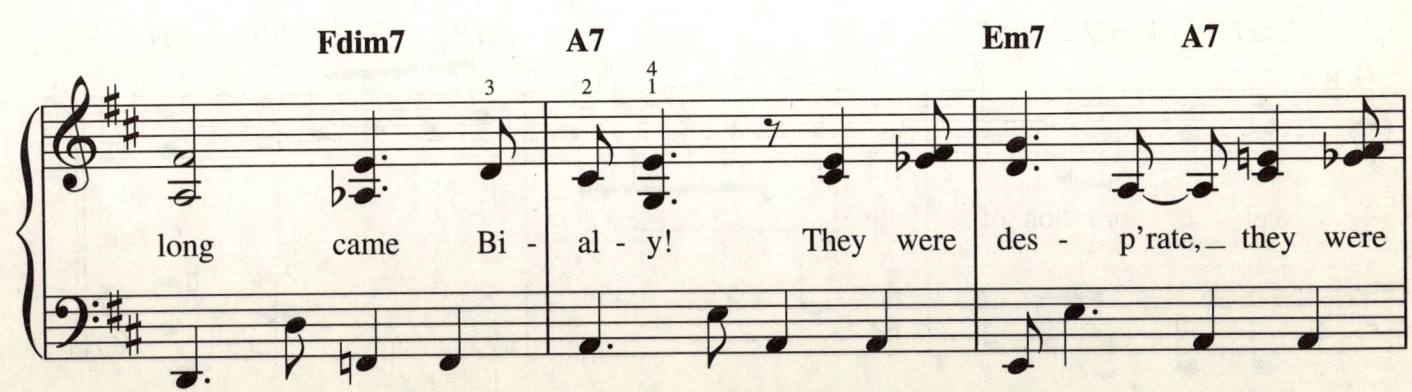

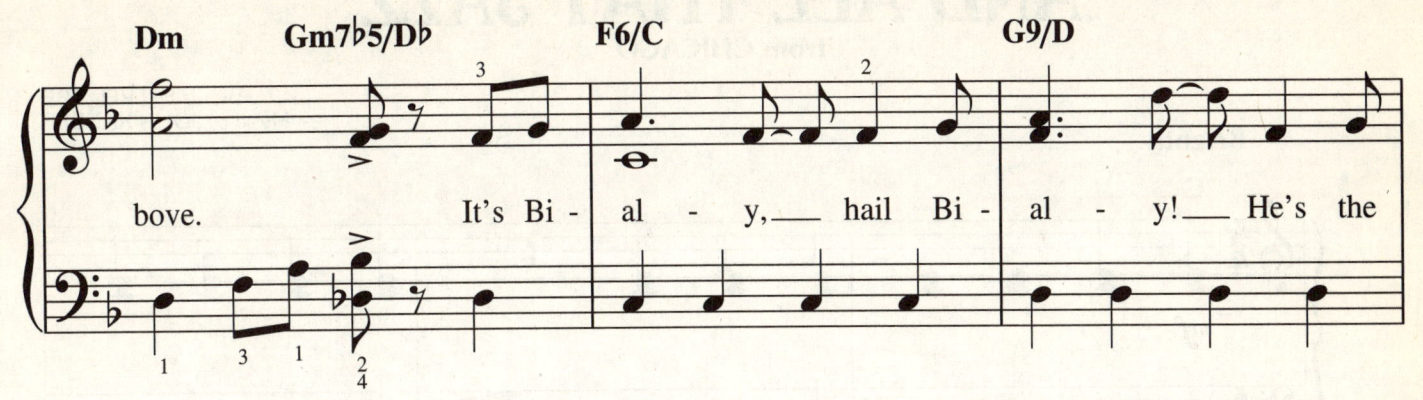
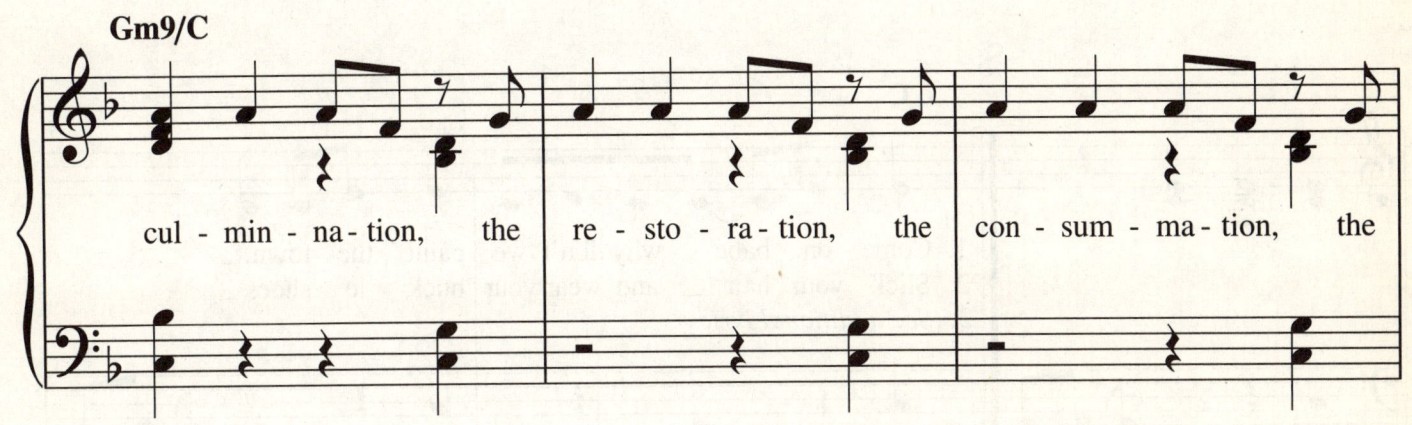
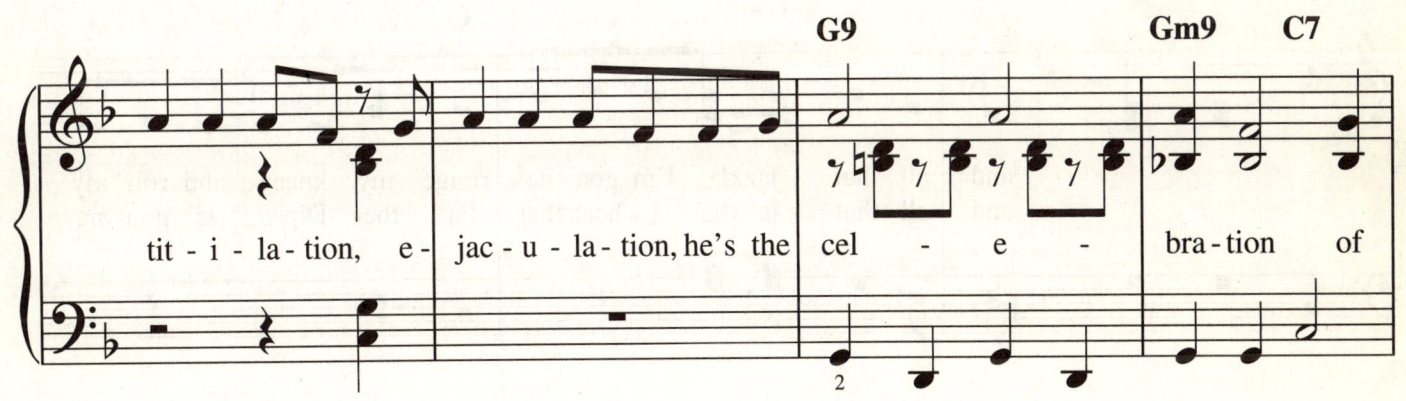

G7
Ab7
Start the car, I know a whoop-ee spot where the gin is cold but the pi-
Hold on, hon, we're gon-na bun-ny hug, 'bought some as-pi-rin down at U-
C
Gm6/Bb
A7
To Coda
an-o's hot. It's just a nois-y hall where there's a night-ly brawl and
nit-ed Drug. In case we shake a-part and want a brand new start and
Ab7
G7
1.
C
all that jazz!
all that
2.
C
A7
D
jazz!
Oh,

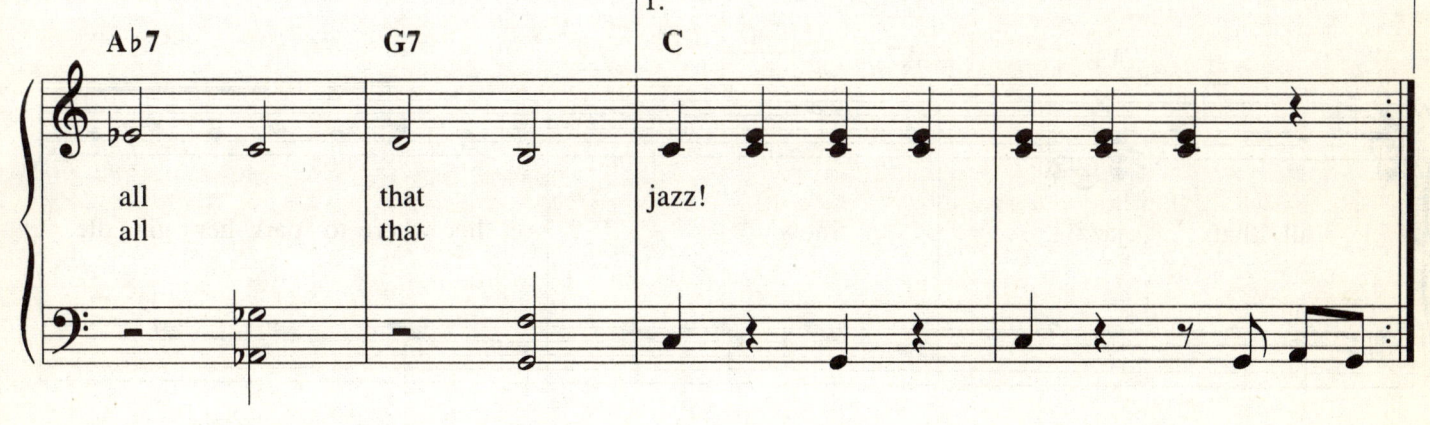

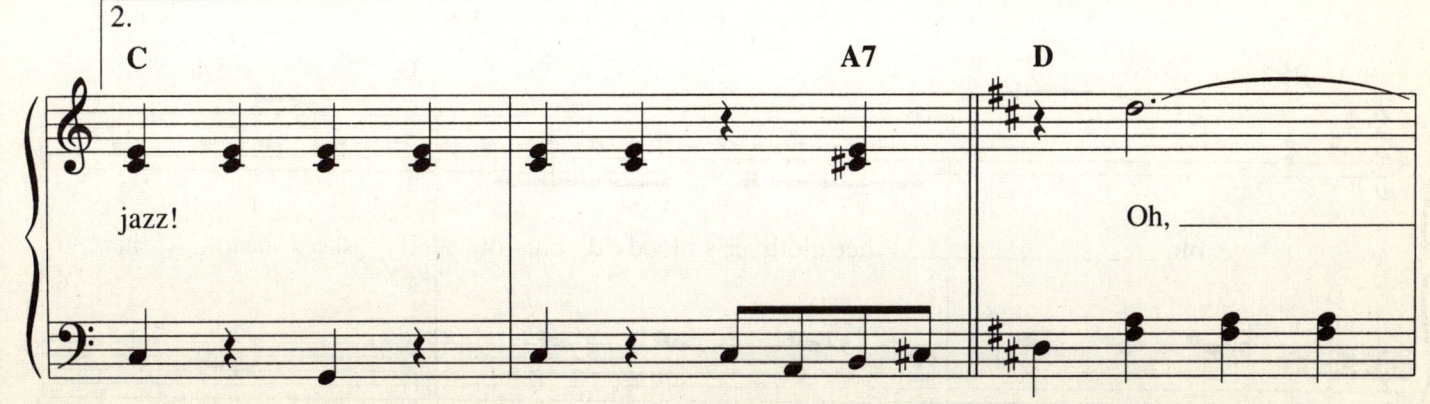

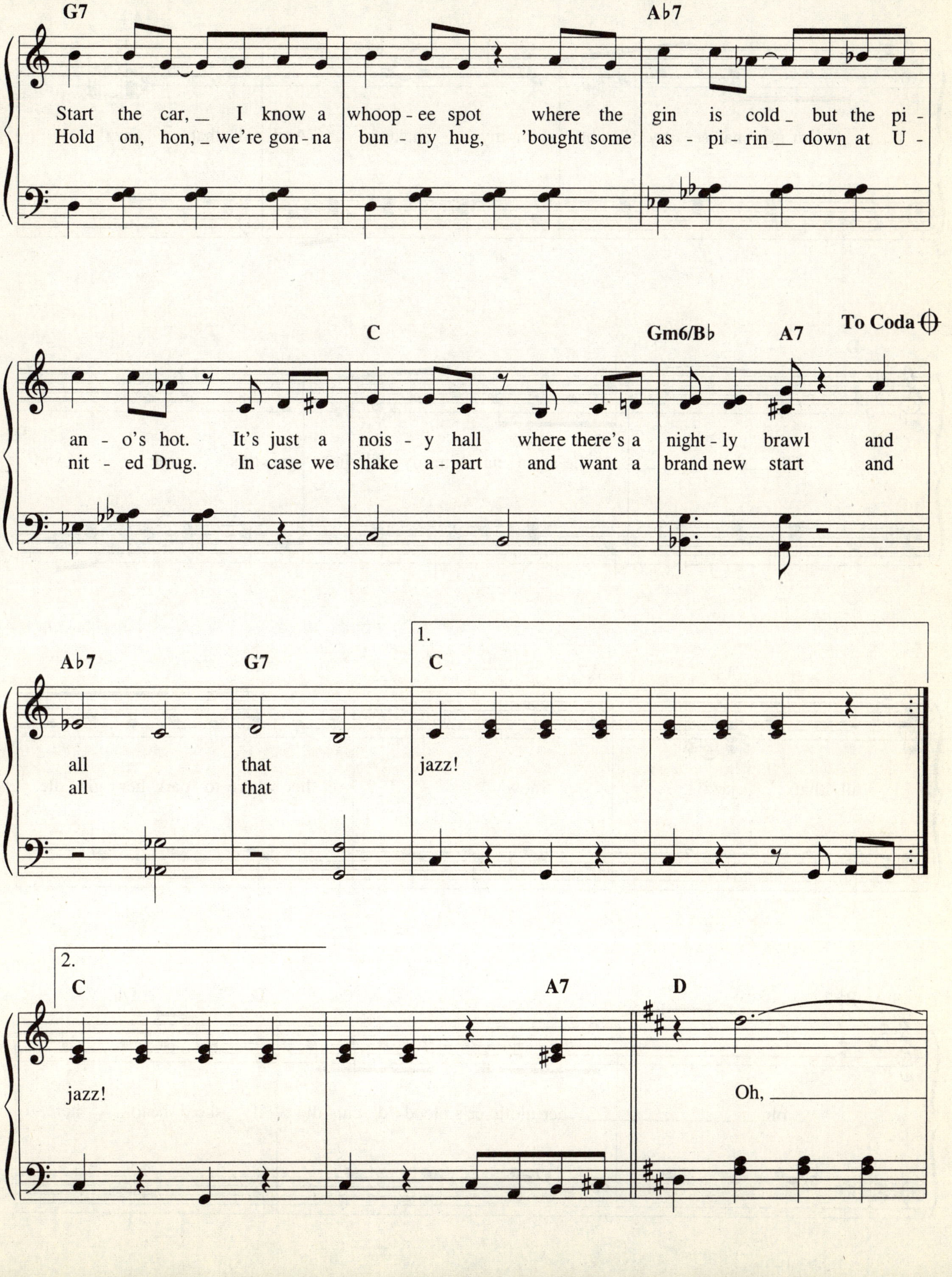

Additional Lyrics

3. Find a flask, we're playing fast and loose
And all that jazz!
Right up here is where I store the juice
And all that jazz!

Come on, babe, we're gonna brush the sky.
I betcha Lucky Lindy never flew so high,
'Cause in the stratosphere how could he lend an ear to
All that jazz!

ANY DREAM WILL DO
from JOSEPH AND THE AMAZING TECHNICOLOR® DREAMCOAT

Music by ANDREW LLOYD WEBBER
Lyrics by TIM RICE

I closed my eyes, drew back the
coat with gol-den

cur - tain, to see for cer - tain
lin - ing, bright col - ours shin - ing,

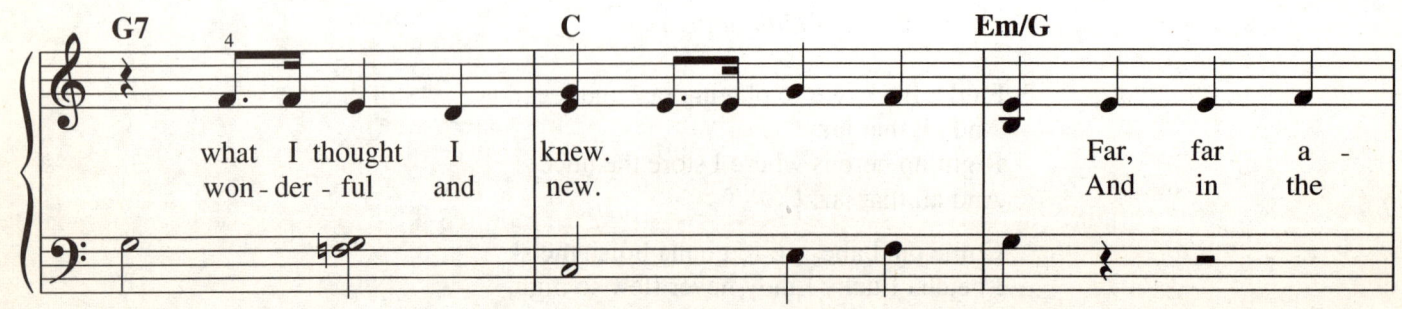

what I thought I knew. Far, far a-
won - der - ful and new. And in the

© Copyright 1969 The Really Useful Group Ltd.
Copyright Renewed
International Copyright Secured   All Rights Reserved

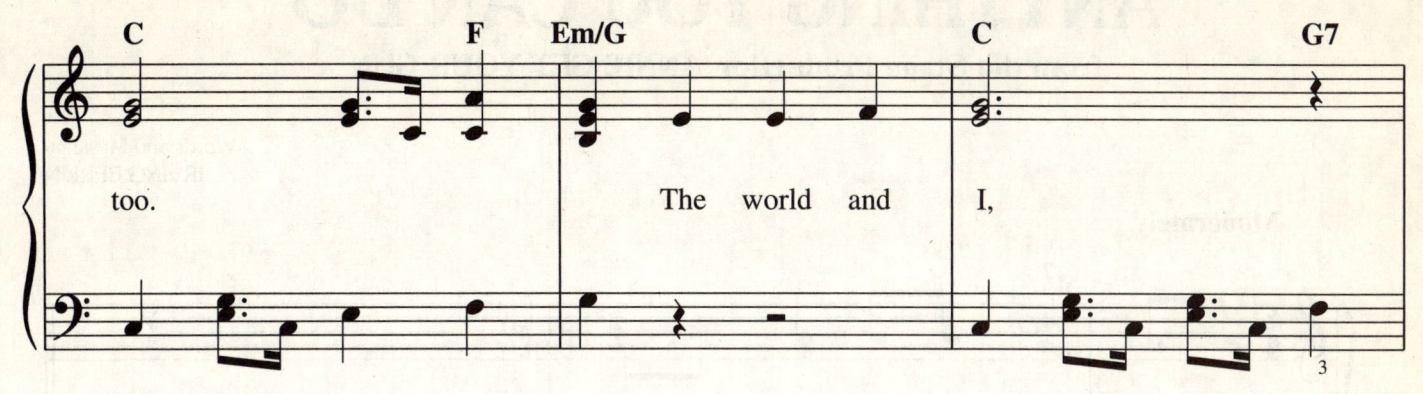

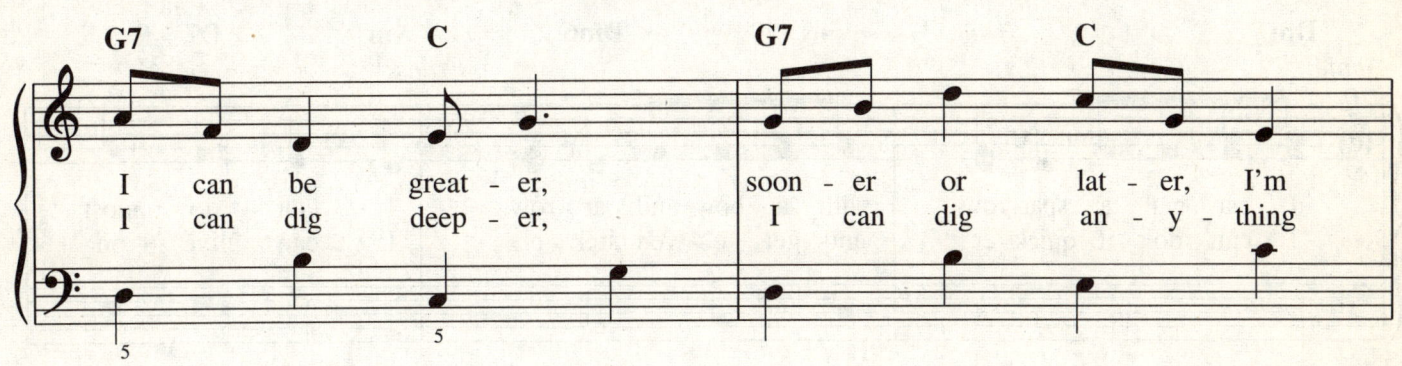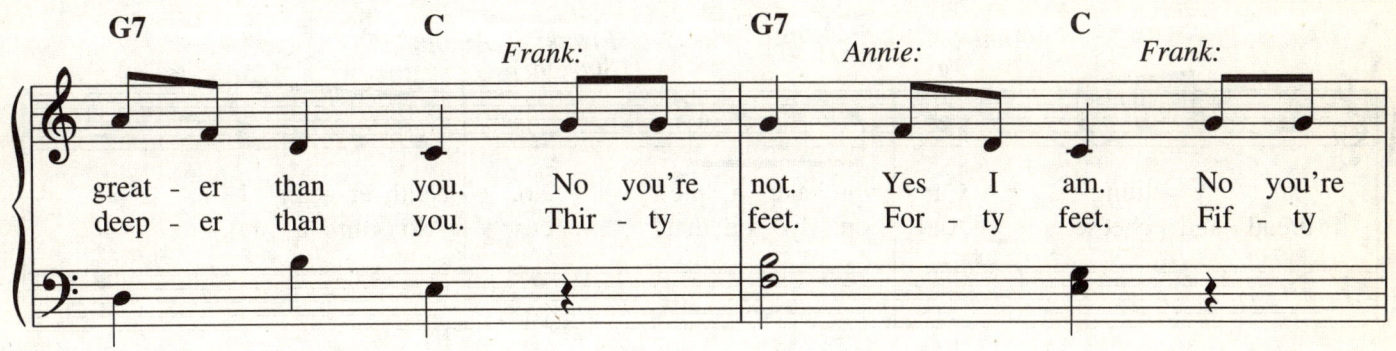

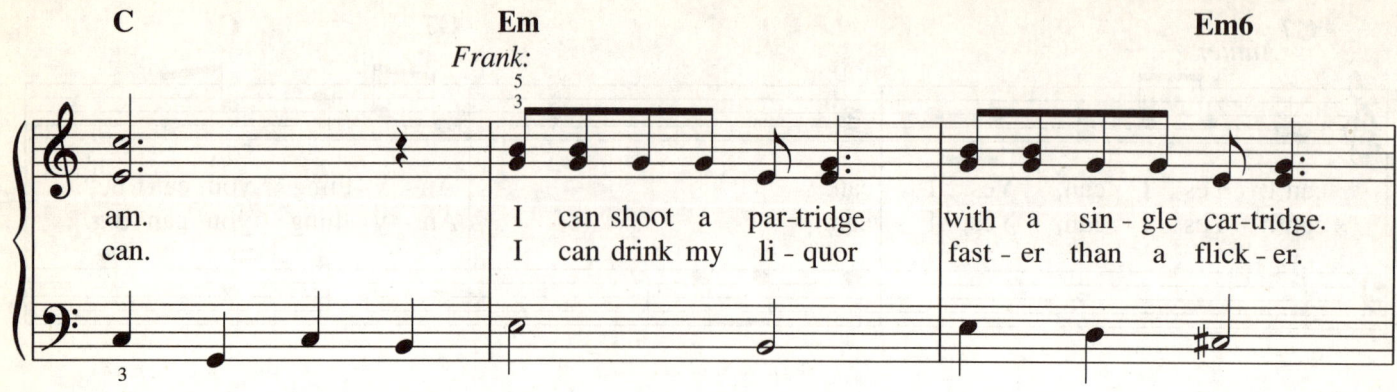

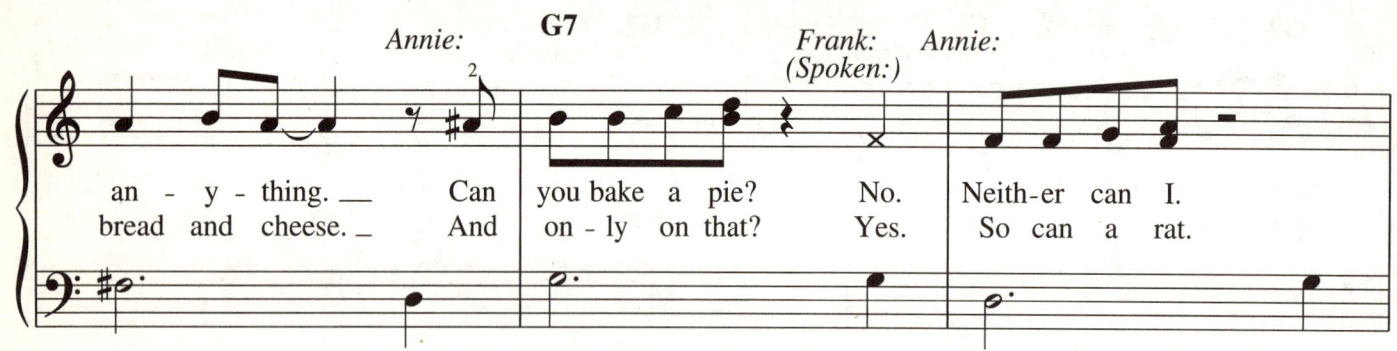
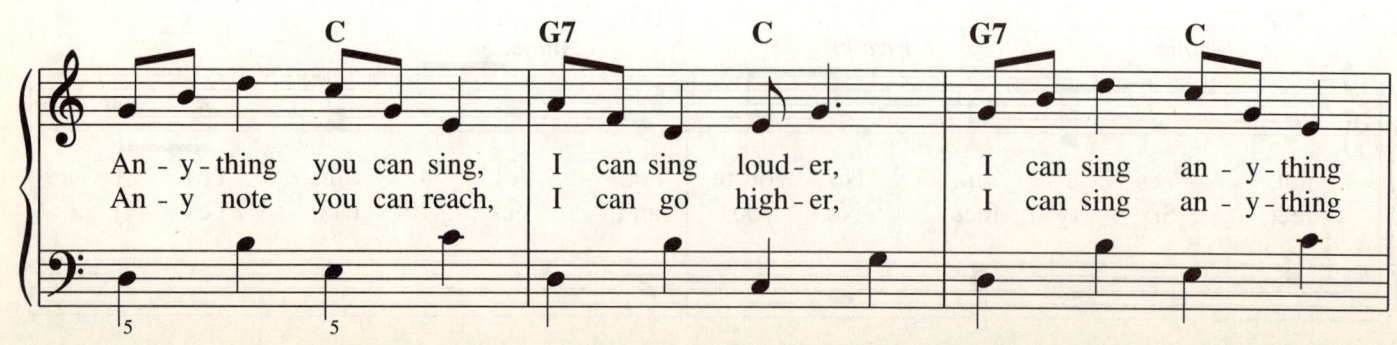

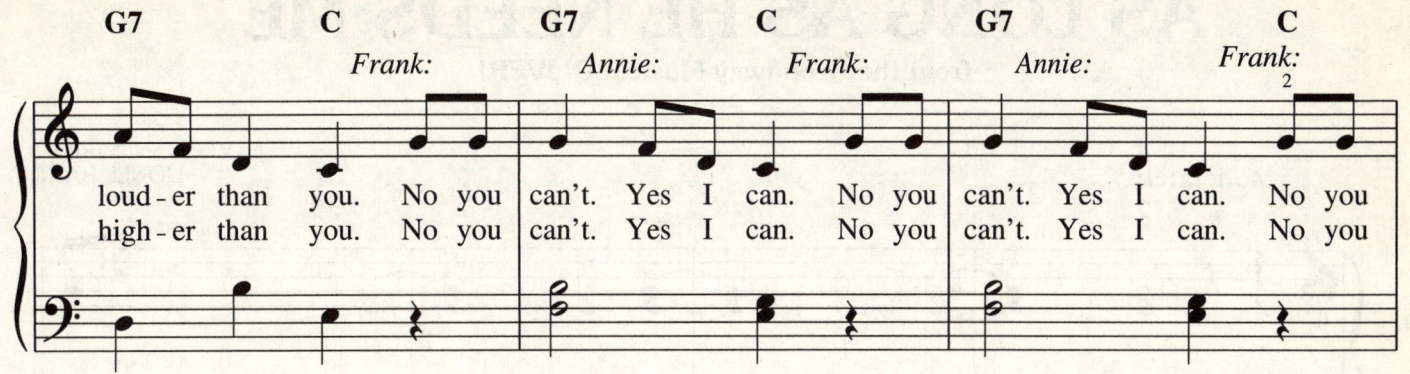

Additional Lyrics

Annie: Anyone you can lick,
I can lick faster,
I can lick anyone faster than you.

Frank: With your fist

Annie: With my feet

Frank: With your feet

Annie: With an axe

Frank: No you can't.

Annie: Yes I can... Yes I can.
Any school where you went,
I could be master,
I could be master much faster than you.

Frank: Can you spell?

Annie: No I can't.

Frank: Can you add?

Annie: No I can't.

Frank: Can you teach?

Annie: Yes I can, Yes I can.

Frank: I could be a racer quite a steeple chaser.

Annie: I can jump a hurdle even with my girdle.

Frank: I can open any safe.

Annie: Without being caught?

Frank: (Spoken:) Yes.

Annie: That's what I thought.
Any note you can hold,
I can hold longer,
I can hold any note longer than you.

Frank: No you can't.

Annie: Yes I can.

Frank: No you can't.

Annie: Yes I can.

Frank: No you can't.

Annie: Yes I can, Yes I can.

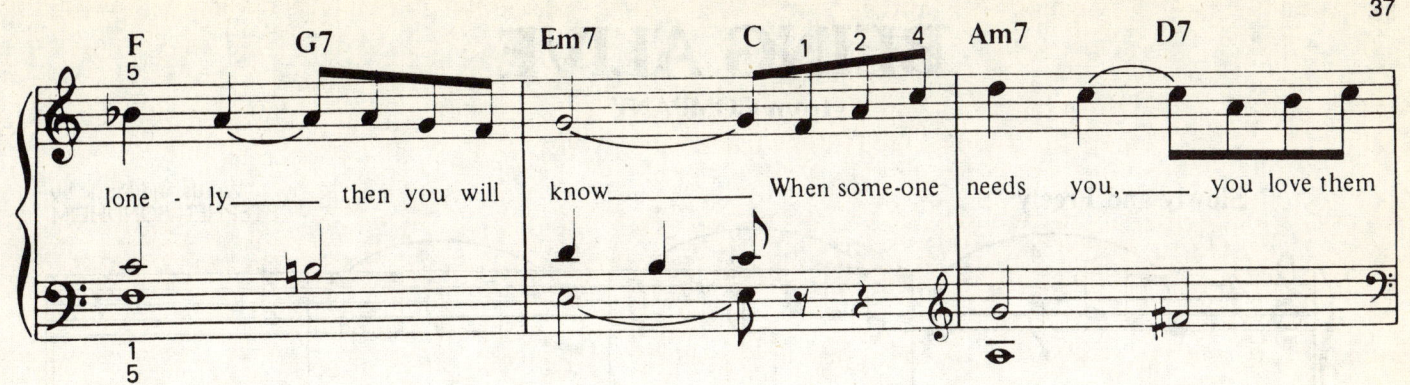
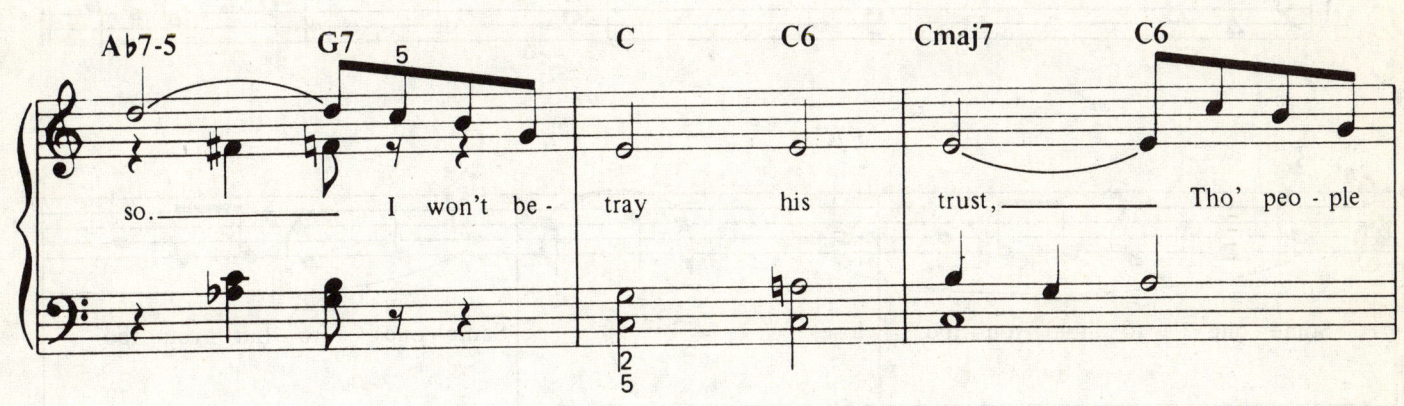
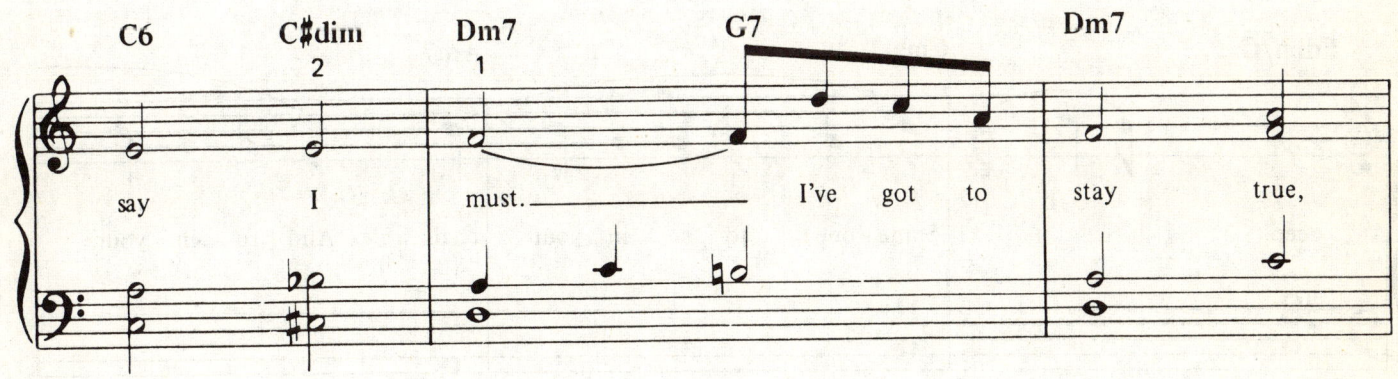
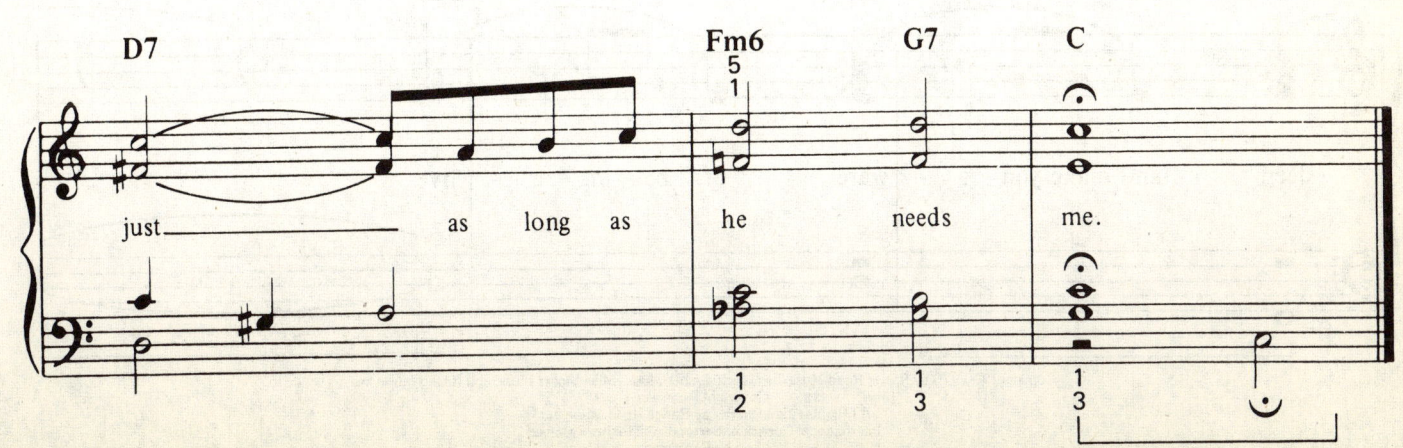

BEING ALIVE
from COMPANY

Words and Music by
STEPHEN SONDHEIM

Slowly and Freely

Some-one to hold you too close, Some-one to hurt you too deep, Some-one to sit in your chair And ru-in your

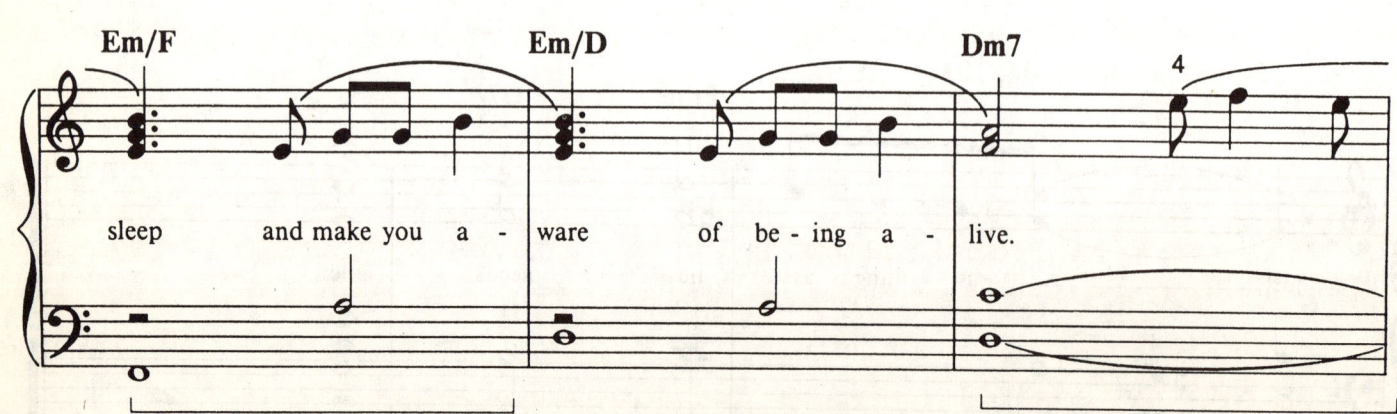

sleep and make you a-ware of be-ing a-live.

Copyright © 1970 by Range Road Music Inc., Jerry Leiber Music, Mike Stoller Music and Rilting Music Inc.
Copyright Renewed
All Rights Administered by Range Road Music Inc.
International Copyright Secured   All Rights Reserved
Used by Permission

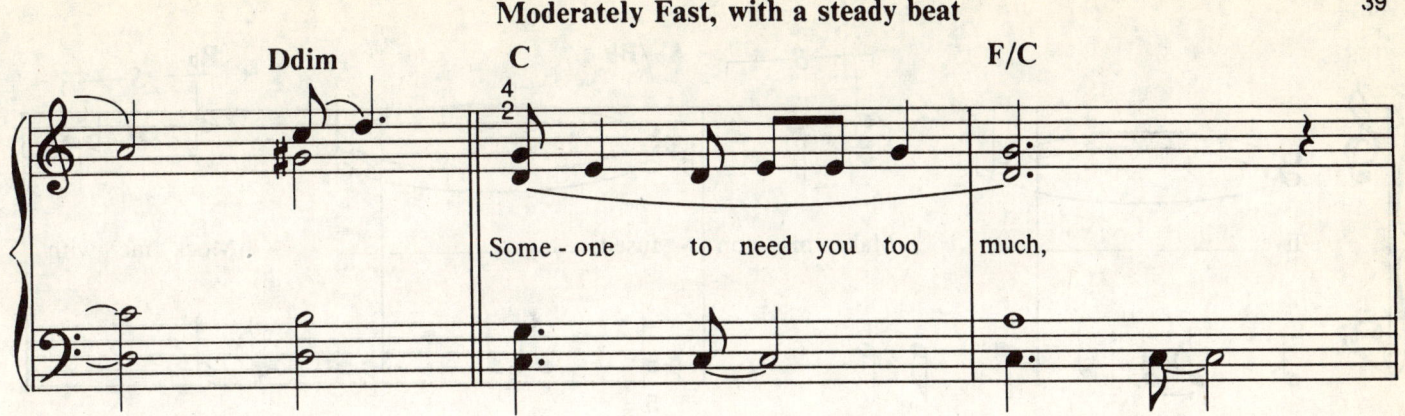
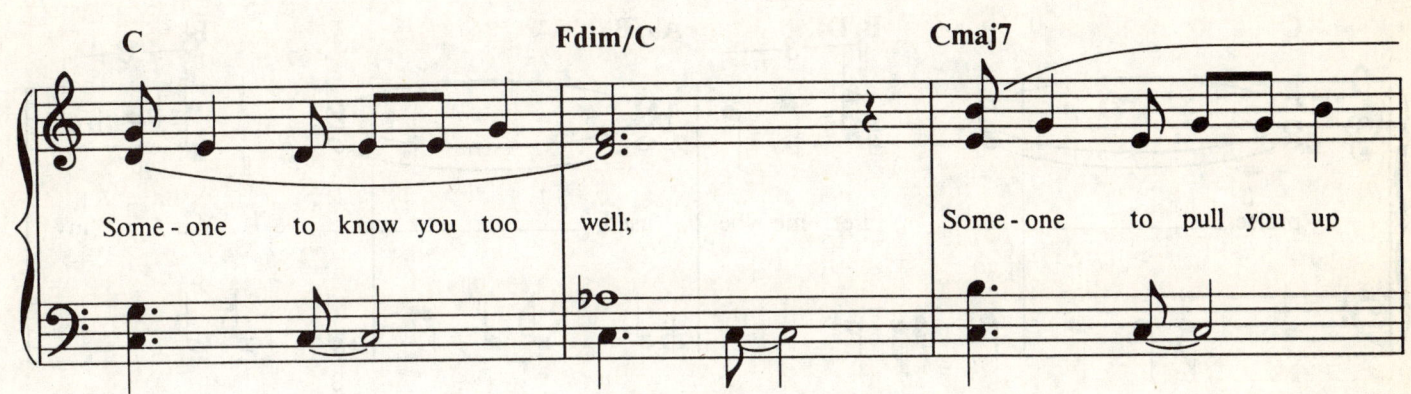

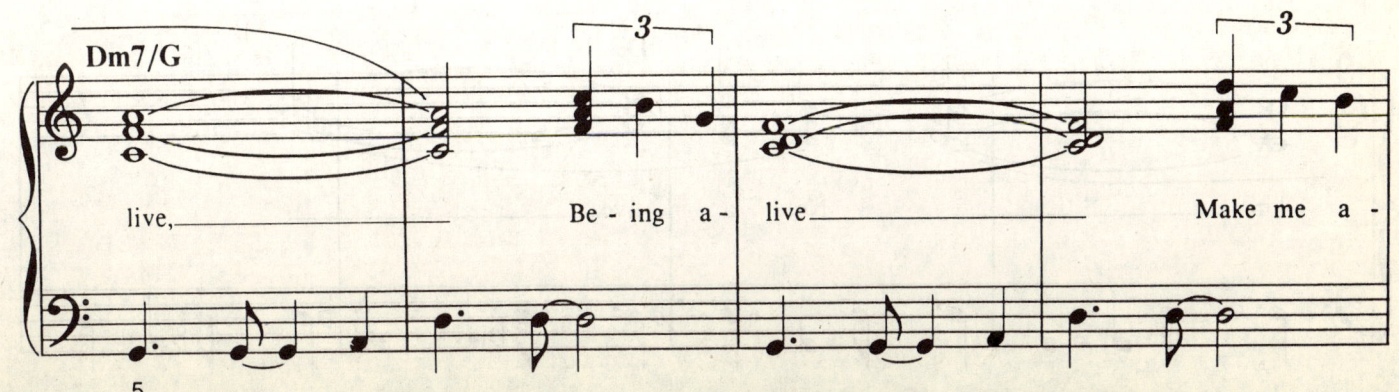

40

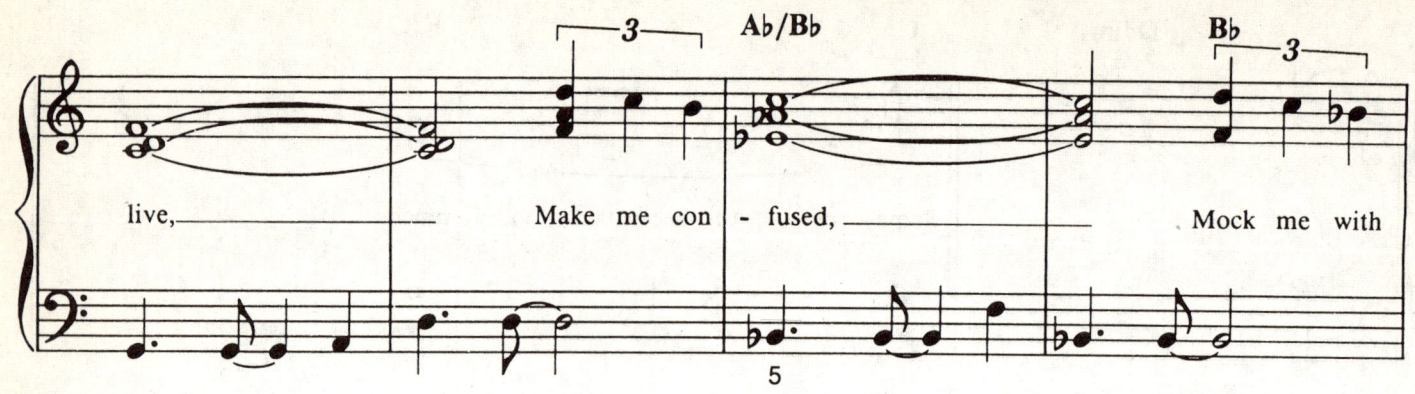

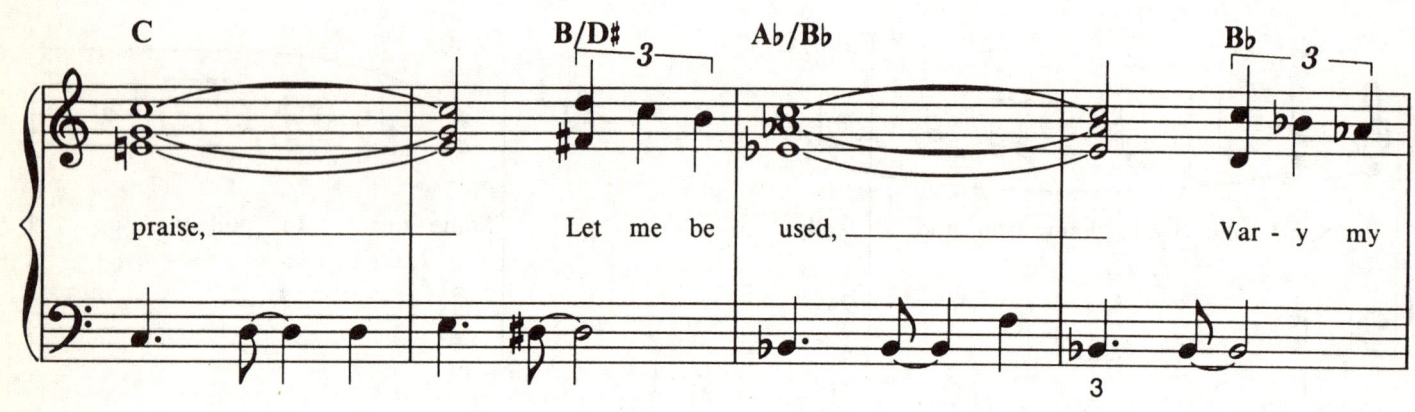

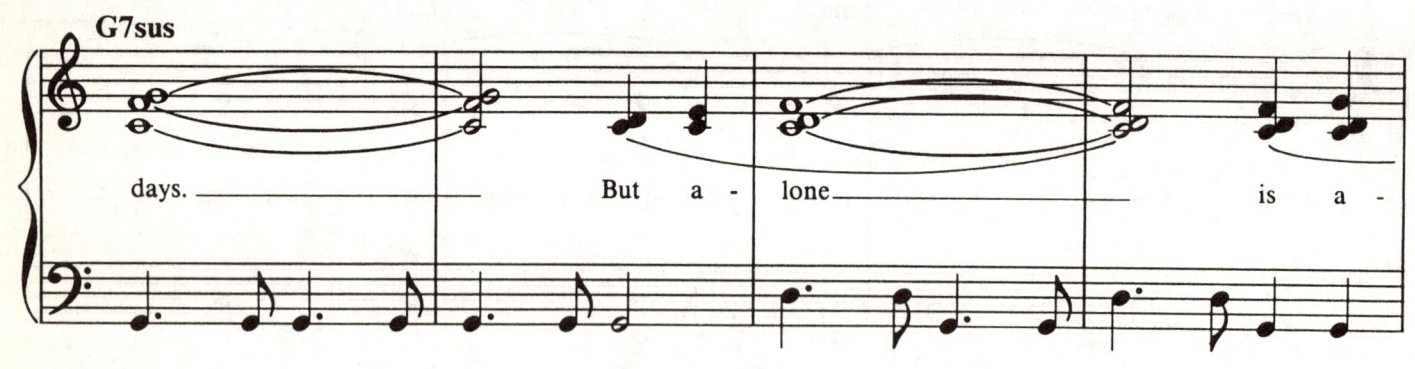

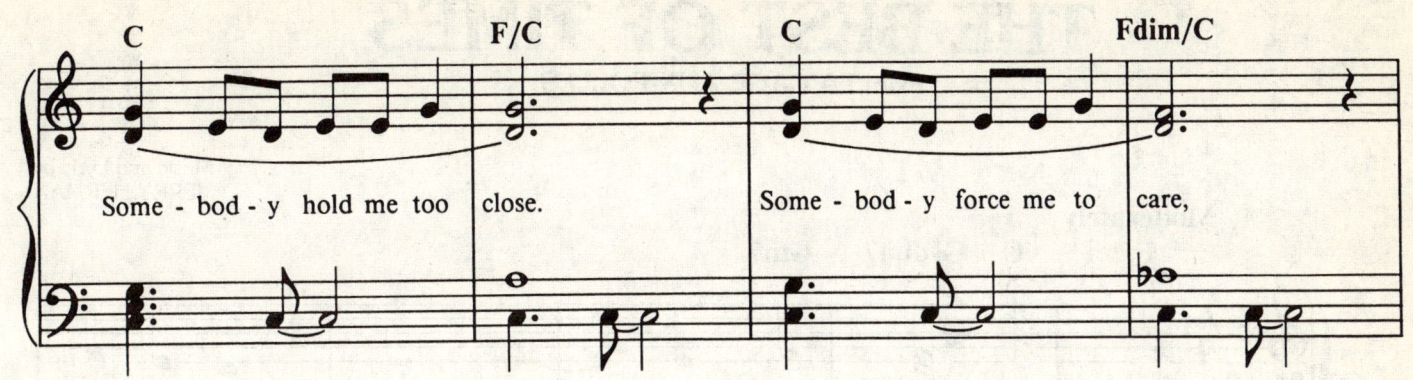

THE BEST OF TIMES
from LA CAGE AUX FOLLES

Music and Lyric by
JERRY HERMAN

© 1983 JERRY HERMAN
All Rights Controlled by Jerryco Music Co.
Exclusive Agent: EDWIN H. MORRIS & COMPANY, A Division of MPL Music Publishing, Inc.
All Rights Reserved

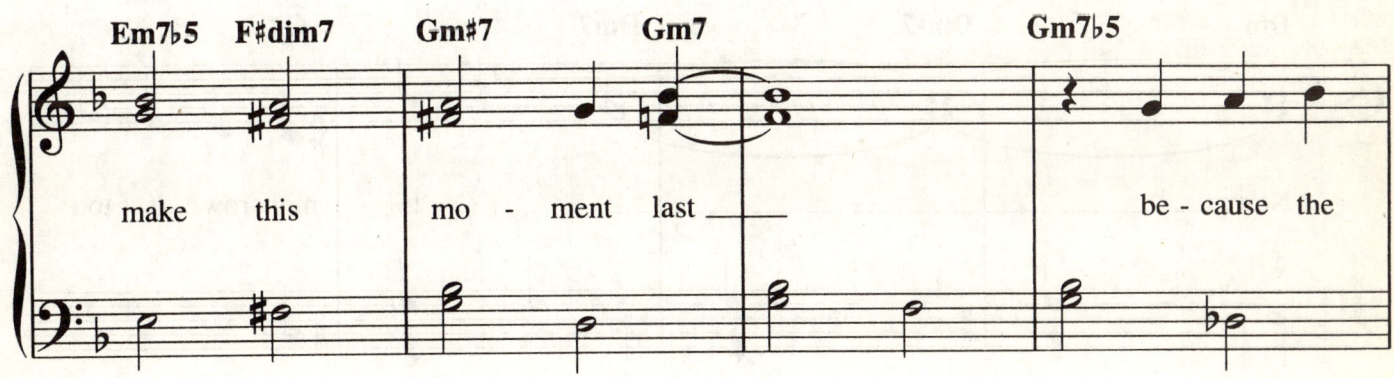
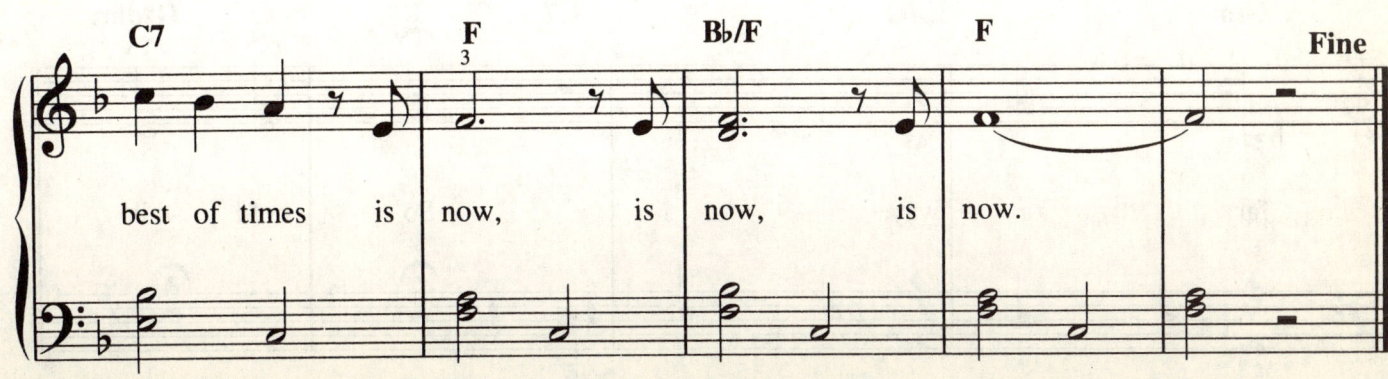

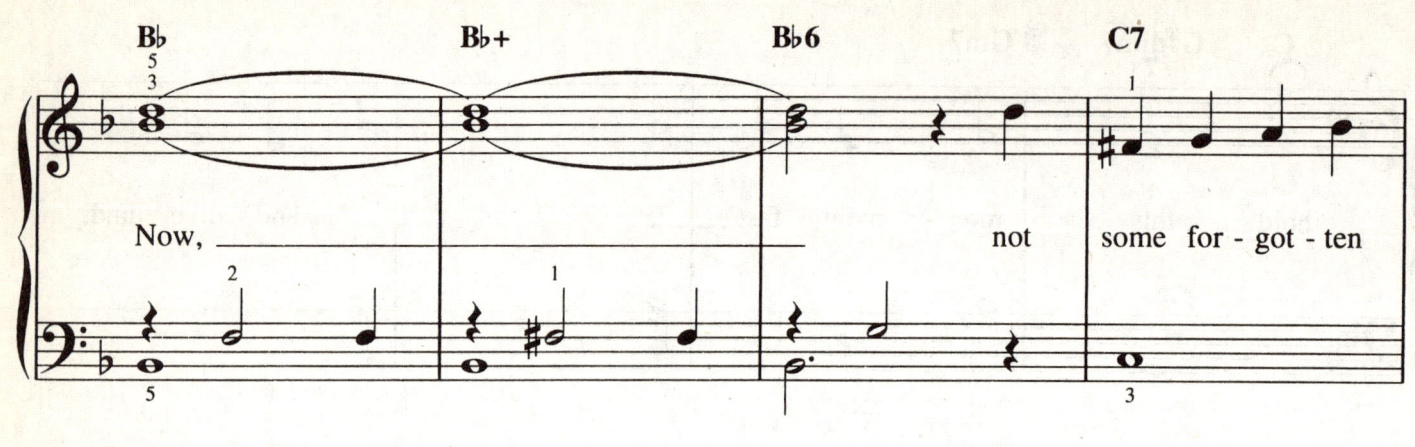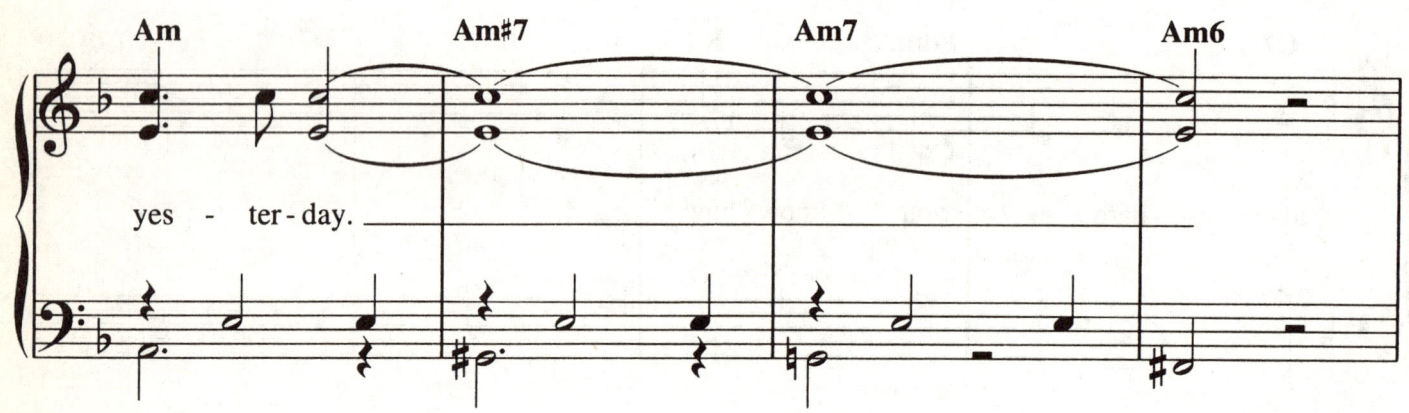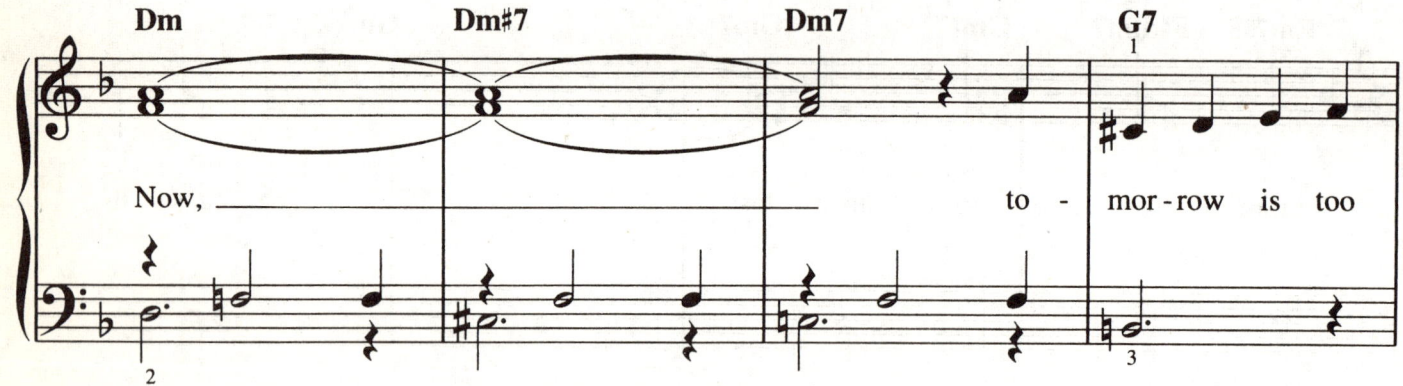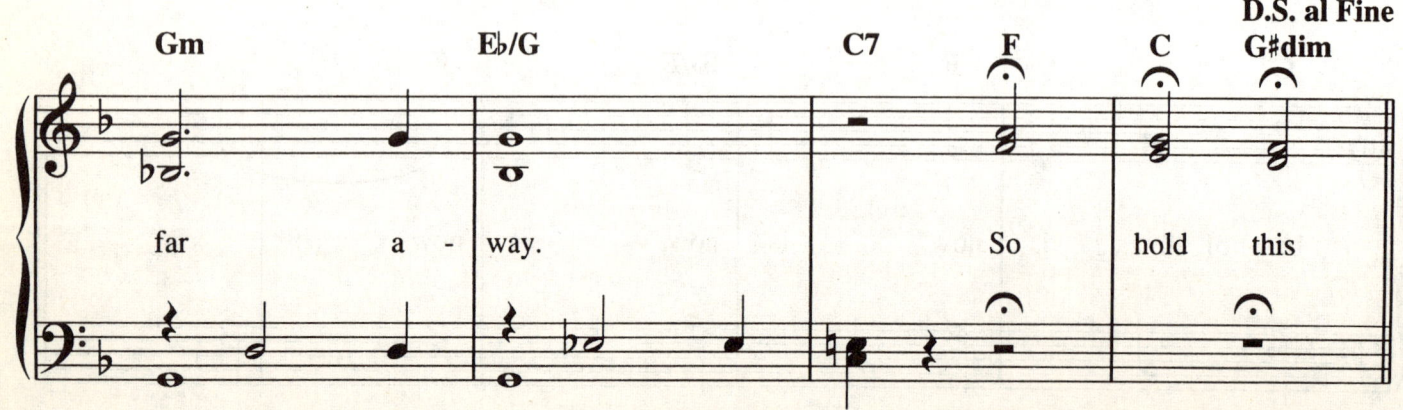

EVERYTHING'S COMING UP ROSES
from GYPSY

Words by STEPHEN SONDHEIM
Music by JULE STYNE

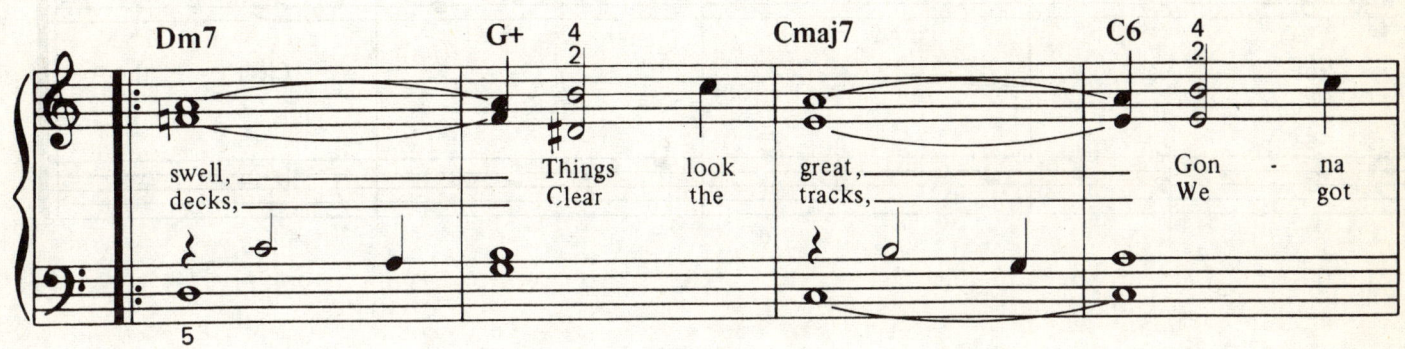
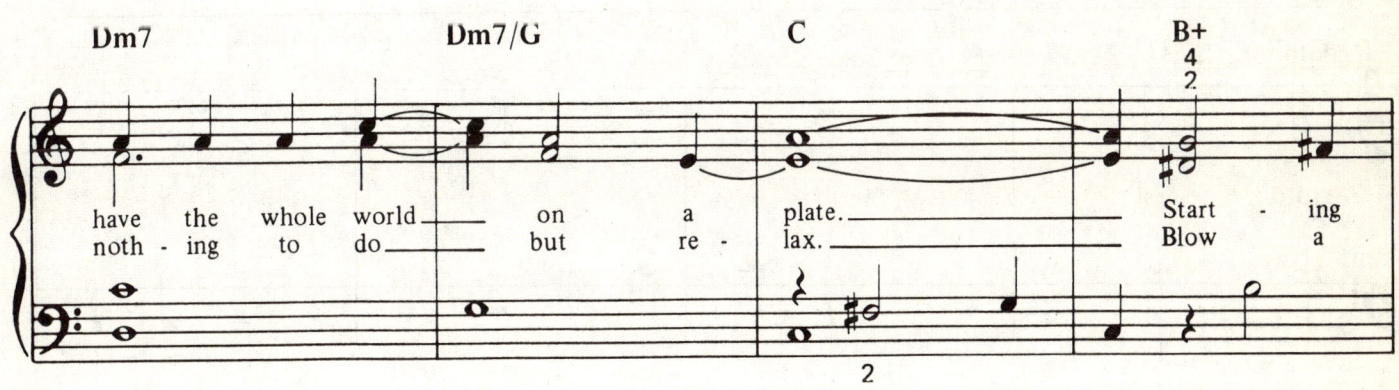
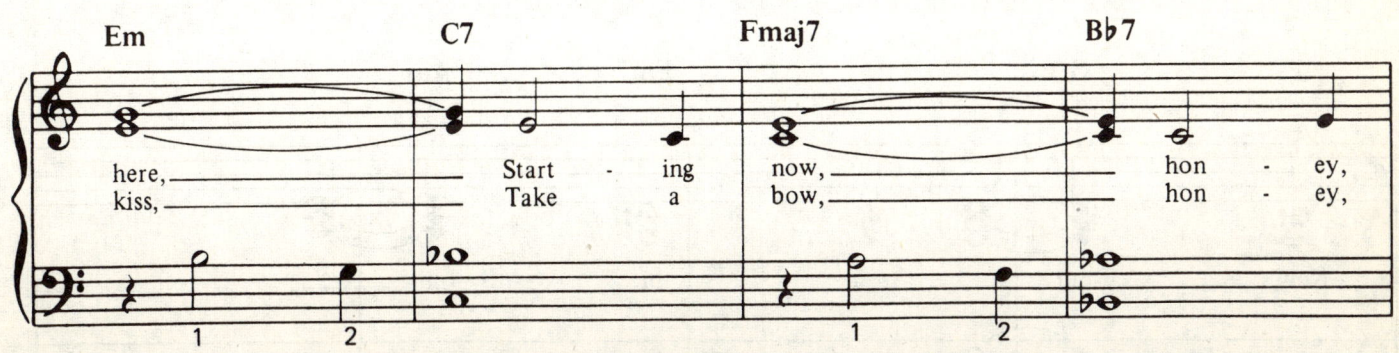

Copyright © 1959 by Stratford Music Corporation and Williamson Music, Inc.
Copyright Renewed
All Rights Administered by Chappell & Co.
International Copyright Secured   All Rights Reserved

EVERYTHING'S COMING UP ROSES

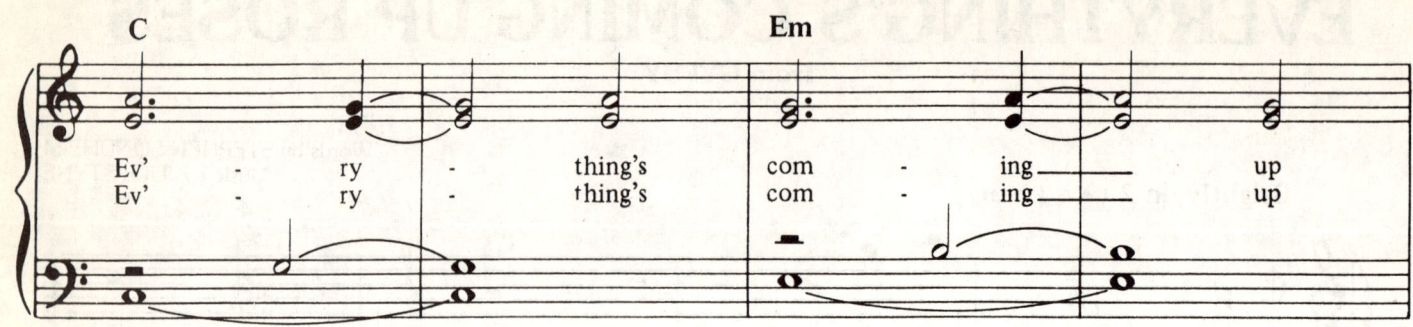

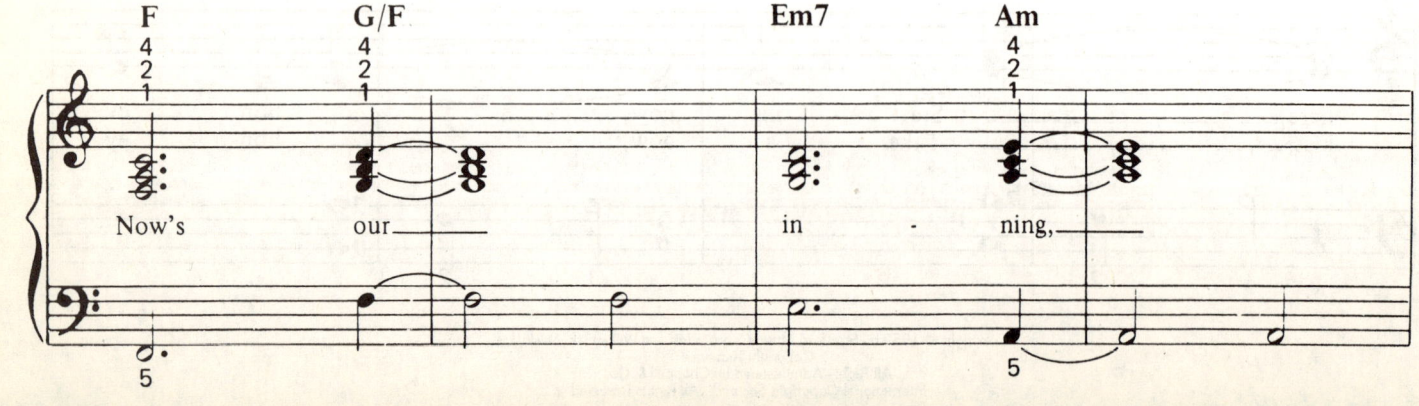

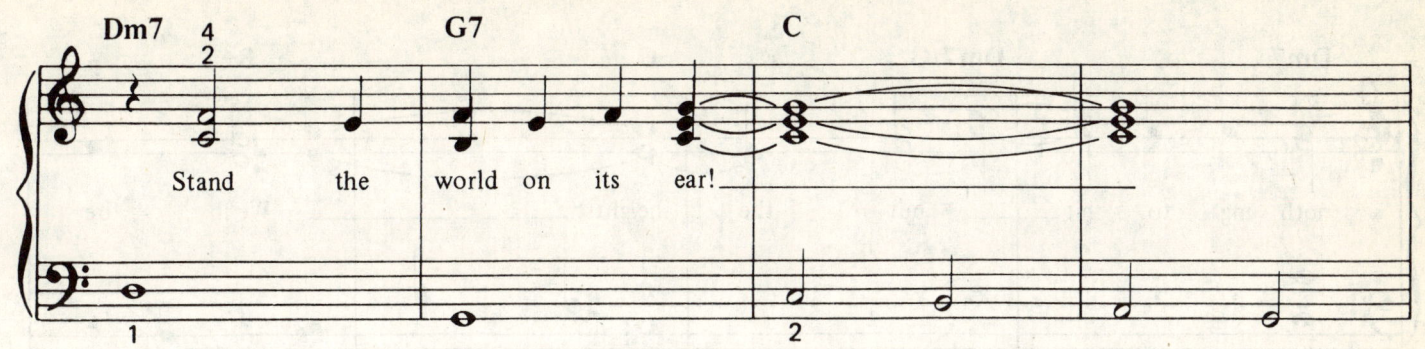
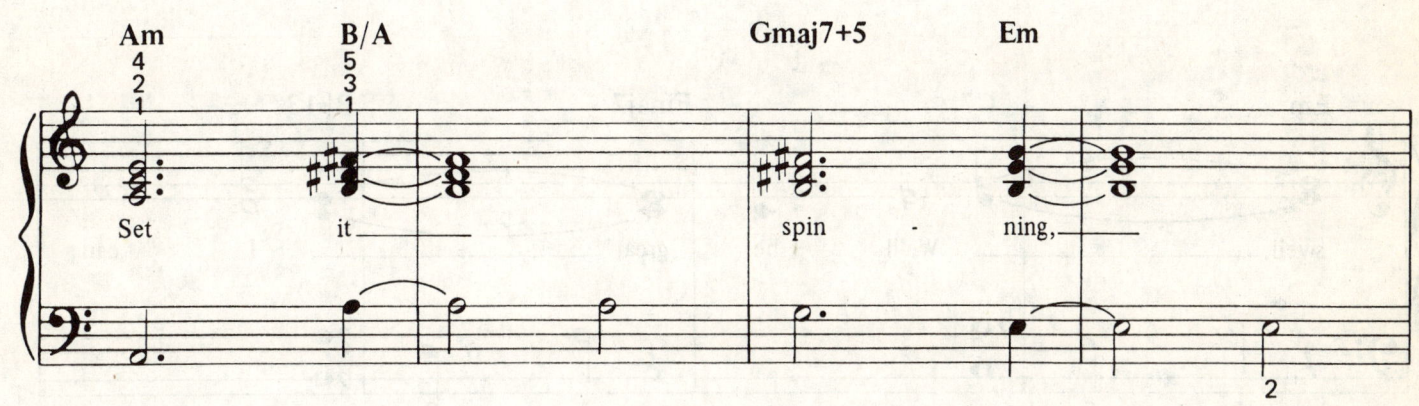

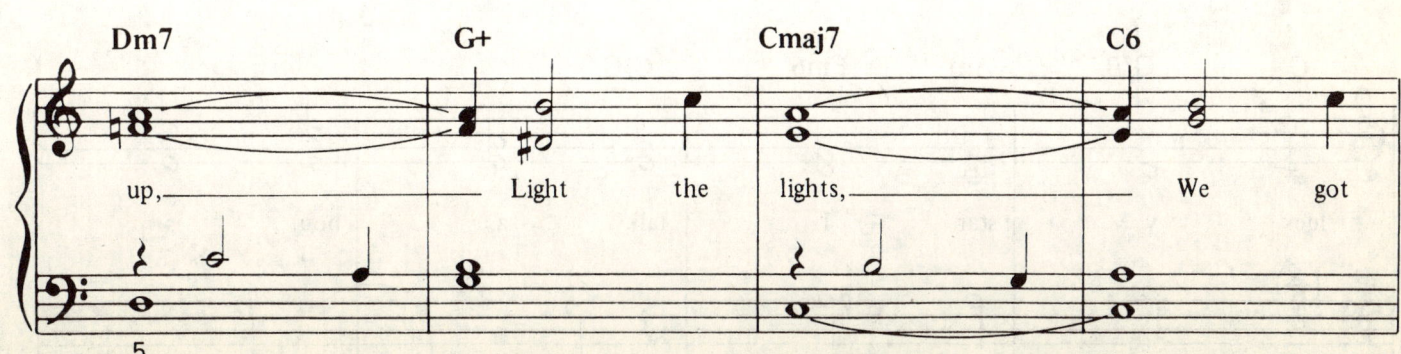

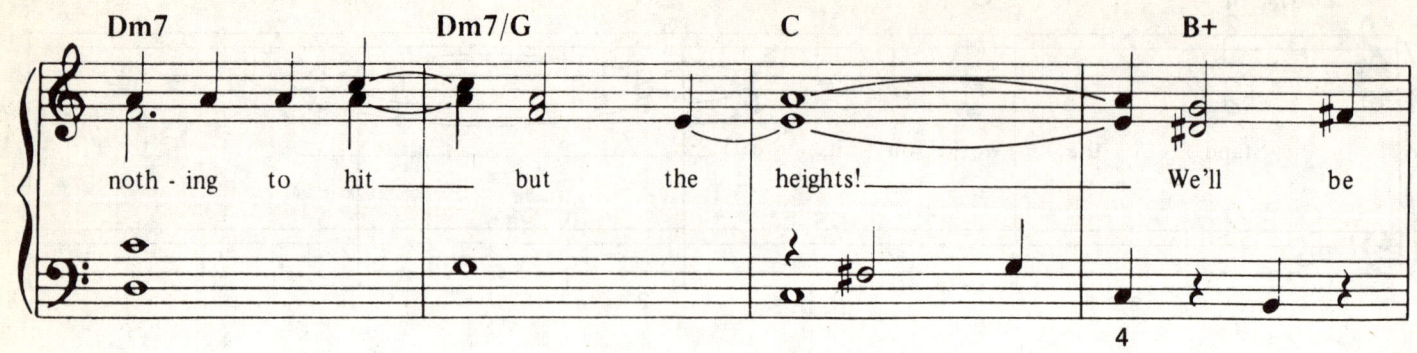

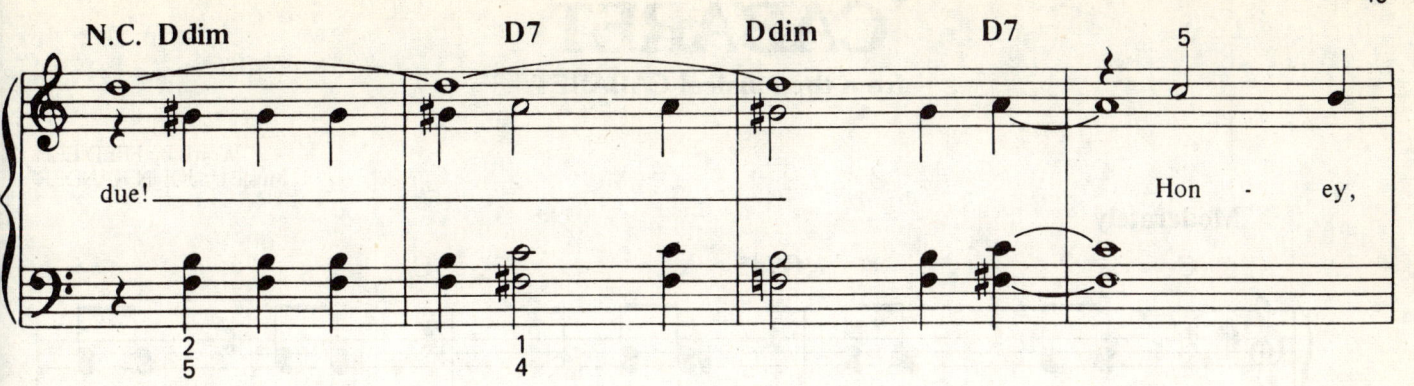
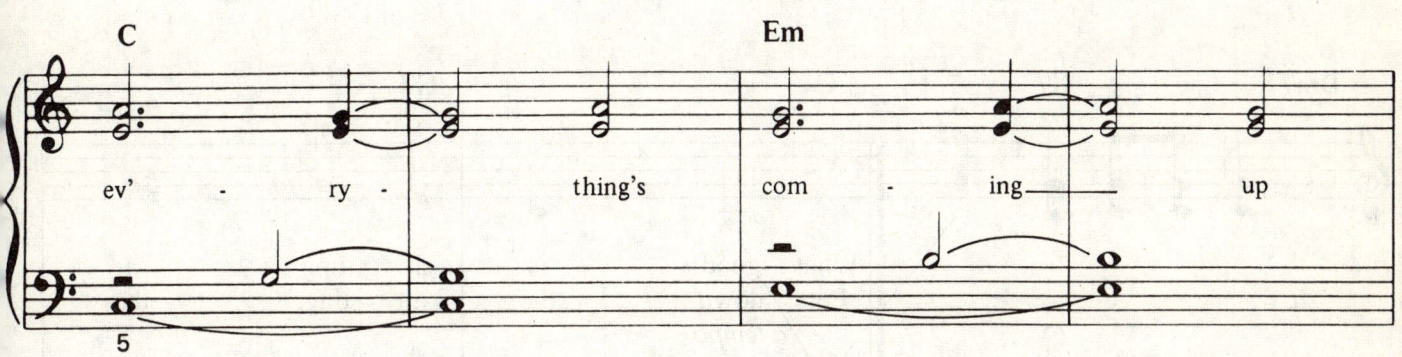
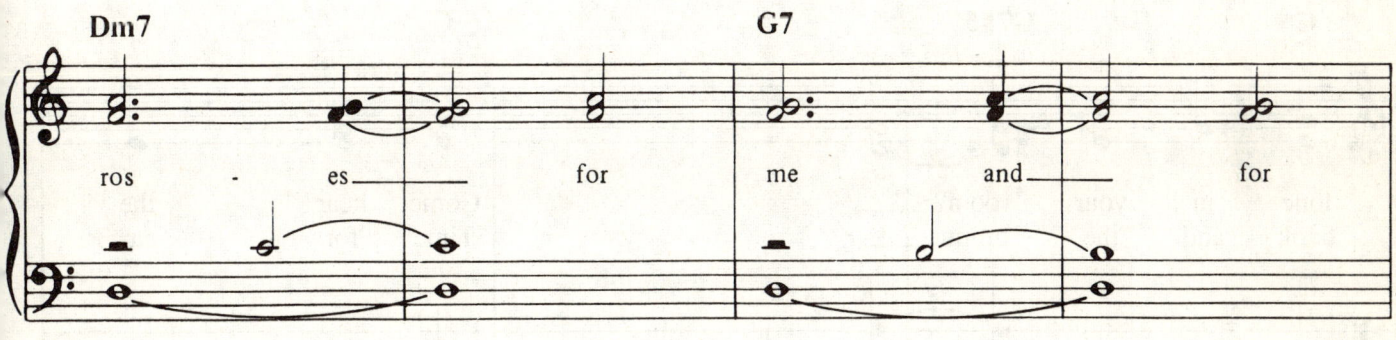

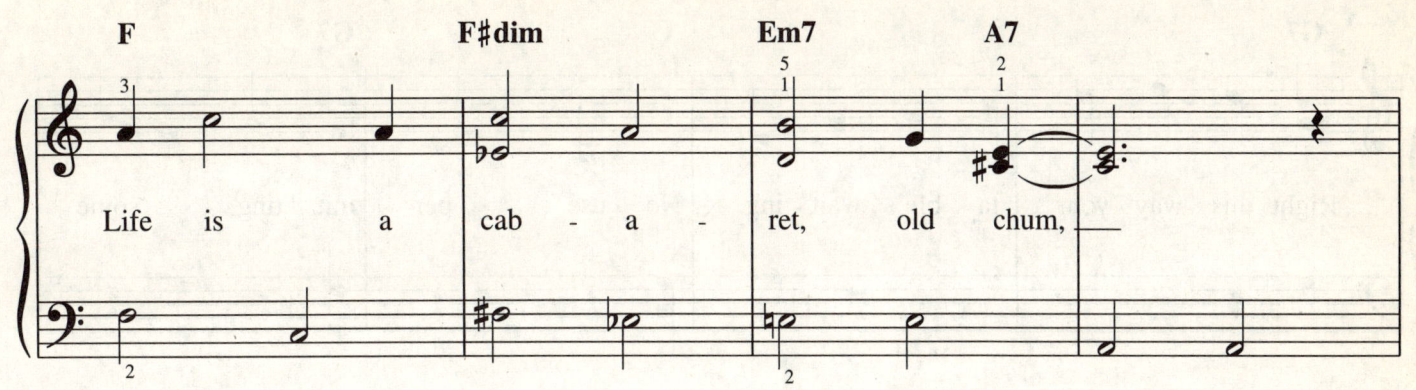
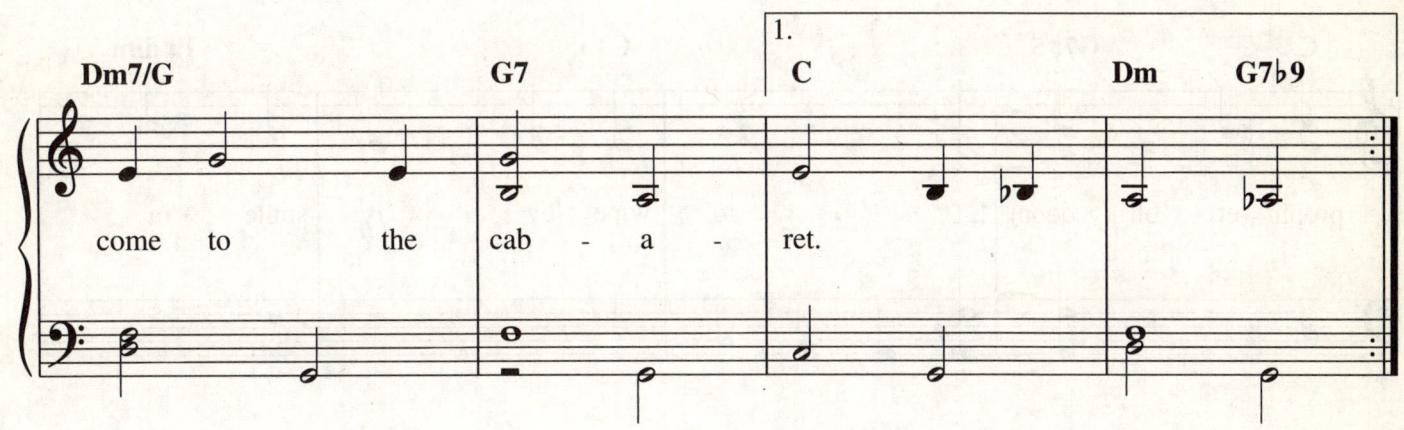

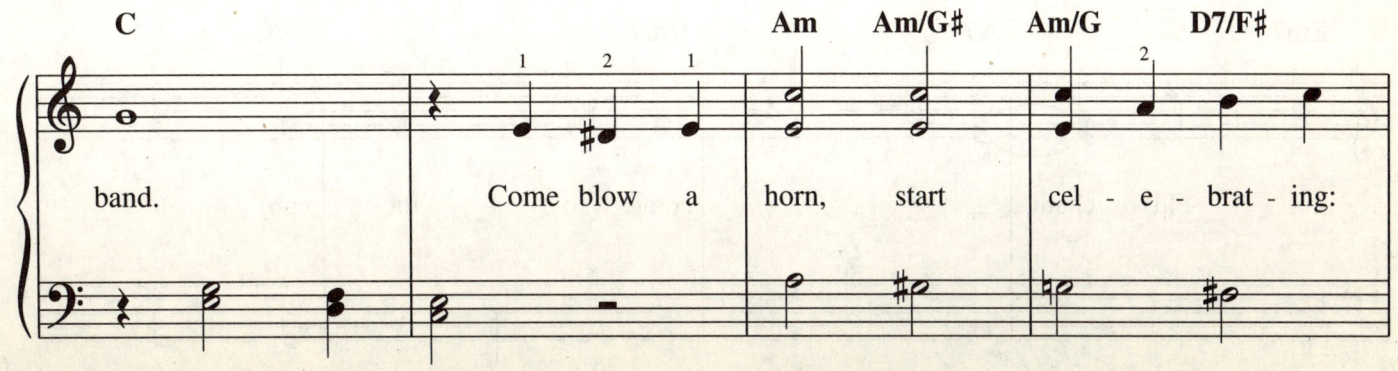

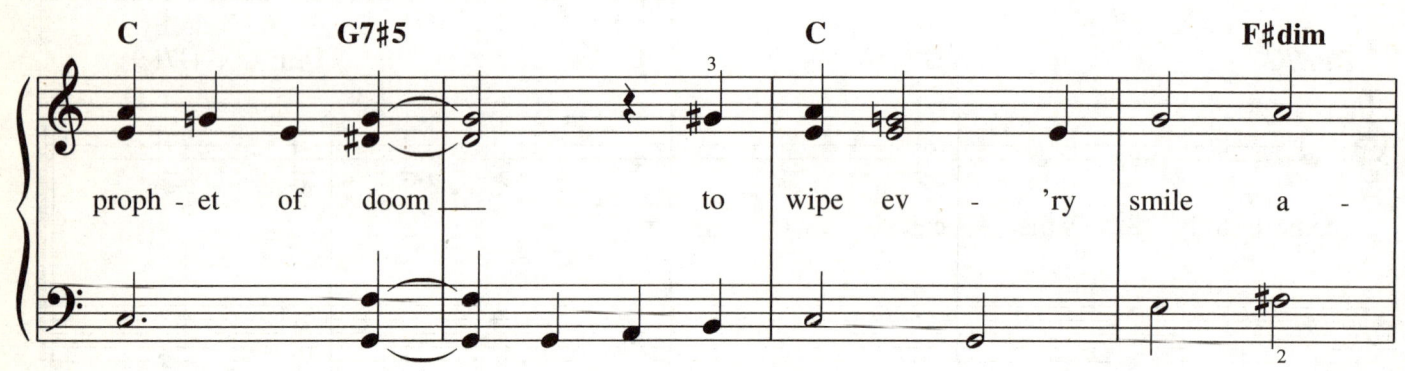
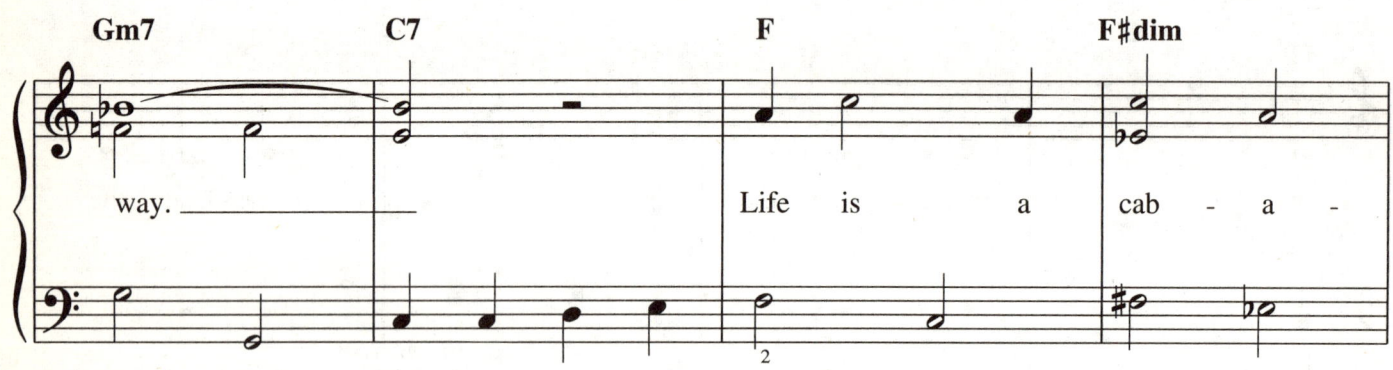

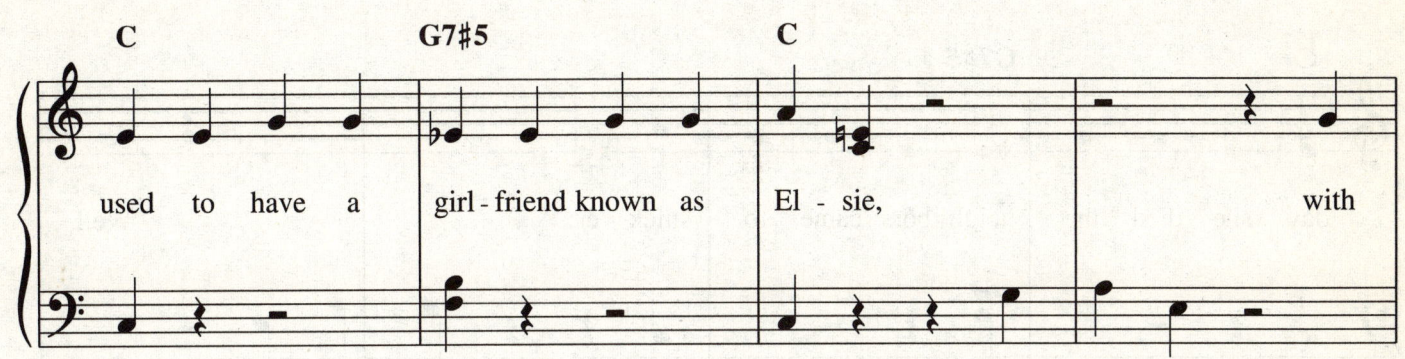
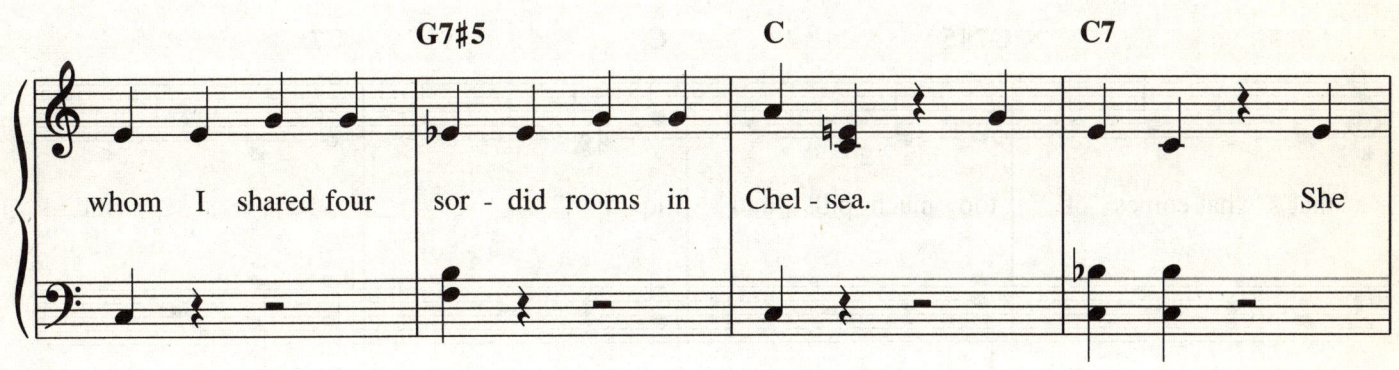
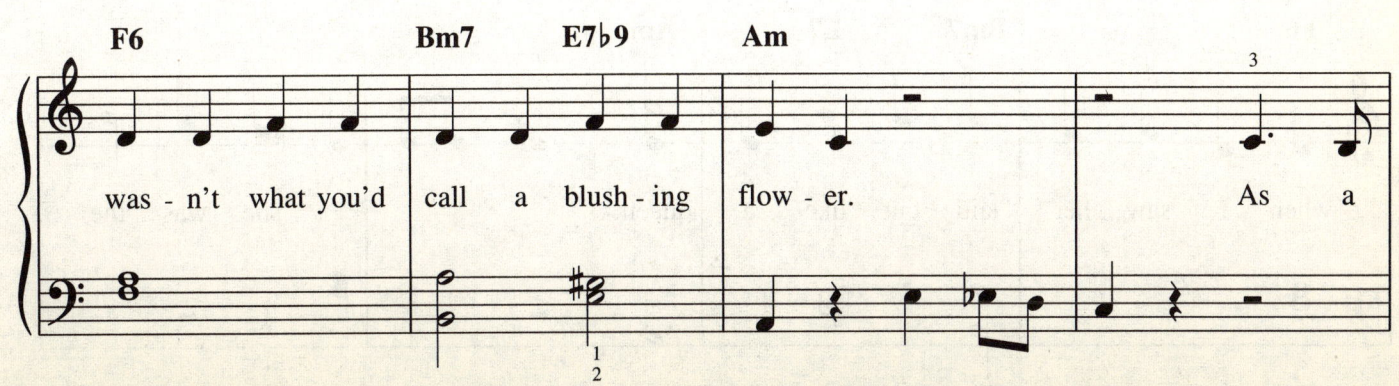

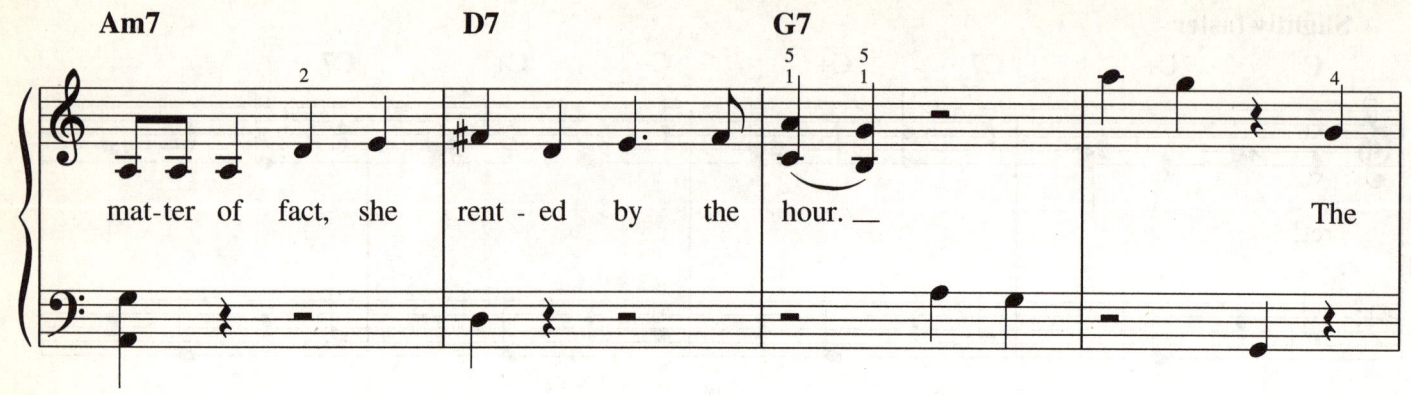
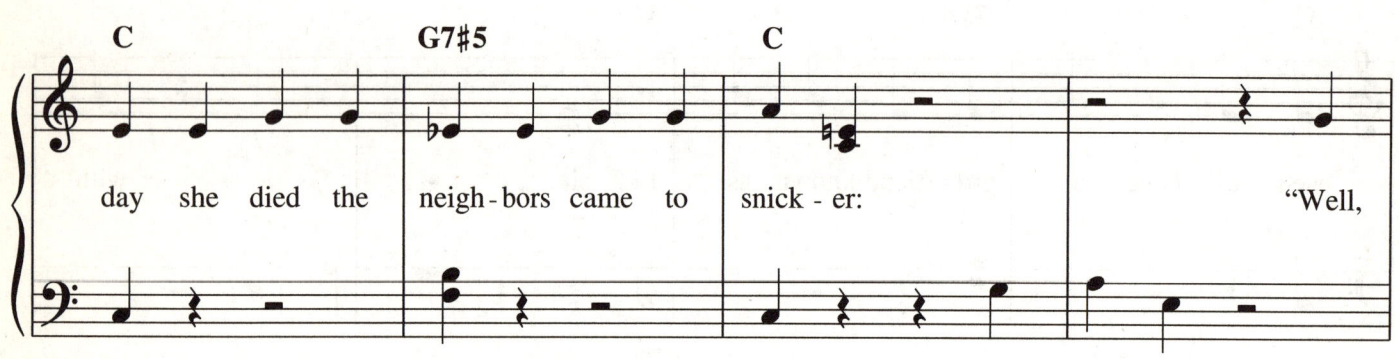

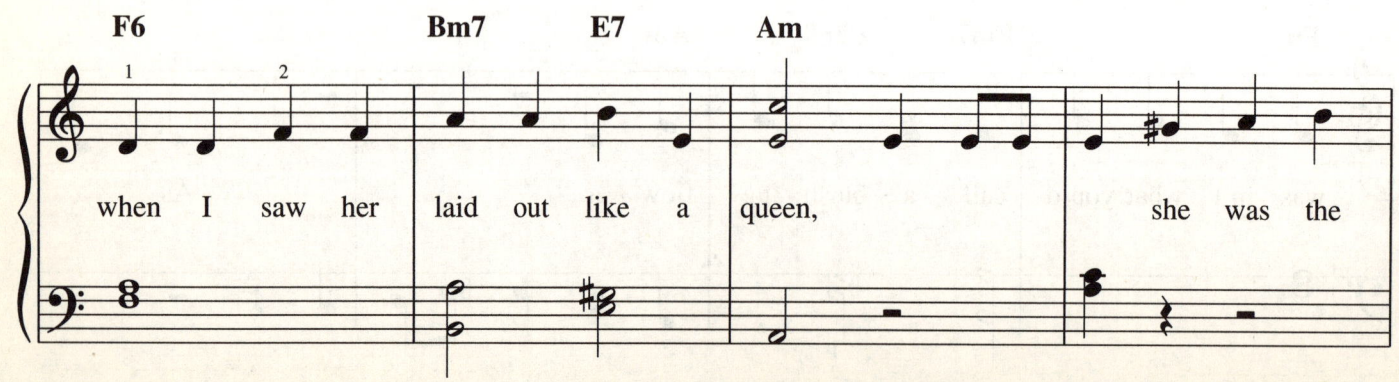

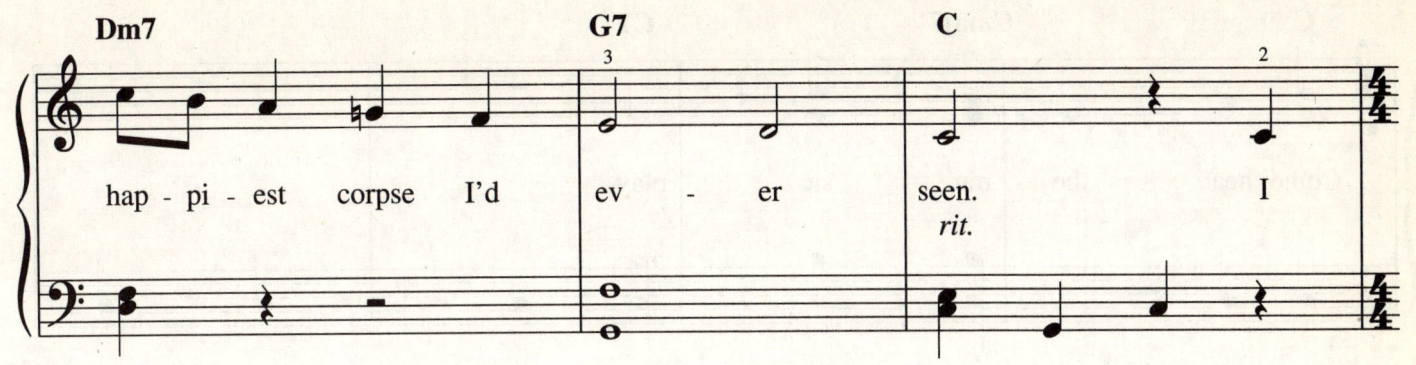
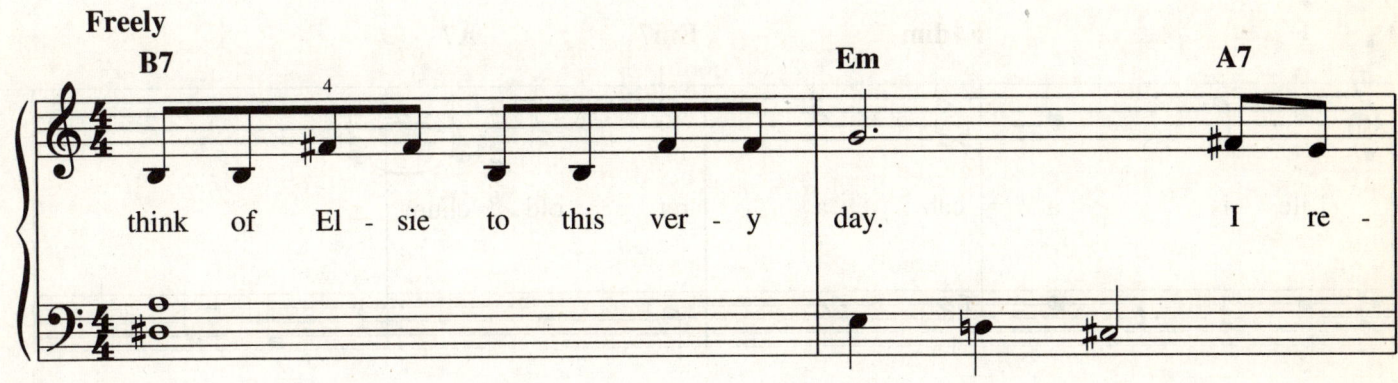

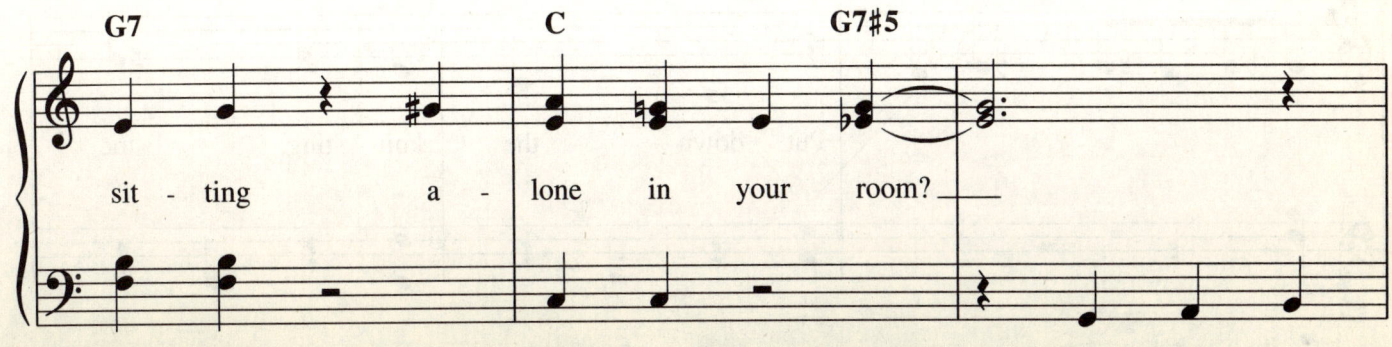

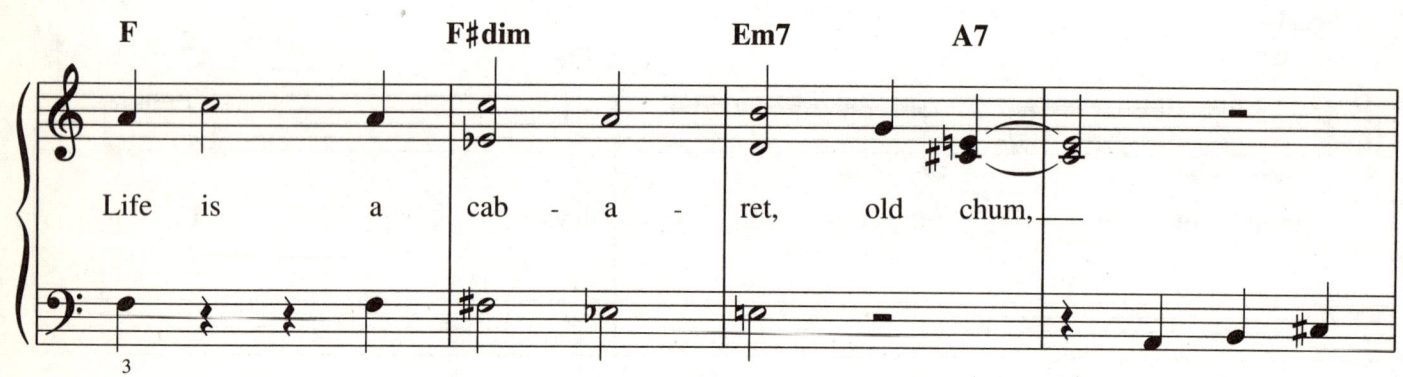
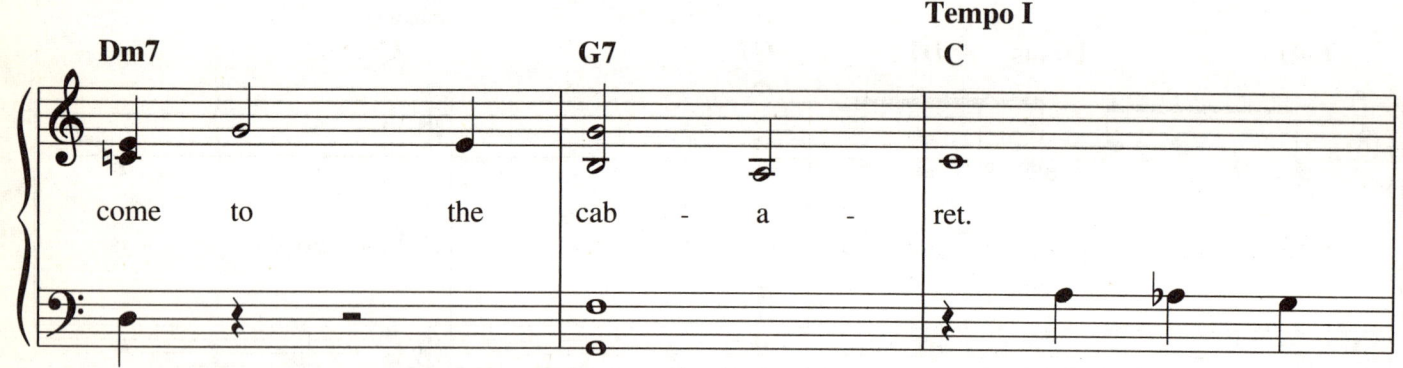
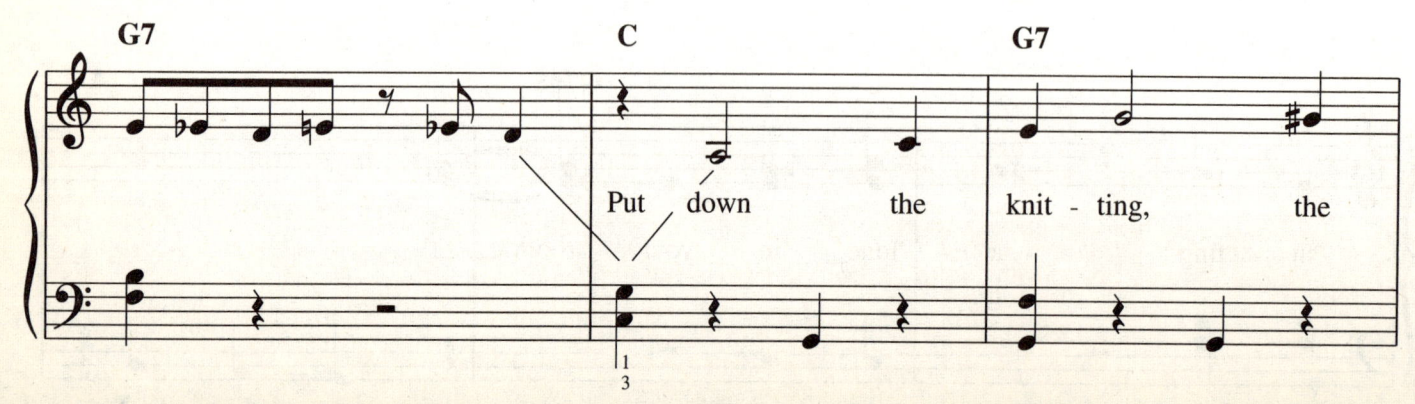

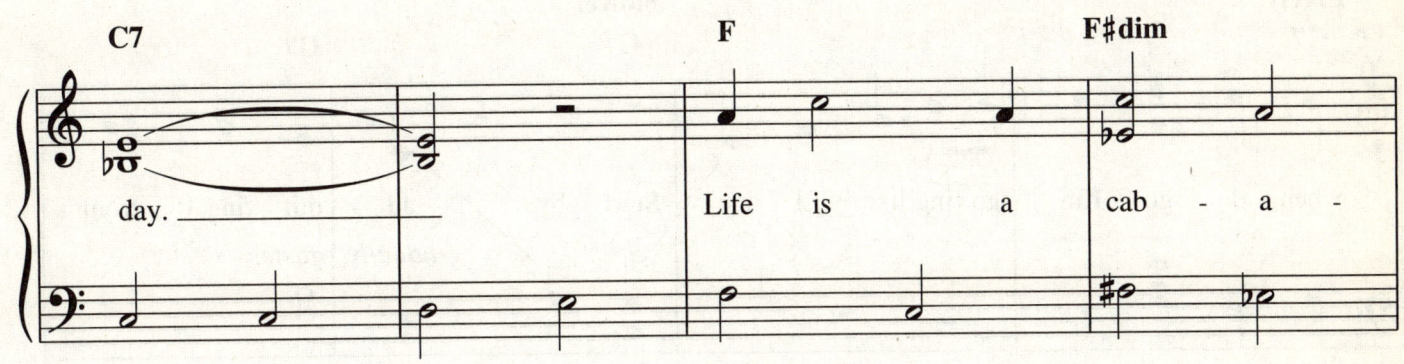

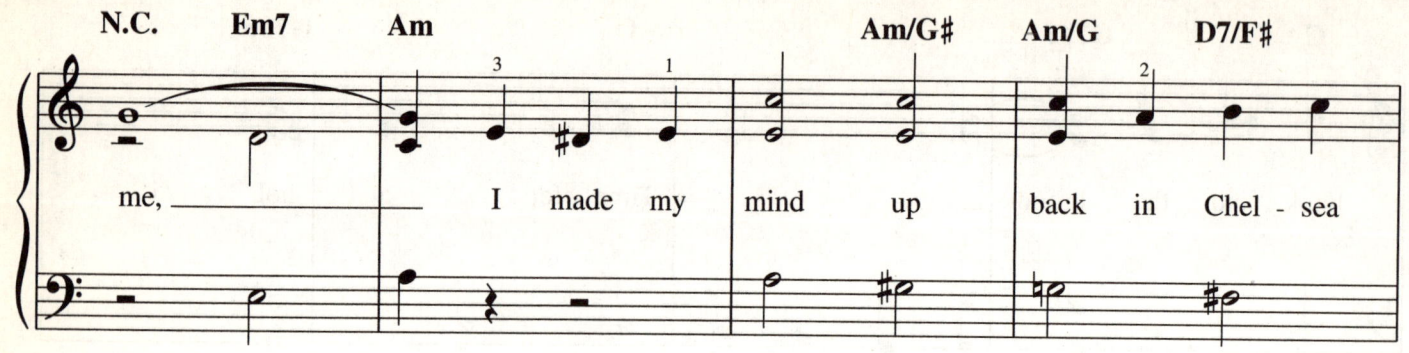

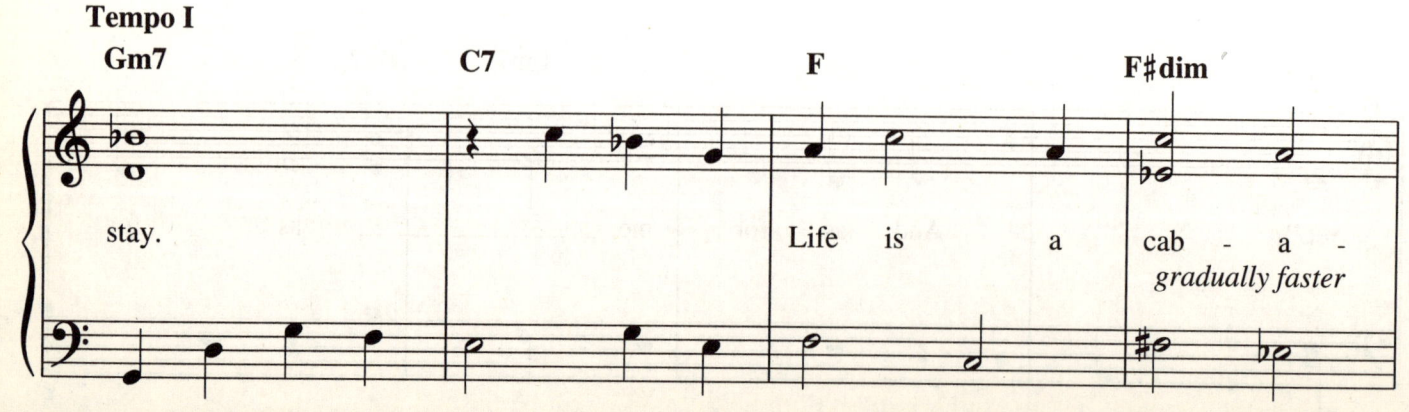

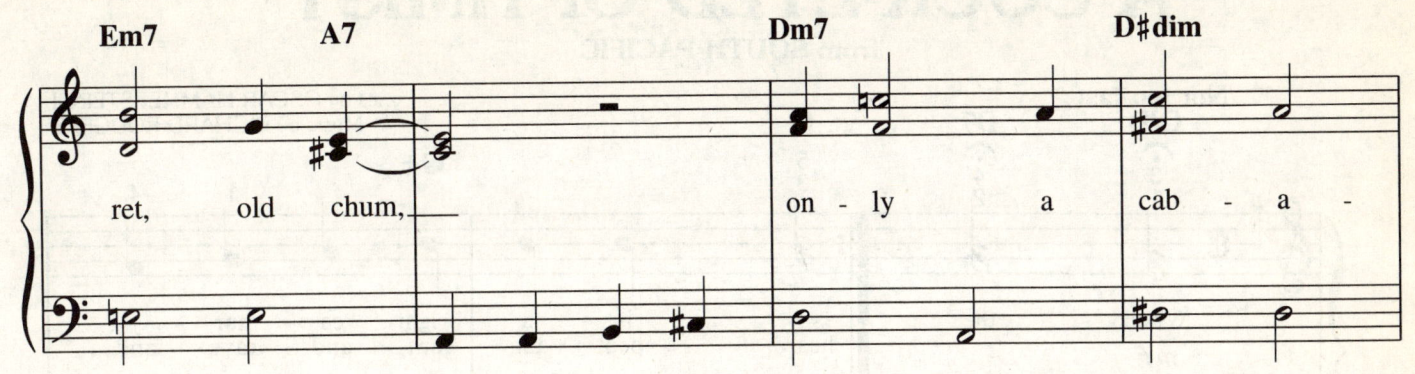
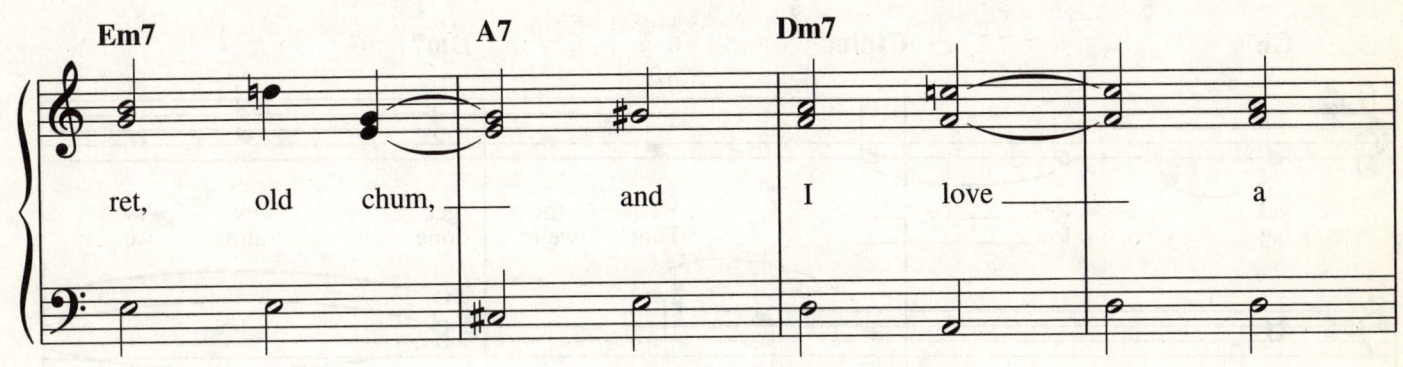
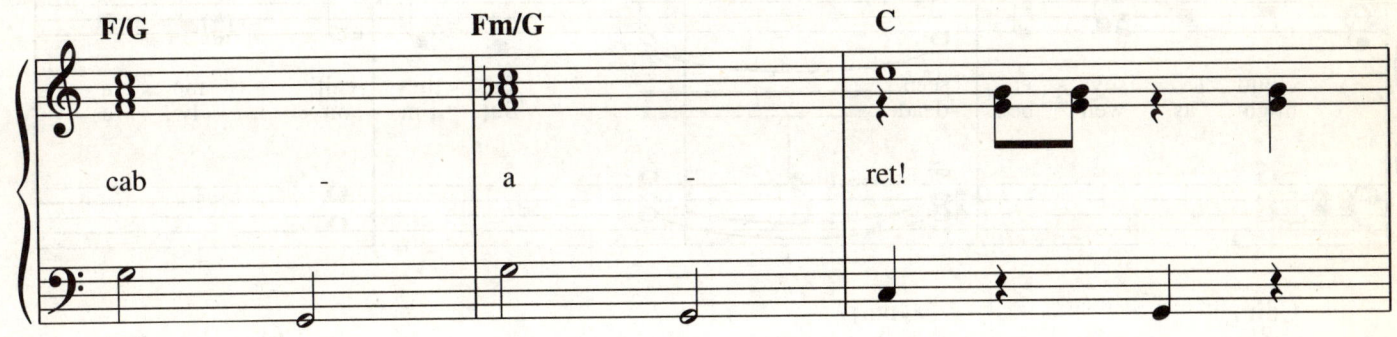

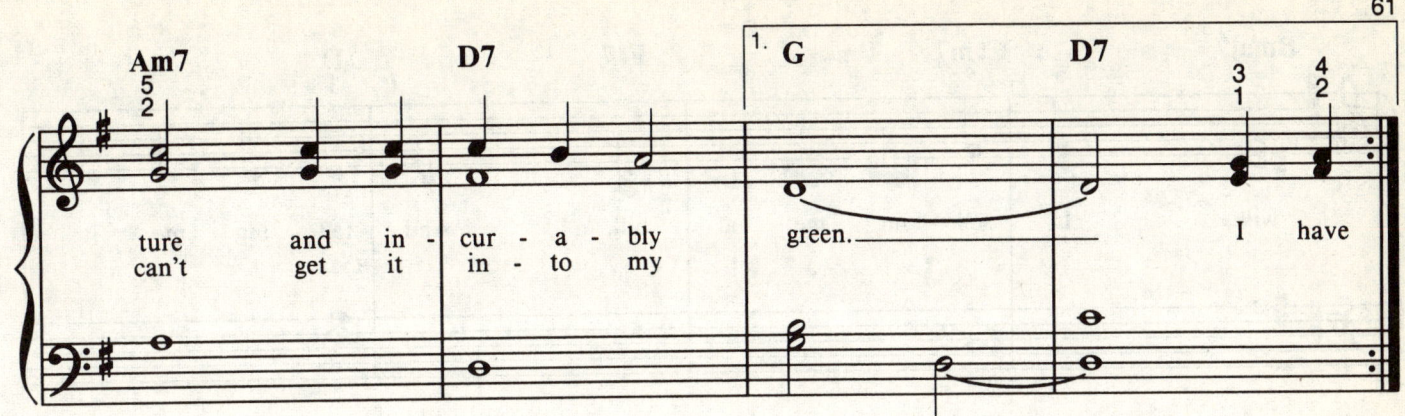
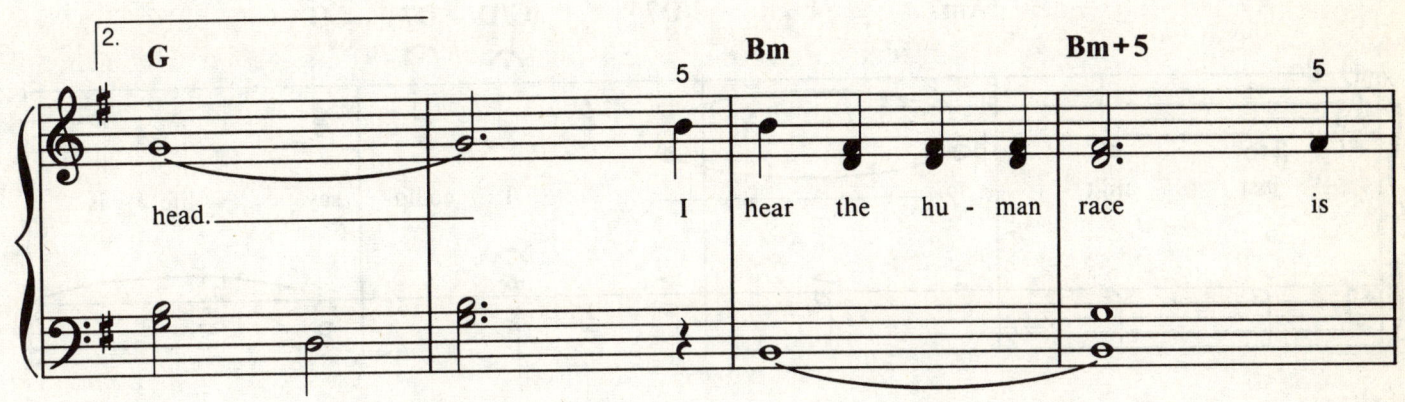

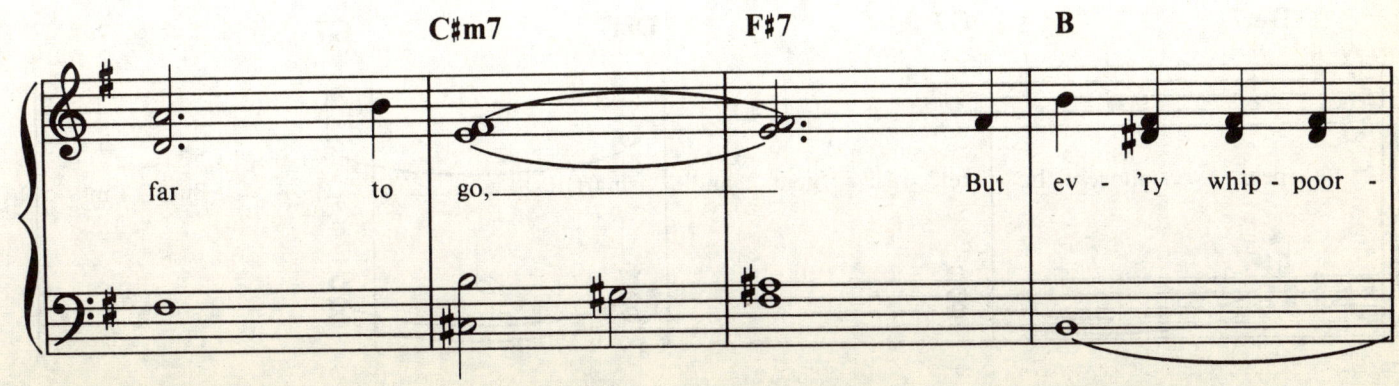

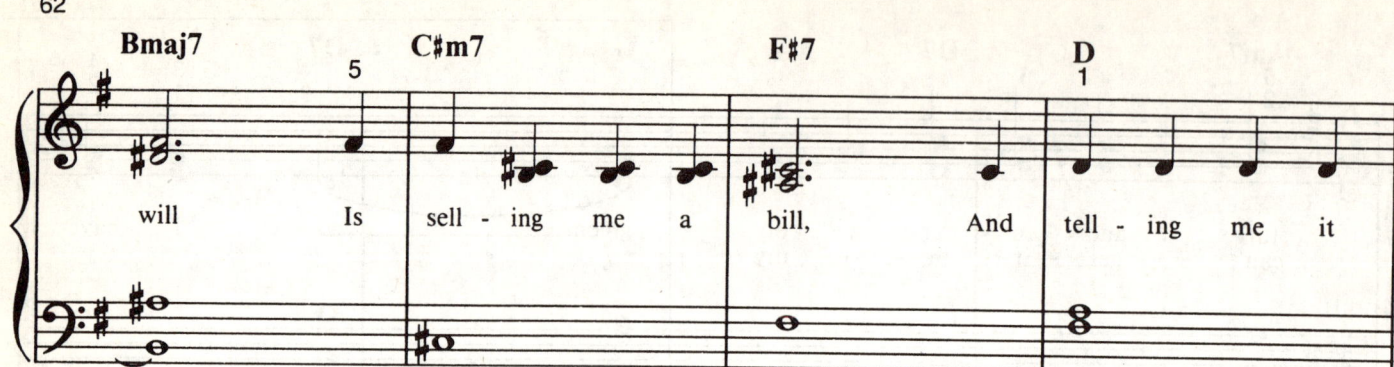

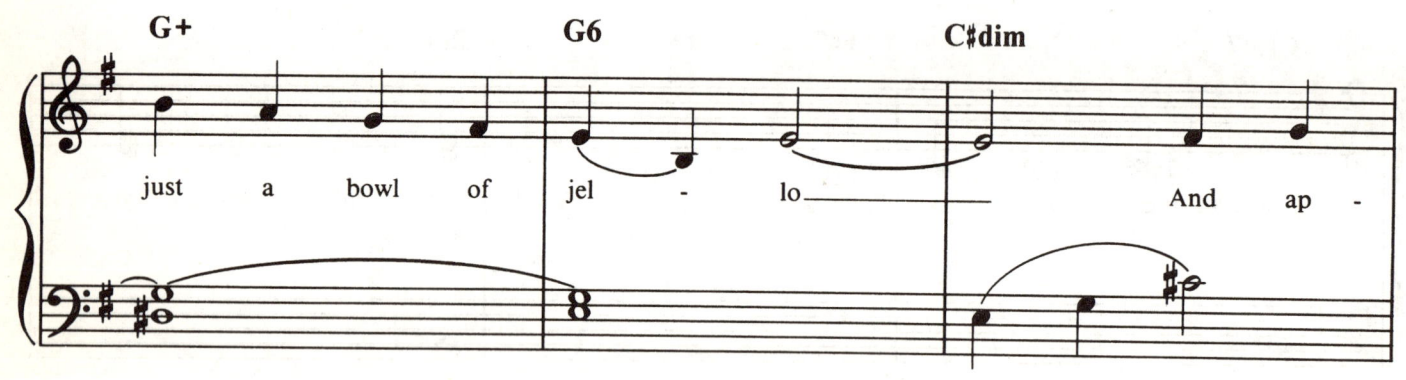

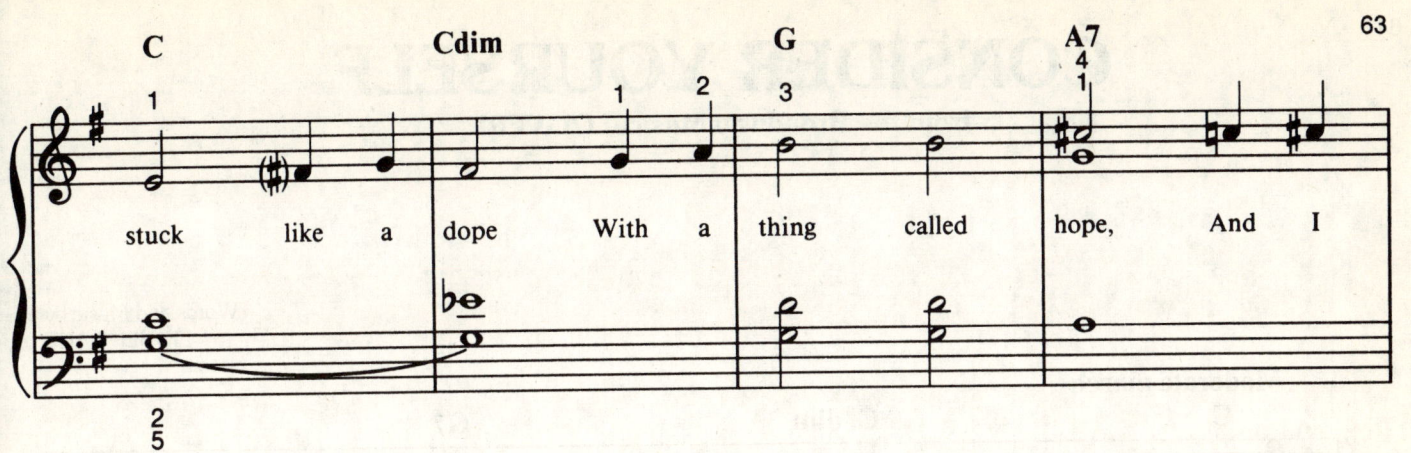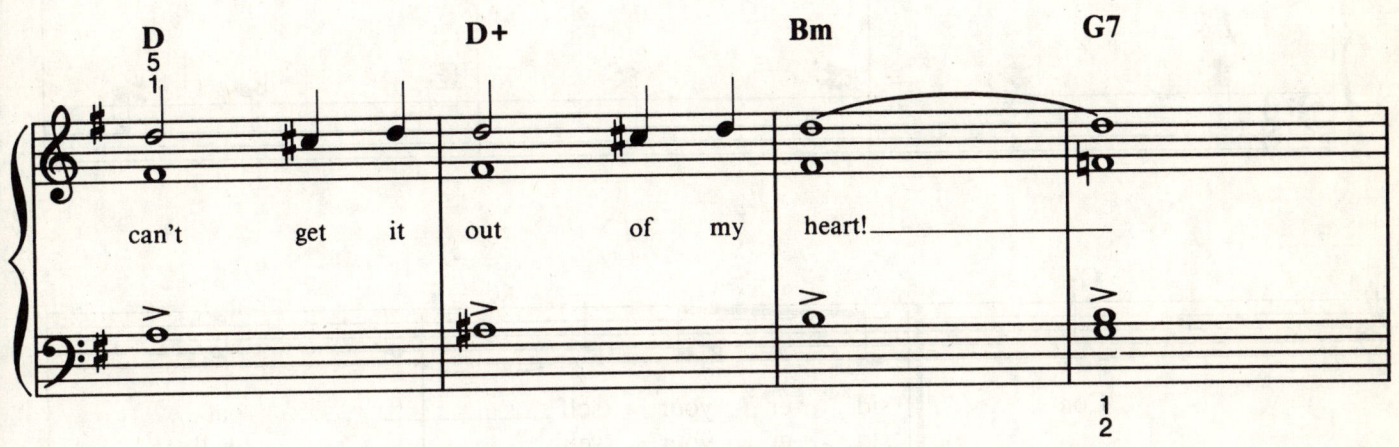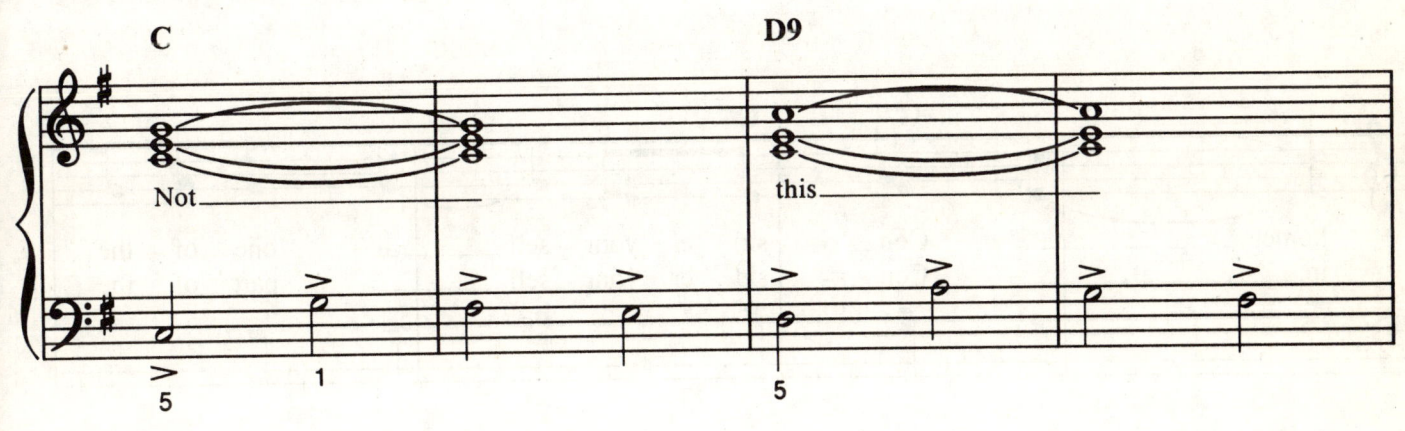

CONSIDER YOURSELF
from the Broadway Musical OLIVER!

Words and Music by
LIONEL BART

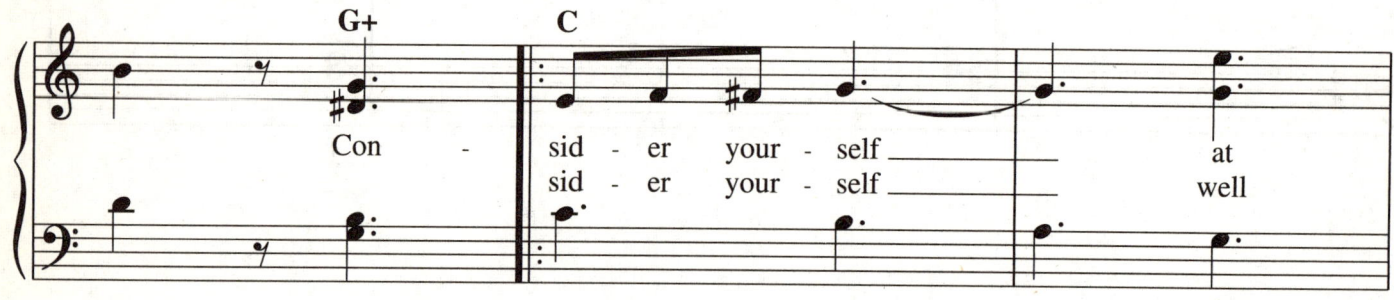
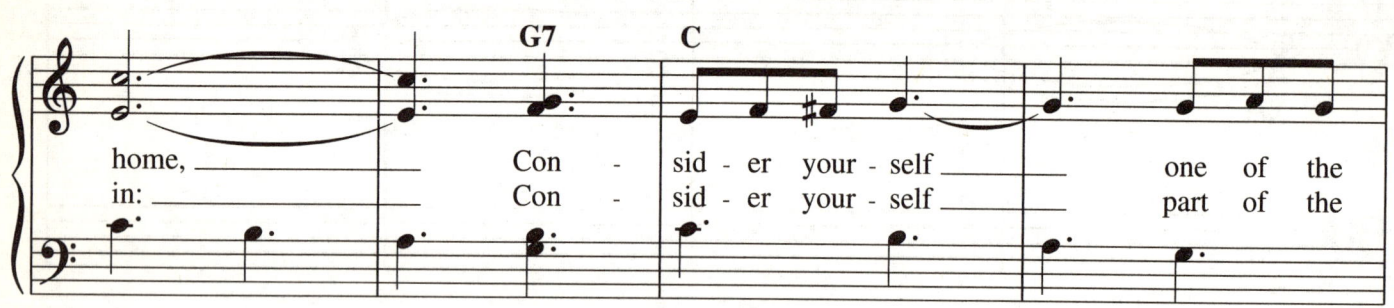

© Copyright 1960 (Renewed) Lakeview Music Co. Ltd., London, England
TRO - Hollis Music, Inc., New York, controls all publication rights for the U.S.A. and Canada
International Copyright Secured
All Rights Reserved Including Public Performance For Profit
Used by Permission

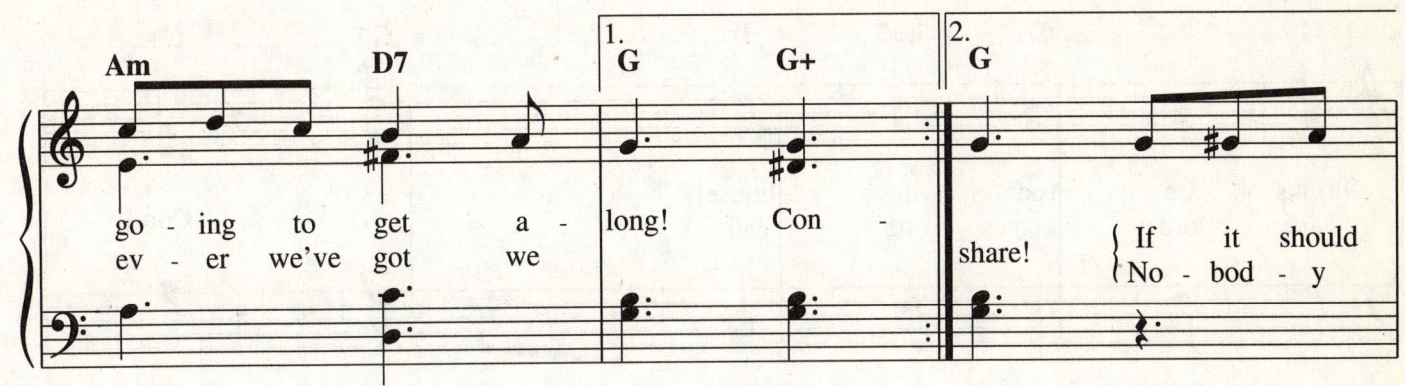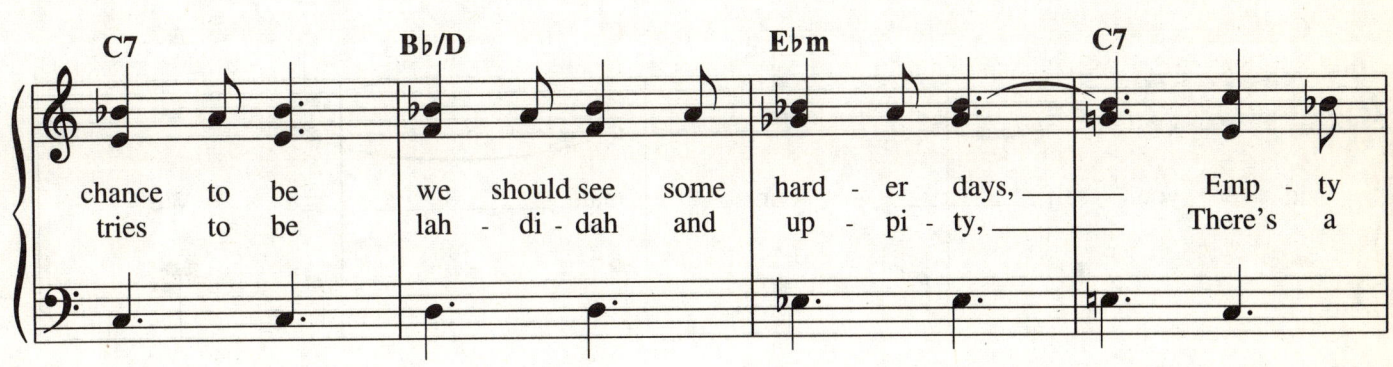

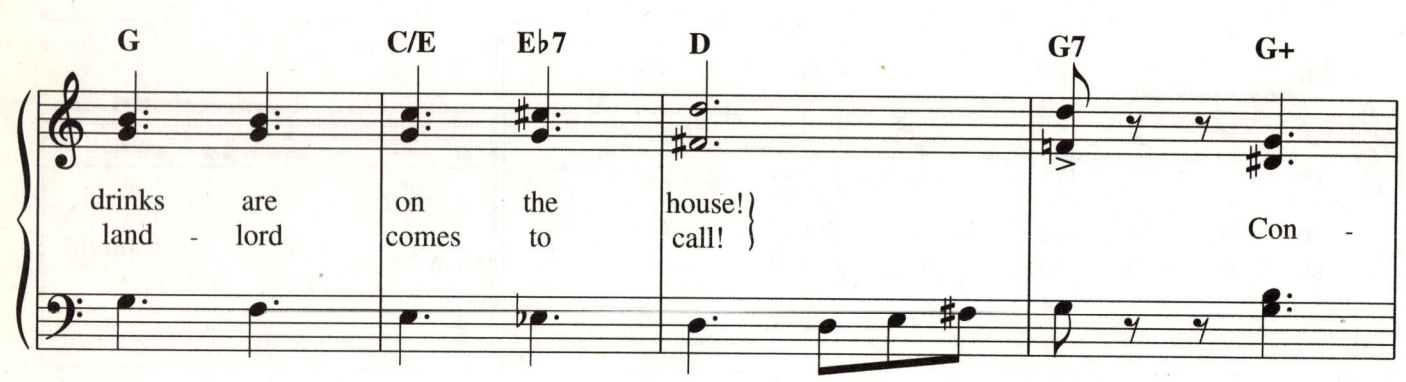

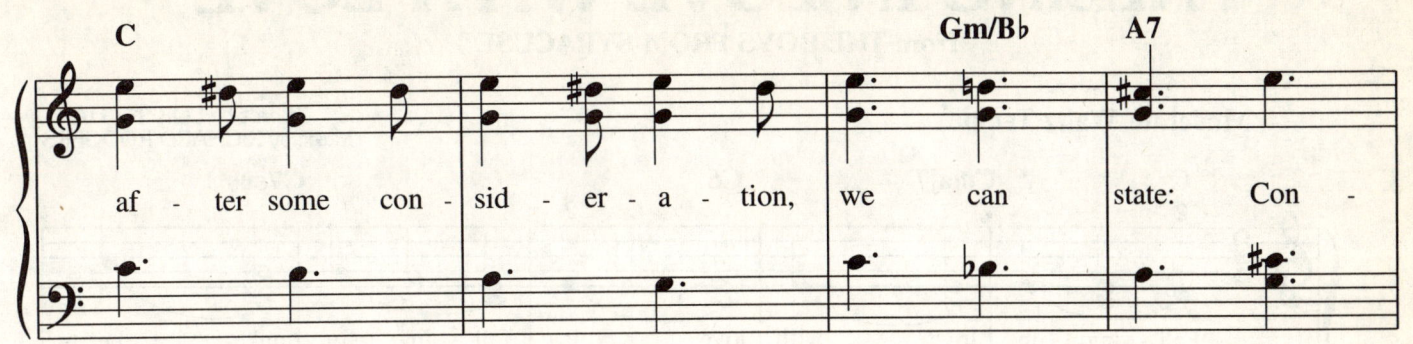
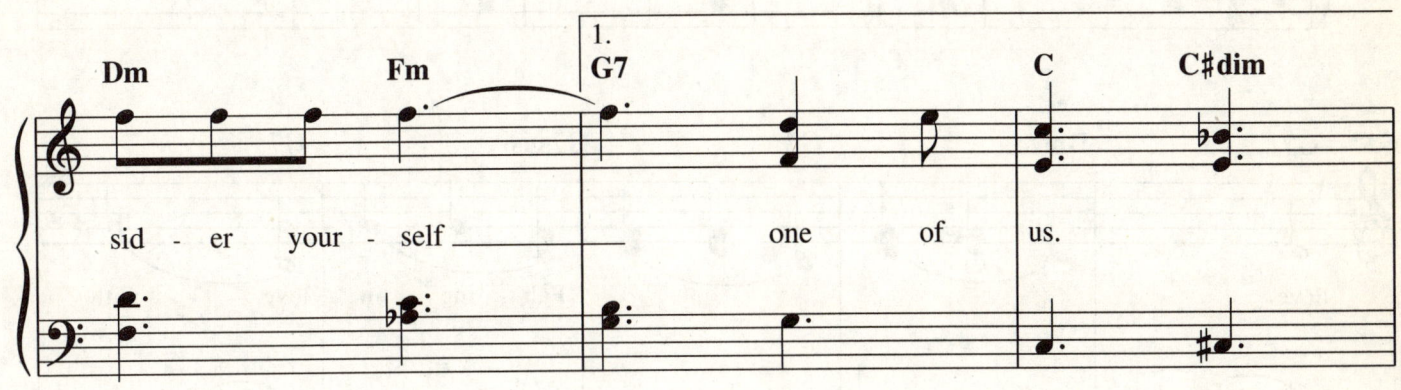

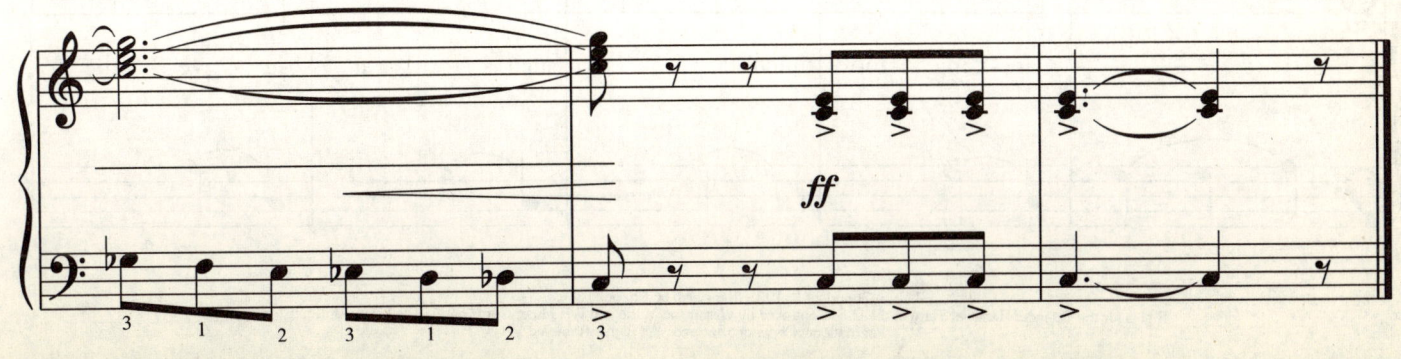

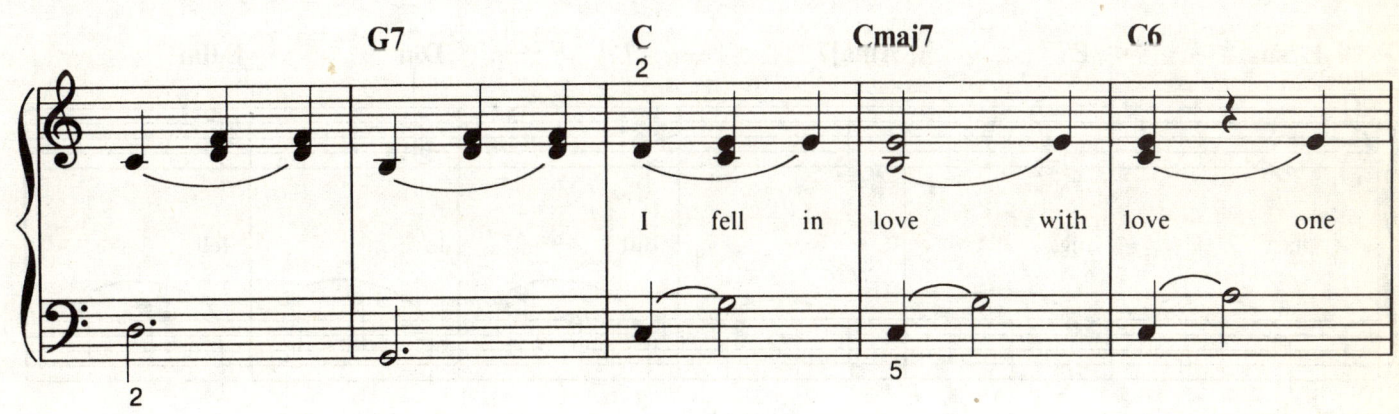
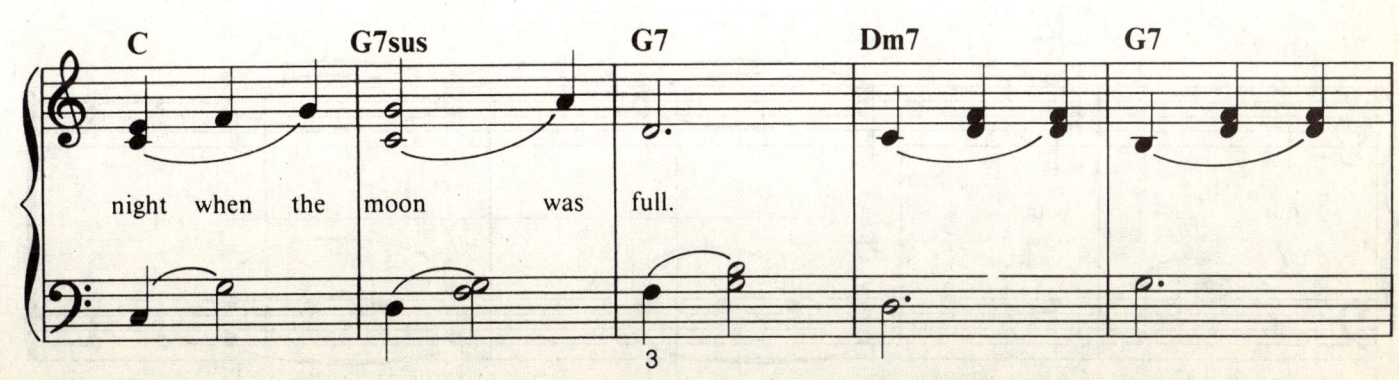

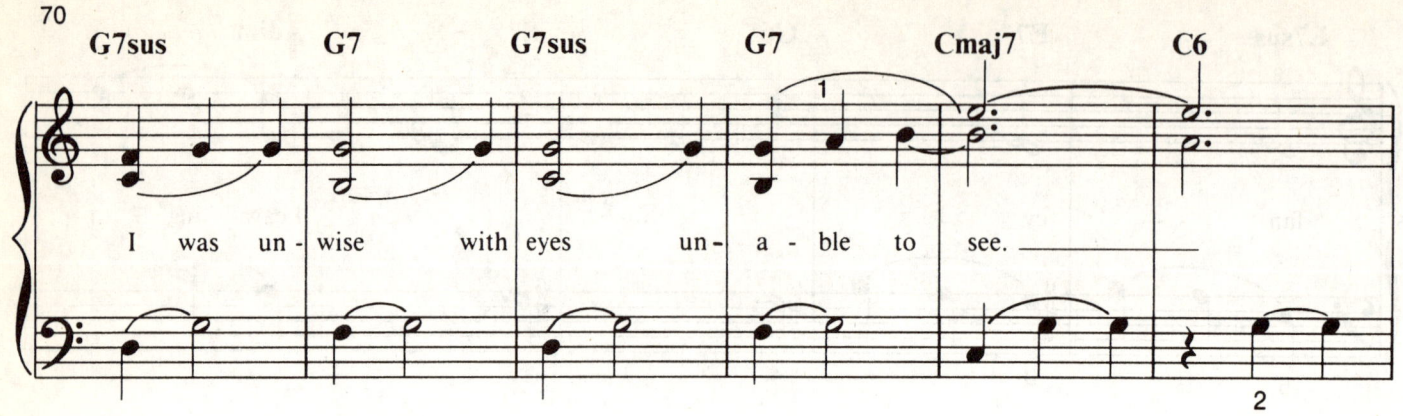
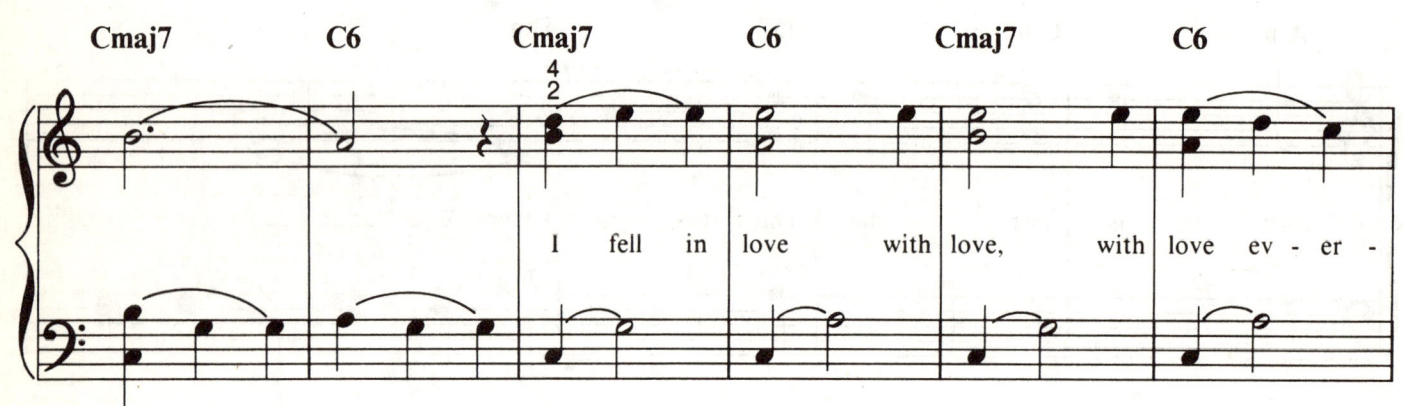

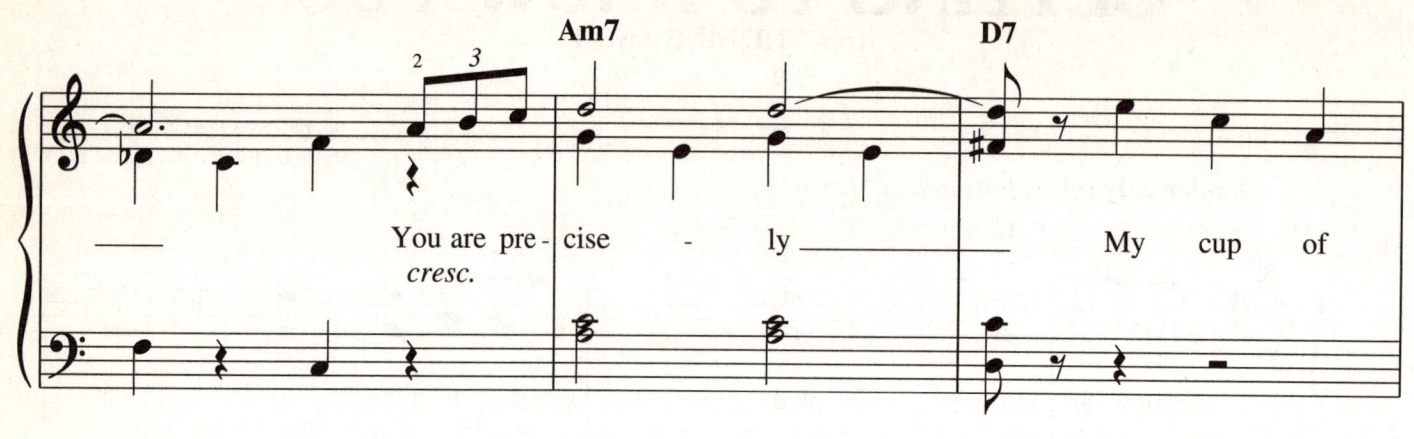

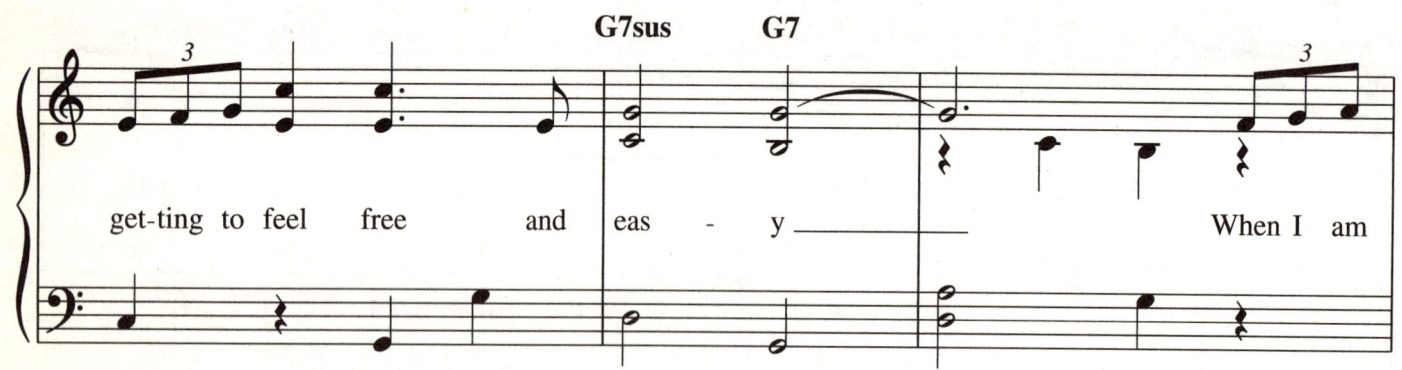
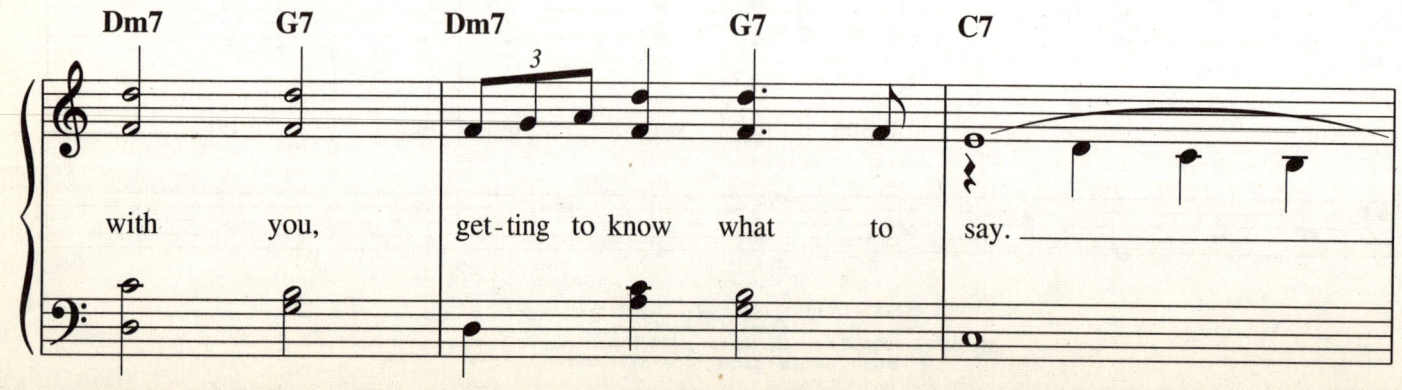

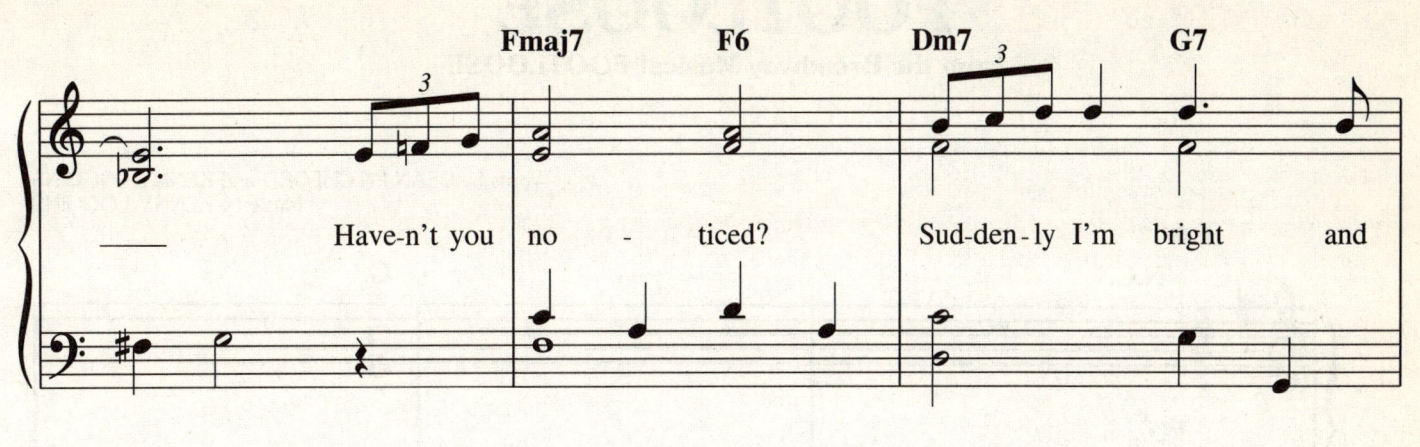

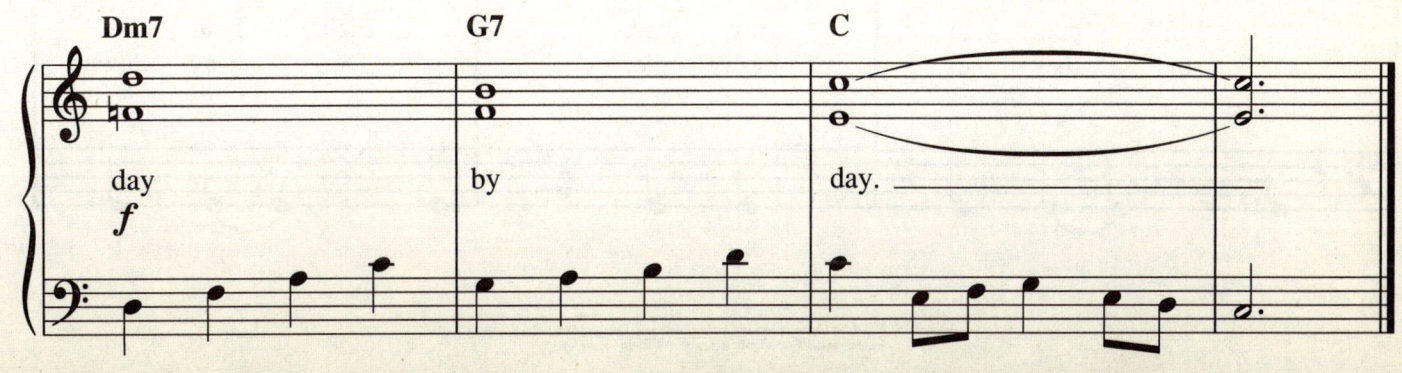

FOOTLOOSE
from the Broadway Musical FOOTLOOSE

Words by DEAN PITCHFORD and KENNY LOGGINS
Music by KENNY LOGGINS

Copyright © 1984 by Famous Music Corporation and Ensign Music Corporation
International Copyright Secured   All Rights Reserved

GUS: THE THEATRE CAT
from CATS

Music by ANDREW LLOYD WEBBER
Text by T.S. ELIOT

Gus is the cat at the the-a-tre door. His
coat's ver-y shab-by, he's thin as a rake. And he

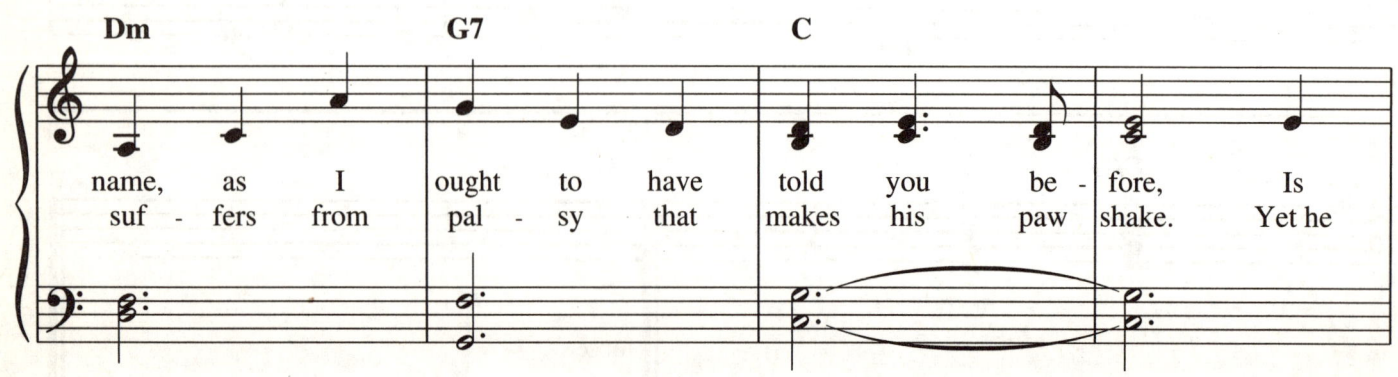

name, as I ought to have told you be-fore, Is
suf-fers from pal-sy that makes his paw shake. Yet he

Music Copyright © 1981 The Really Useful Group Ltd.
Text Copyright © 1939 T.S. Eliot; this edition of the text © 1981 Set Copyrights Ltd.
All Rights in the text Controlled by Faber and Faber Ltd. and Administered for the United States and Canada by R&H Music Co.
International Copyright Secured   All Rights Reserved

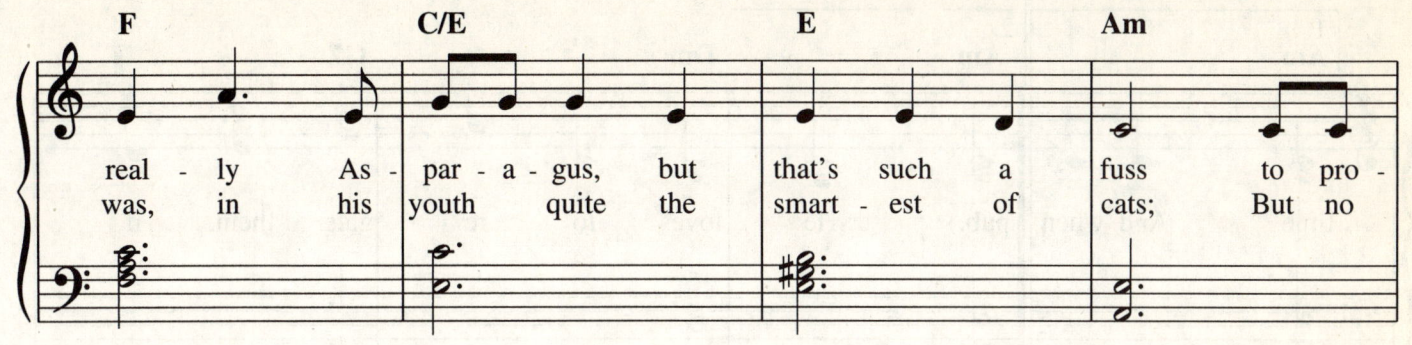

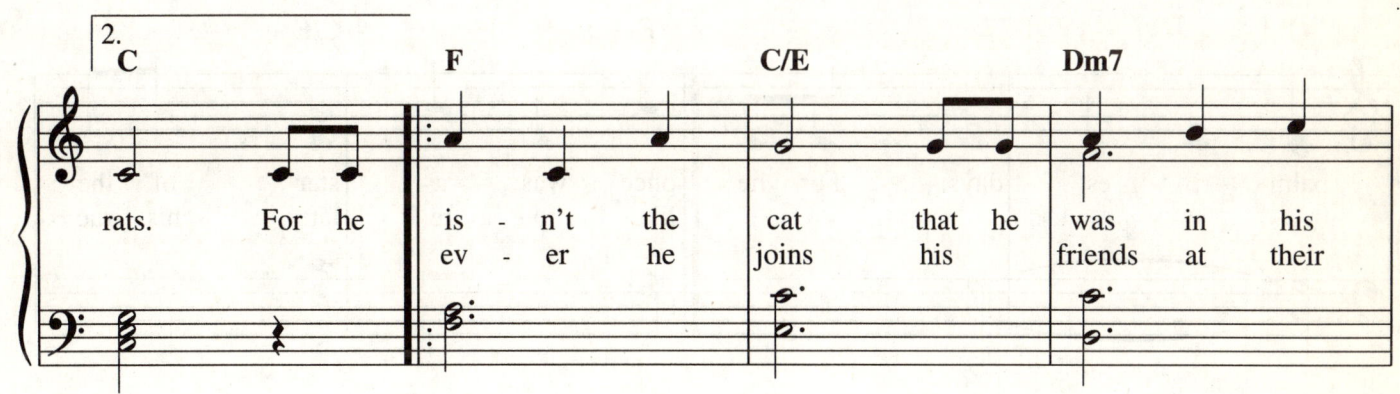
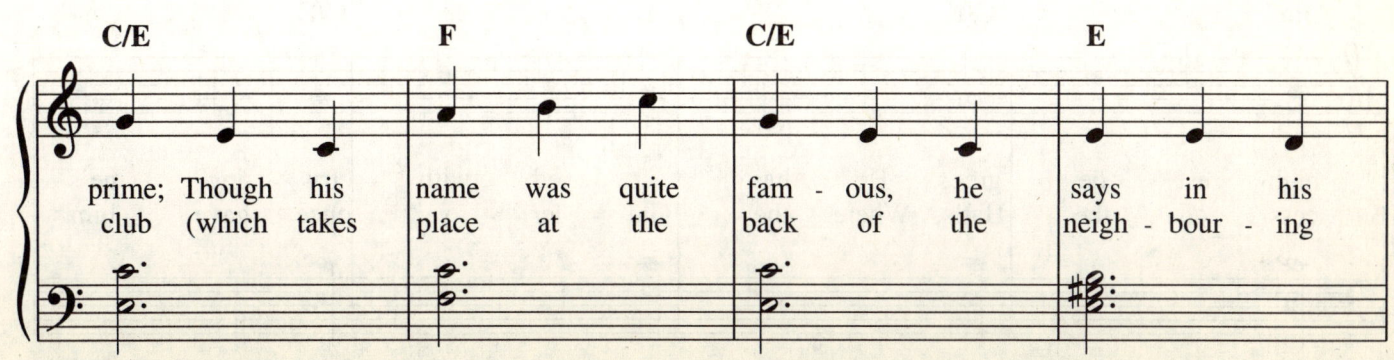

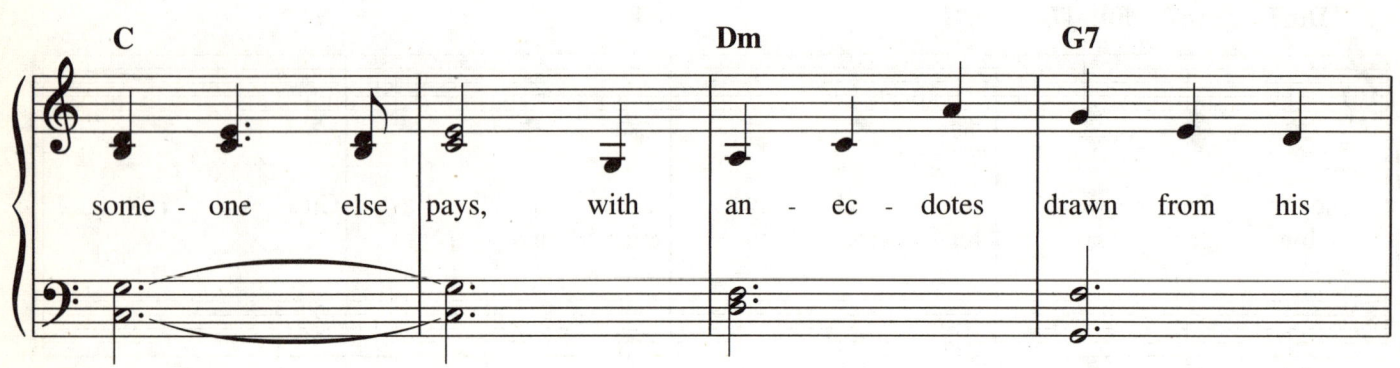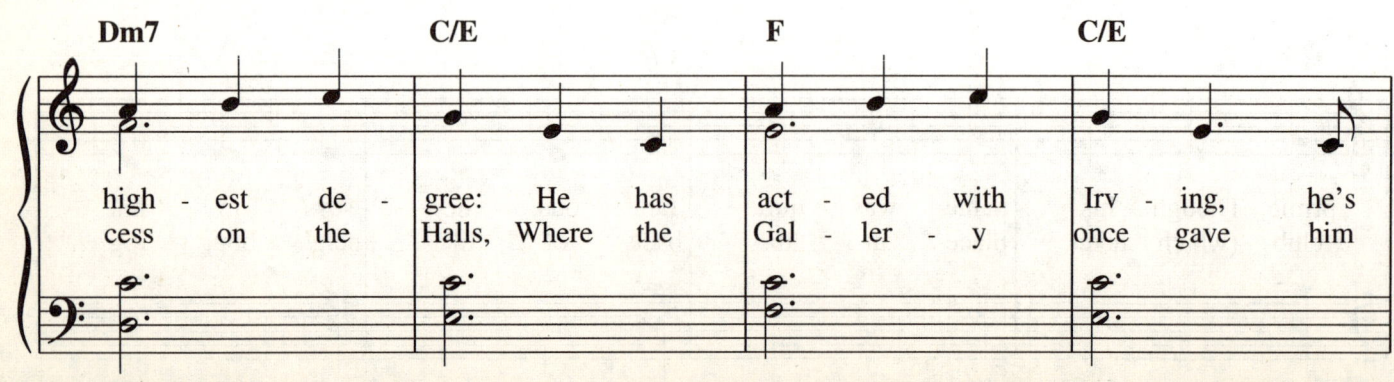

GUYS AND DOLLS
from GUYS AND DOLLS

By FRANK LOESSER

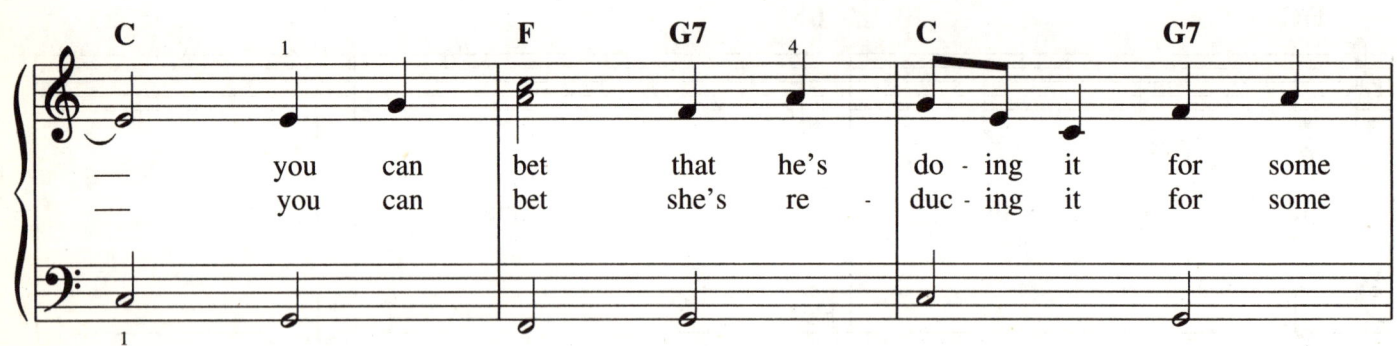

© 1950 (Renewed) FRANK MUSIC CORP.
All Rights Reserved

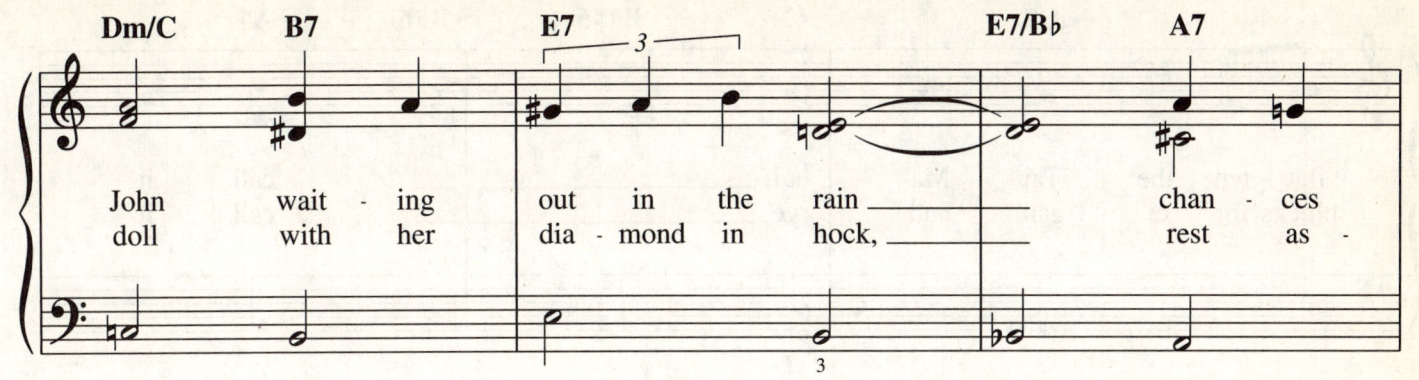

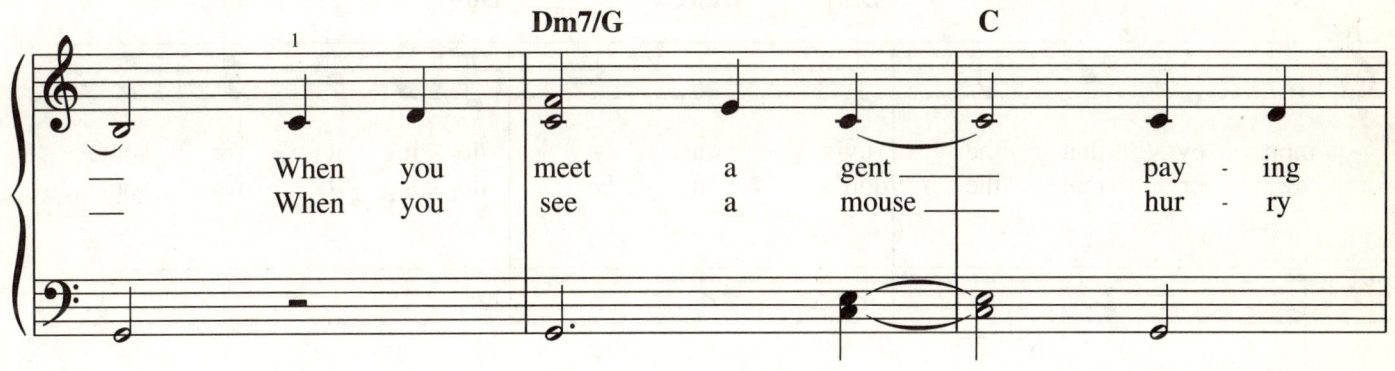
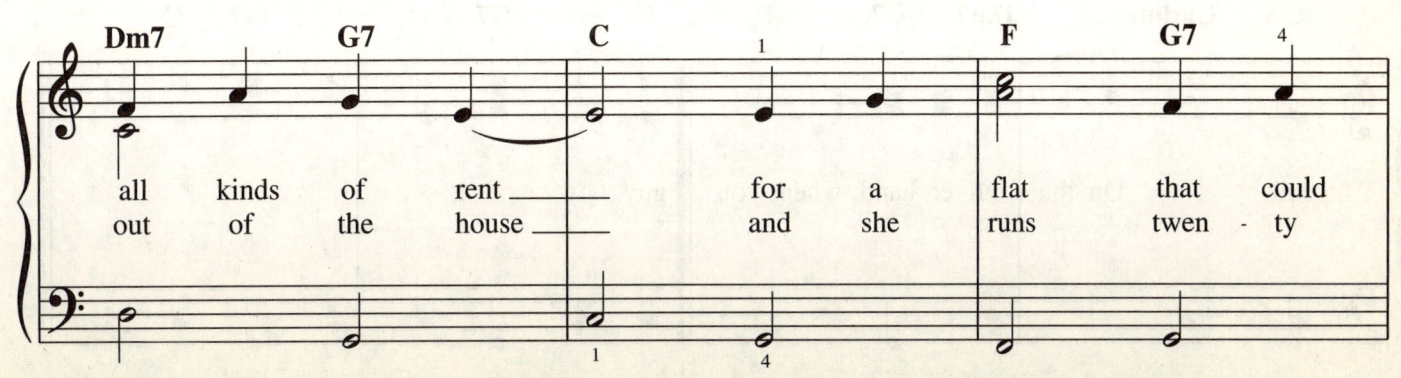

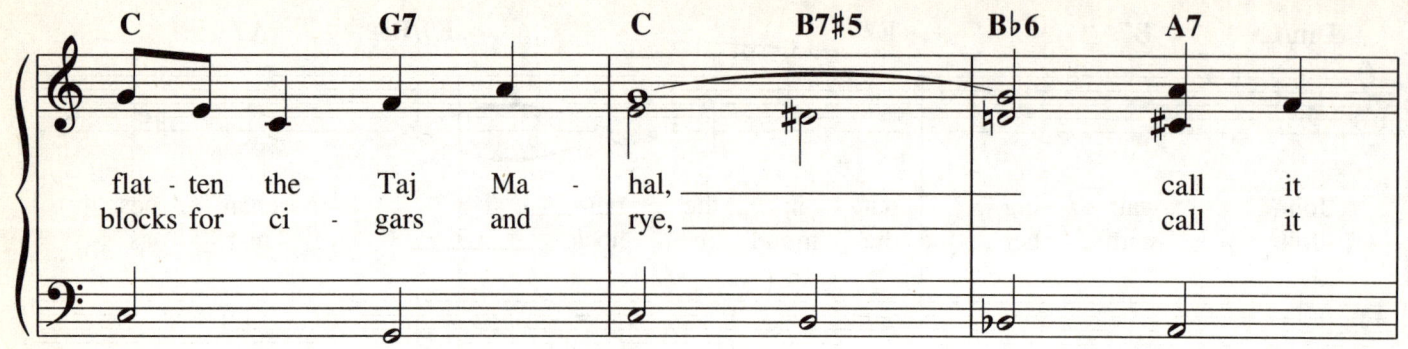

I AIN'T DOWN YET
from THE UNSINKABLE MOLLY BROWN

By MEREDITH WILLSON

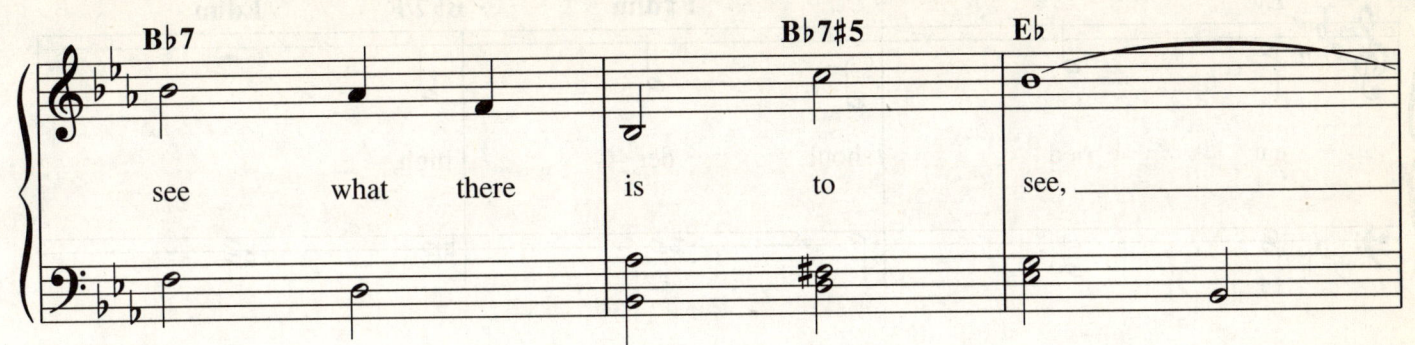
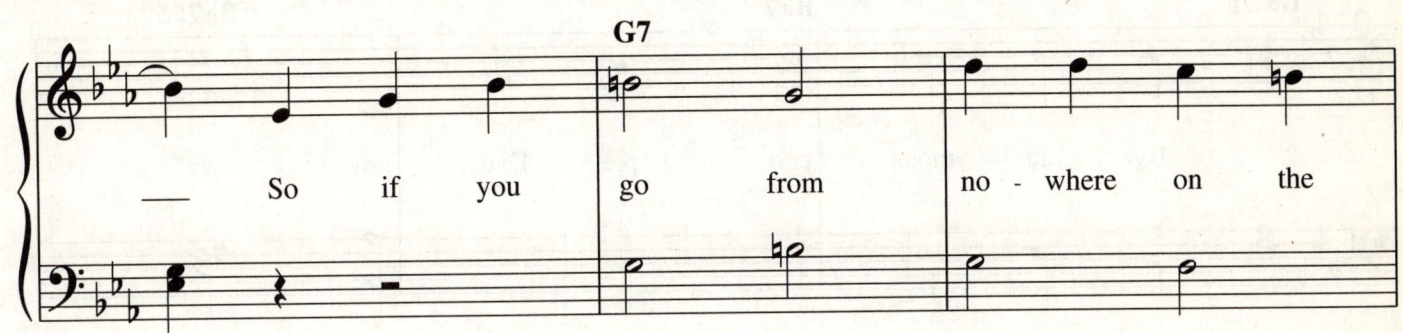
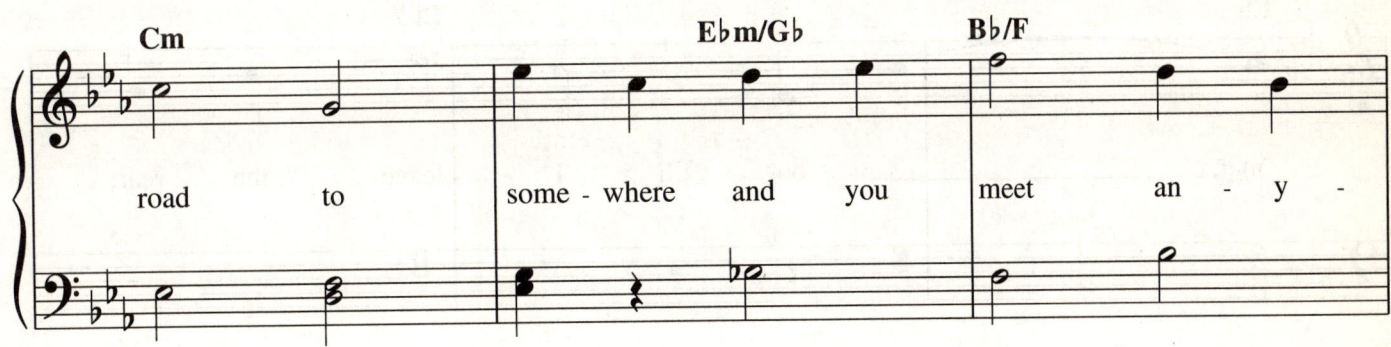
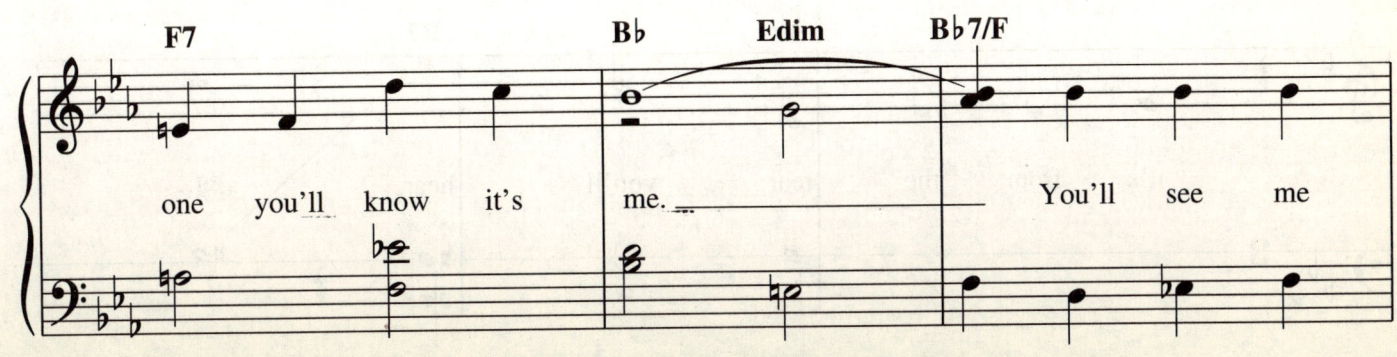

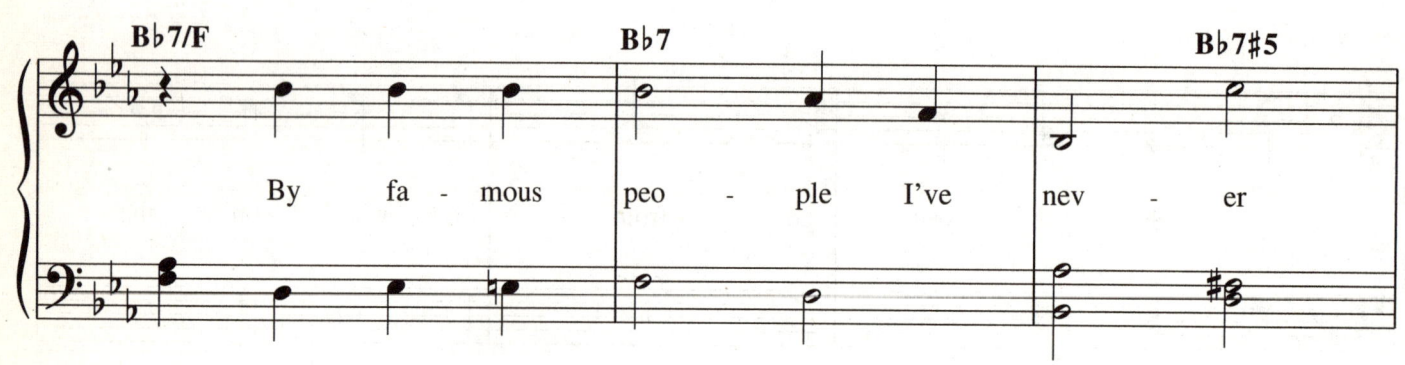

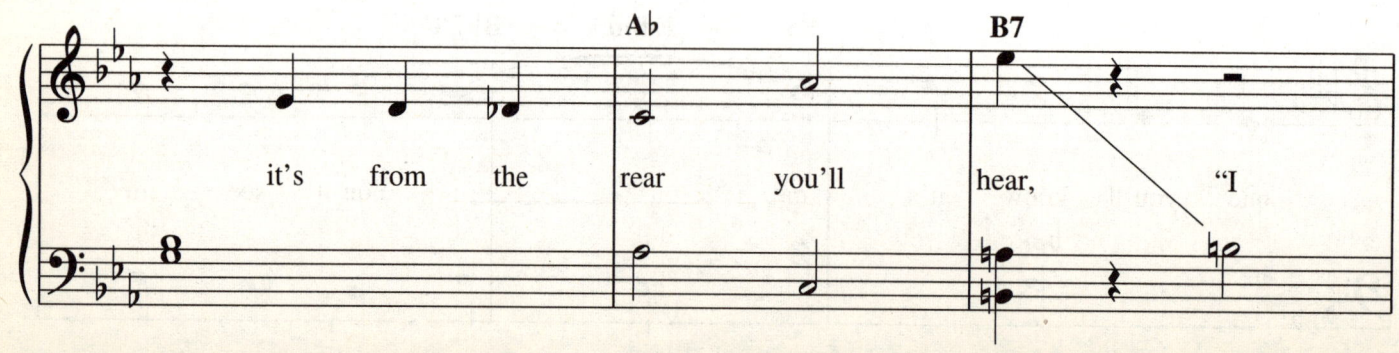

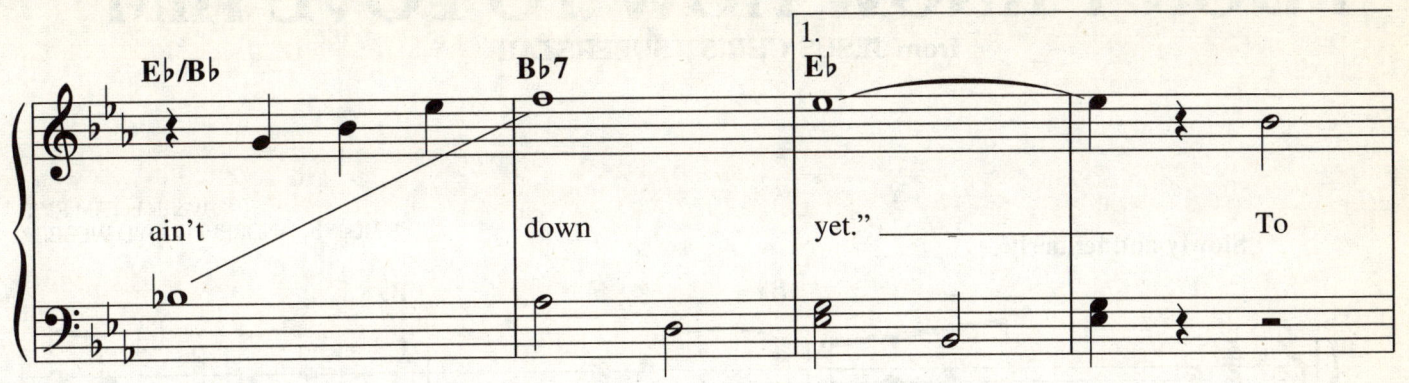
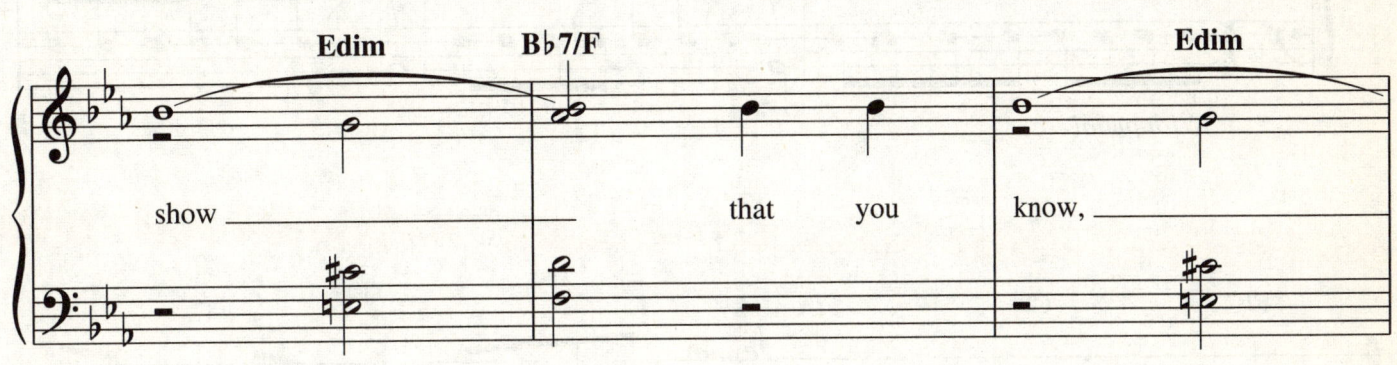
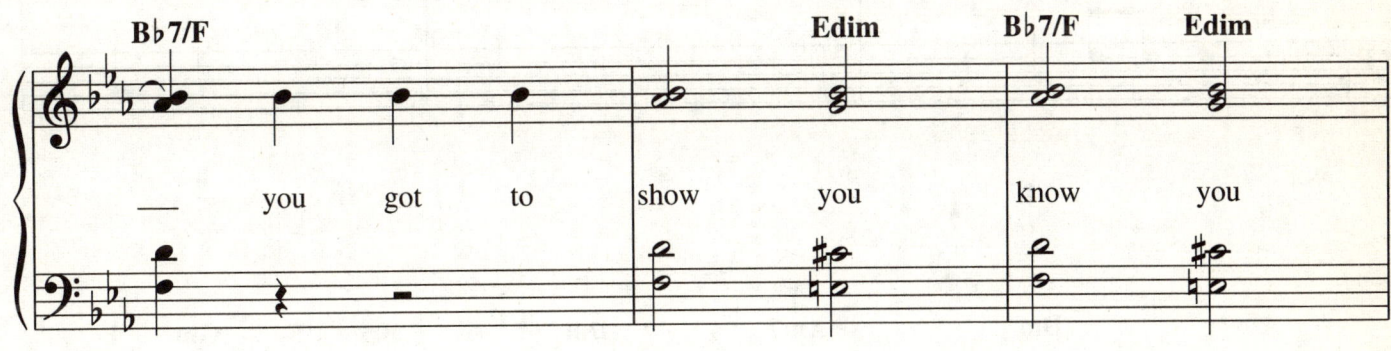
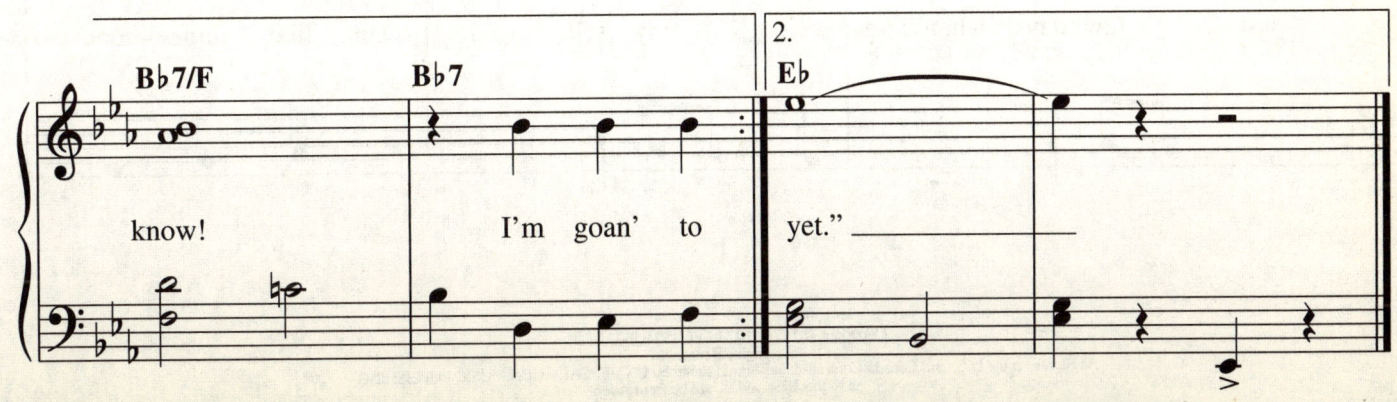

I DON'T KNOW HOW TO LOVE HIM

from JESUS CHRIST SUPERSTAR

Words by TIM RICE
Music by ANDREW LLOYD WEBBER

Copyright © 1970, 1971 LEEDS MUSIC LTD.
Copyrights Renewed
All Rights for the U.S. and Canada Controlled and Administered by UNIVERSAL - MCA MUSIC PUBLISHING
All Rights Reserved   Used by Permission

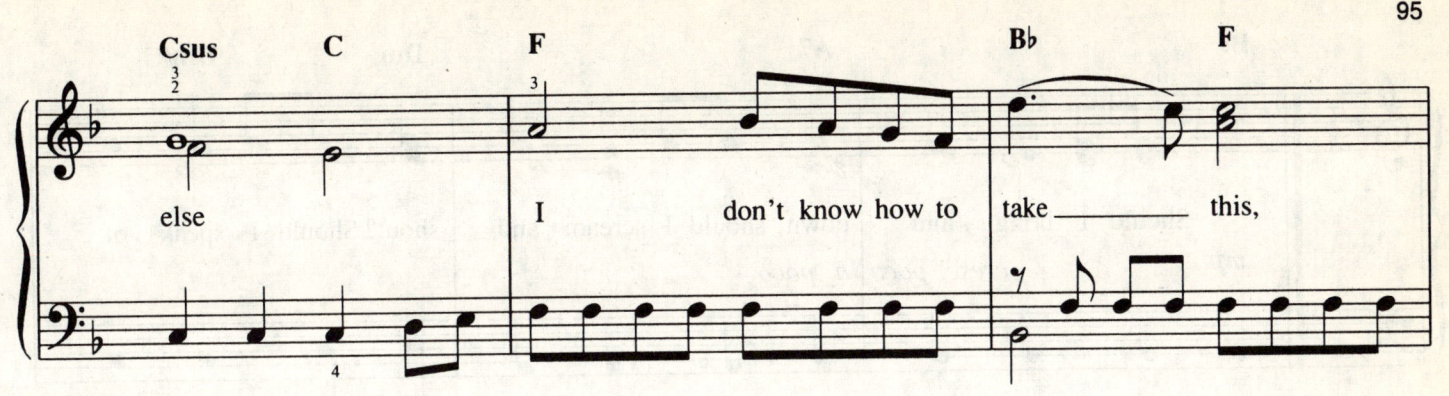
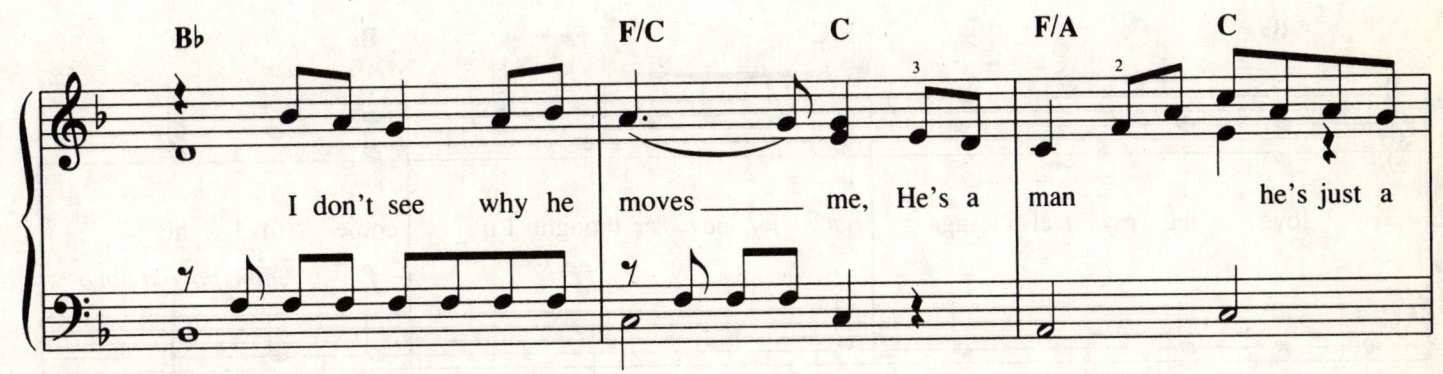

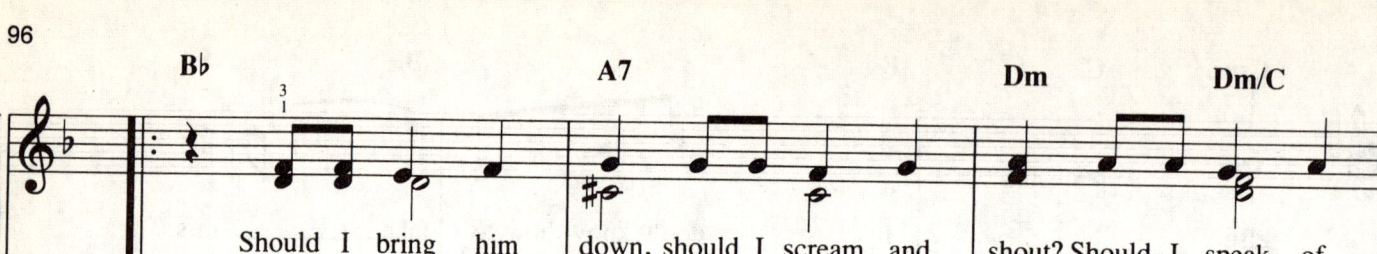

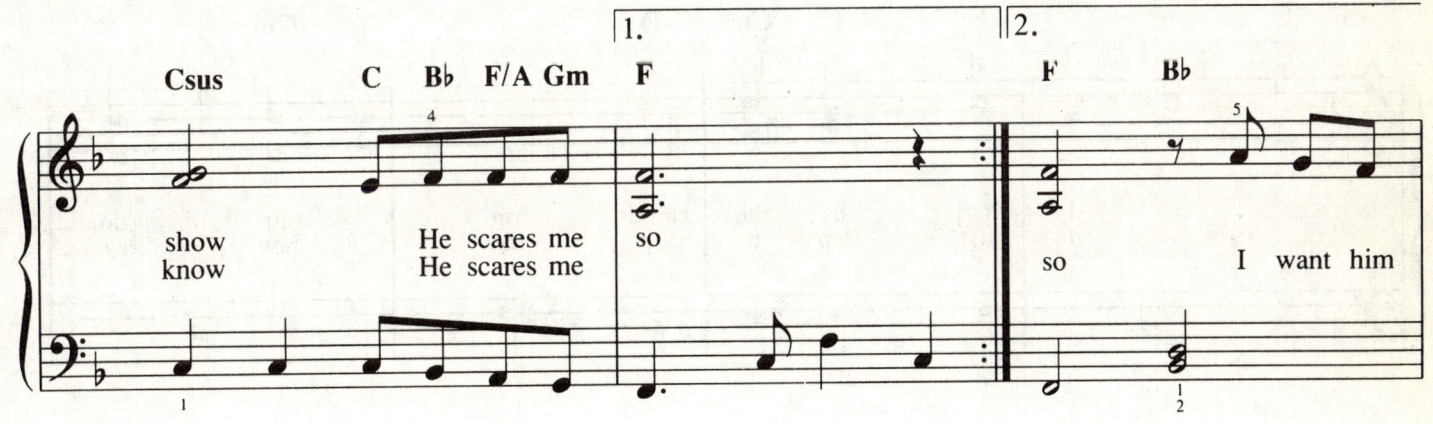

I ENJOY BEING A GIRL
from FLOWER DRUM SONG

Lyrics by OSCAR HAMMERSTEIN II
Music by RICHARD RODGERS

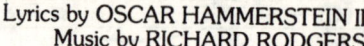

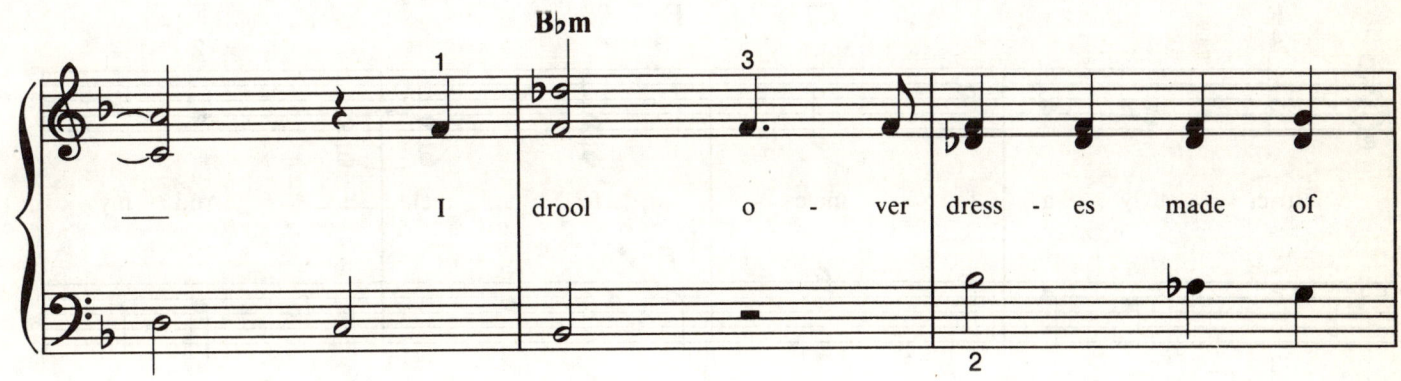

A♭
G7
ho - urs
With a pound and a half of
cream up - on my face!
C7
I'm
F
C7
F
strict - ly a fe - male fe - male
And my
Gm
C7
C
fu - ture I hope will be
In the

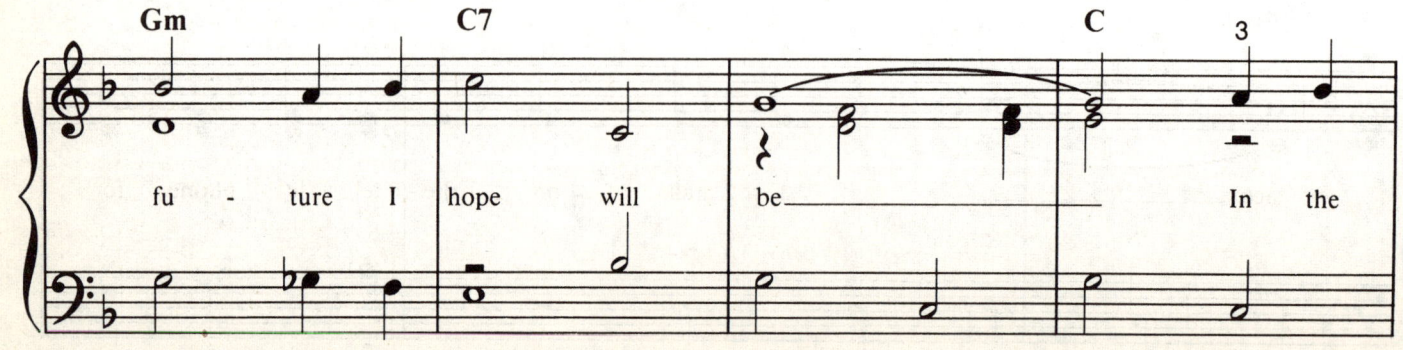

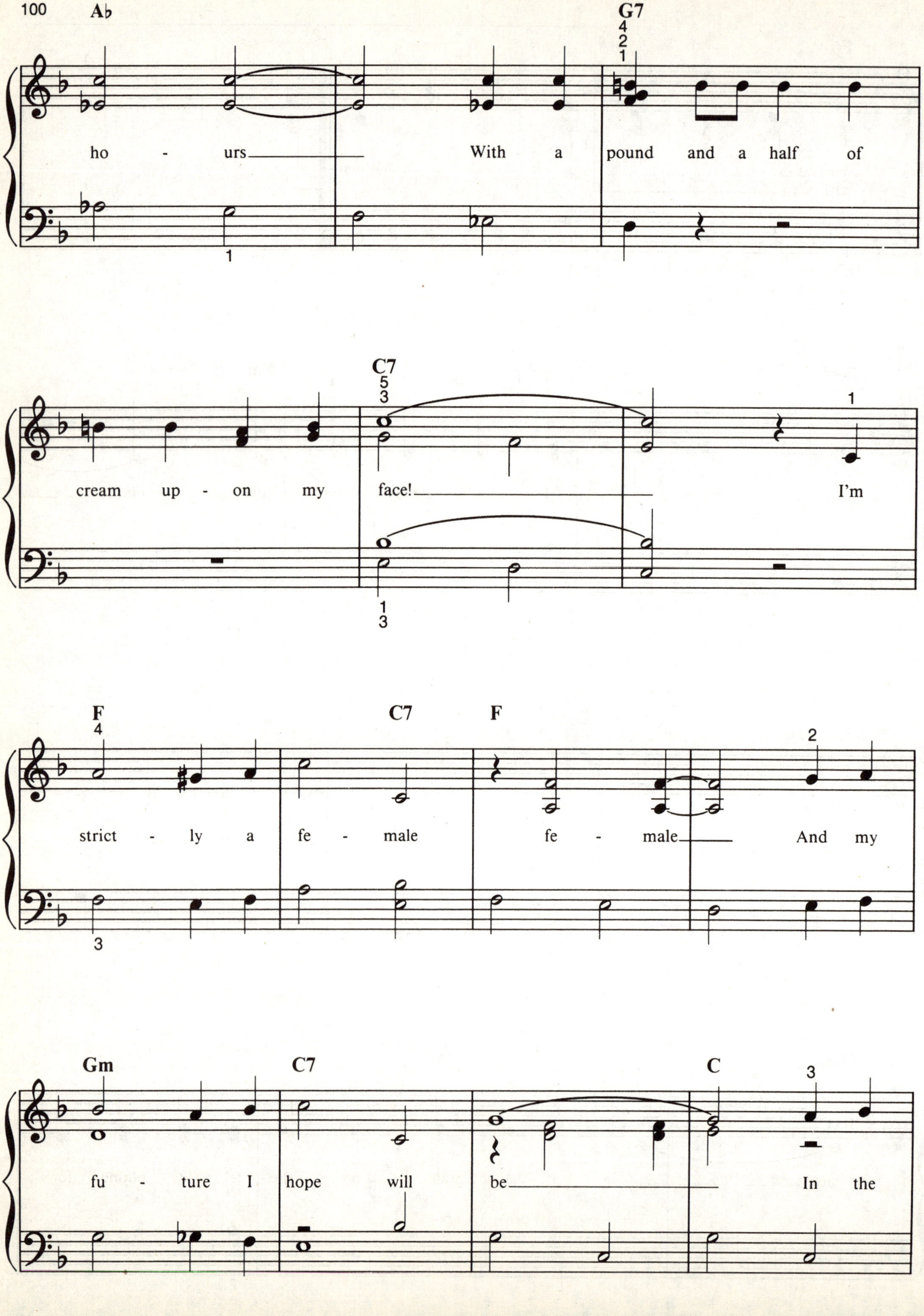

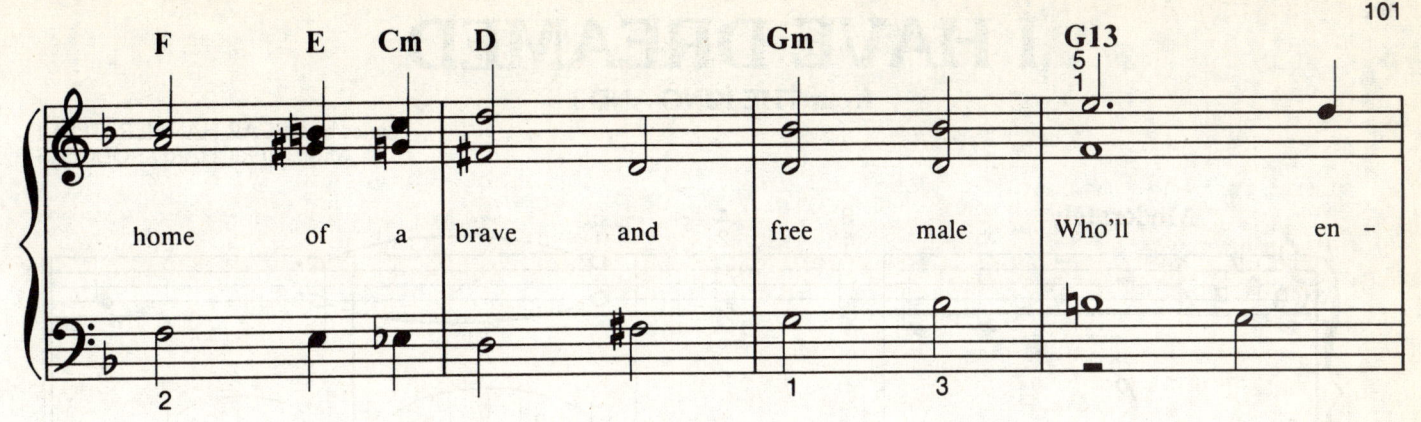
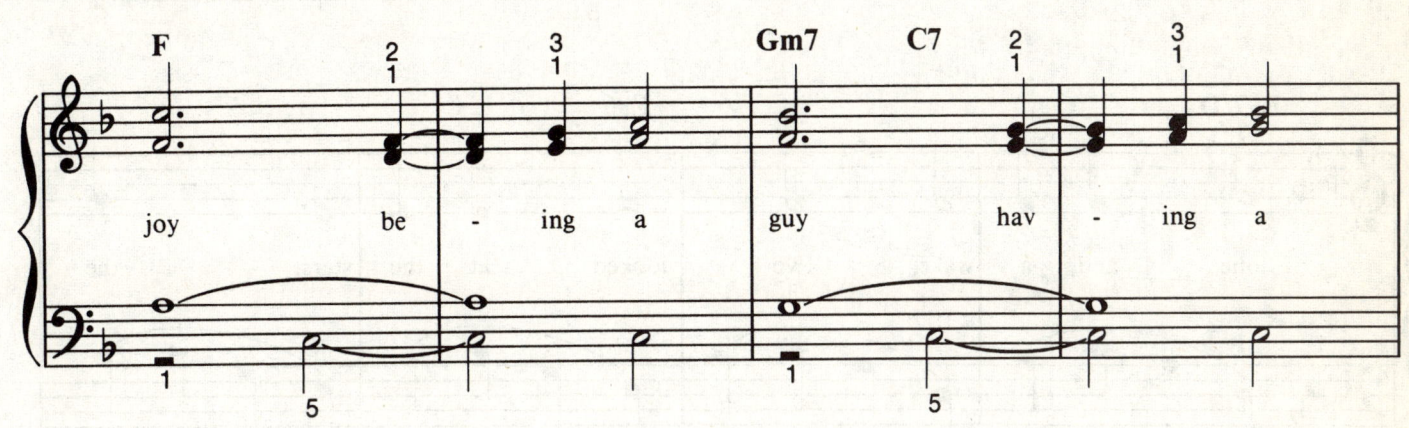
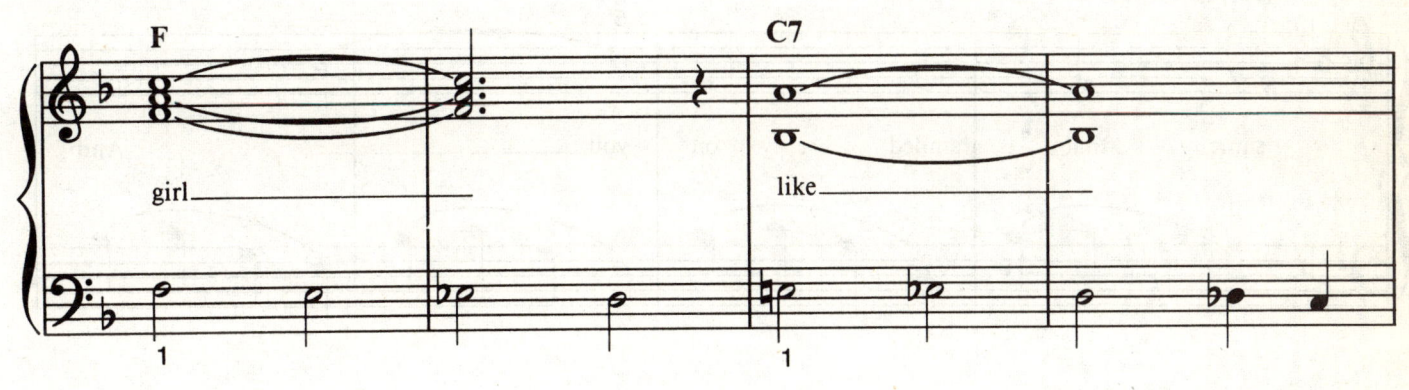

I HAVE DREAMED
from THE KING AND I

Lyrics by OSCAR HAMMERSTEIN II
Music by RICHARD RODGERS

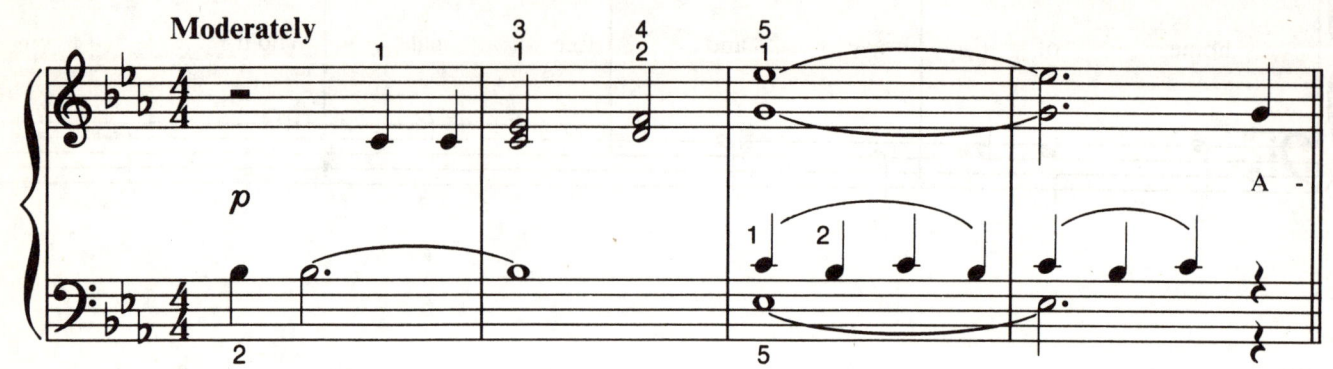

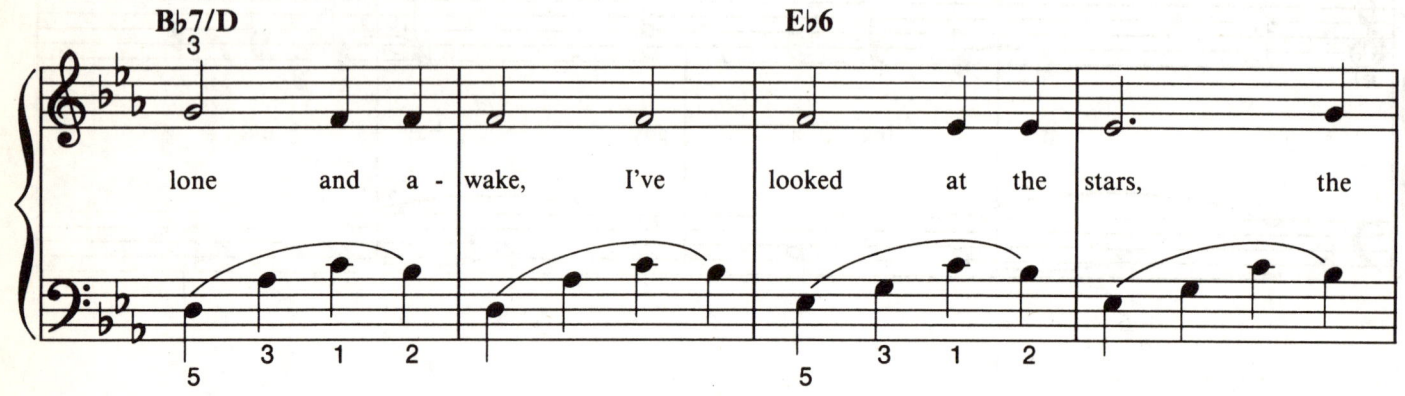
A- lone and a- wake, I've looked at the stars, the

same that smiled on you. And

time and a- gain, I've thought all the things that

Copyright © 1951 by Richard Rodgers and Oscar Hammerstein II
Copyright Renewed
WILLIAMSON MUSIC owner of publication and allied rights throughout the world
International Copyright Secured   All Rights Reserved

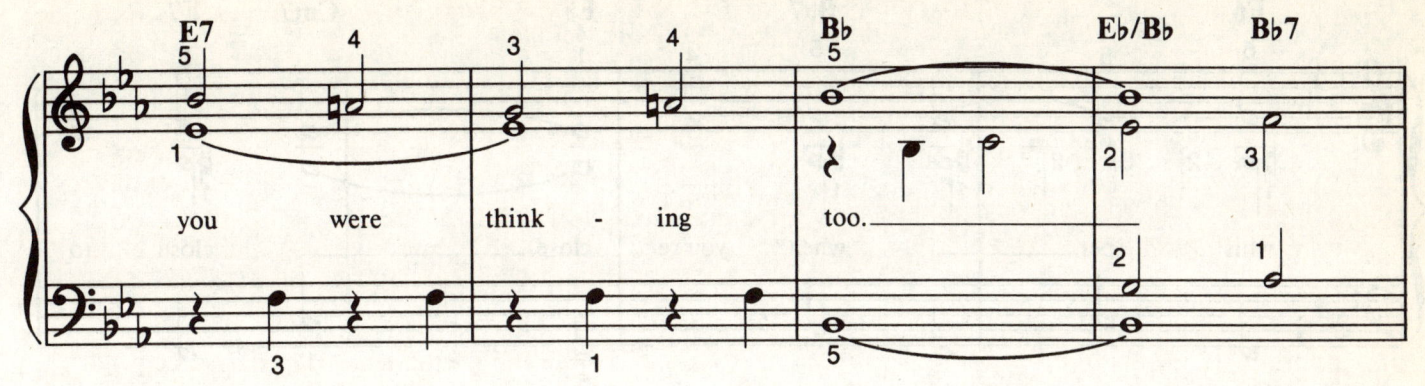
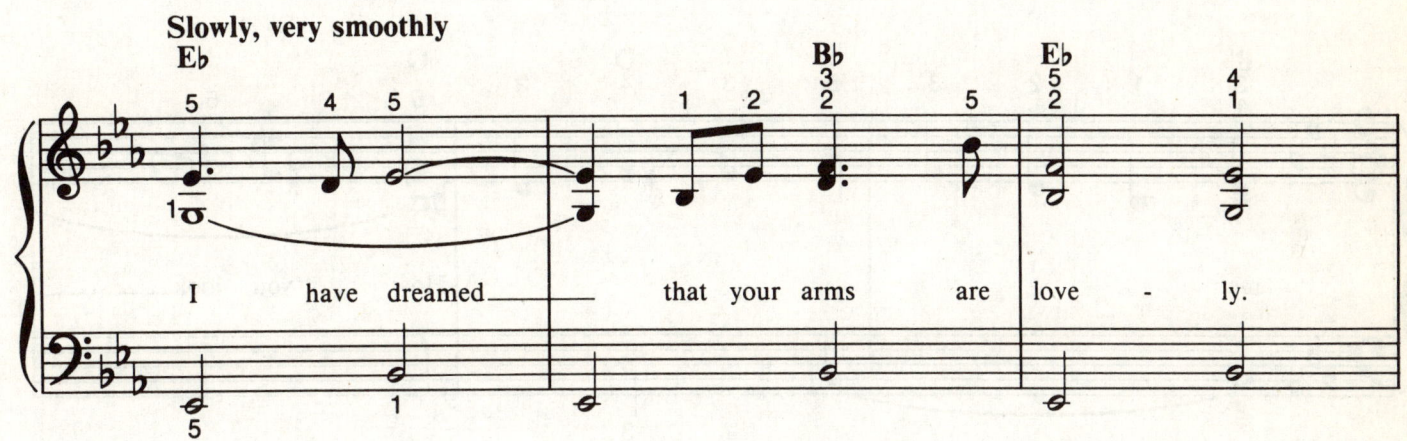

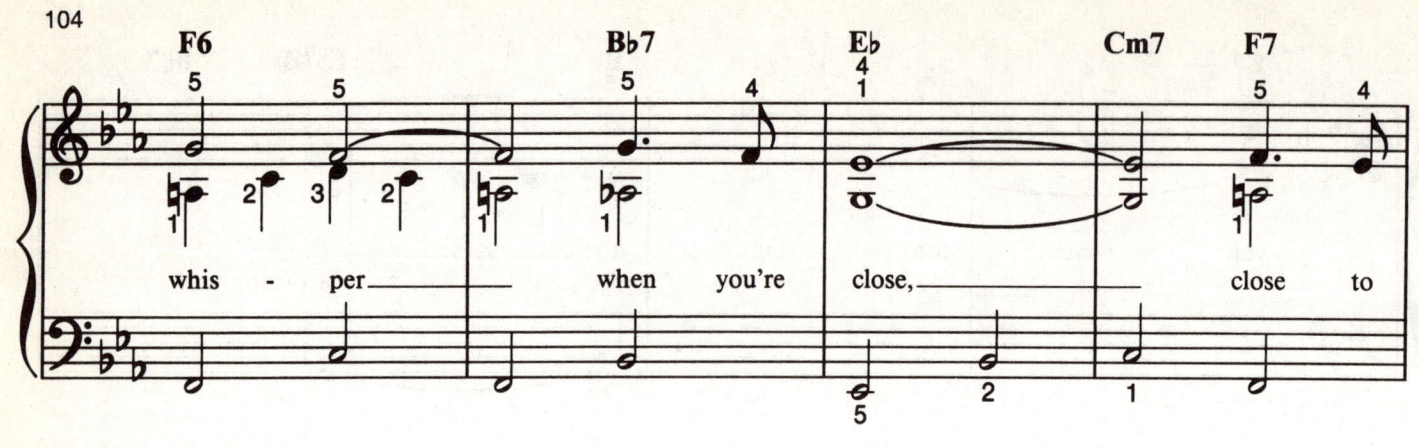
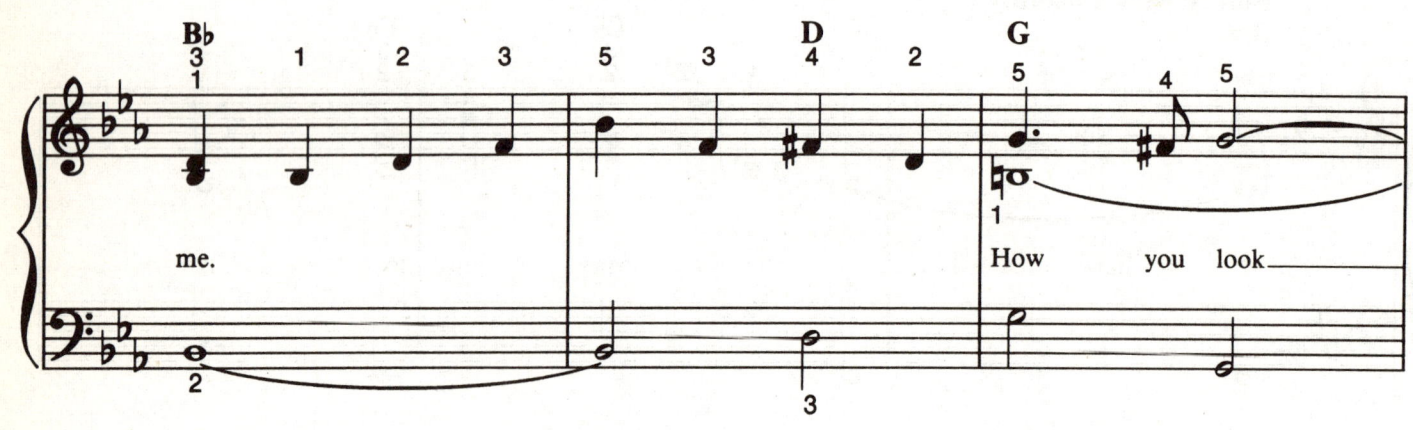

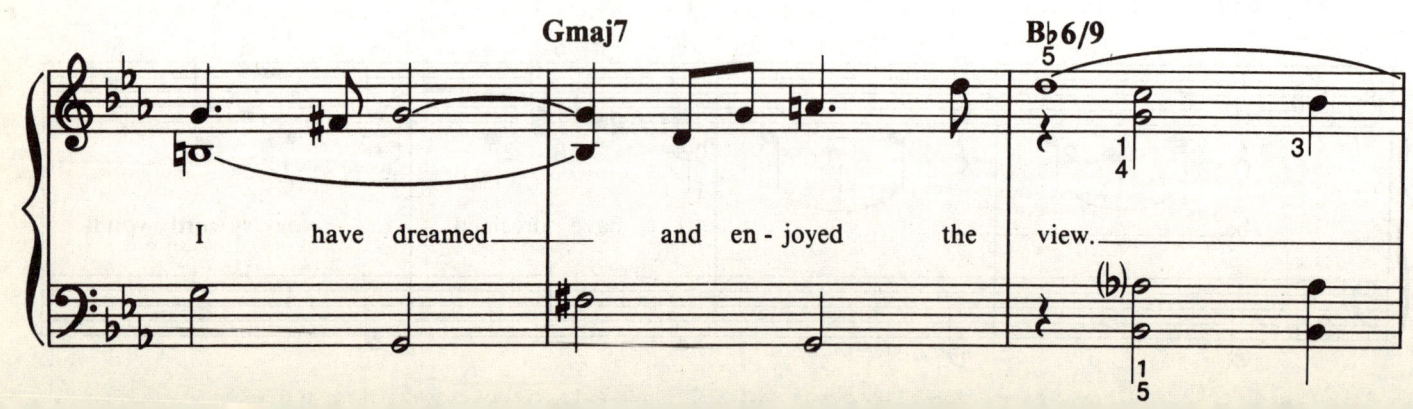

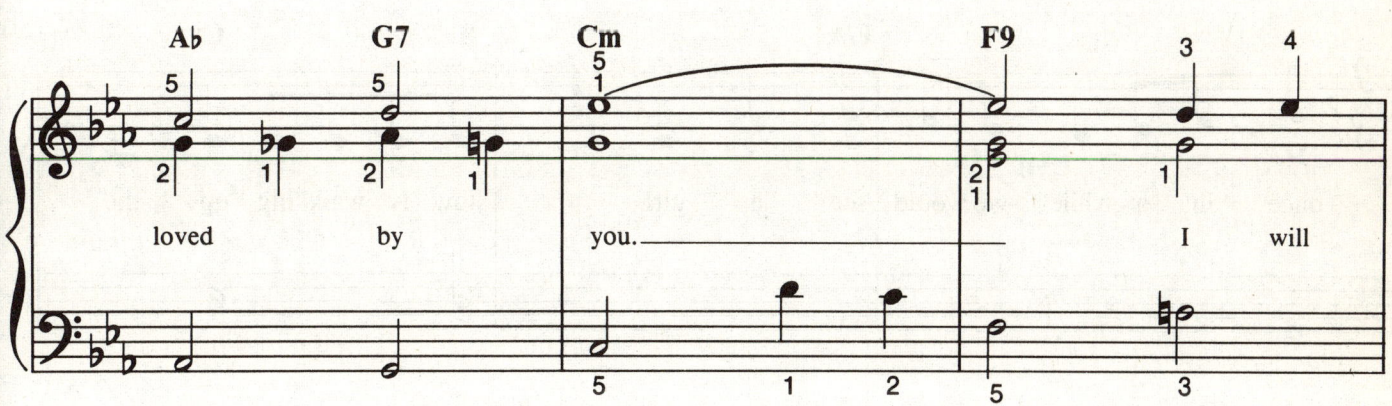
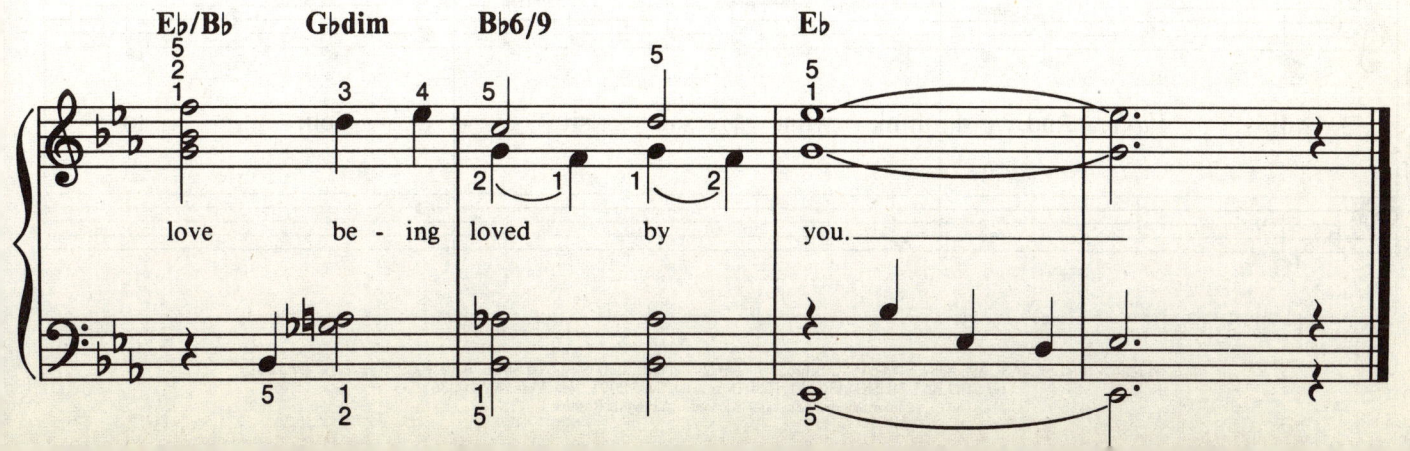

I WILL NEVER LEAVE YOU
from SIDE SHOW

Words by BILL RUSSELL
Music by HENRY KRIEGER

Daisy: If we stood on our tip-toes,

we could peek o-ver the sill. And

once in a-while we would see a girl slow-ly walk-ing up the

hill. *Violet:* And we'd think what a sad sit-u-a-tion, to

© 1994 MIROKU MUSIC (ASCAP)/Administered by A. Schroeder International LLC, 200 West 51st Street, Suite 1009, New York, NY 10019
and STILLBILL MUSIC (ASCAP), 1500 Broadway, Suite 2001, New York, NY 10036
International Copyright Secured   All Rights Reserved

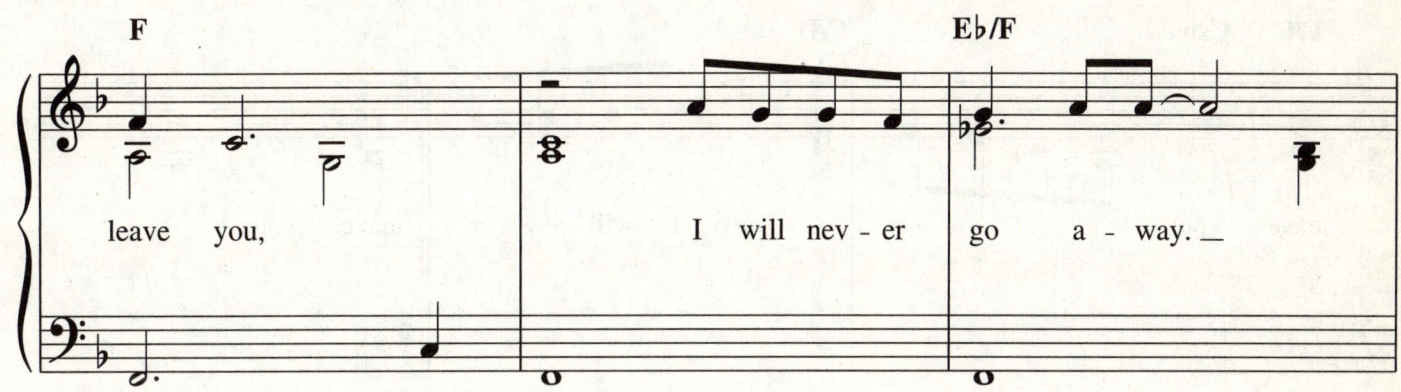

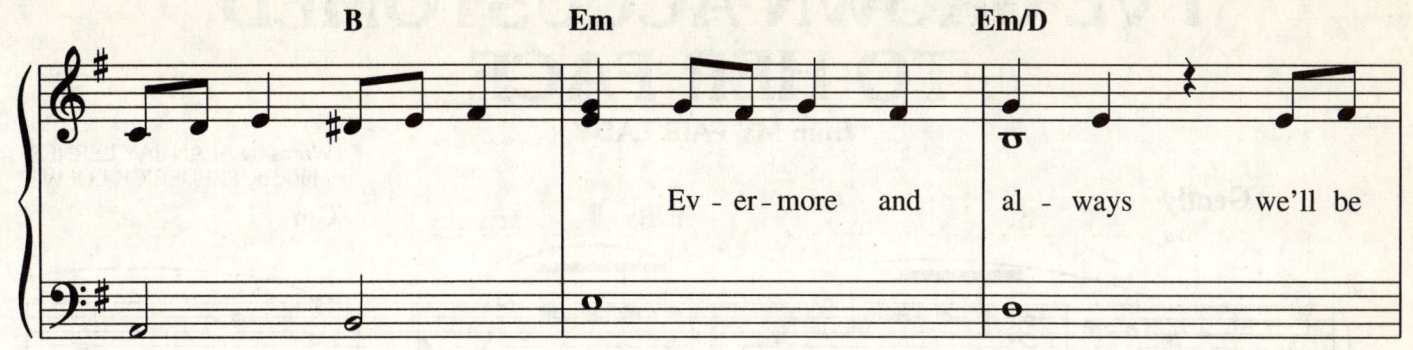
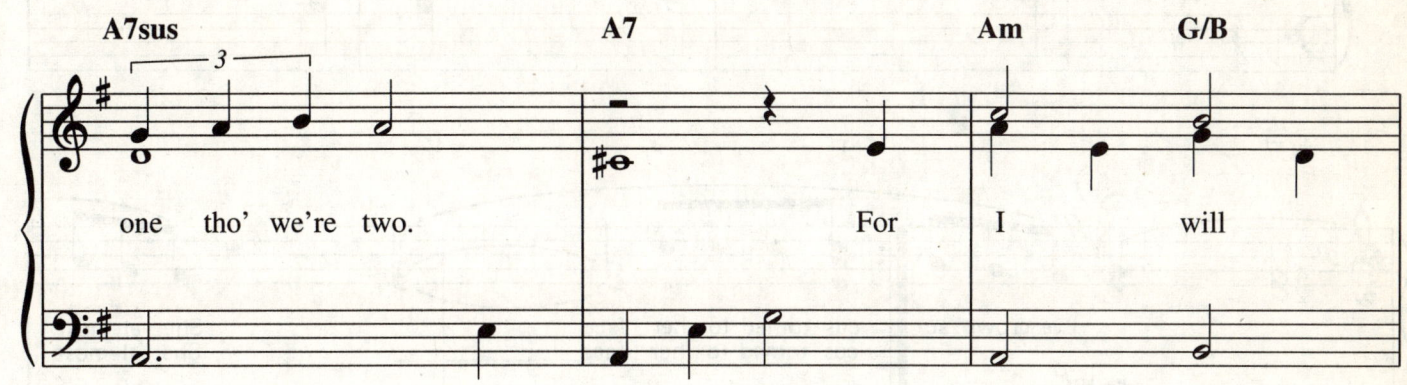

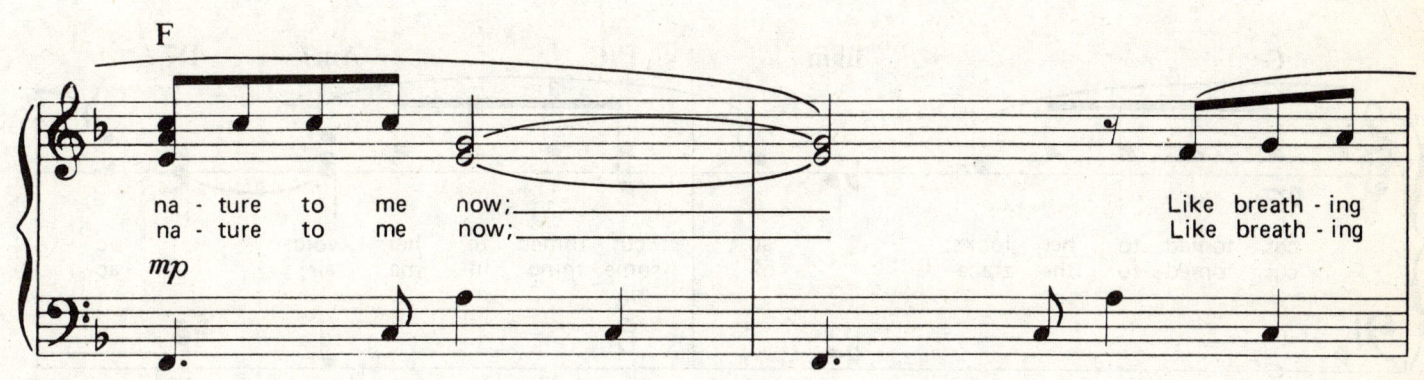

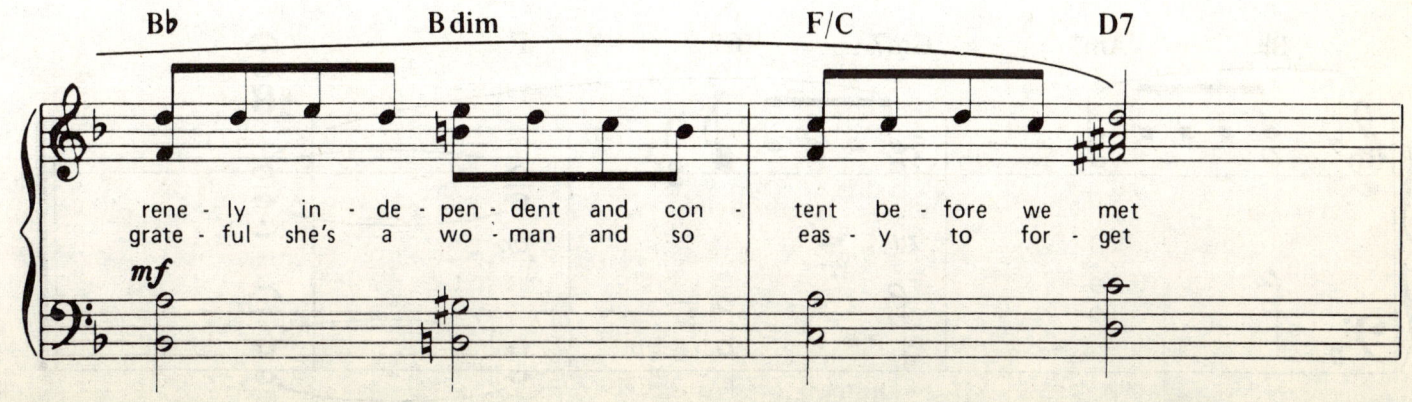

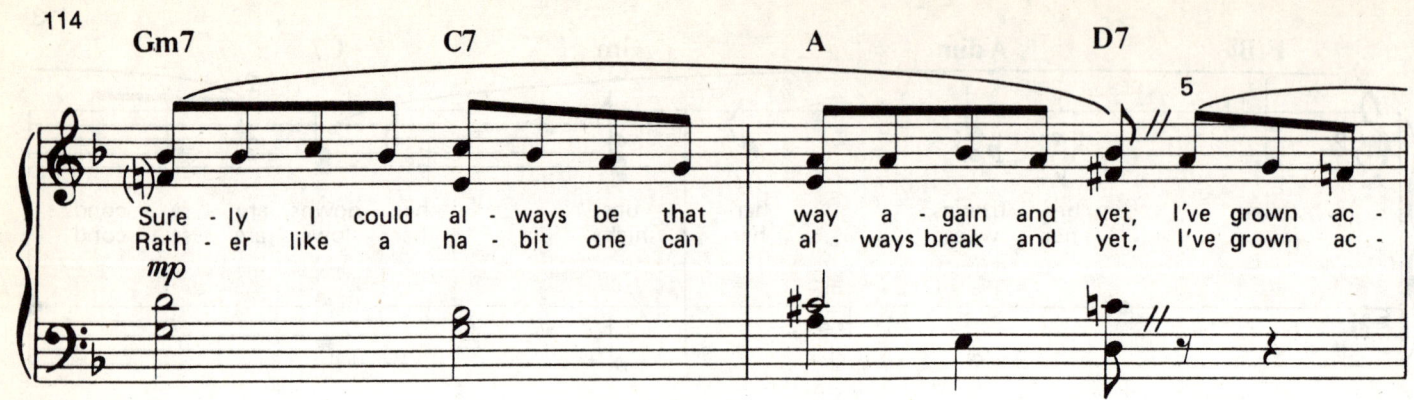
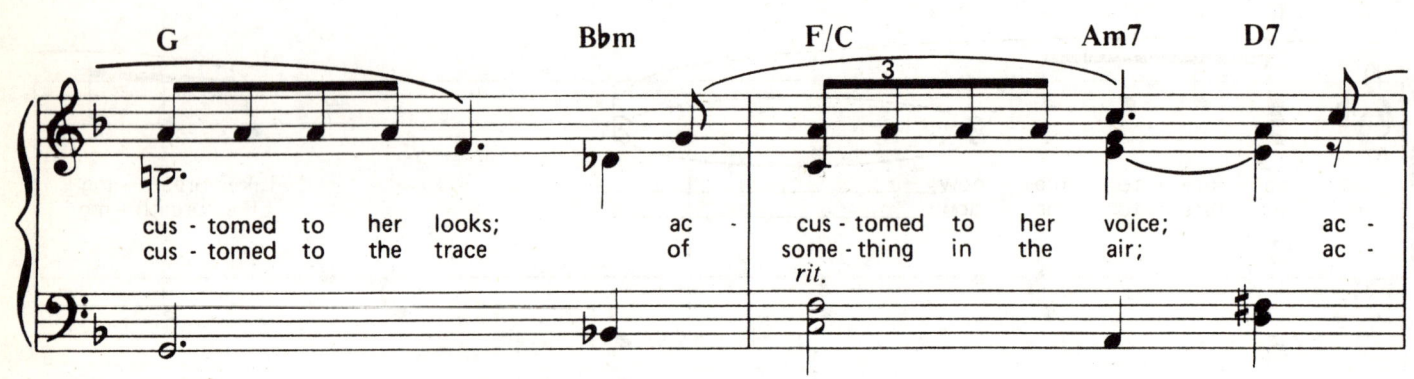

IF HE WALKED INTO MY LIFE
from MAME

IF I CAN'T LOVE HER

from Walt Disney's BEAUTY AND THE BEAST: THE BROADWAY MUSICAL

Music by ALAN MENKEN
Lyrics by TIM RICE

Beast: And in my twist-ed face

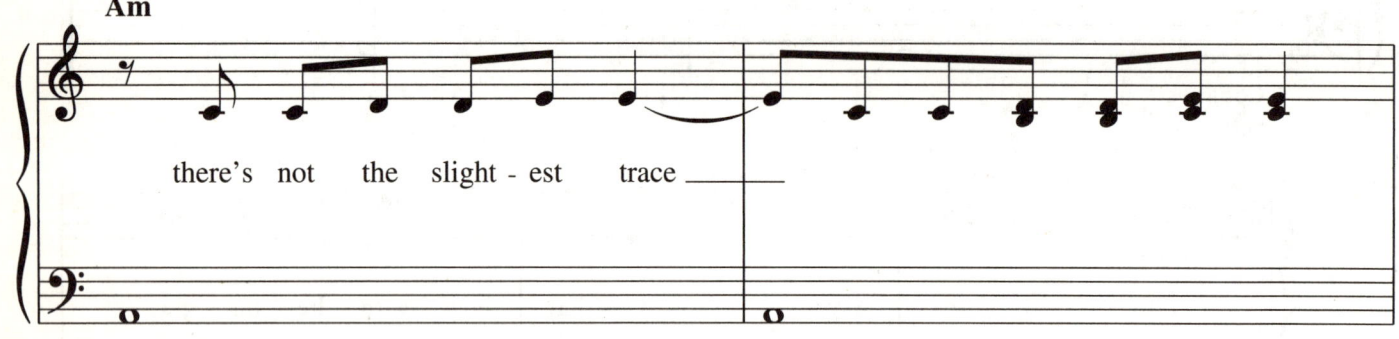

there's not the slight-est trace

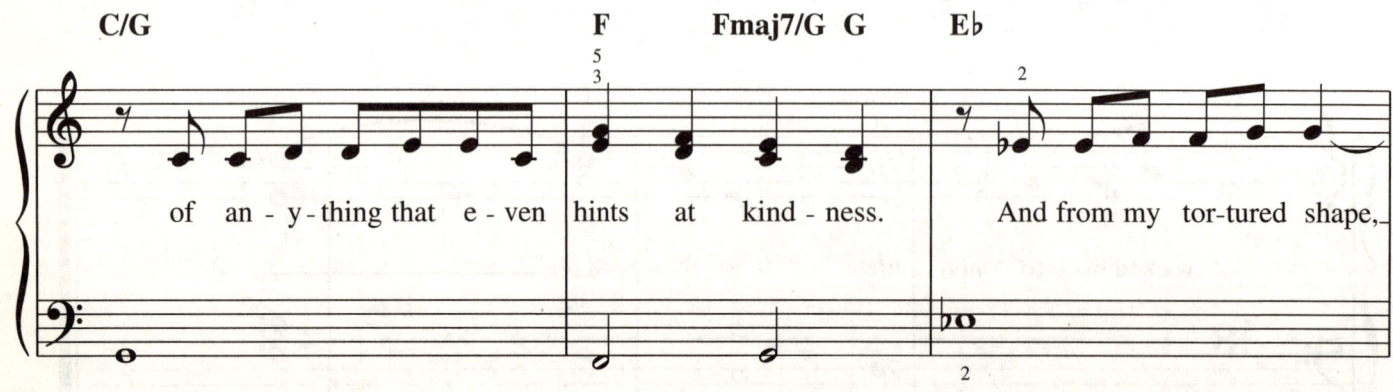

of an-y-thing that e-ven hints at kind-ness. And from my tor-tured shape,

© 1994 Wonderland Music Company, Inc., Menken Music, Trunksong Music Ltd. and Walt Disney Music Company
All Rights Reserved   Used by Permission

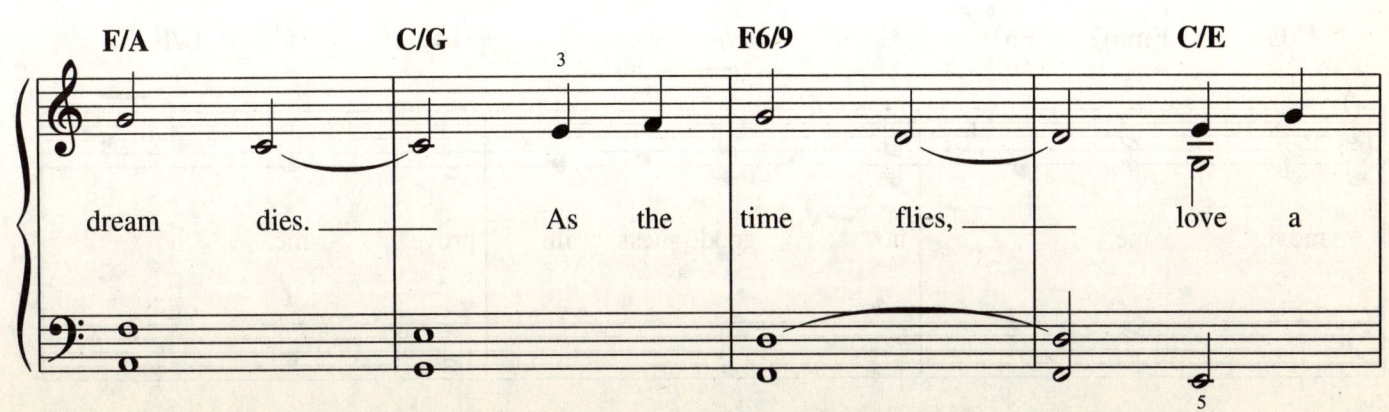

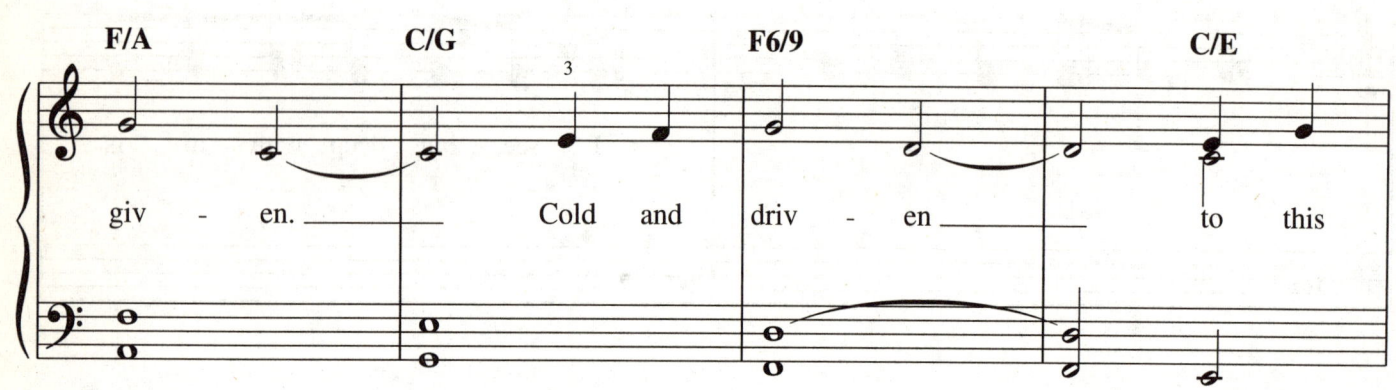

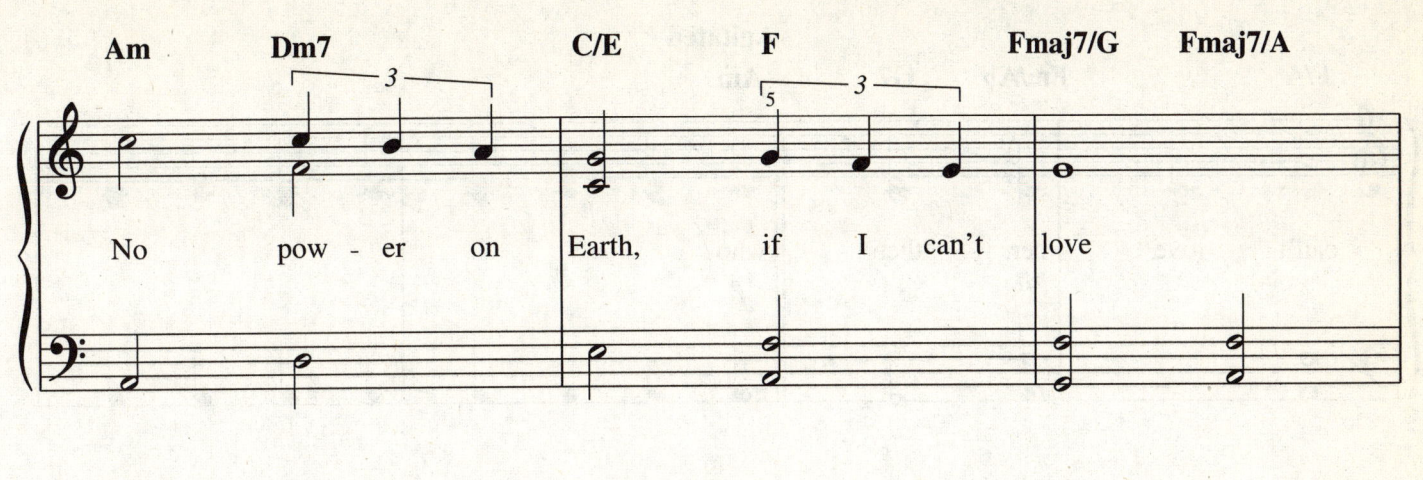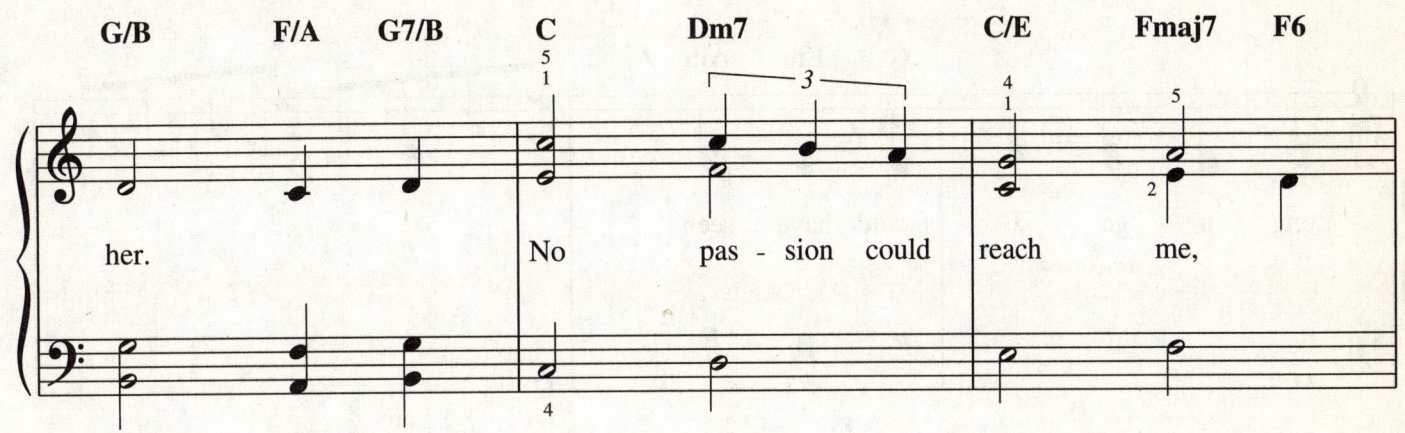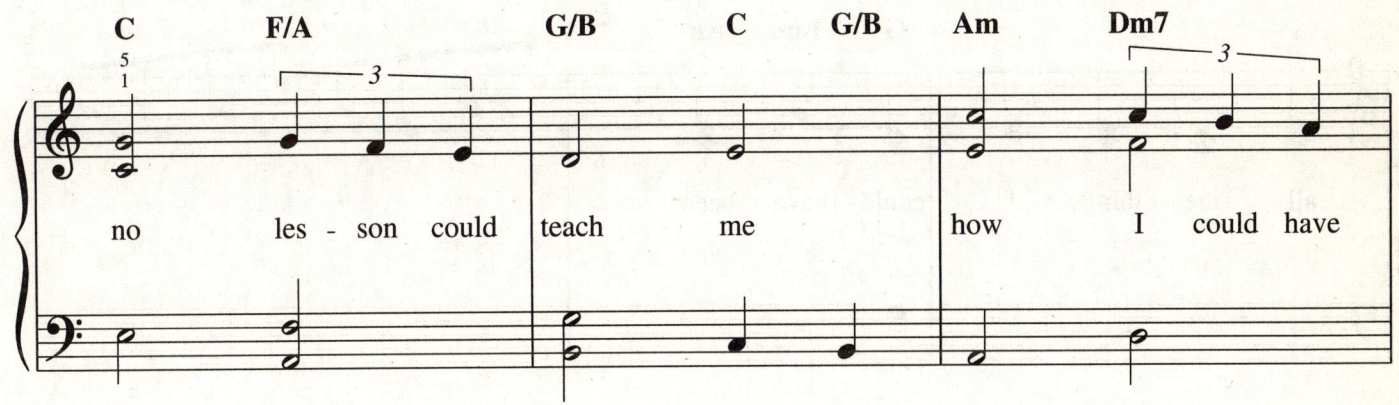

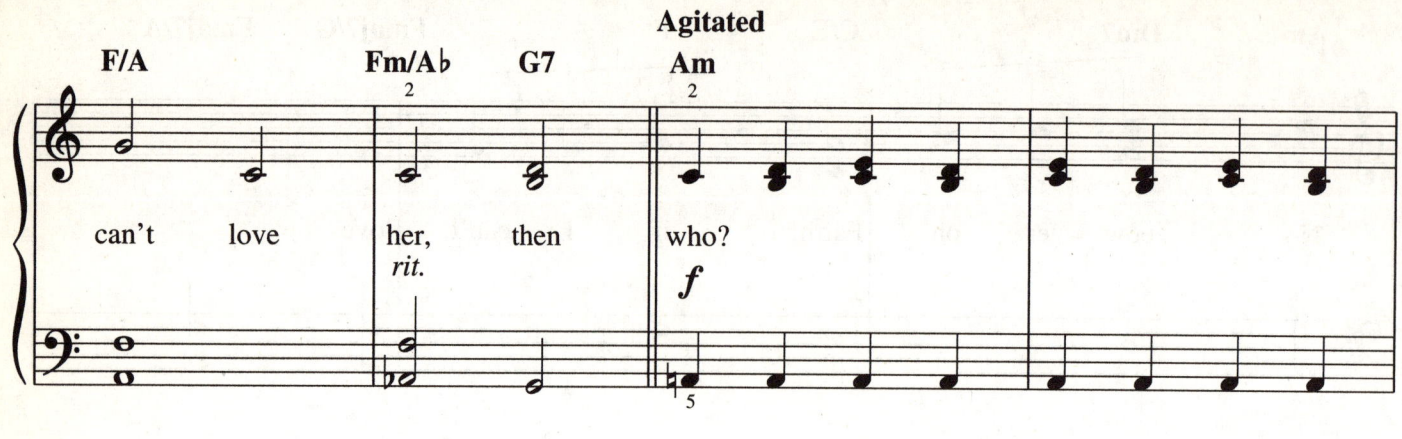
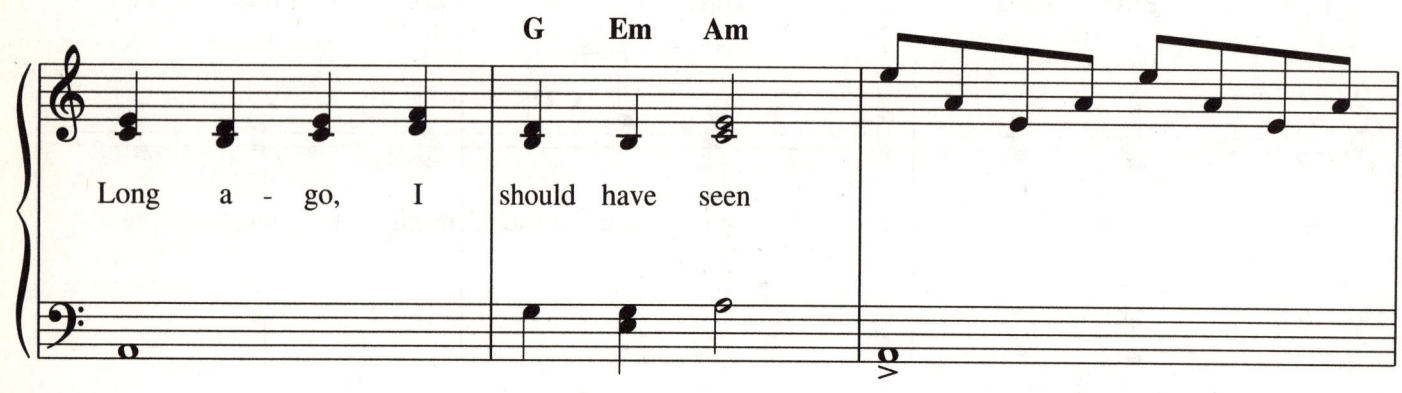
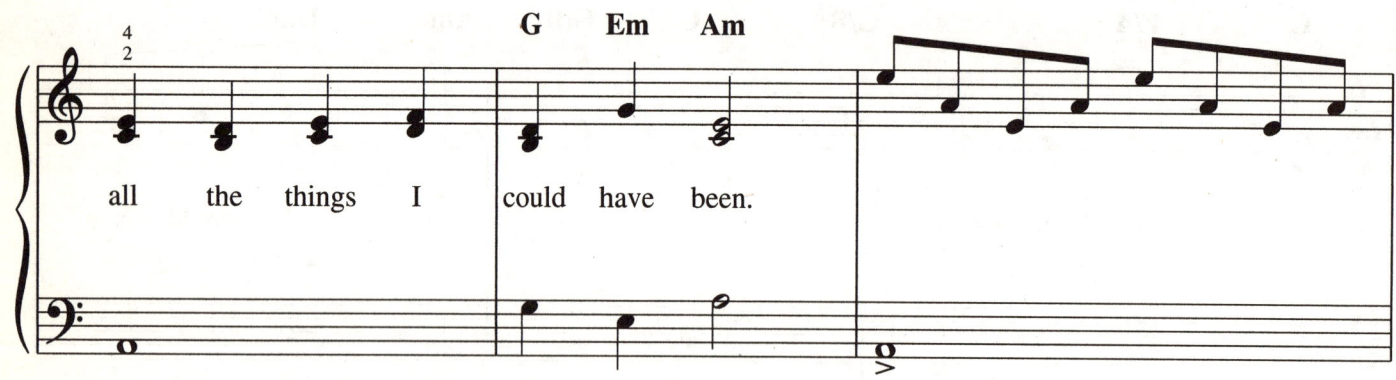
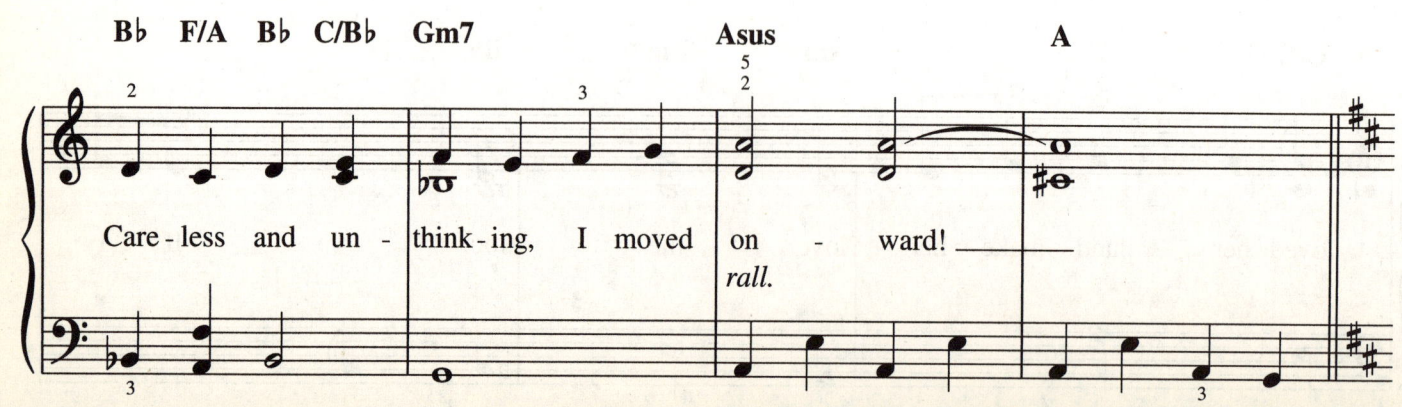

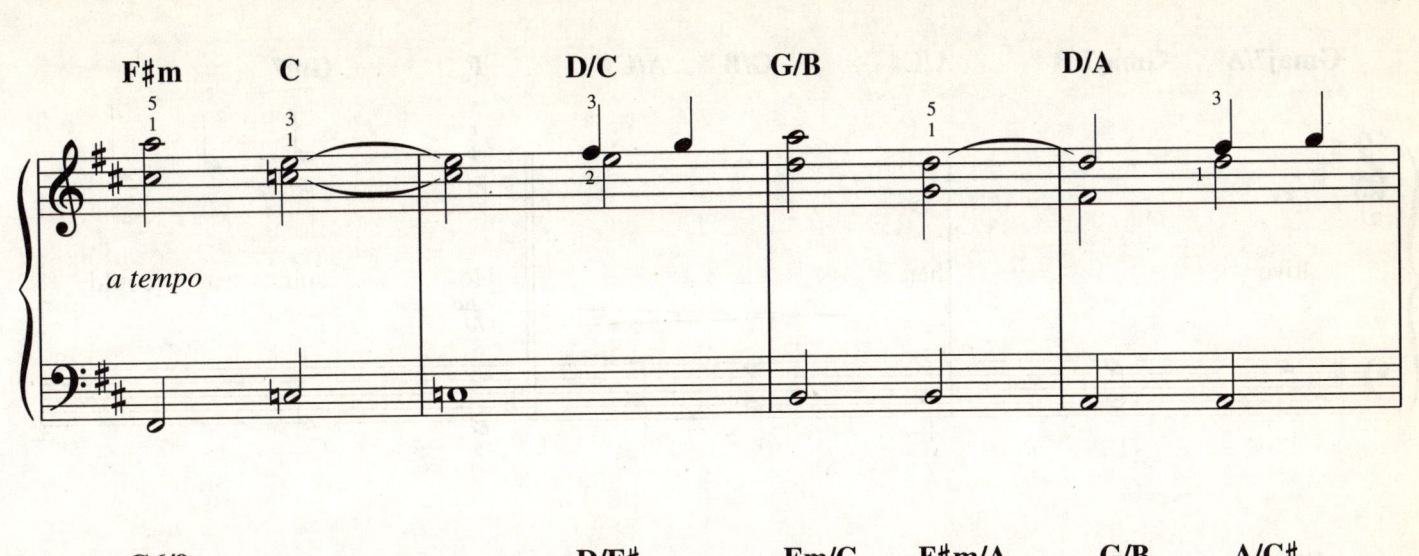
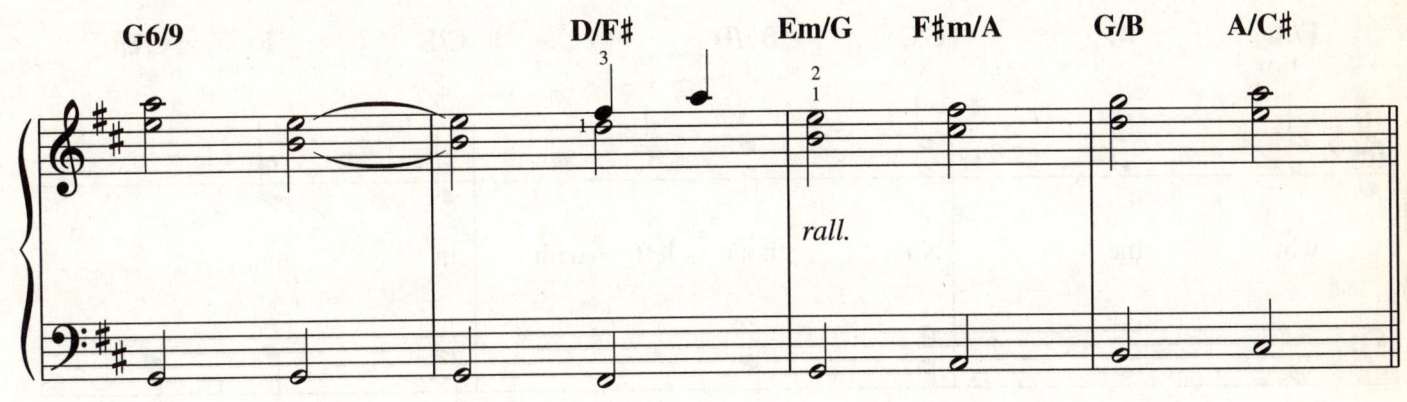
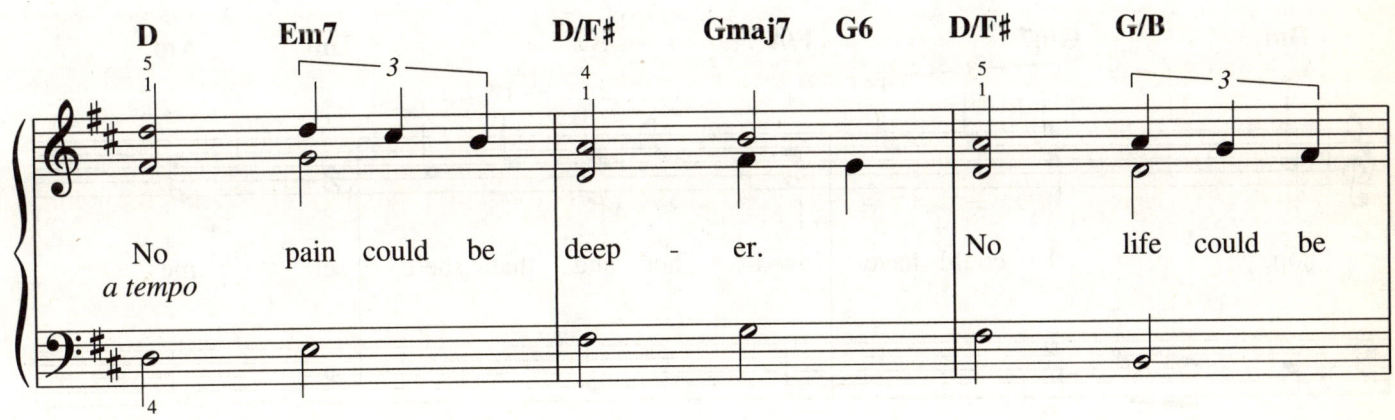
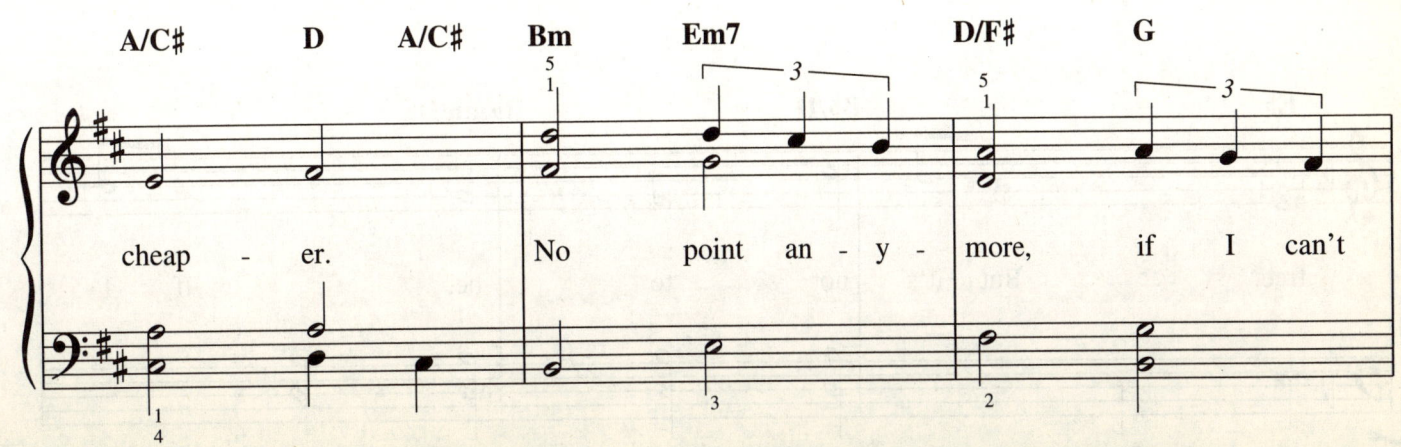

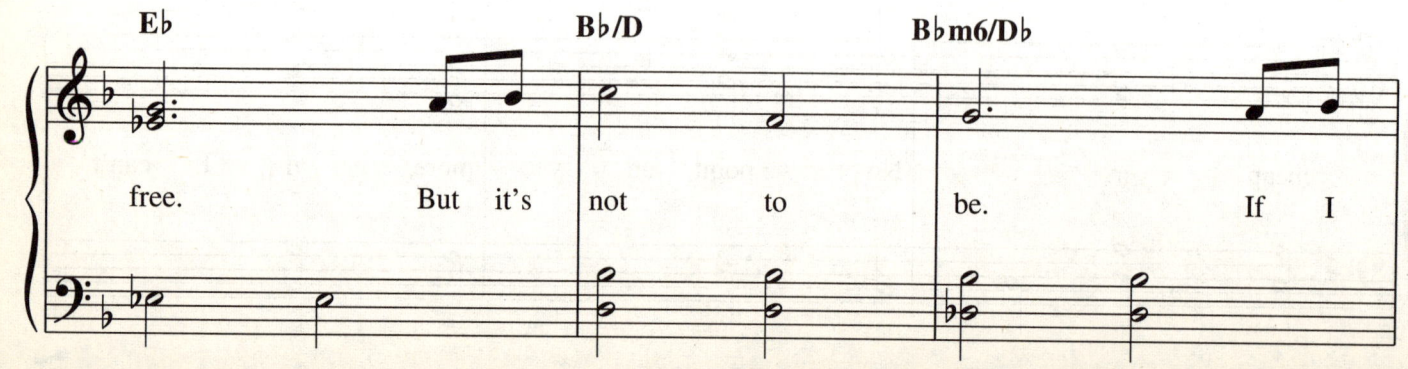

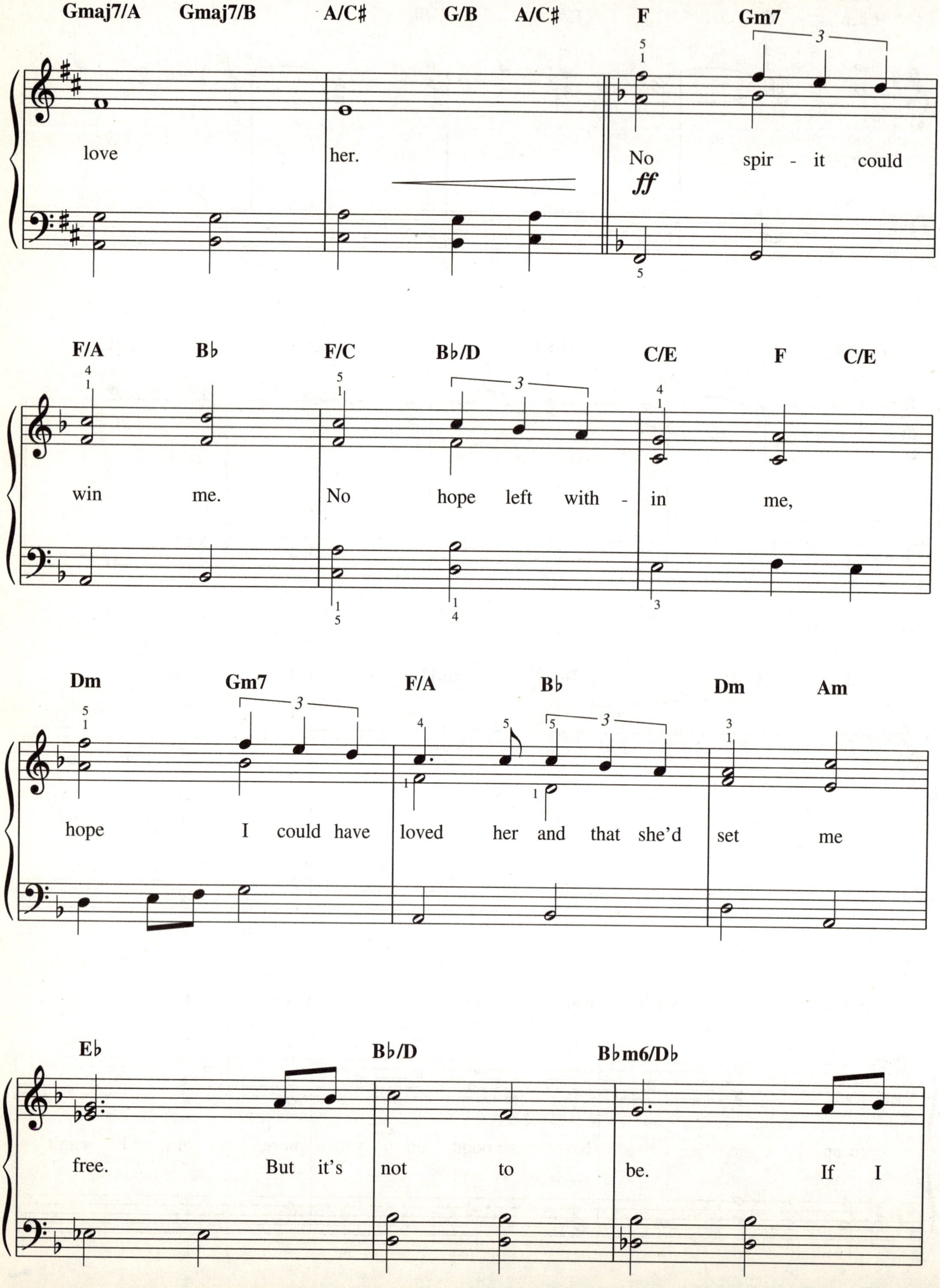
Gmaj7/A Gmaj7/B A/C# G/B A/C# F Gm7
love her. No spir - it could
ff
F/A B♭ F/C B♭/D C/E F C/E
win me. No hope left with - in me,
Dm Gm7 F/A B♭ Dm Am
hope I could have loved her and that she'd set me
E♭ B♭/D B♭m6/D♭
free. But it's not to be. If I

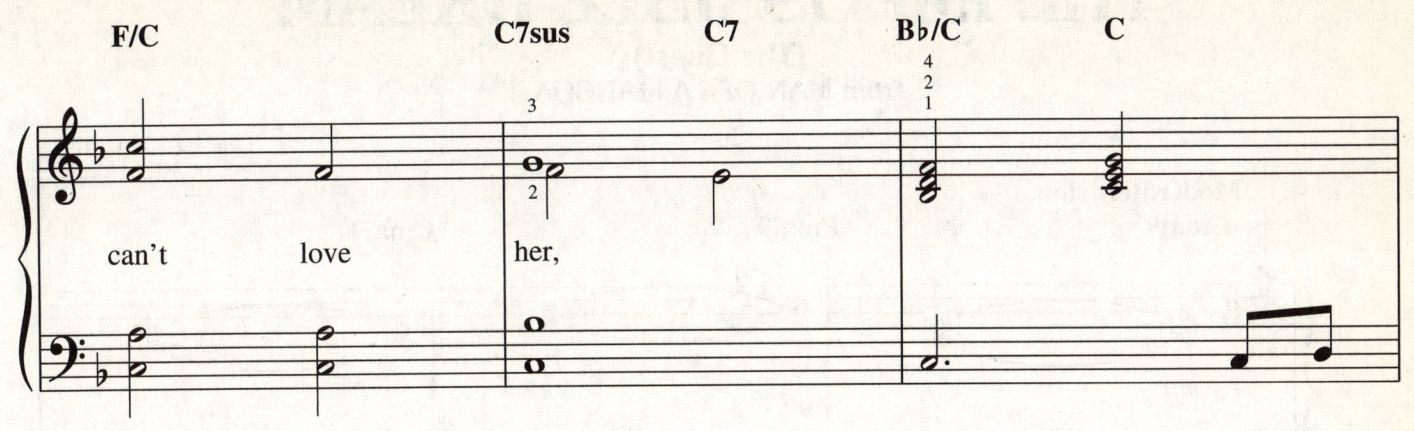
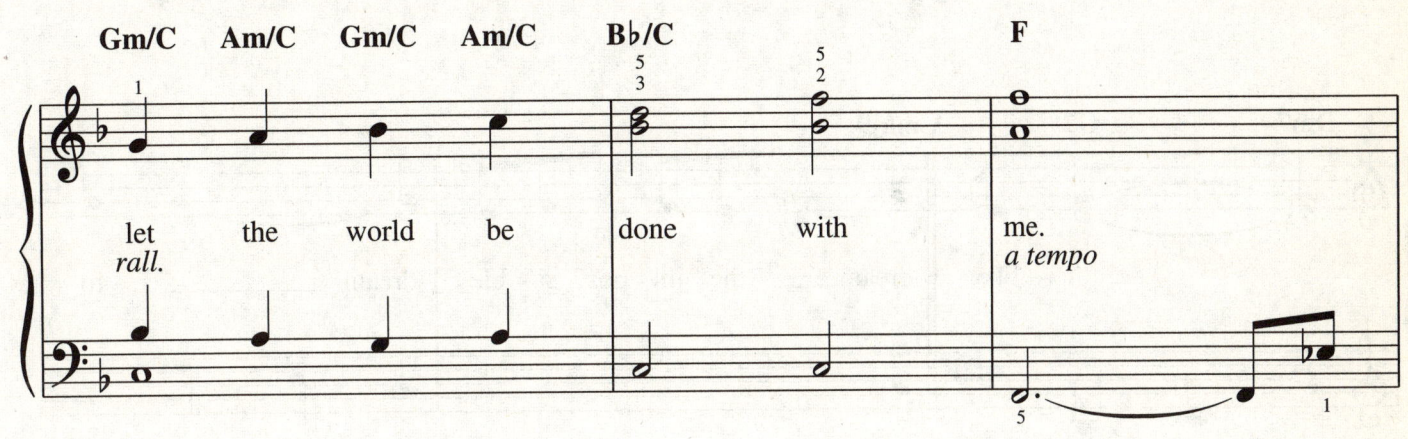

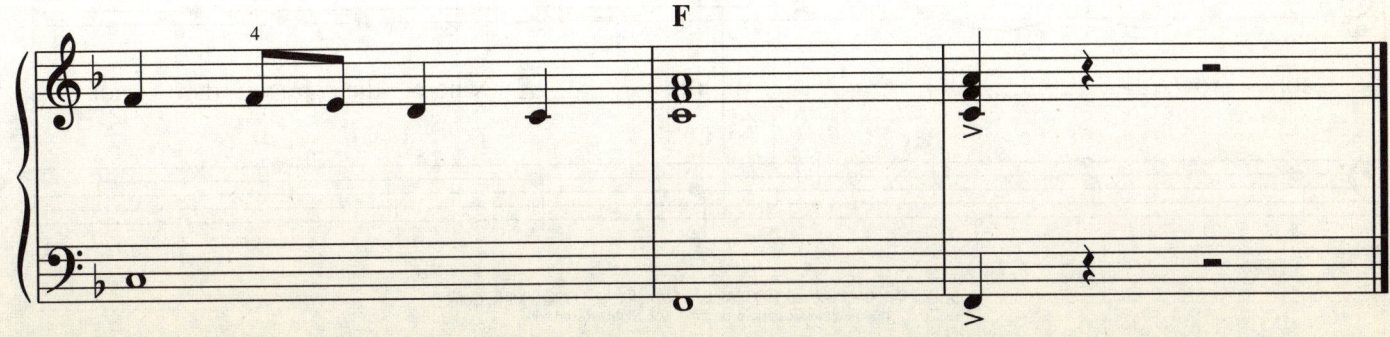

THE IMPOSSIBLE DREAM
(The Quest)
from MAN OF LA MANCHA

Lyric by JOE DARION
Music by MITCH LEIGH

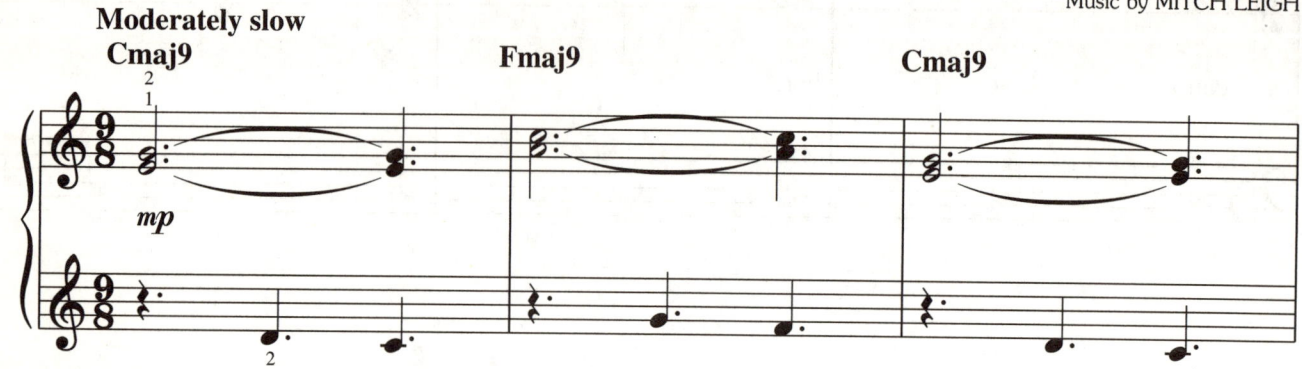

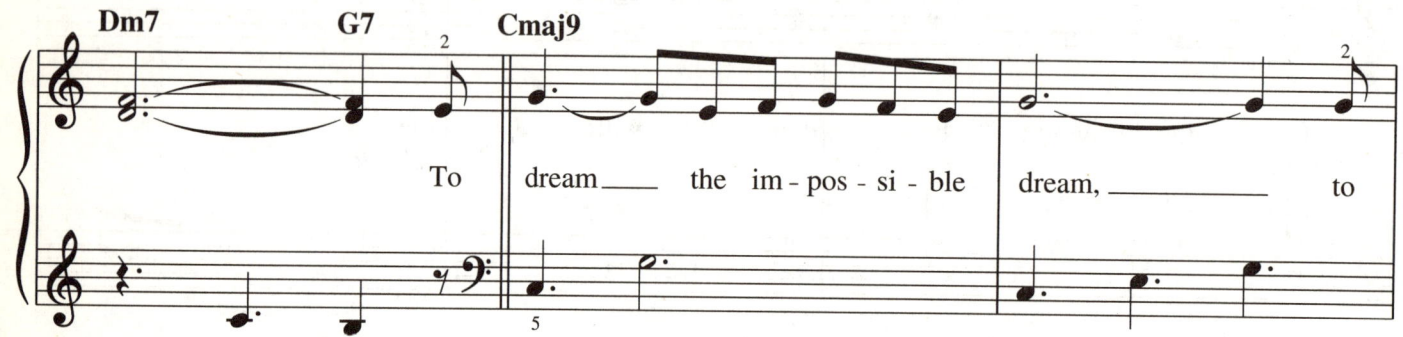

To dream ___ the im-pos-si-ble dream, ___ to

fight ___ the un-beat-a-ble foe, ___ to bear ___ the un-bear-a-ble

sor-row, ___ to run ___ where the brave dare not

Copyright © 1965 (Renewed 1994) Andrew Scott, Inc. and Helena Music Corp.
International Copyright Secured   All Rights Reserved

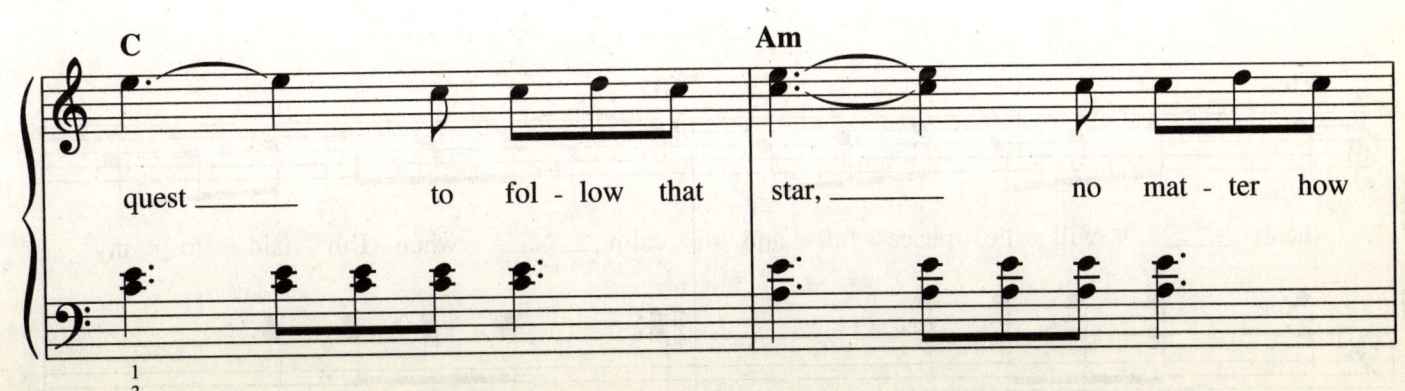

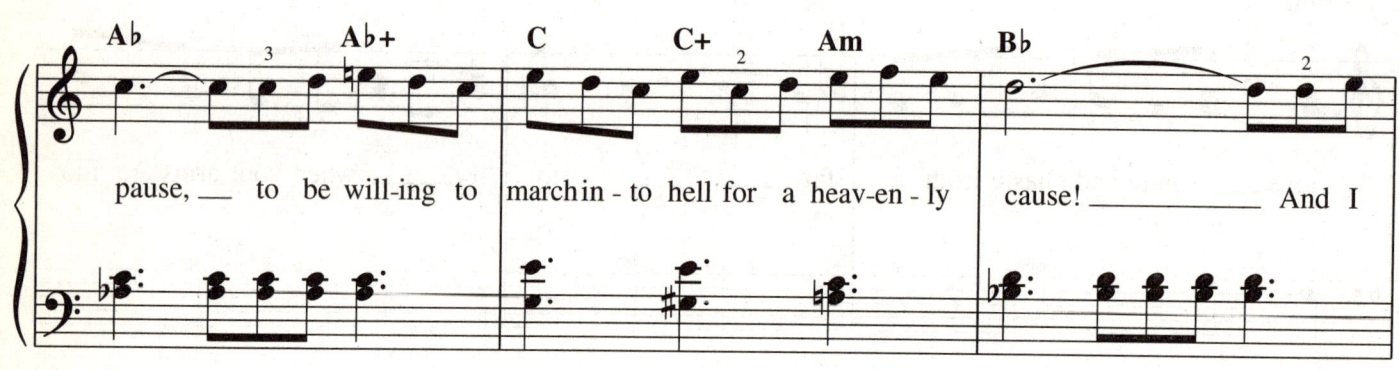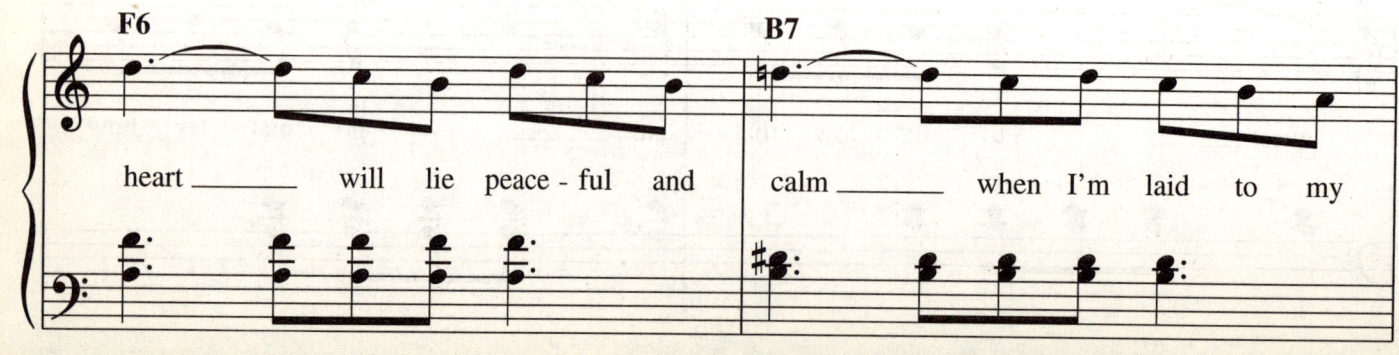

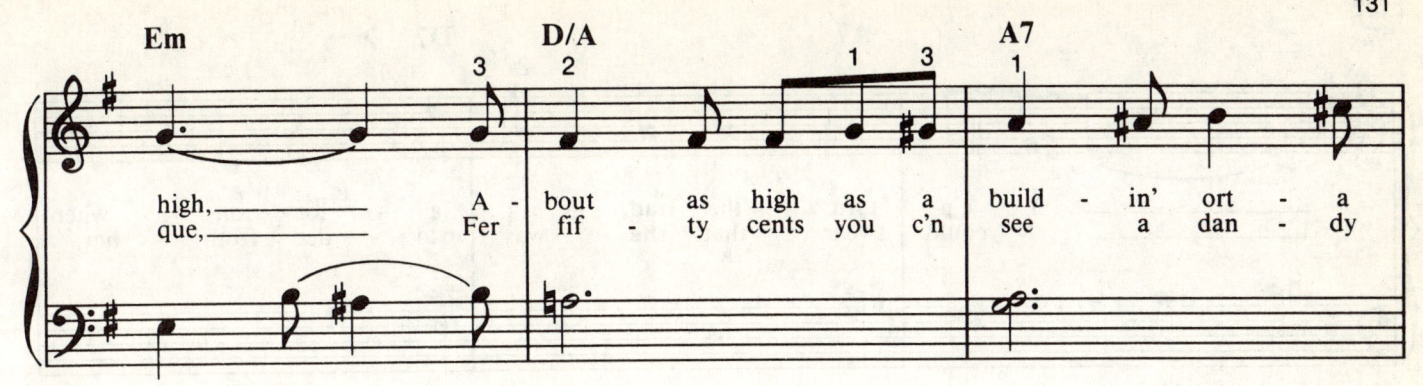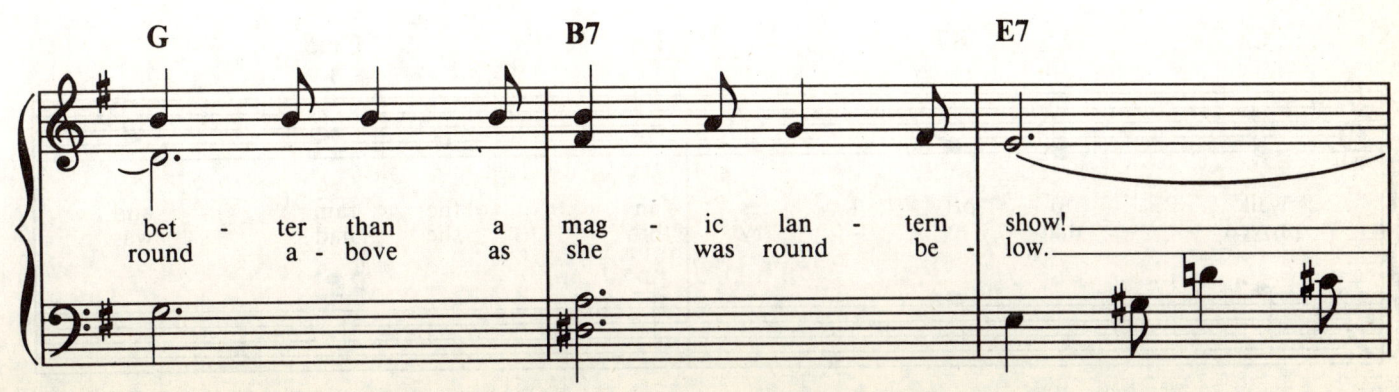

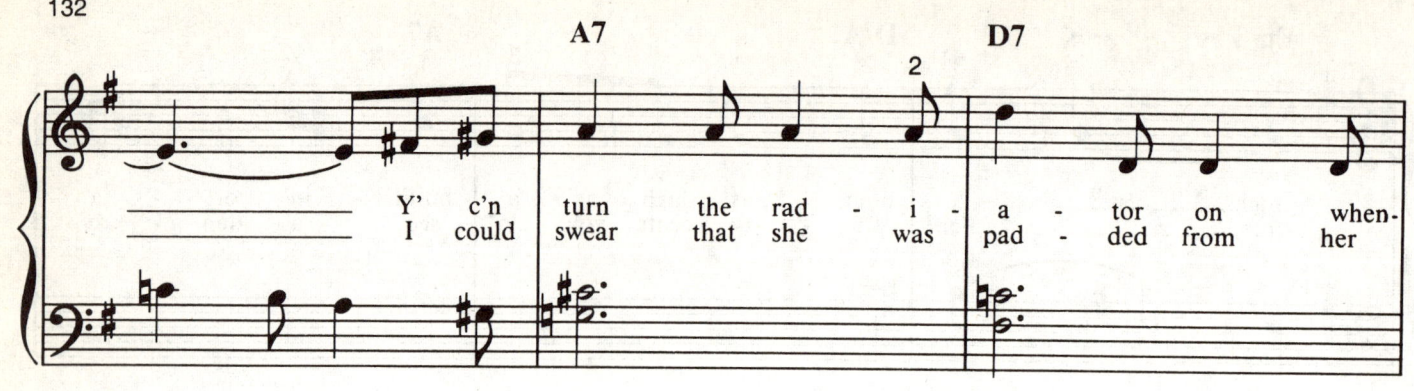
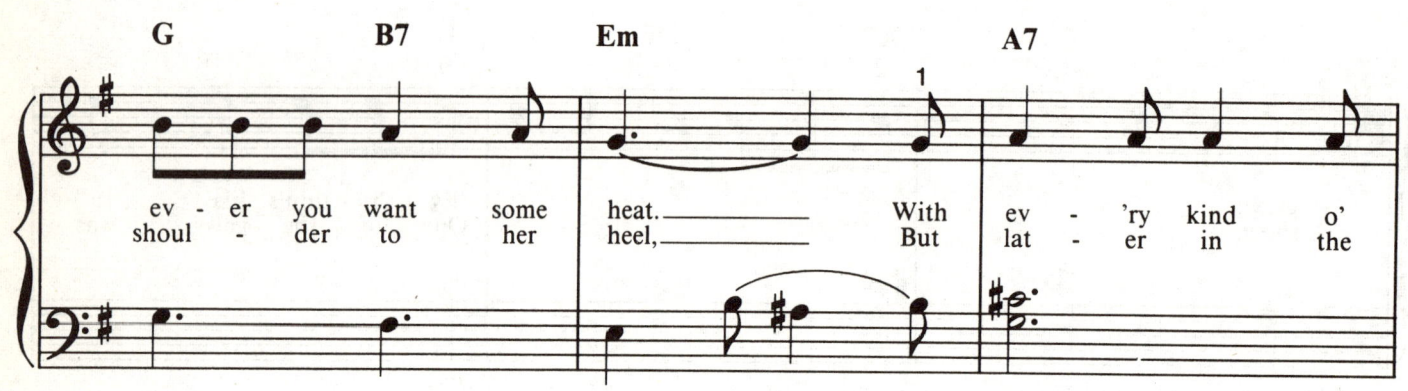
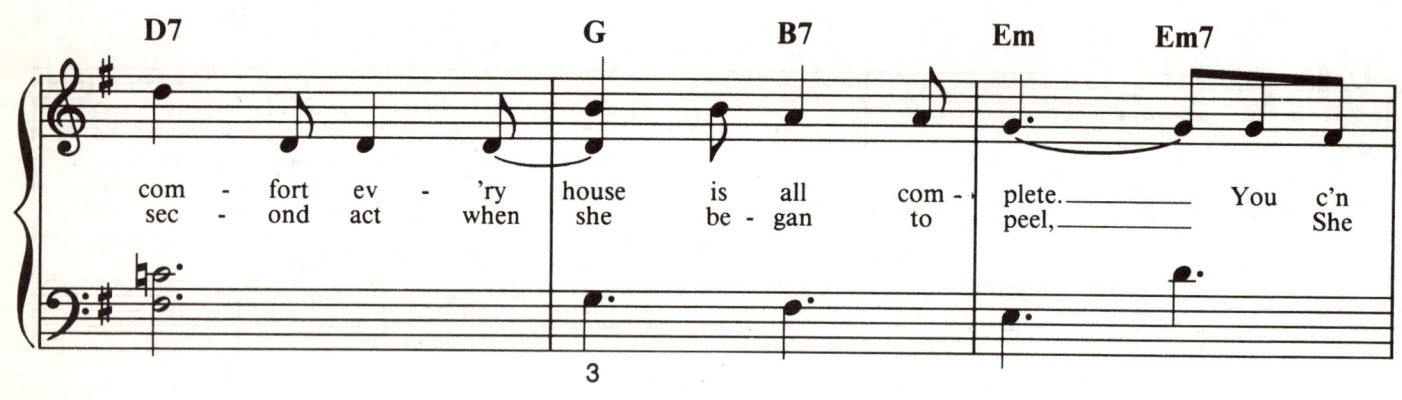

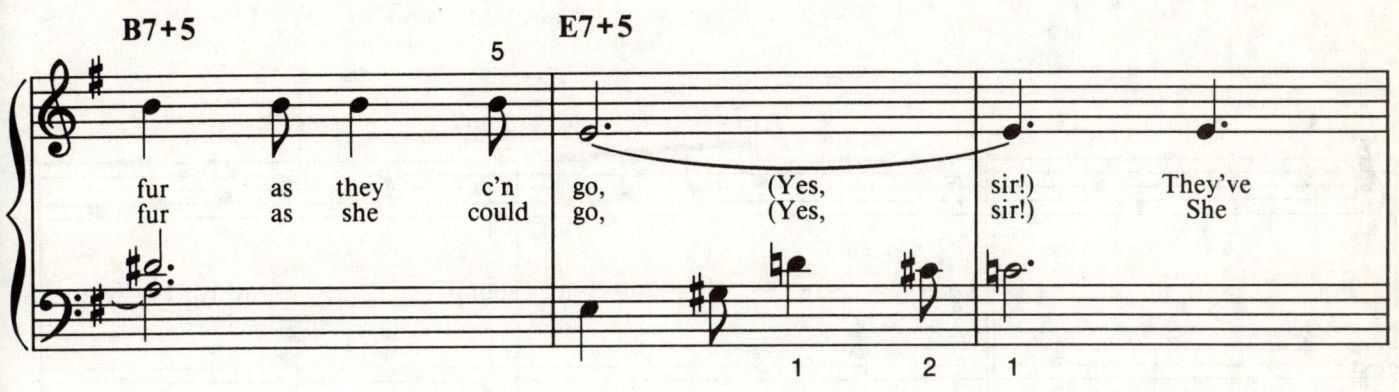

LEANING ON A LAMP POST
from ME AND MY GIRL

By NOEL GAY

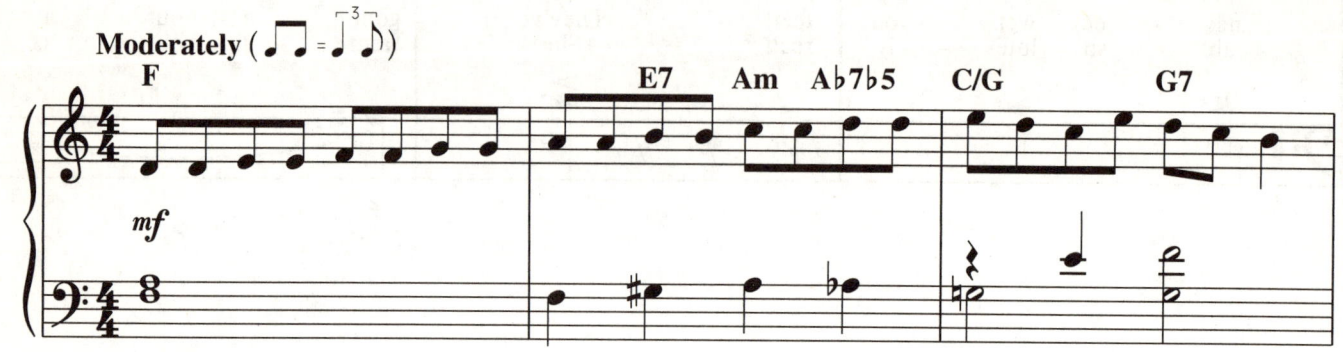

Lean - ing on a lamp, May - be you

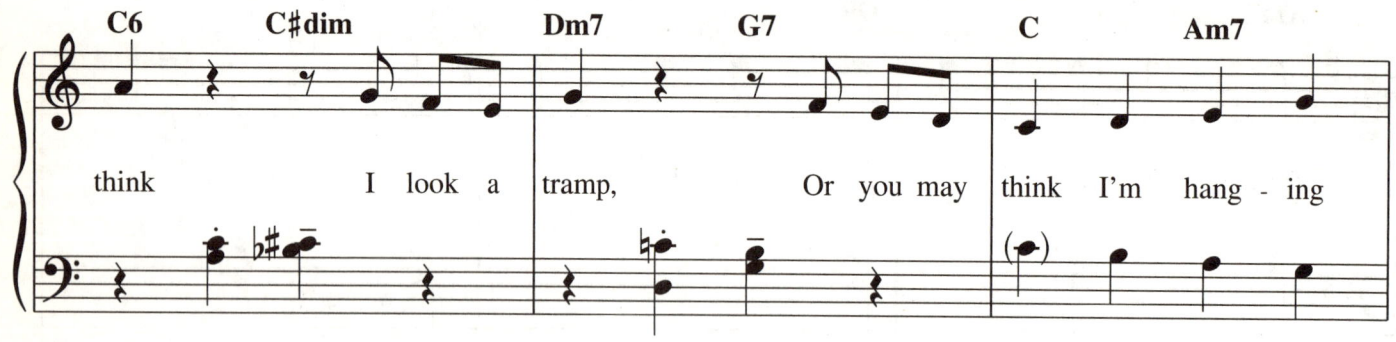

think I look a tramp, Or you may think I'm hang - ing

'round to steal a car. But

Copyright © 1937 (Renewed) Richard Armitage Ltd.
All Rights for the U.S. and Canada Controlled by Music Sales Corporation (ASCAP)
International Copyright Secured   All Rights Reserved
Reprinted by Permission

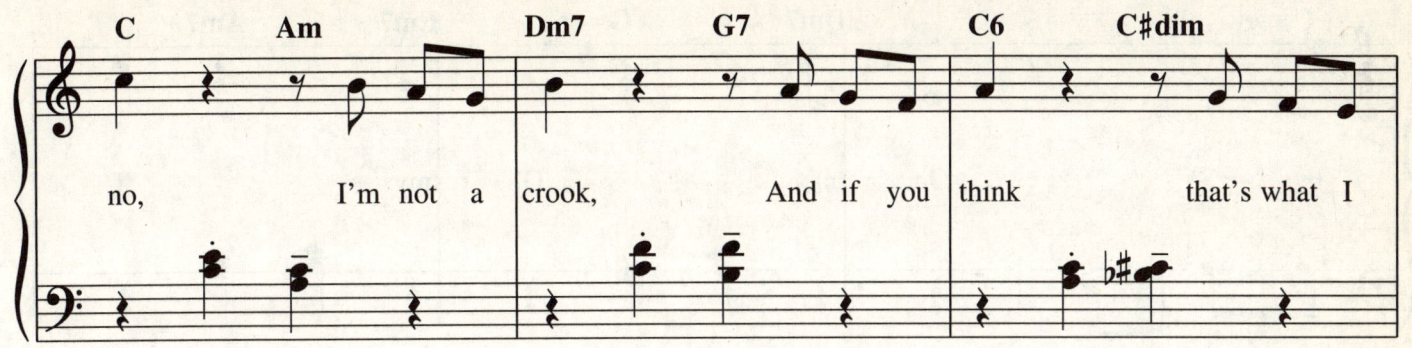
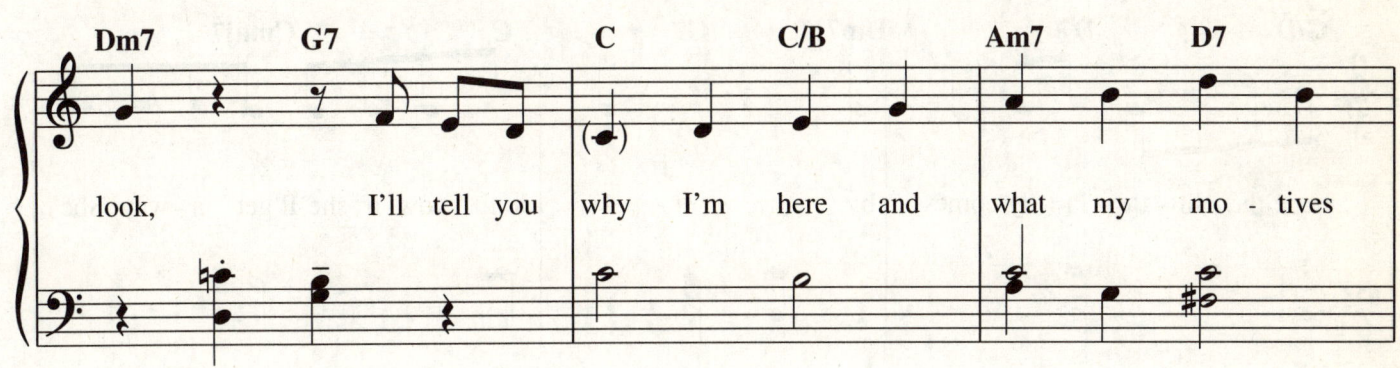
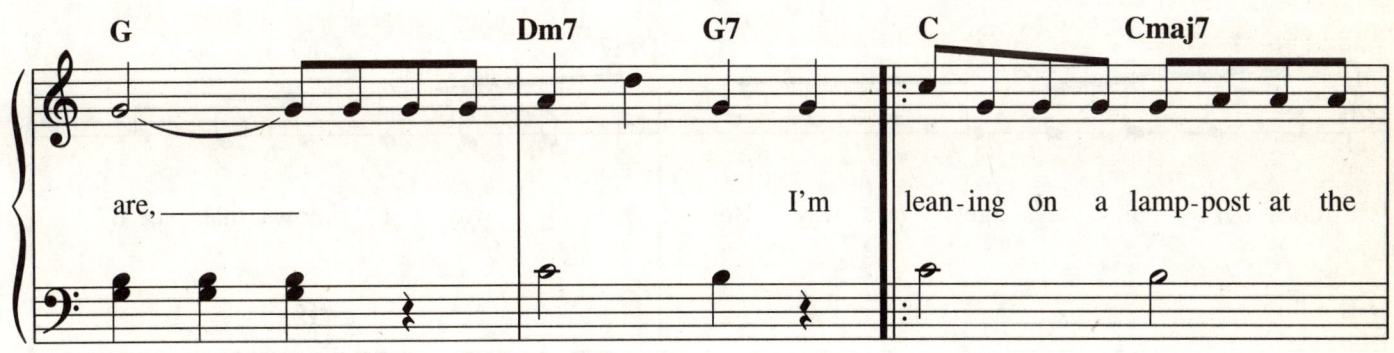

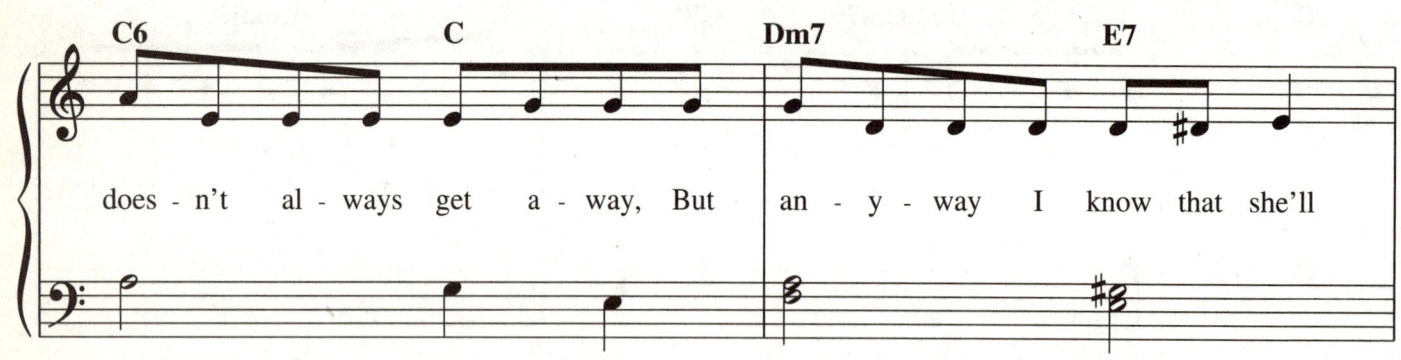

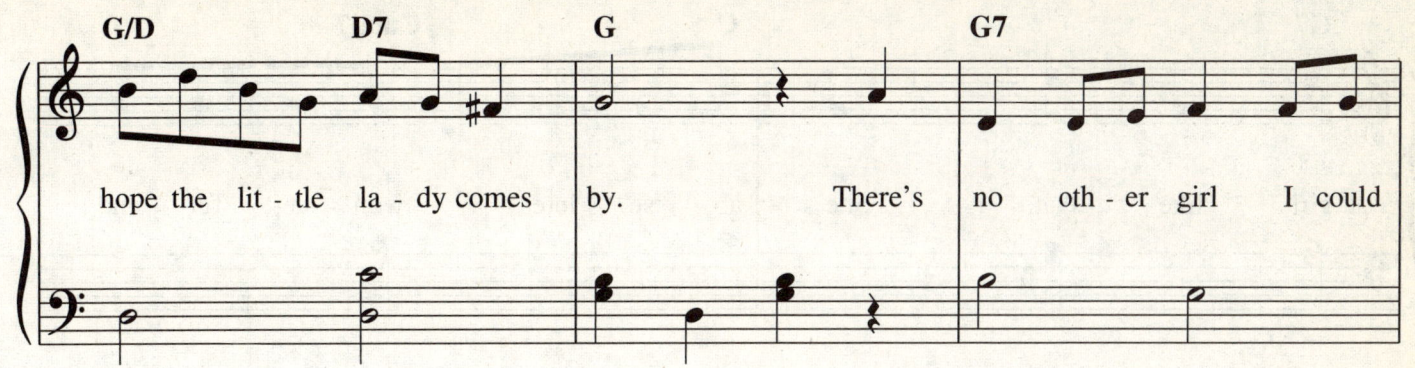
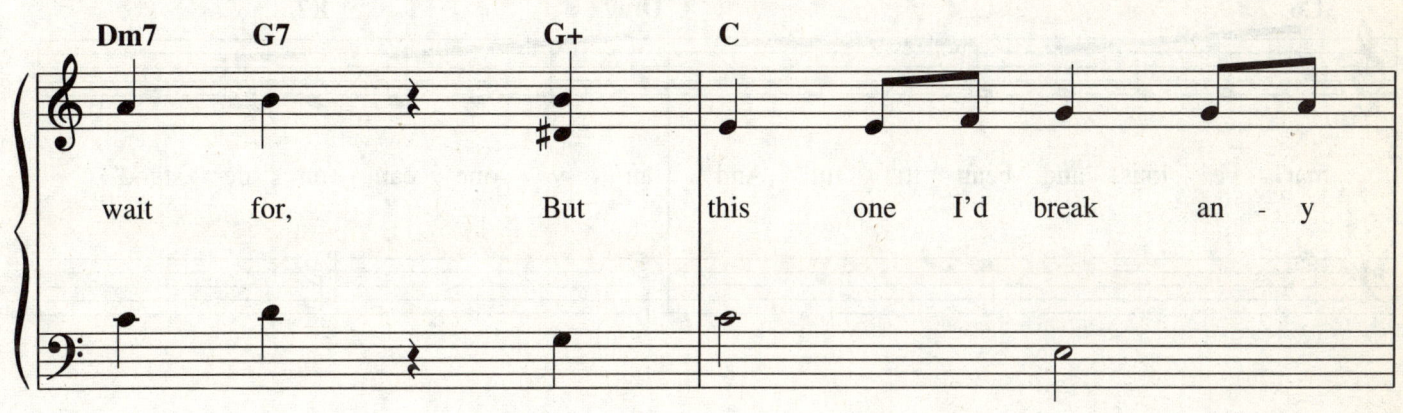

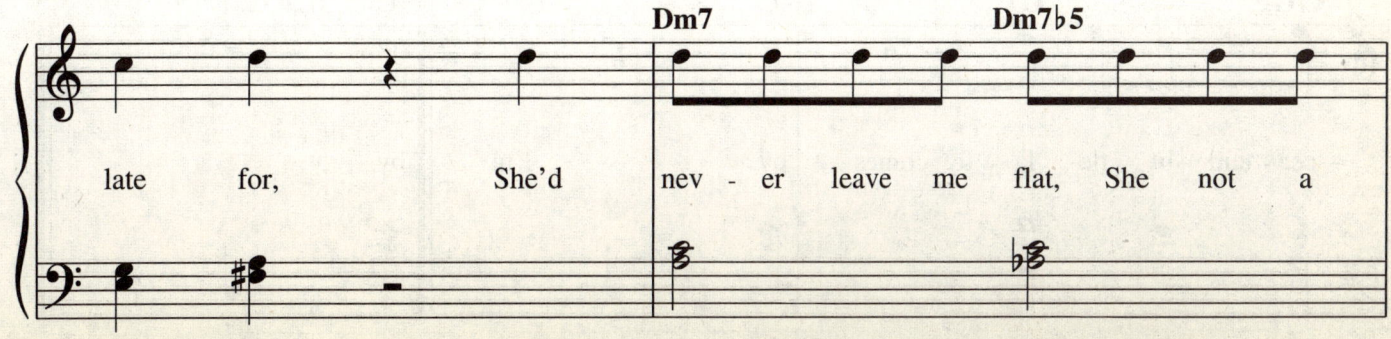

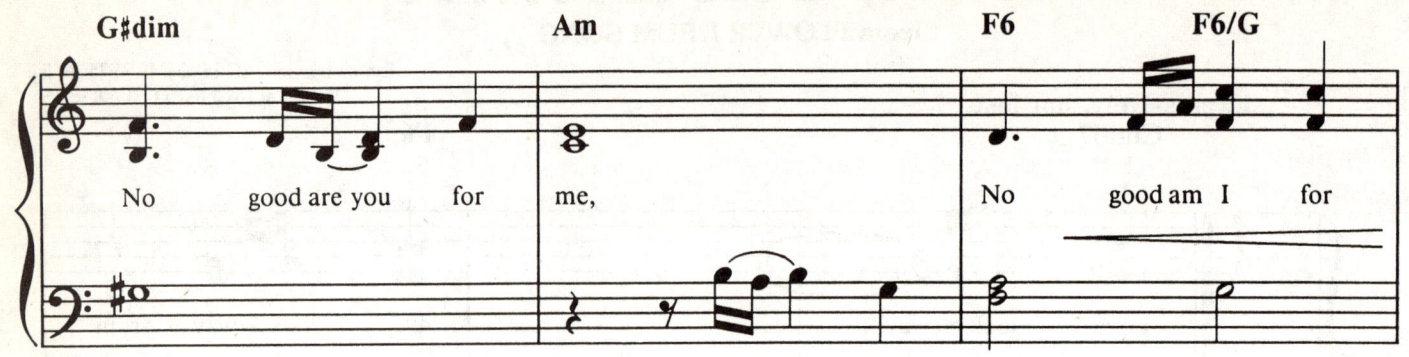

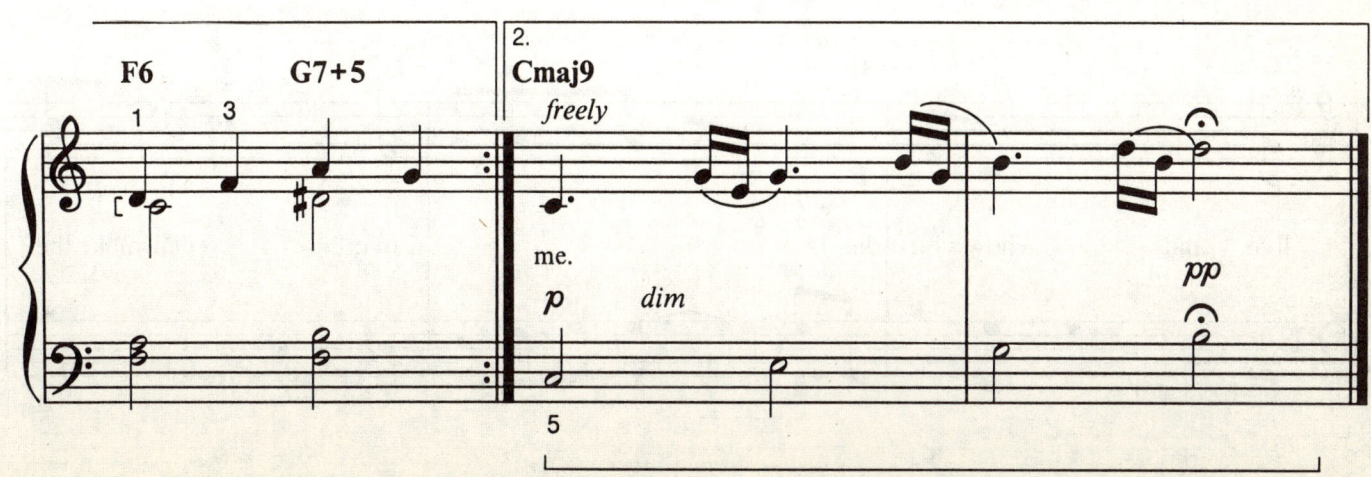

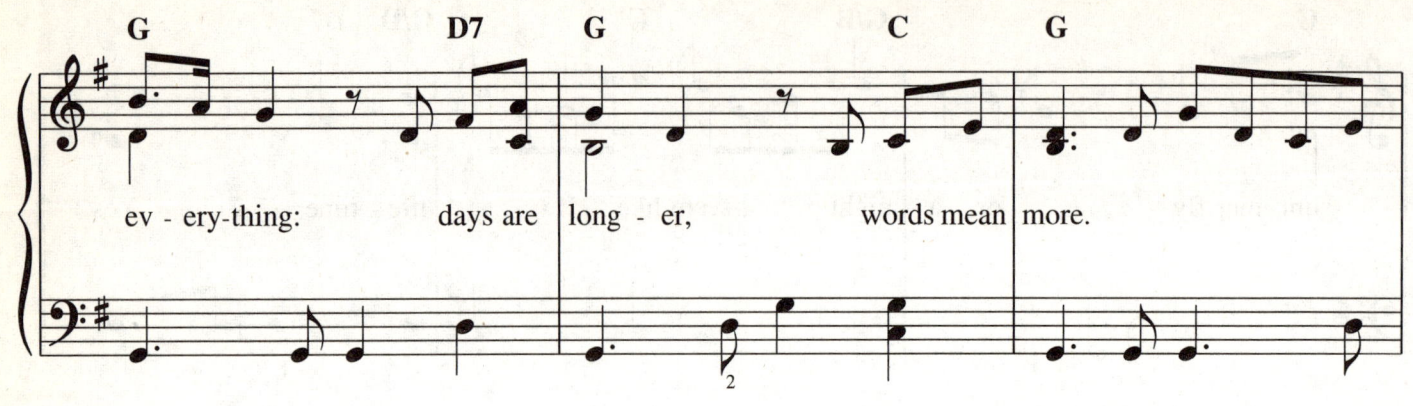

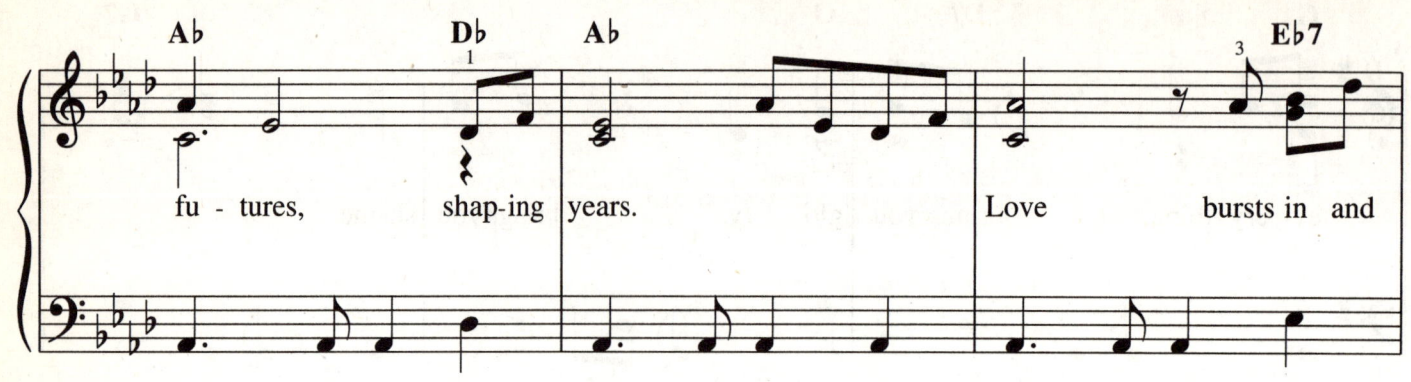

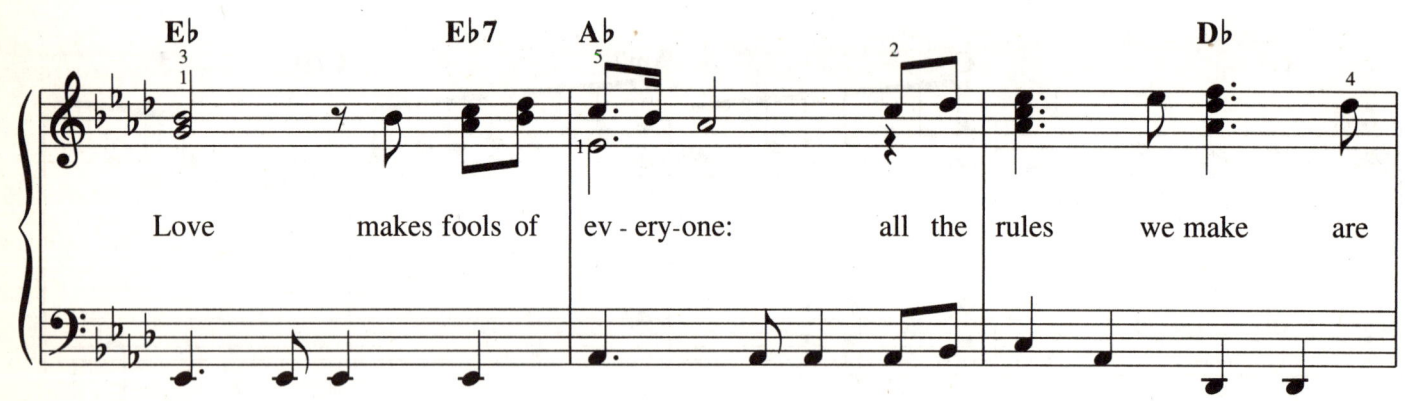
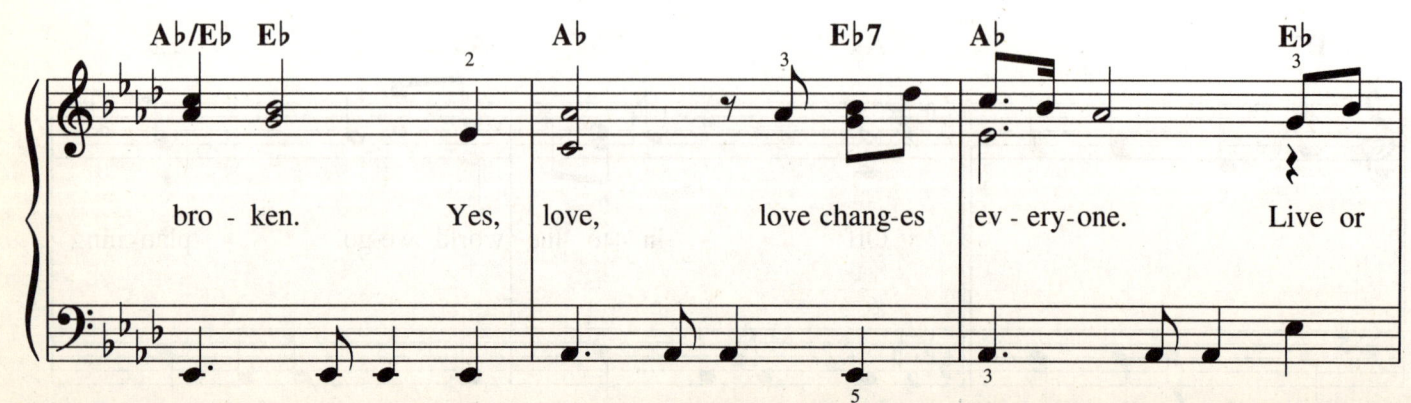

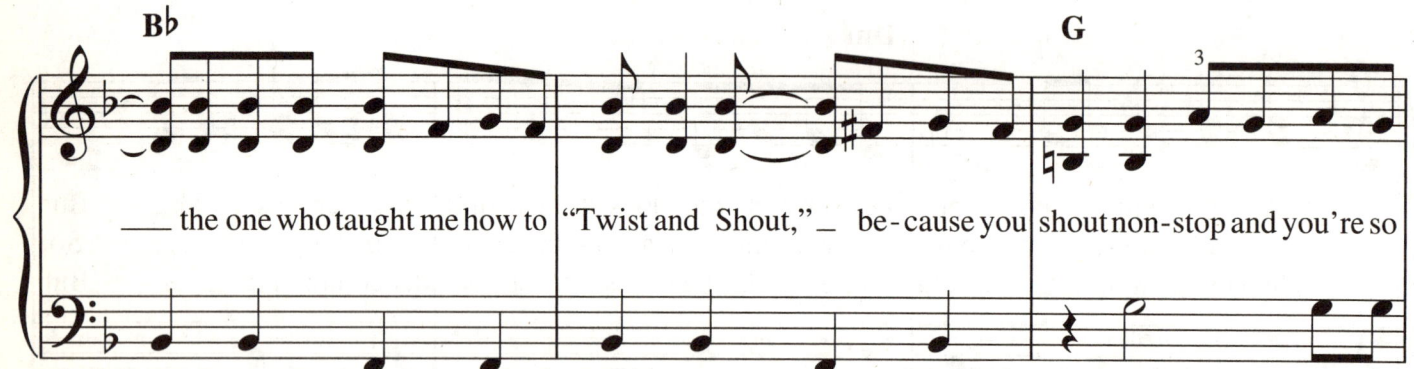

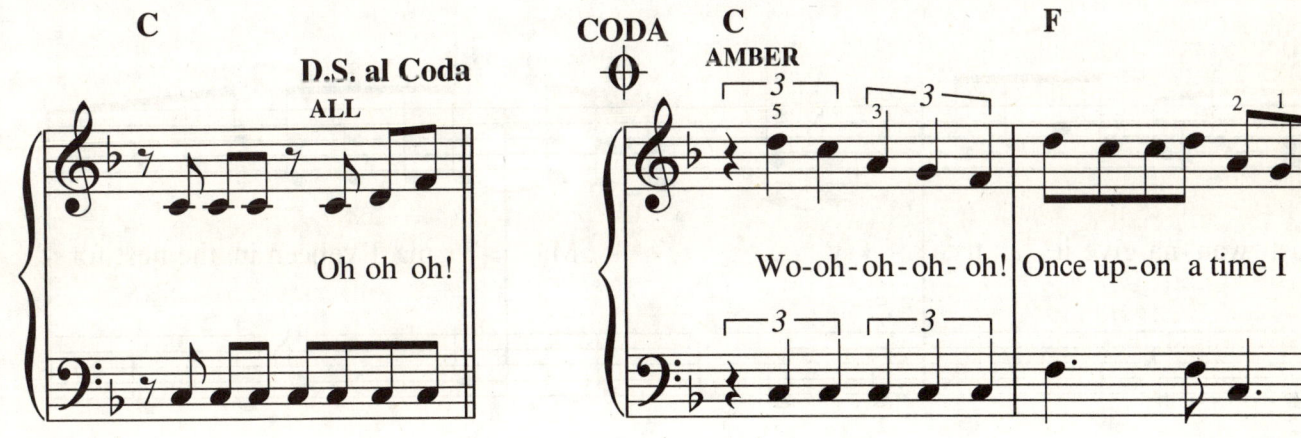

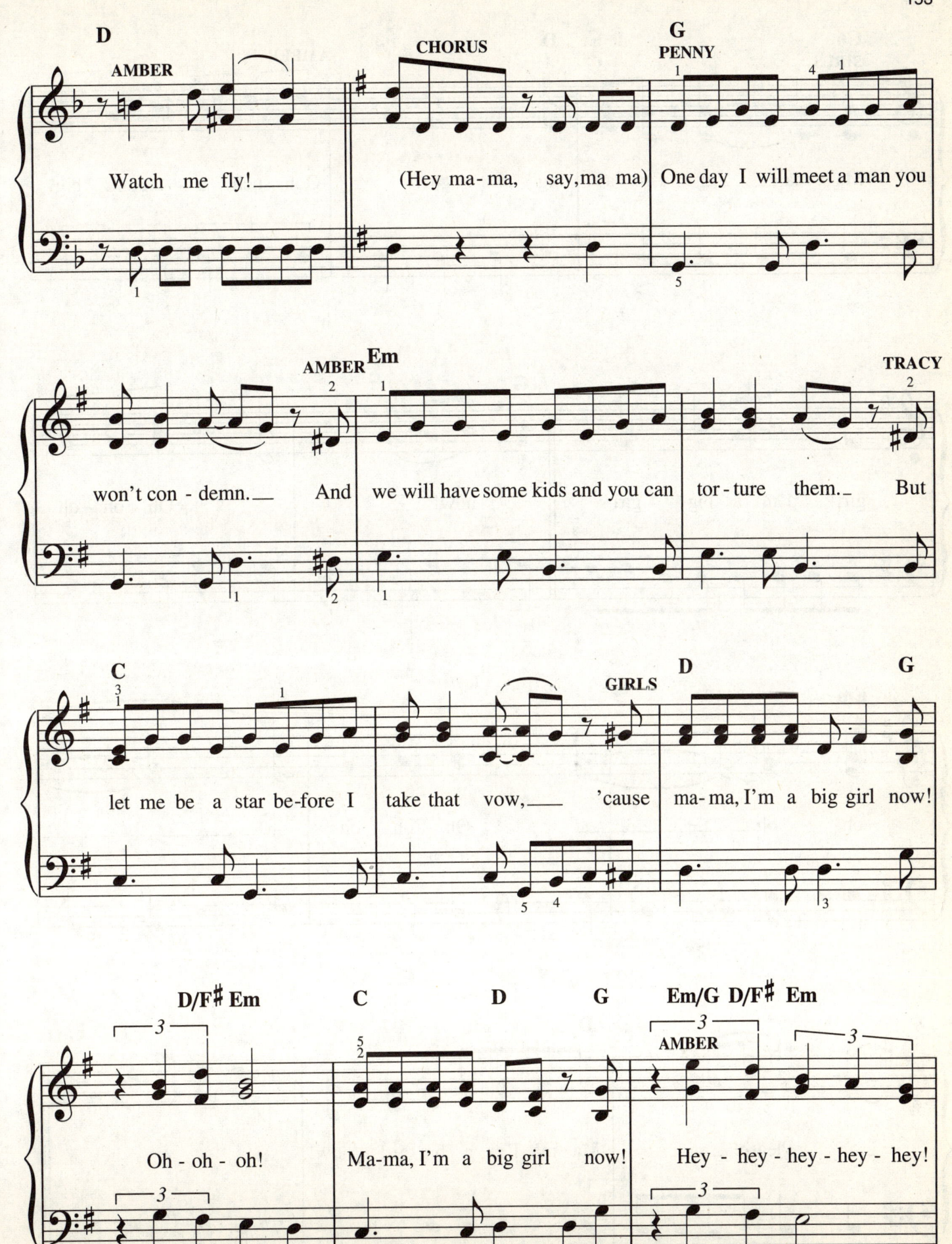

MAME
from MAME

Music and Lyric by
JERRY HERMAN

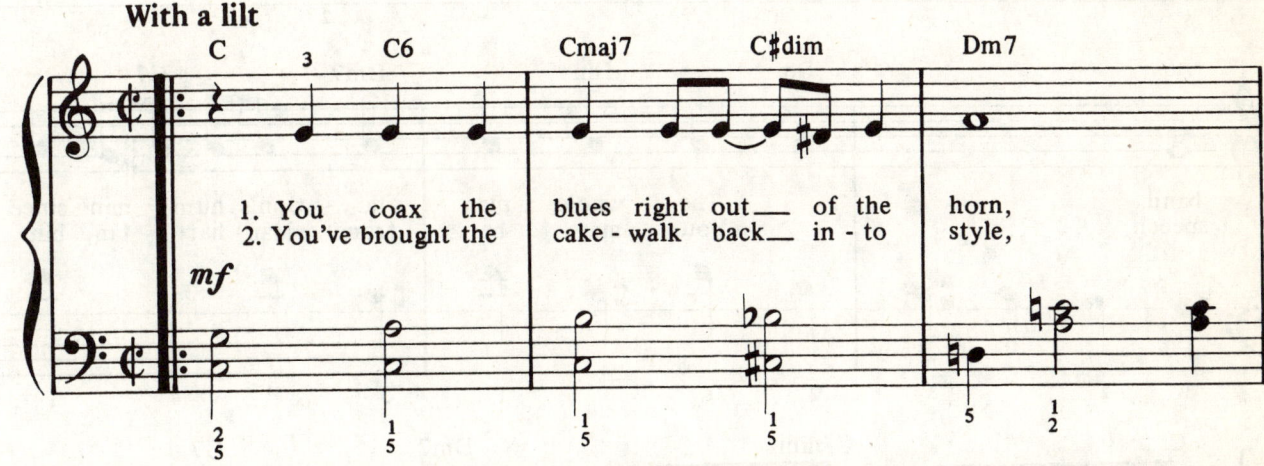
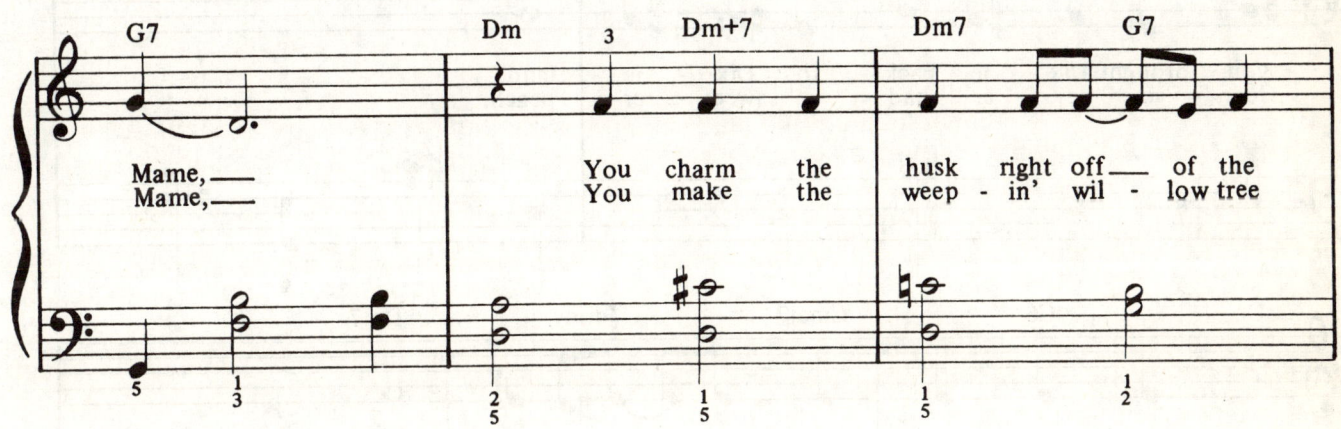
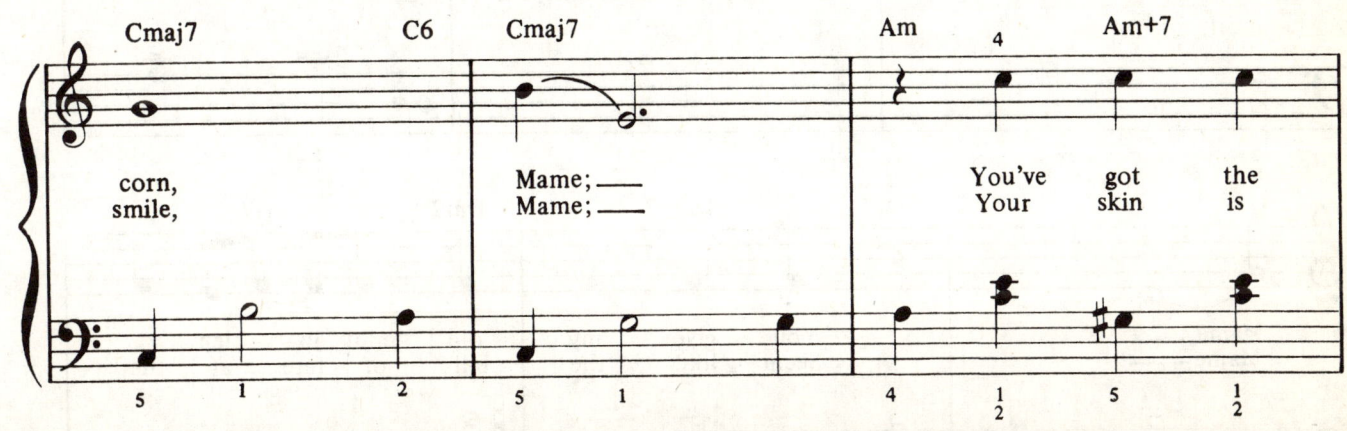

1. You coax the blues right out of the horn, Mame, You charm the husk right off of the corn, Mame;
2. You've brought the cake-walk back into style, Mame, You make the weepin' willow tree smile, Mame; You've got the / Your skin is

© 1966 (Renewed) JERRY HERMAN
All Rights Controlled by Jerryco Music Co.
Exclusive Agent: EDWIN H. MORRIS & COMPANY, A Division of MPL Music Publishing, Inc.
All Rights Reserved

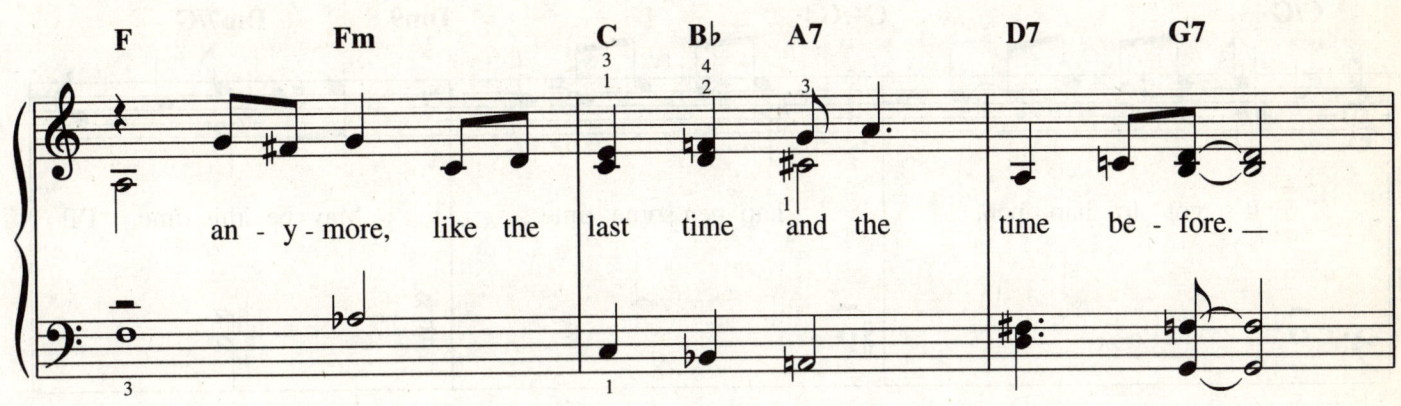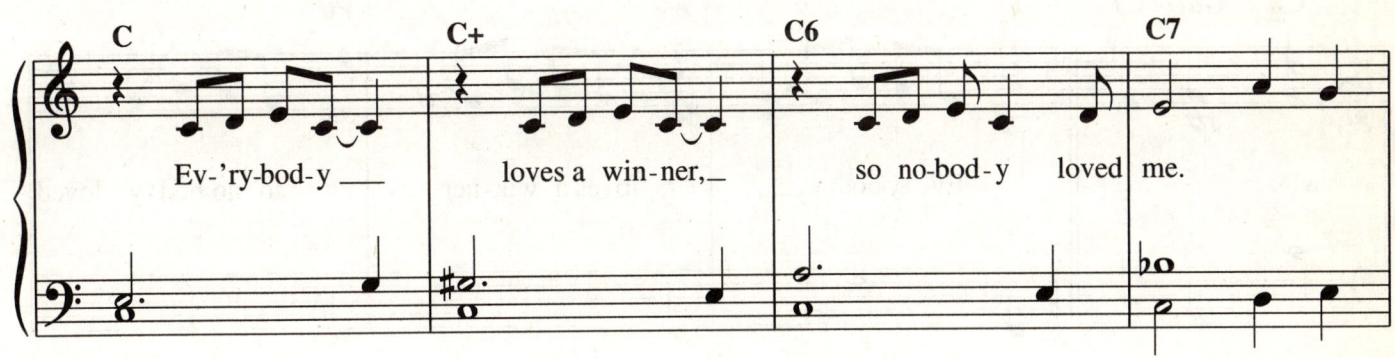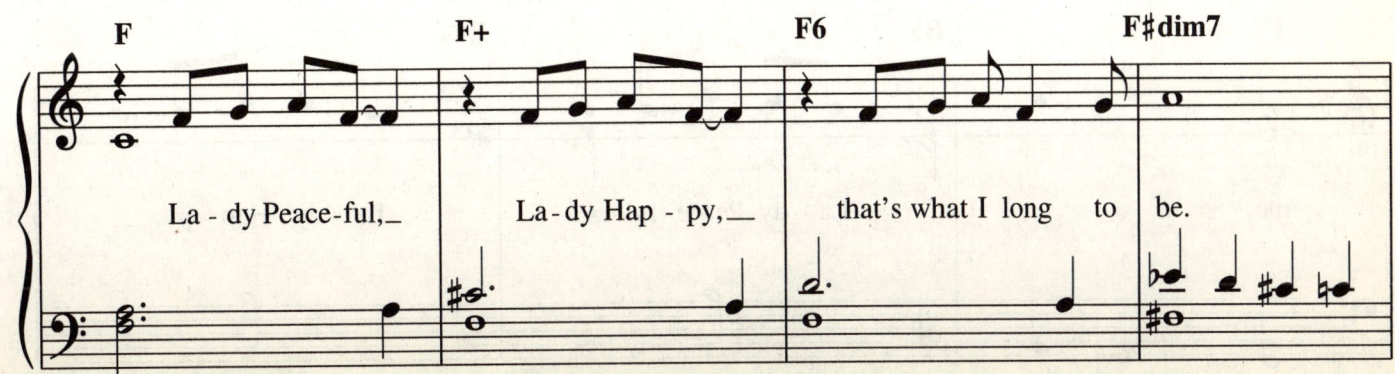

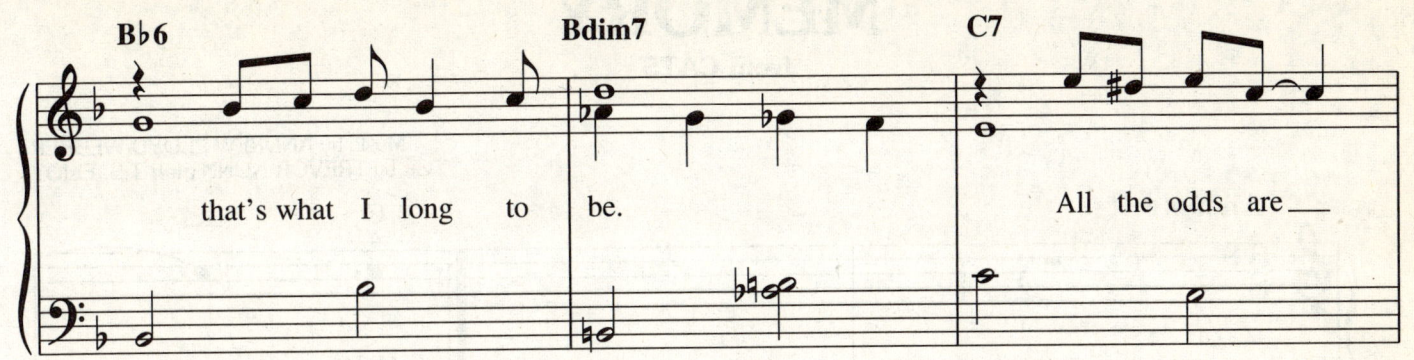

MEMORY
from CATS

Music by ANDREW LLOYD WEBBER
Text by TREVOR NUNN after T.S. ELIOT

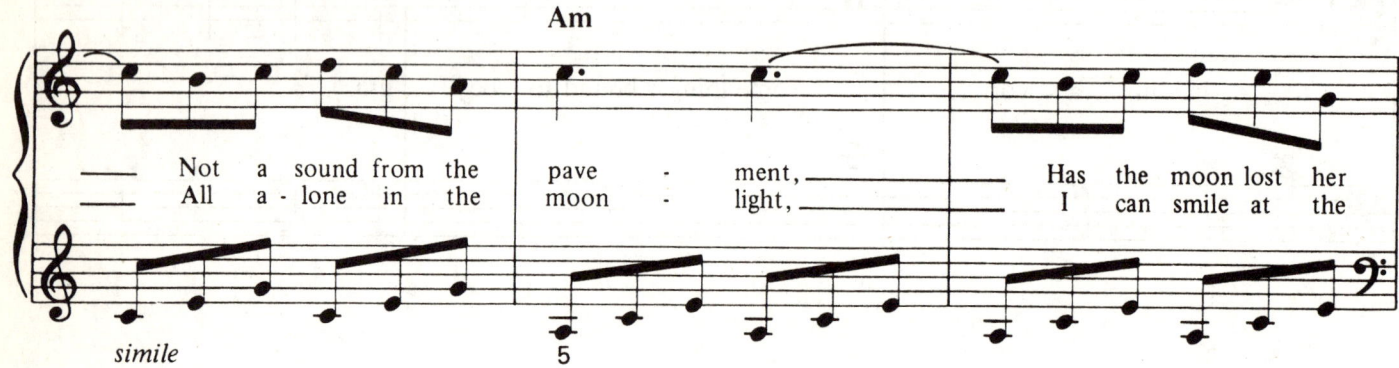

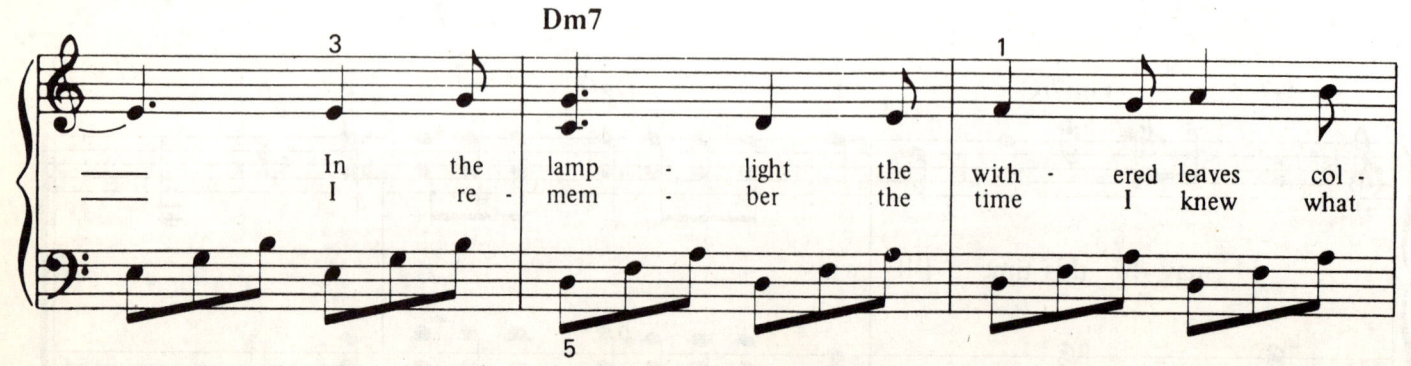

Music Copyright © 1981 The Really Useful Group Ltd.
Text Copyright © 1981 Trevor Nunn and Set Copyrights Ltd.
All Rights in the text Controlled by Faber and Faber Ltd. and Administered for the United States and Canada by R&H Music Co.
International Copyright Secured   All Rights Reserved

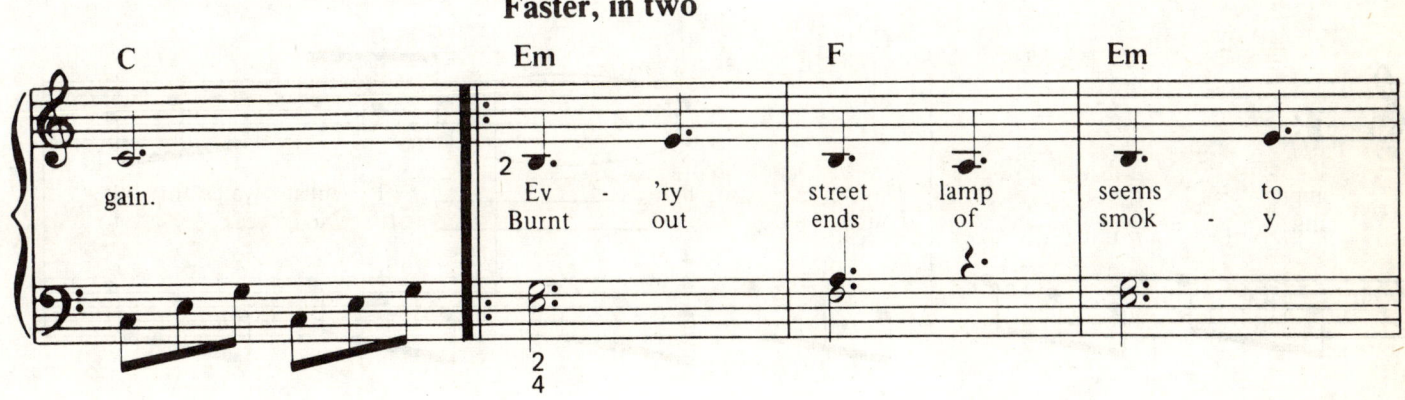

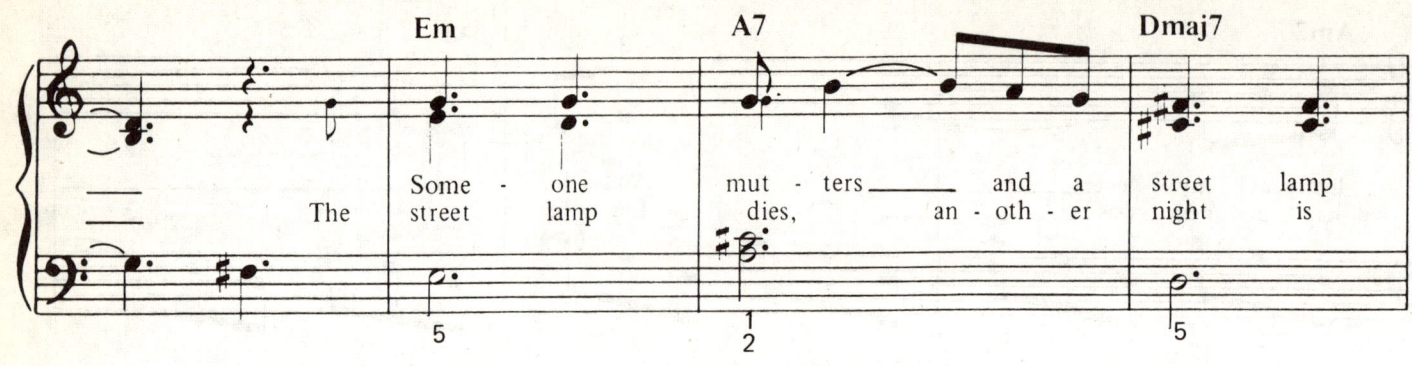

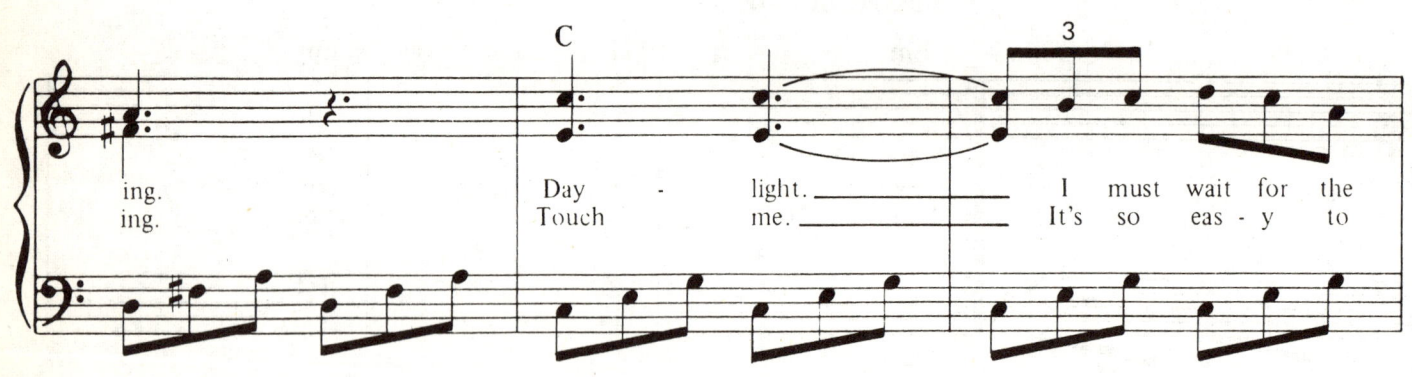

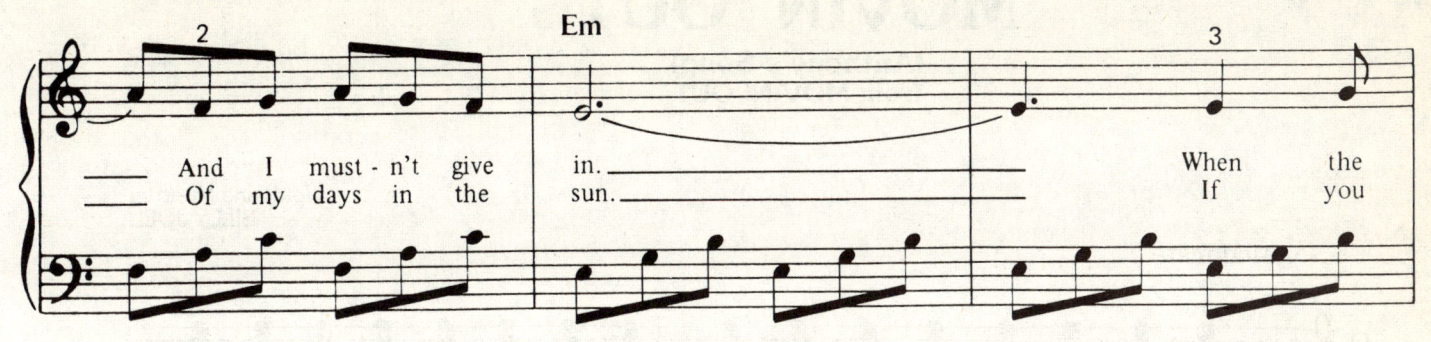

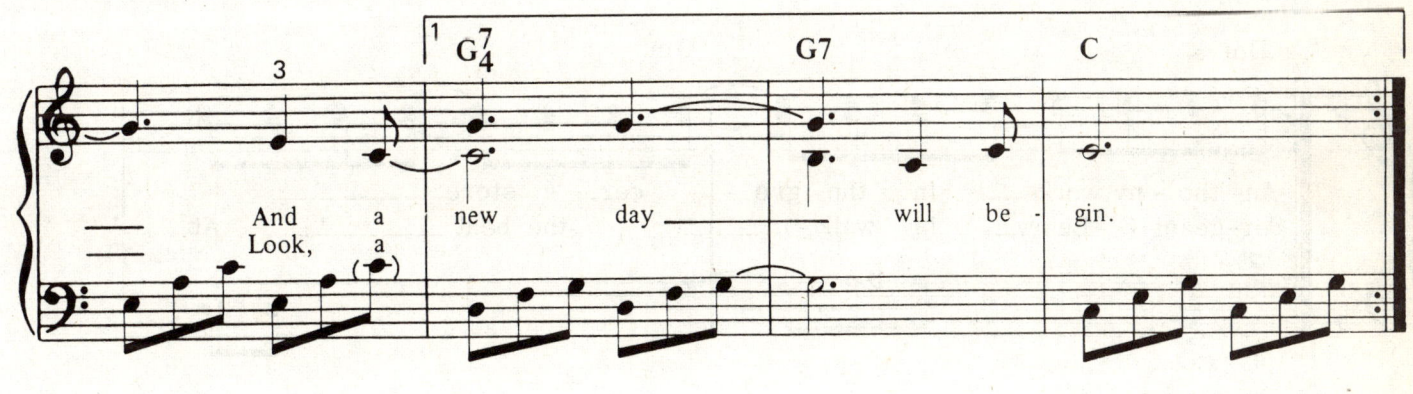
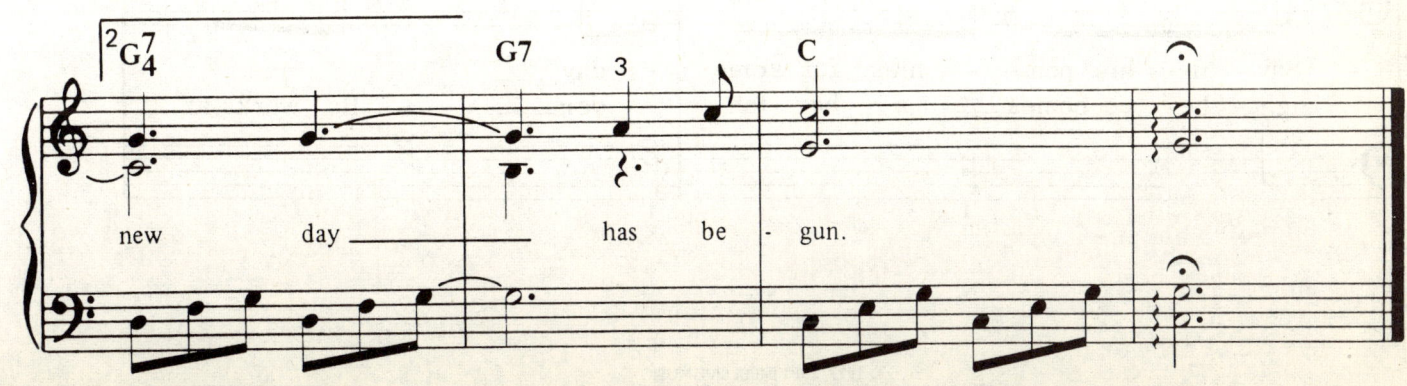

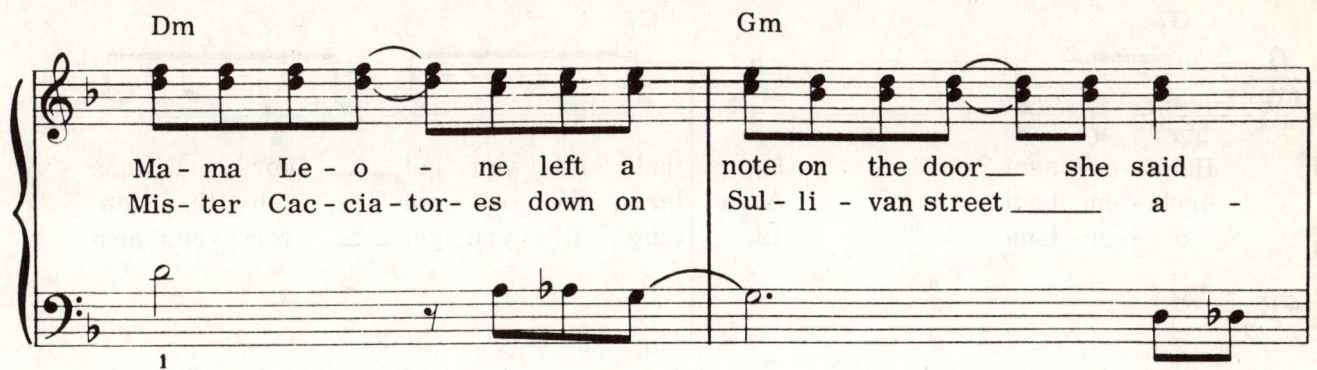

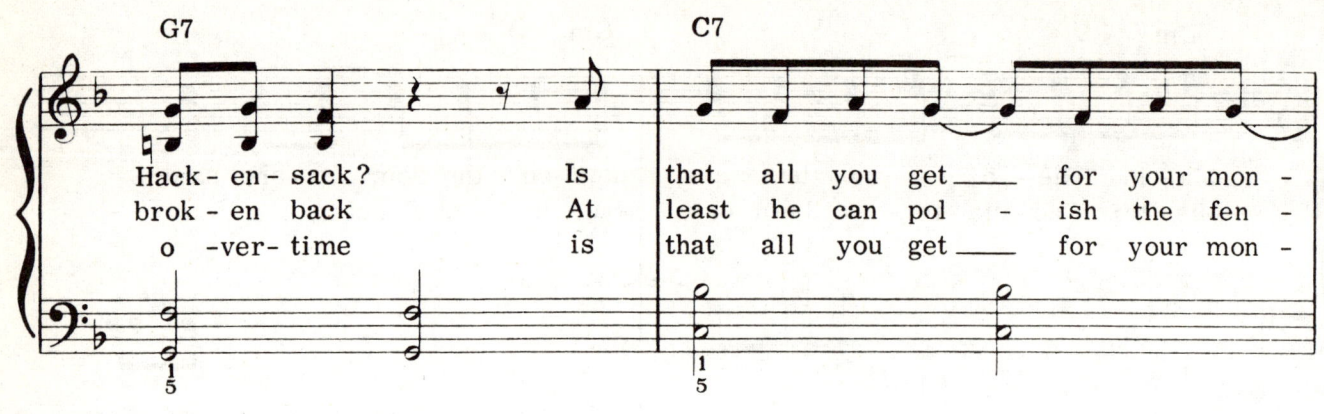

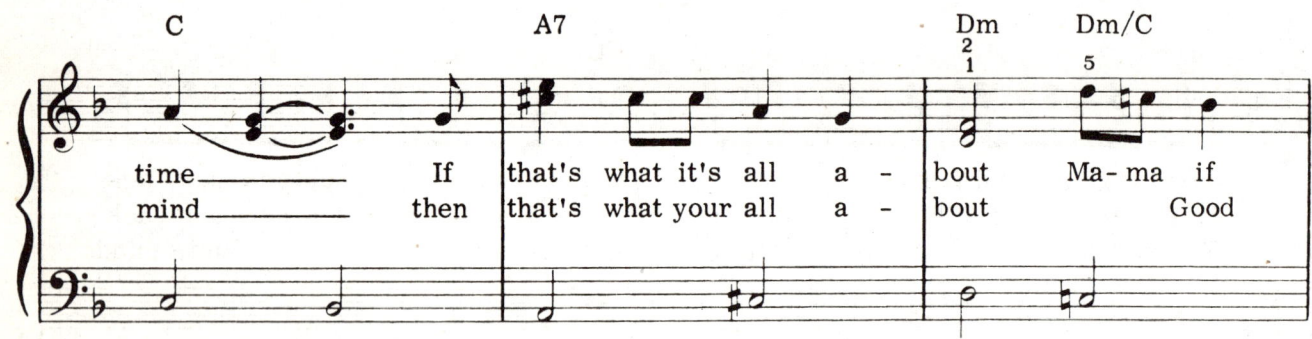
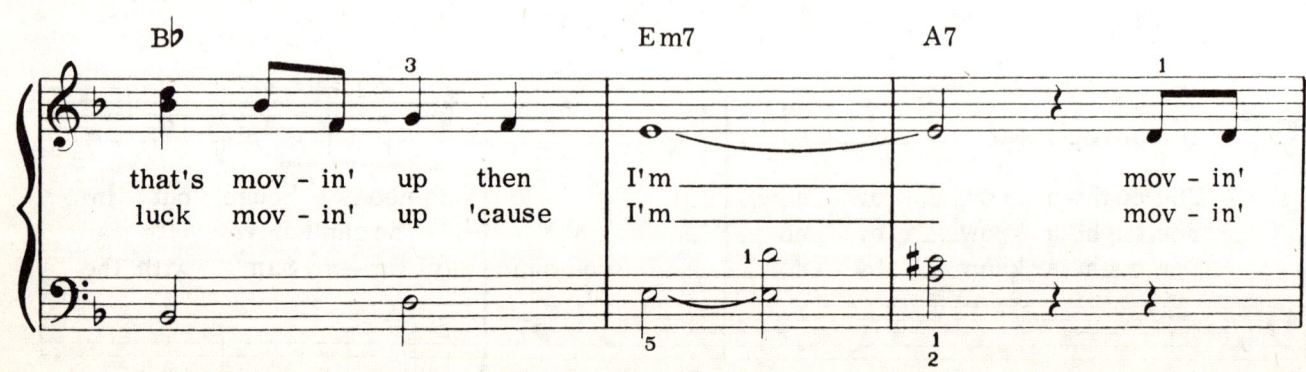

MY CUP RUNNETH OVER
from I DO! I DO!

Words by TOM JONES
Music by HARVEY SCHMIDT

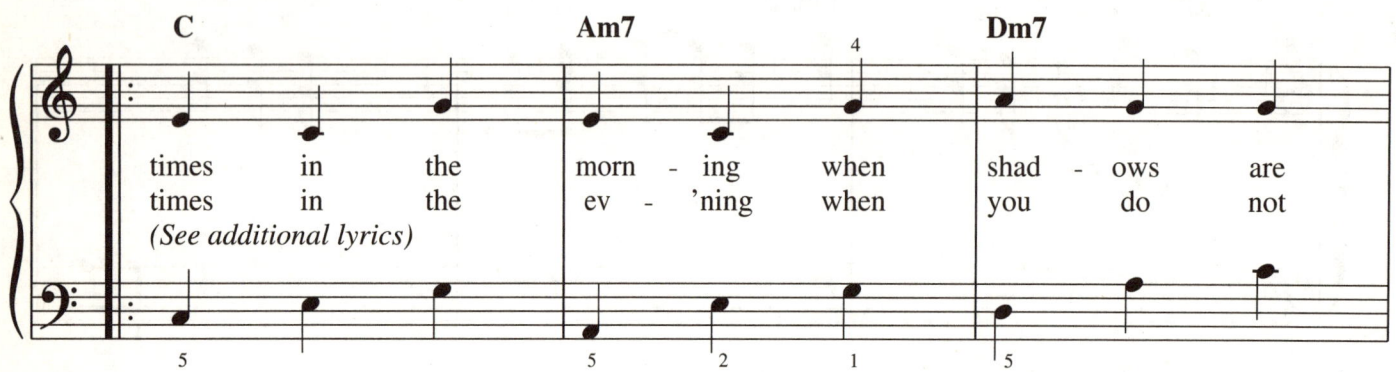

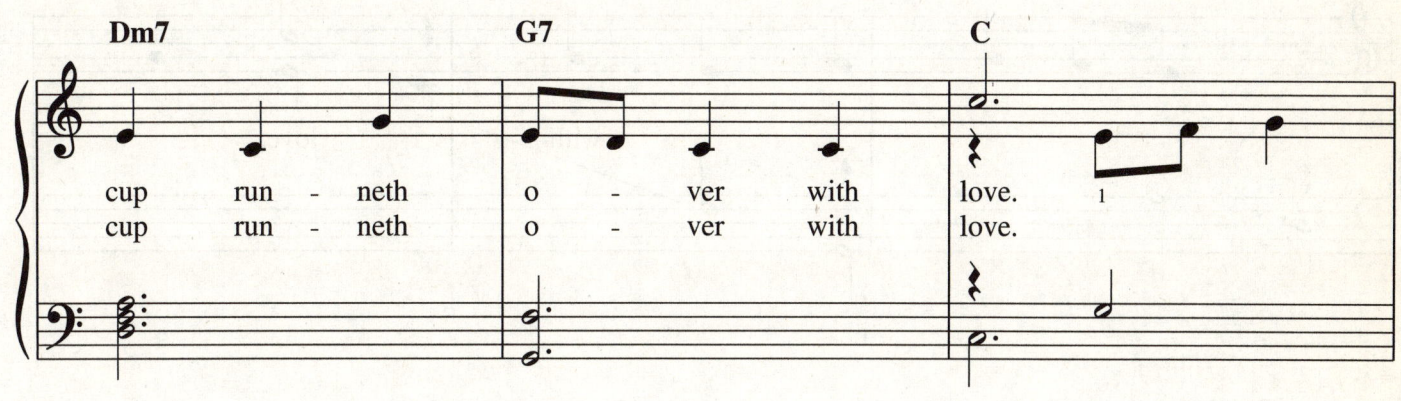

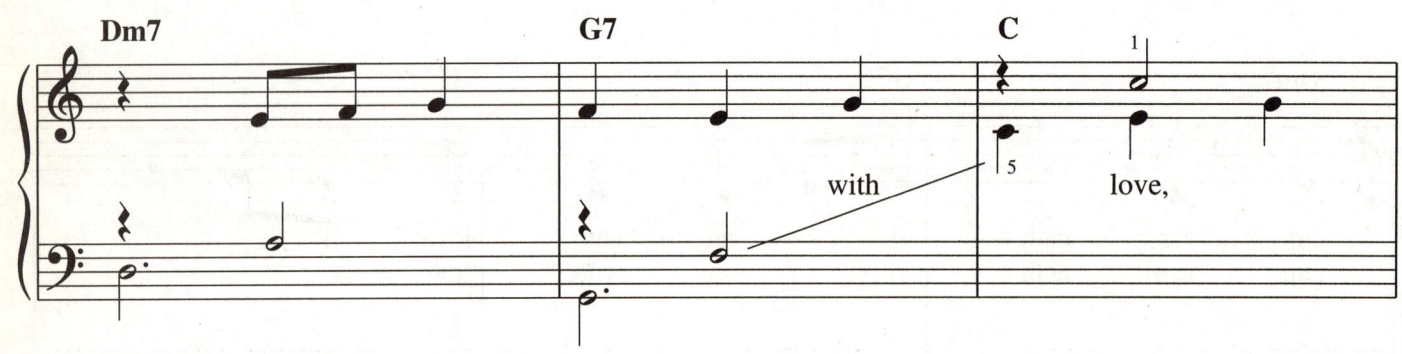

Additional Lyrics

In only a moment we both will be old;
We won't even notice the world turning cold.
And so in this moment with sunlight above,
My cup runneth over with love, with love.

OKLAHOMA
from OKLAHOMA!

Lyrics by OSCAR HAMMERSTEIN II
Music by RICHARD RODGERS

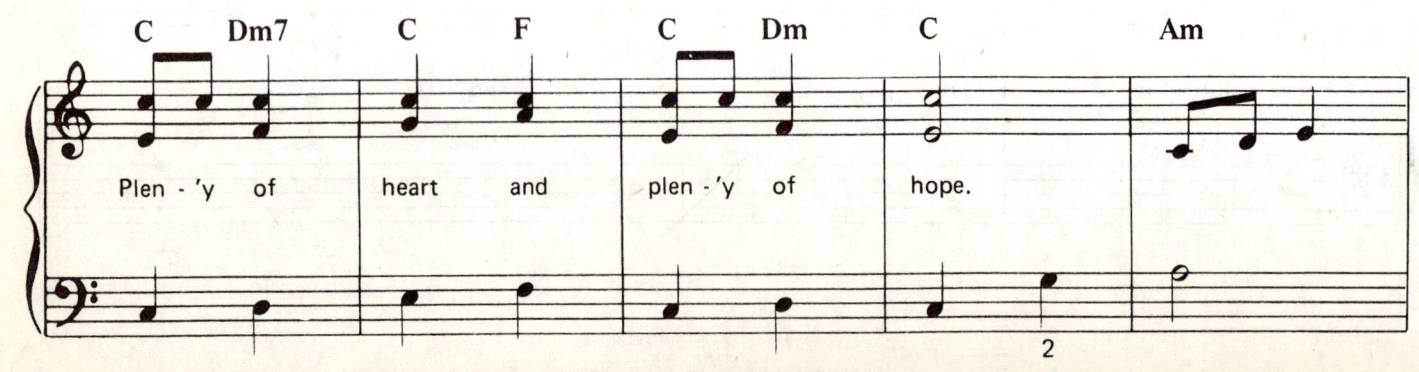

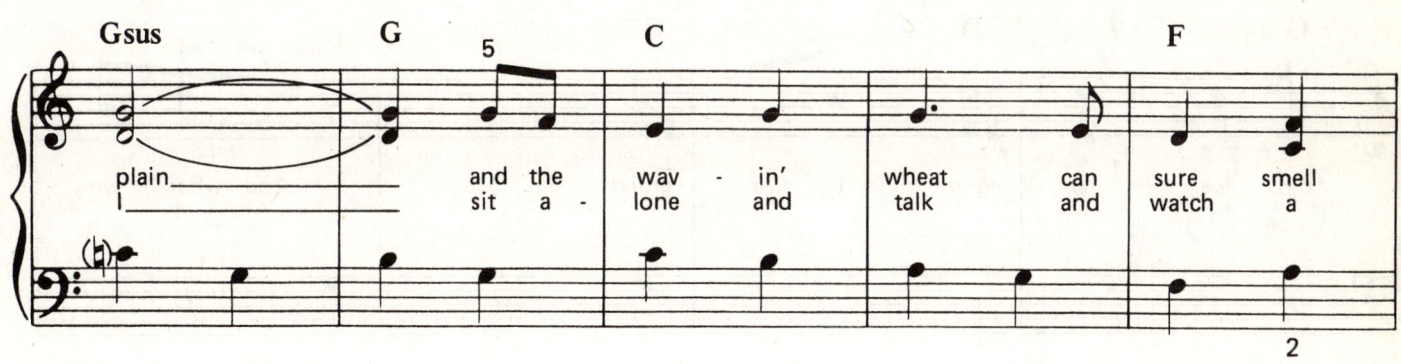

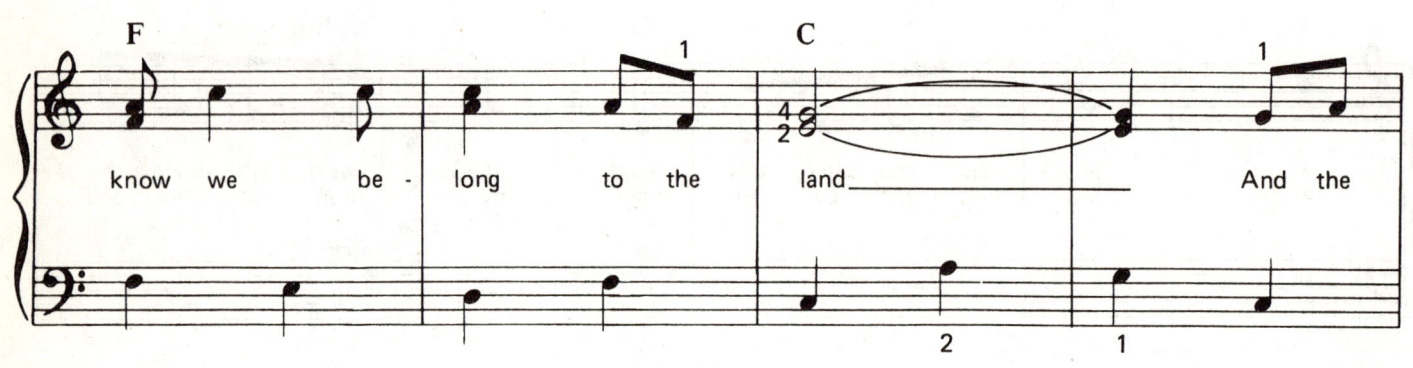

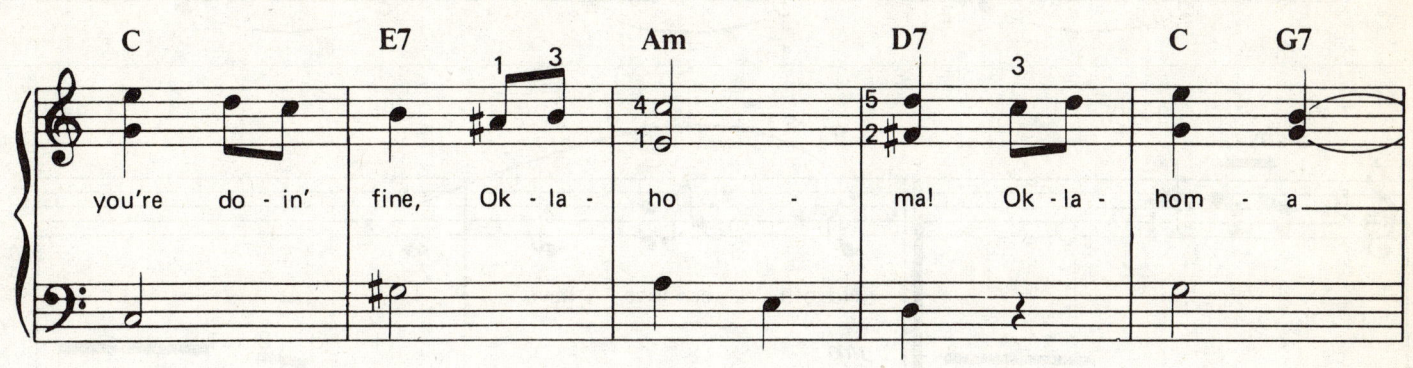

NO OTHER LOVE
from ME AND JULIET

Lyrics by OSCAR HAMMERSTEIN II
Music by RICHARD RODGERS

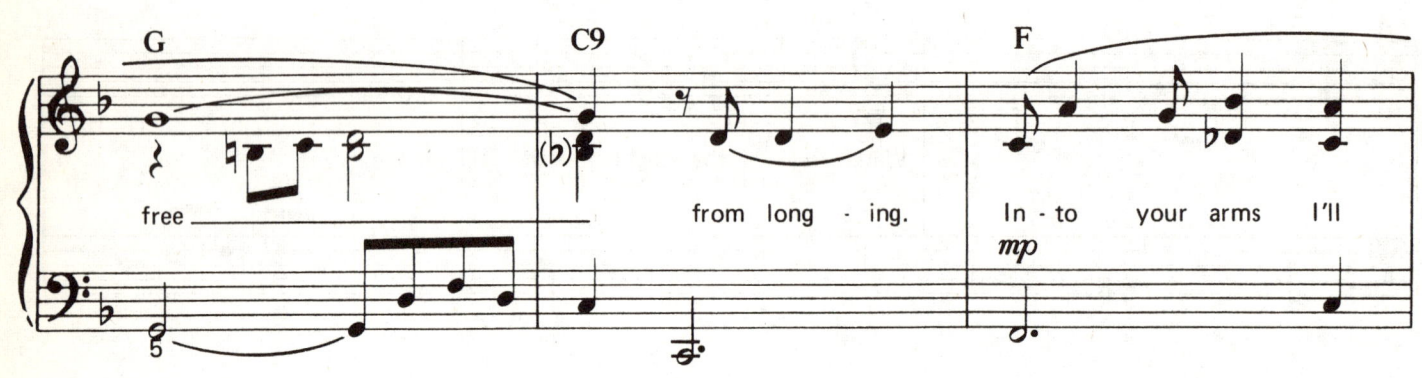

OL' MAN RIVER
from SHOW BOAT

Lyrics by OSCAR HAMMERSTEIN II
Music by JEROME KERN

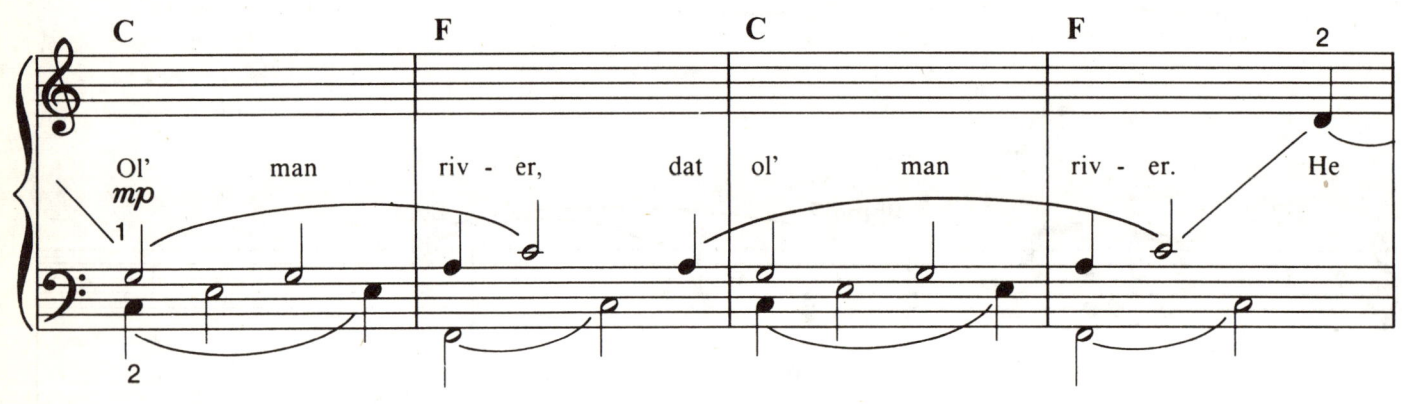

Copyright © 1927 UNIVERSAL - POLYGRAM INTERNATIONAL PUBLISHING, INC.
Copyright Renewed
All Rights Reserved   Used by Permission

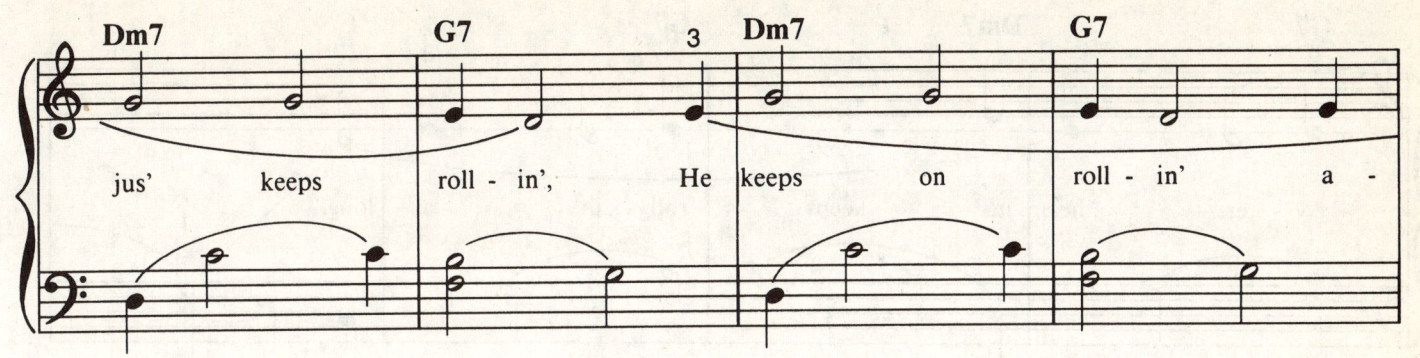
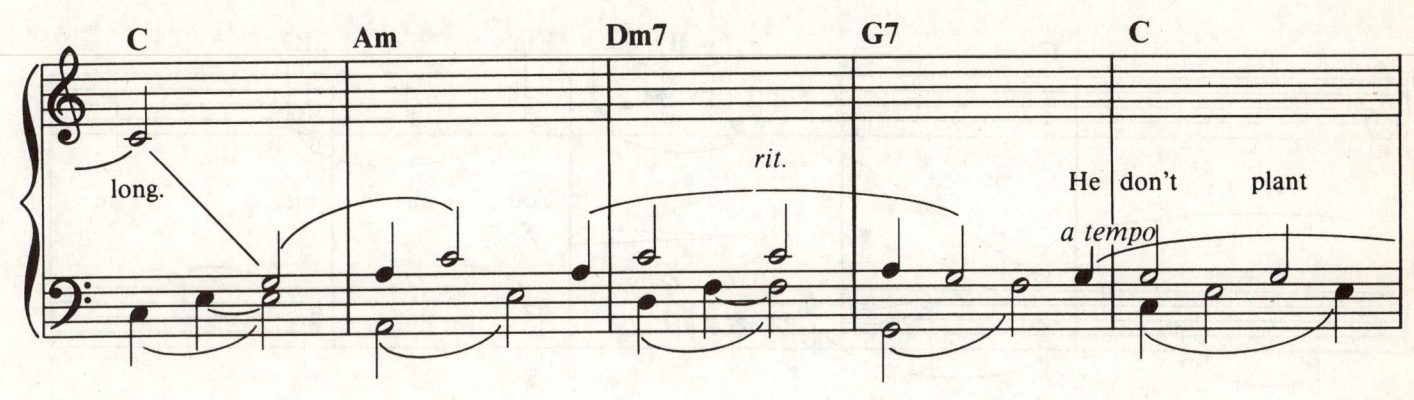
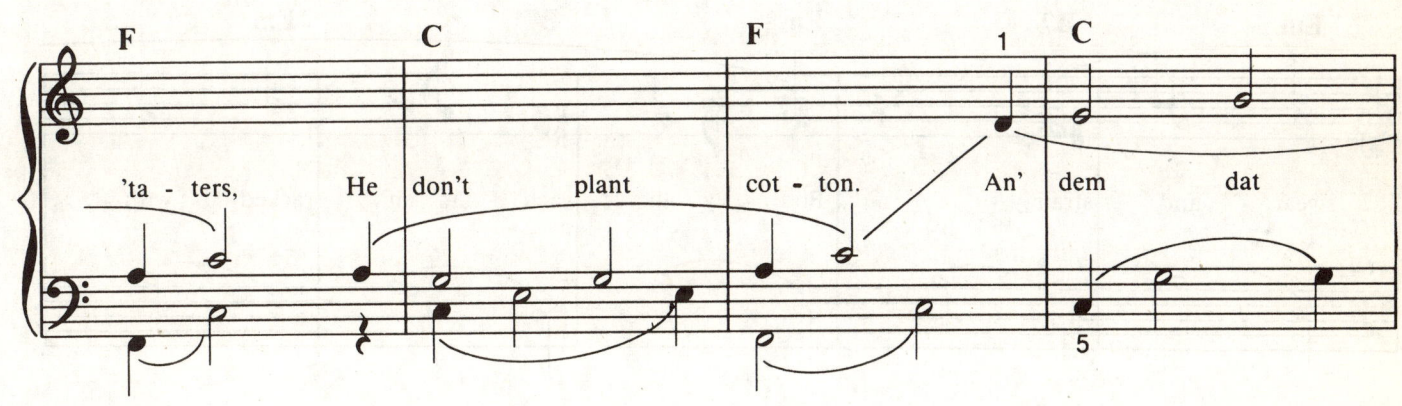
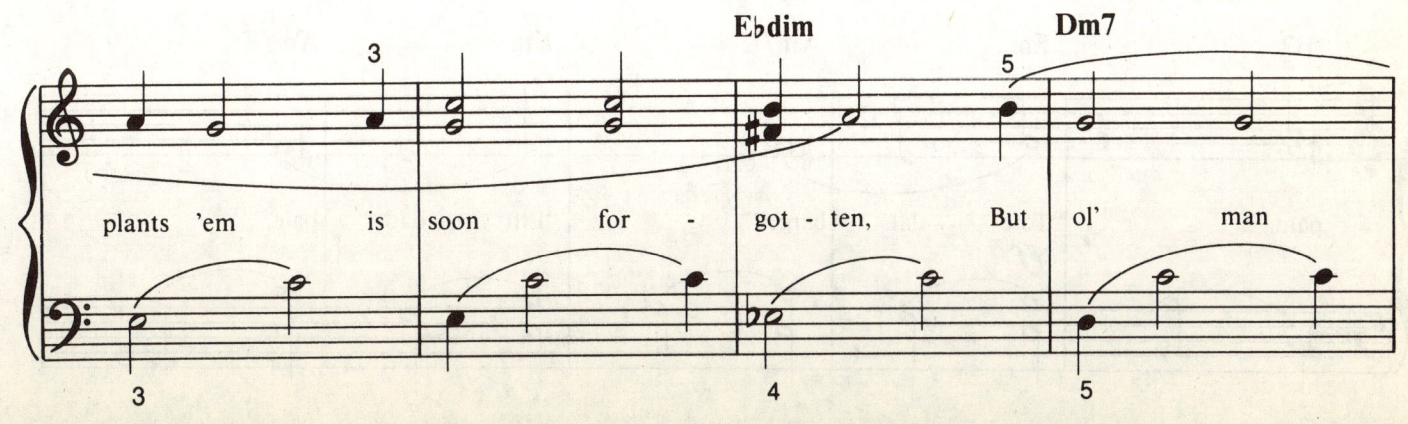

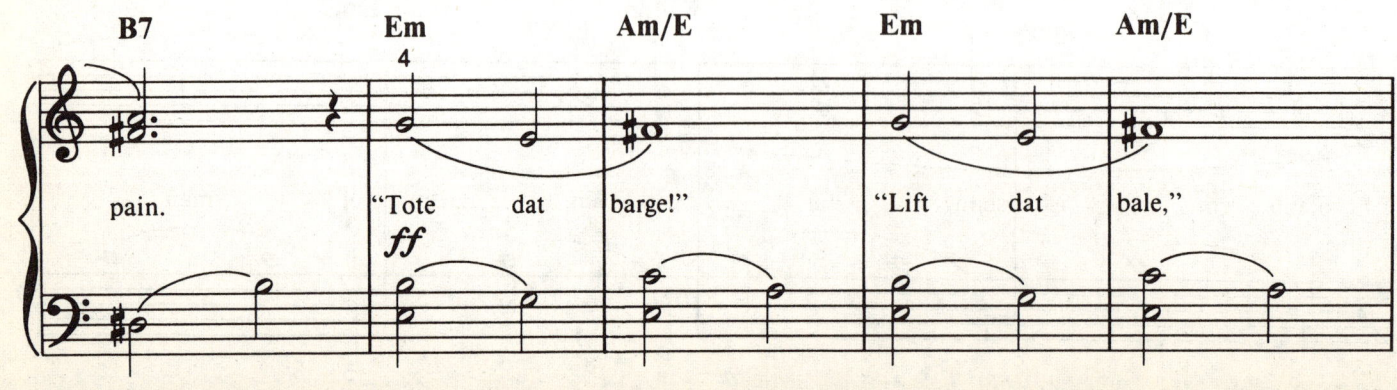

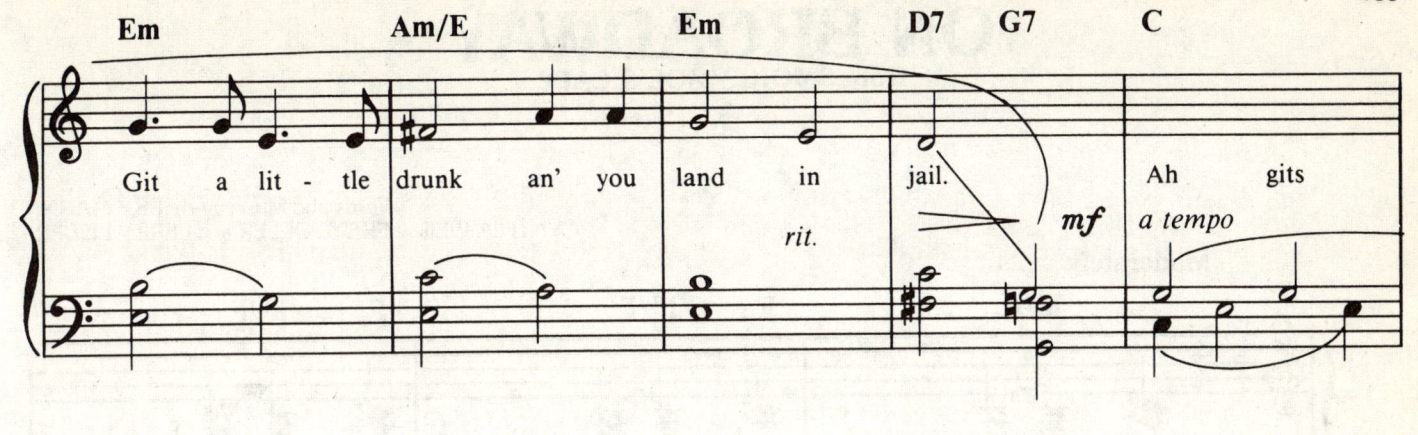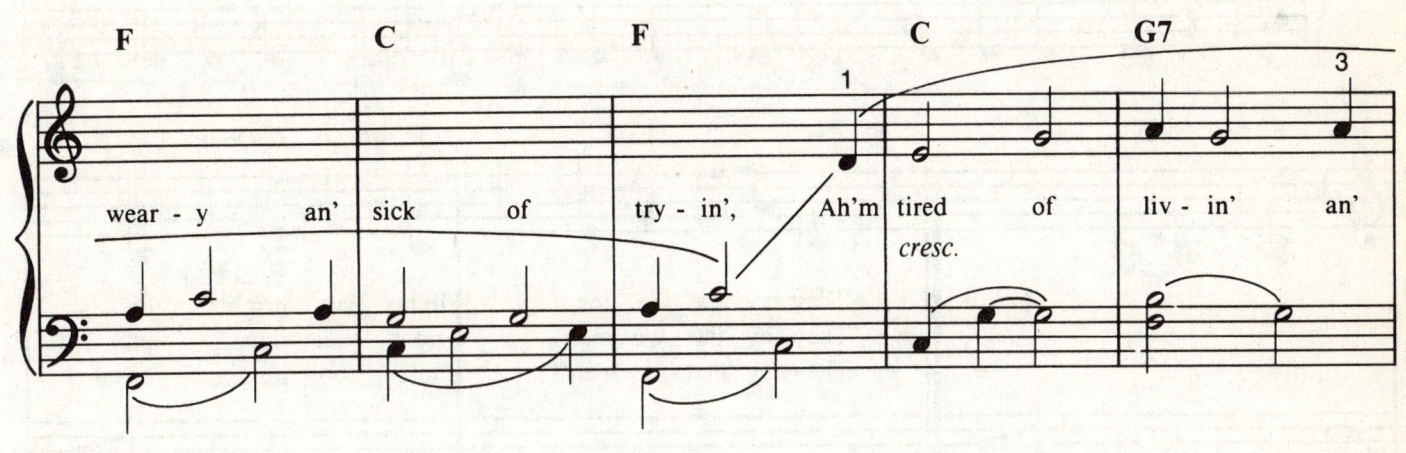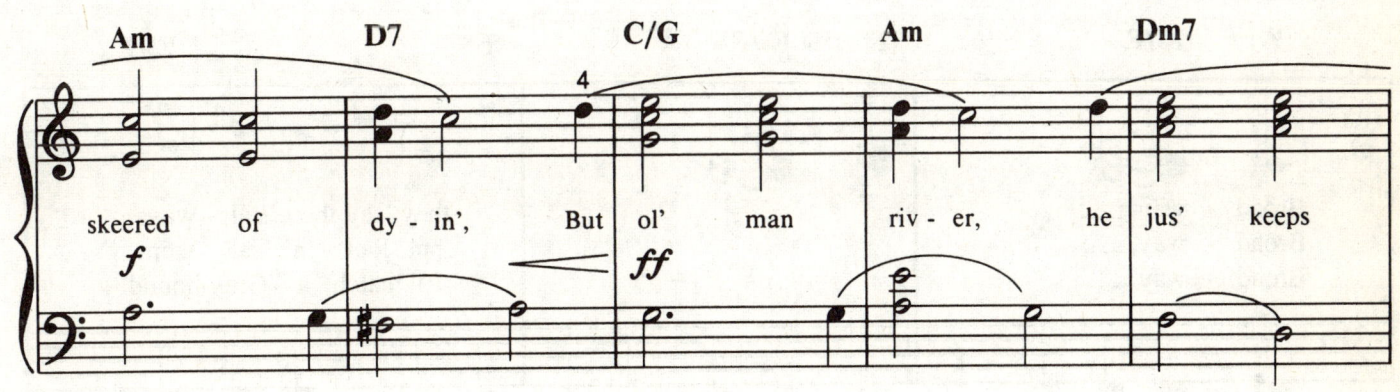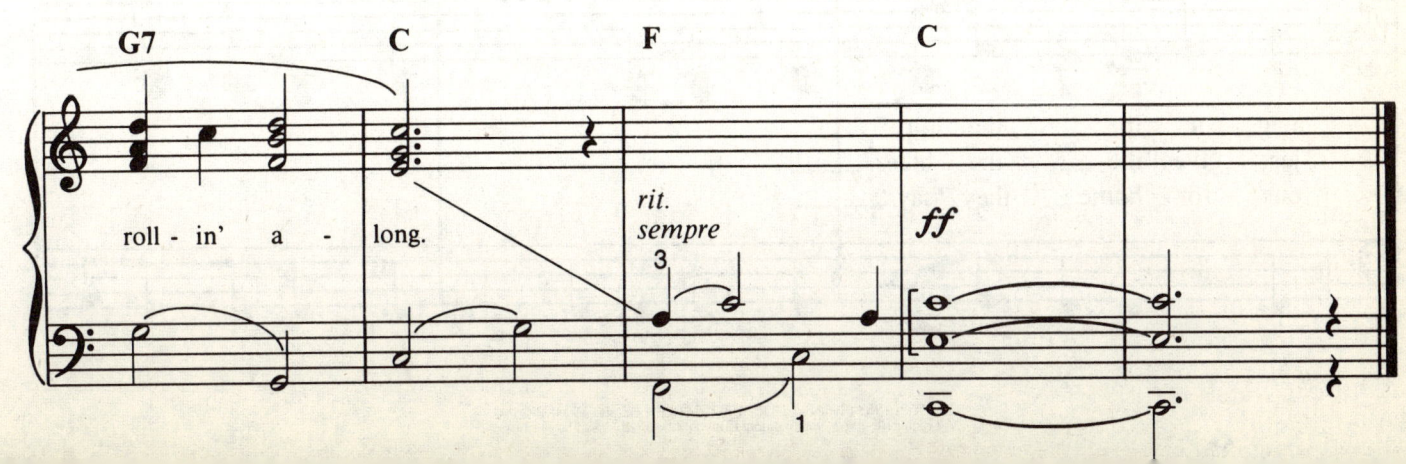

ONE
from A CHORUS LINE

Music by MARVIN HAMLISCH
Lyric by EDWARD KLEBAN

© 1975 (Renewed) MARVIN HAMLISCH and EDWARD KLEBAN
All Rights Controlled by WREN MUSIC CO. and AMERICAN COMPASS MUSIC CORP.
All Rights Reserved

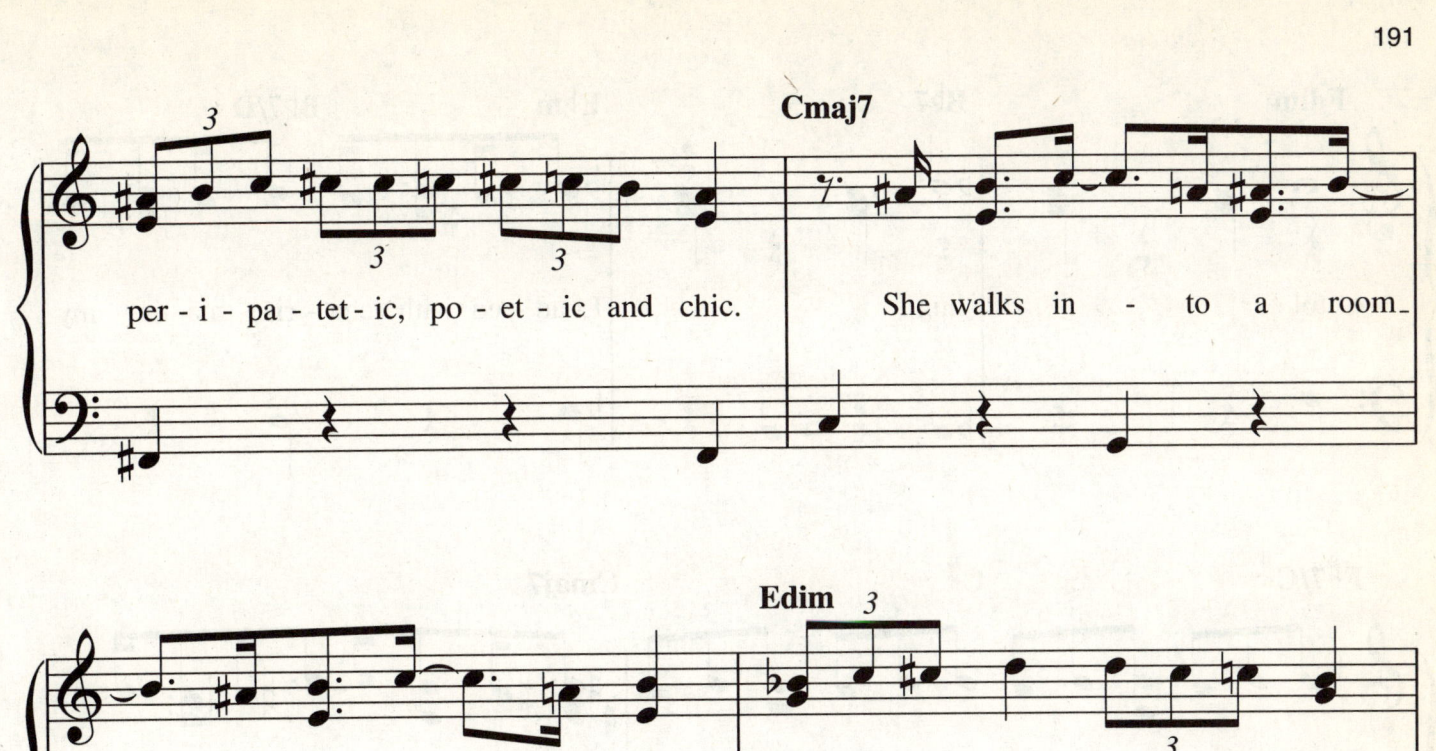

Fdim
Bb7
Ebm
Bb7/D
tol - ling.
Load - ed with cha - ris - ma is my
F#7/C#
C#
Cmaj7
jaun - ti - ly, saun - ter - ing, am - bl - ing sham - bl - er.
She walks in - to a room
and you know you must
F#7
shuf - fle a - long, join the pa - rade.
She's the quin - tes-sense of mak - ing the grade.
F
This is what - cha call

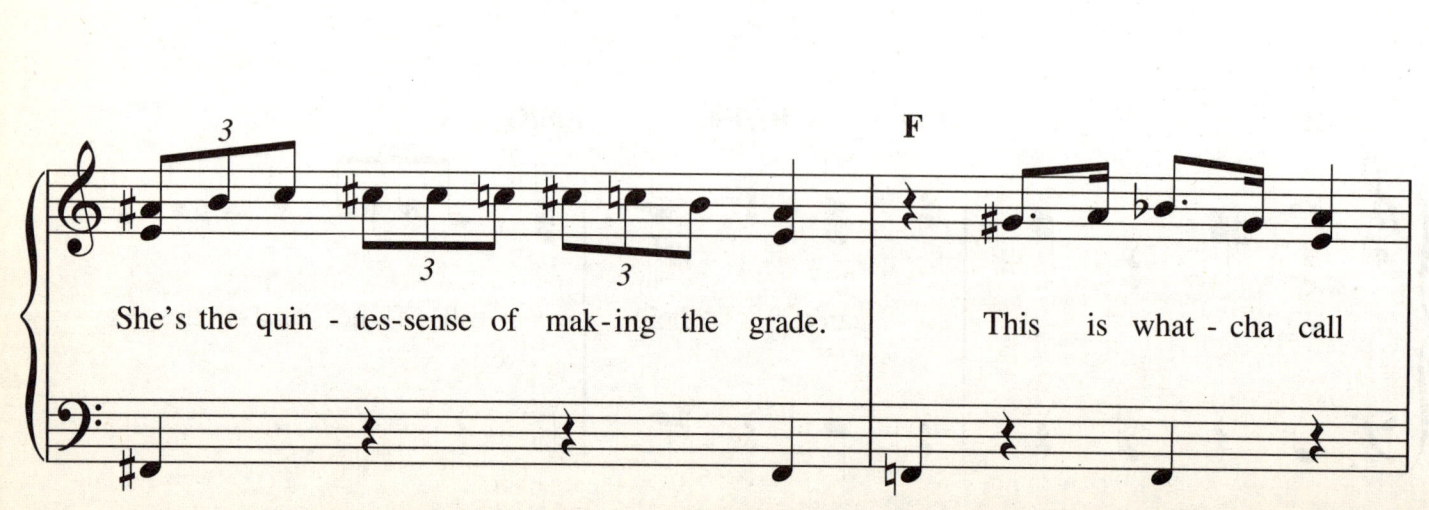

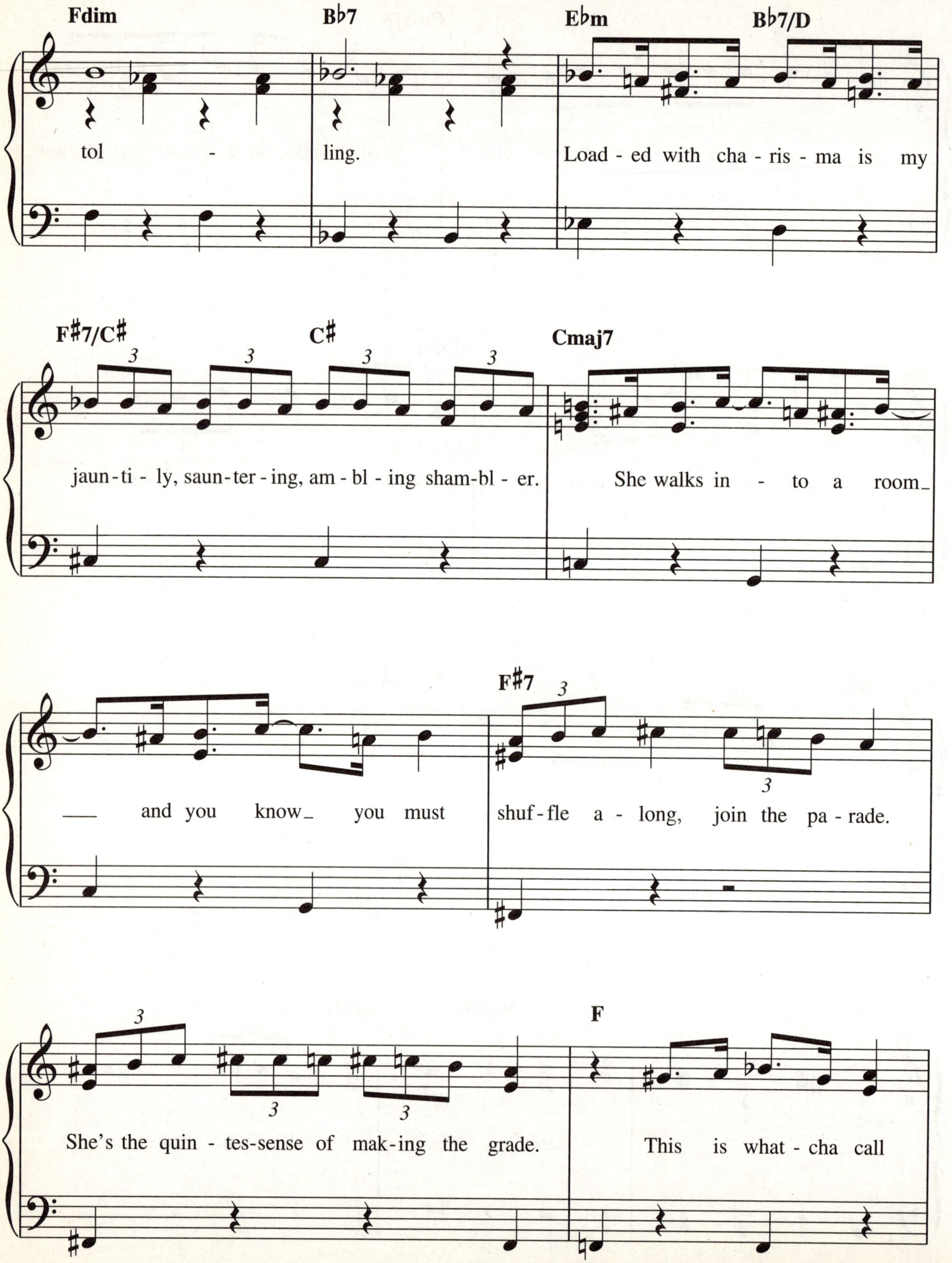

PEOPLE
from FUNNY GIRL

Words by BOB MERRILL
Music by JULE STYNE

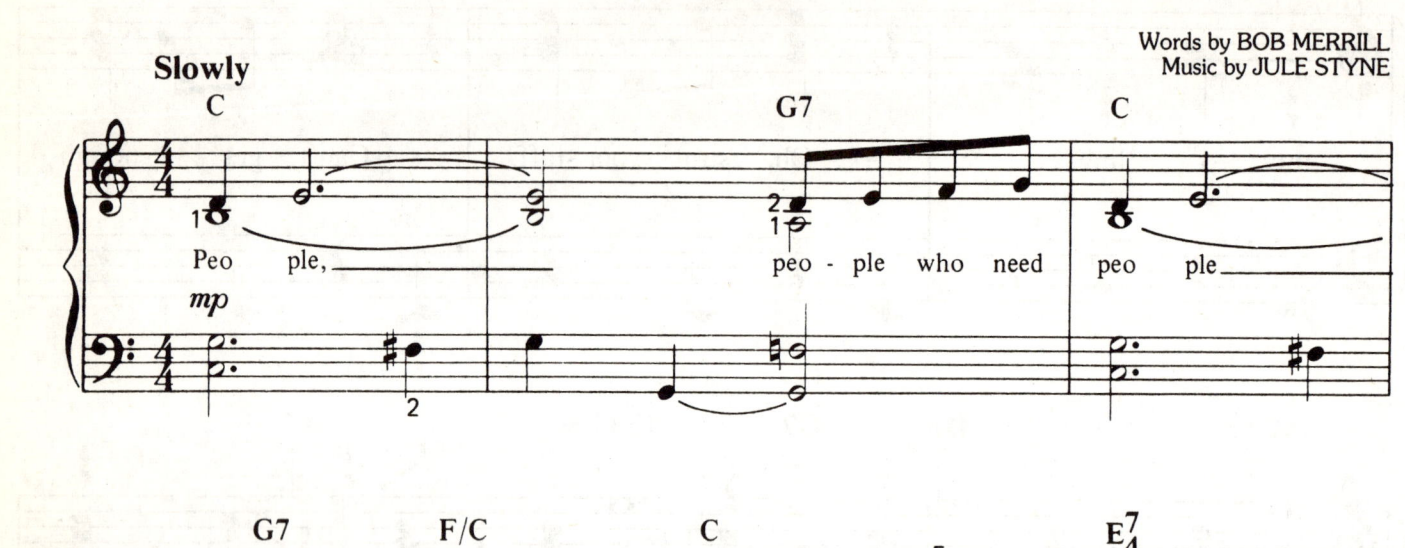

Copyright © 1963, 1964 by Bob Merrill and Jule Styne
Copyright Renewed
All Rights Administered by Chappell & Co.
International Copyright Secured   All Rights Reserved

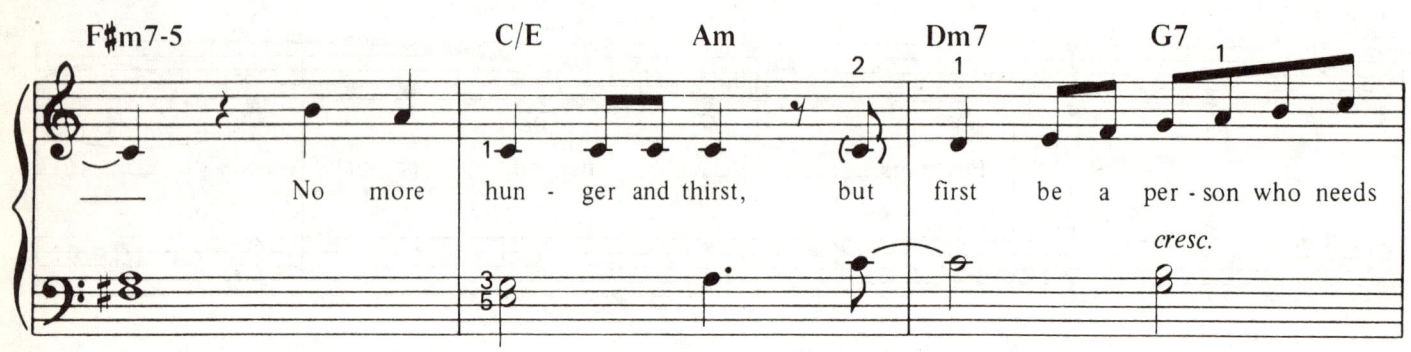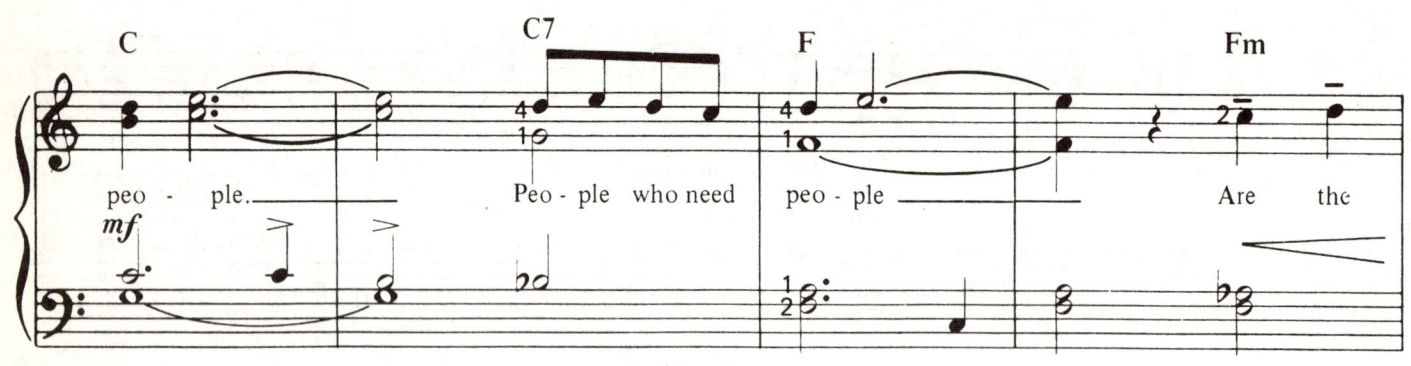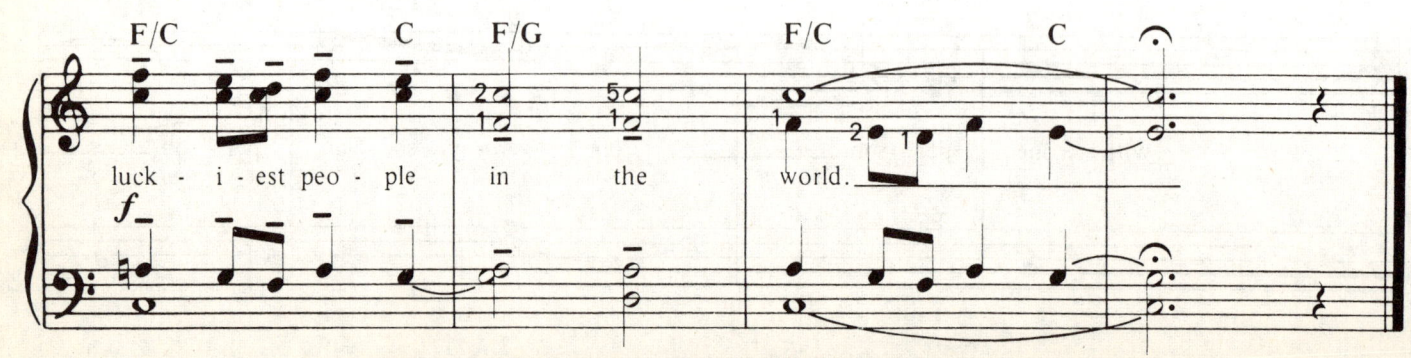

RIVER IN THE RAIN
from BIG RIVER

Words and Music by
ROGER MILLER

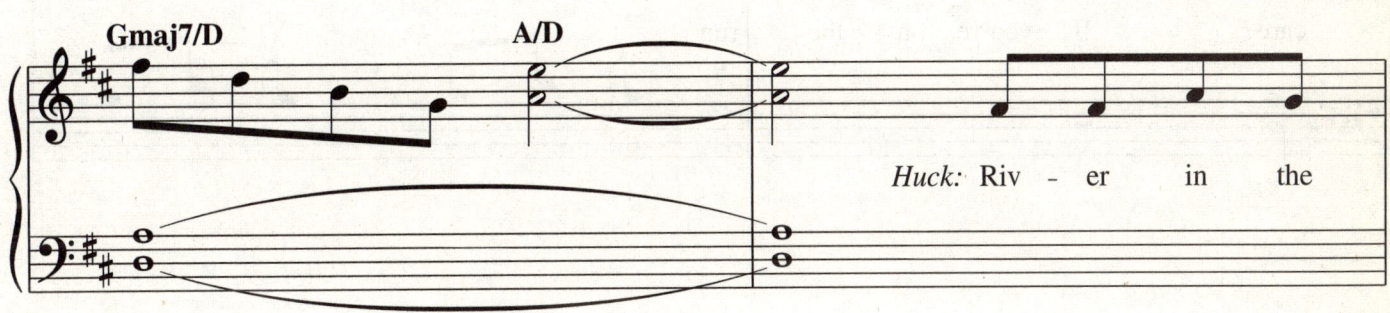

Copyright © 1985 Sony/ATV Songs LLC and Roger Miller Music
All Rights Administered by Sony/ATV Music Publishing, 8 Music Square West, Nashville, TN 37203
International Copyright Secured   All Rights Reserved

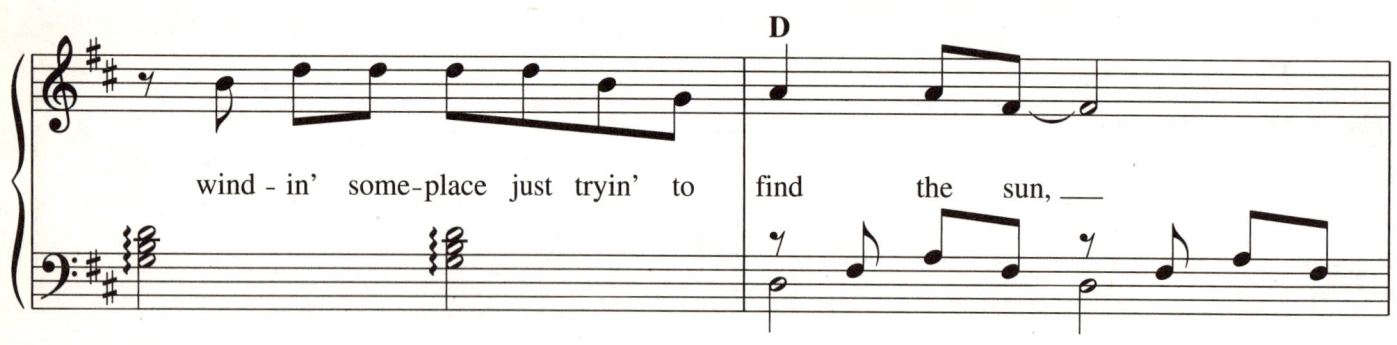

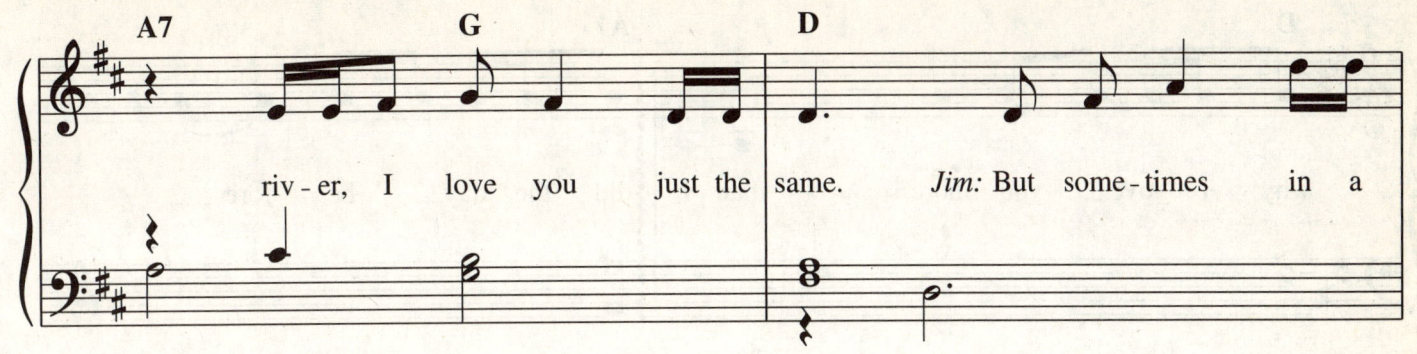

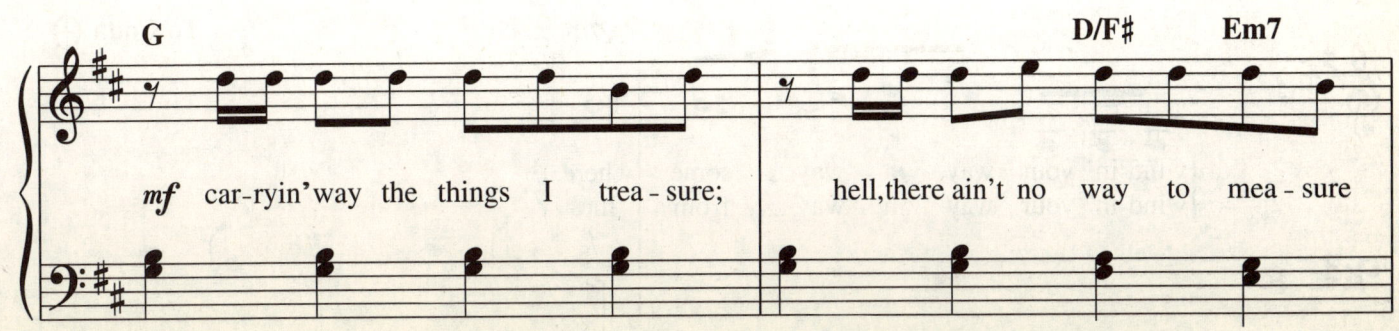

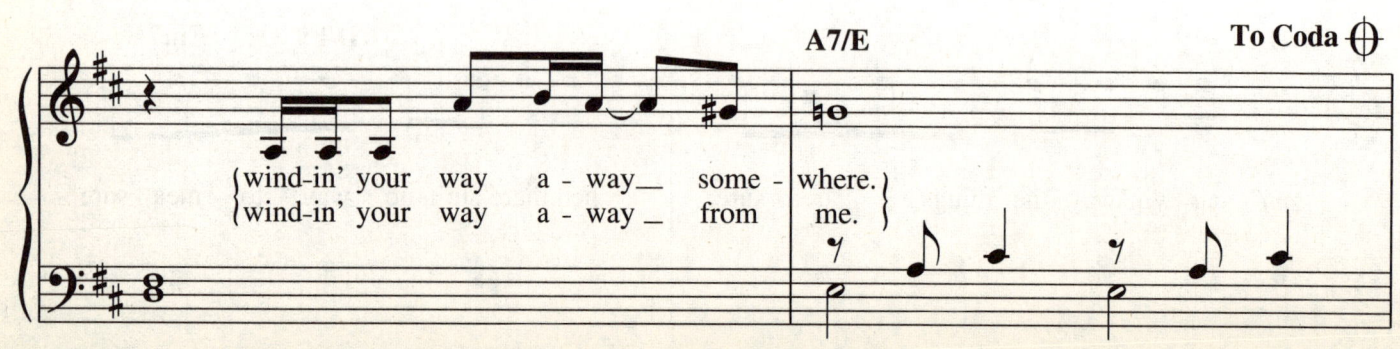

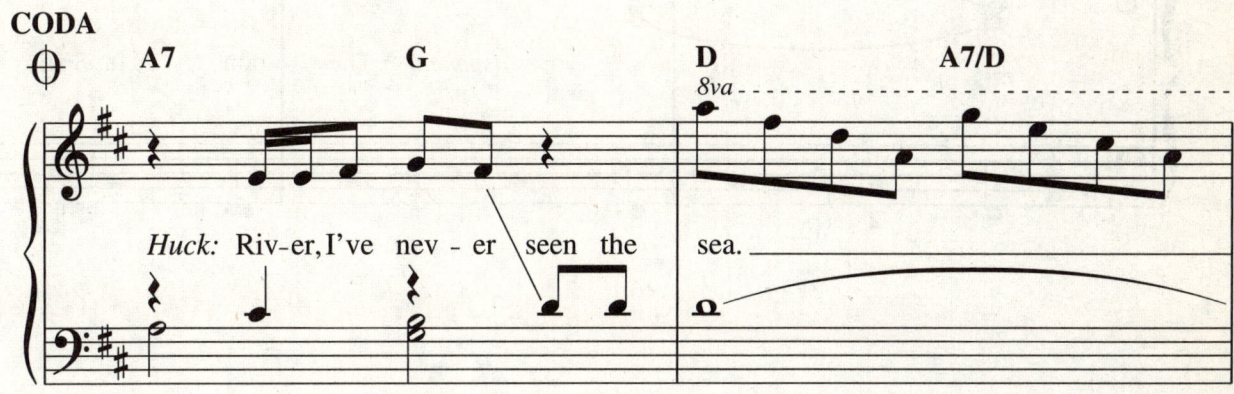

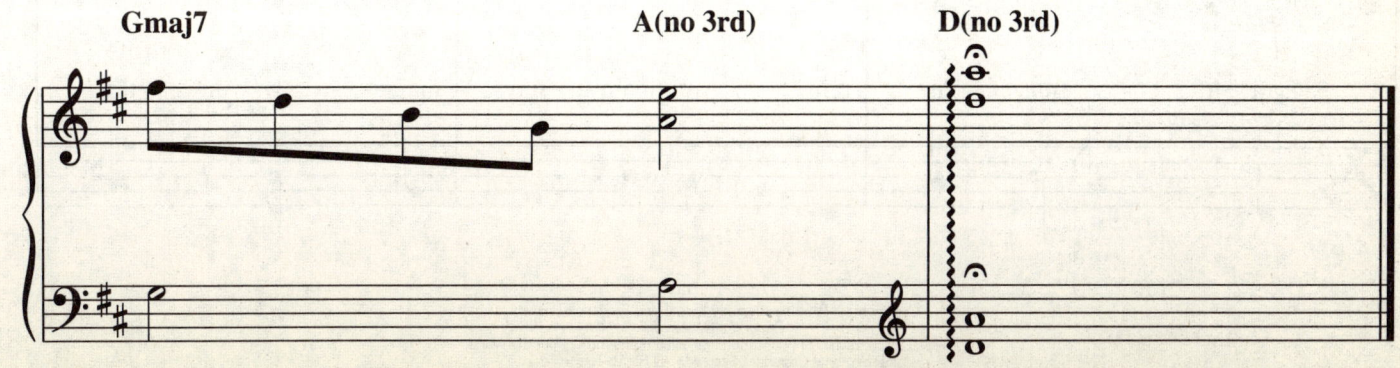

THE RAIN IN SPAIN
from MY FAIR LADY

Words by ALAN JAY LERNER
Music by FREDERICK LOEWE

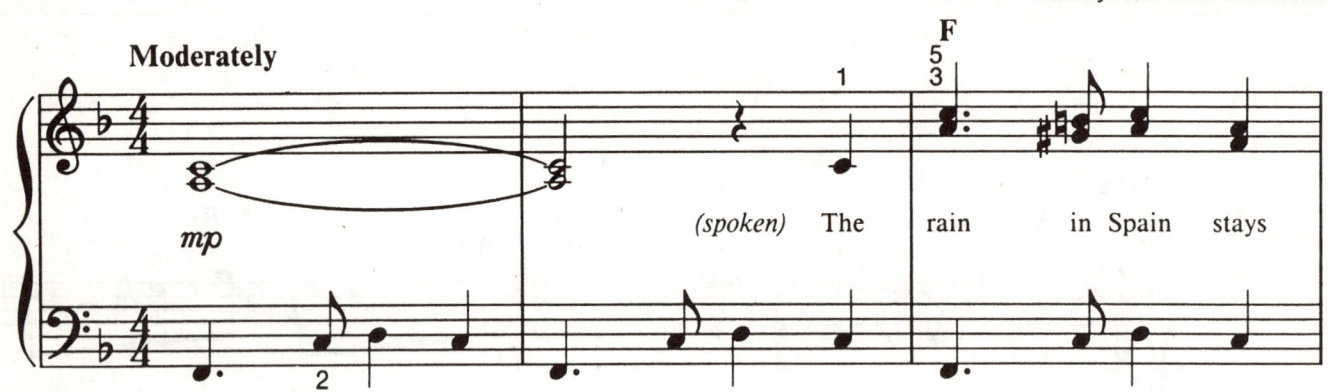

Copyright © 1956 by Alan Jay Lerner and Frederick Loewe
Copyright Renewed
Chappell & Co. owner of publication and allied rights throughout the world
International Copyright Secured   All Rights Reserved

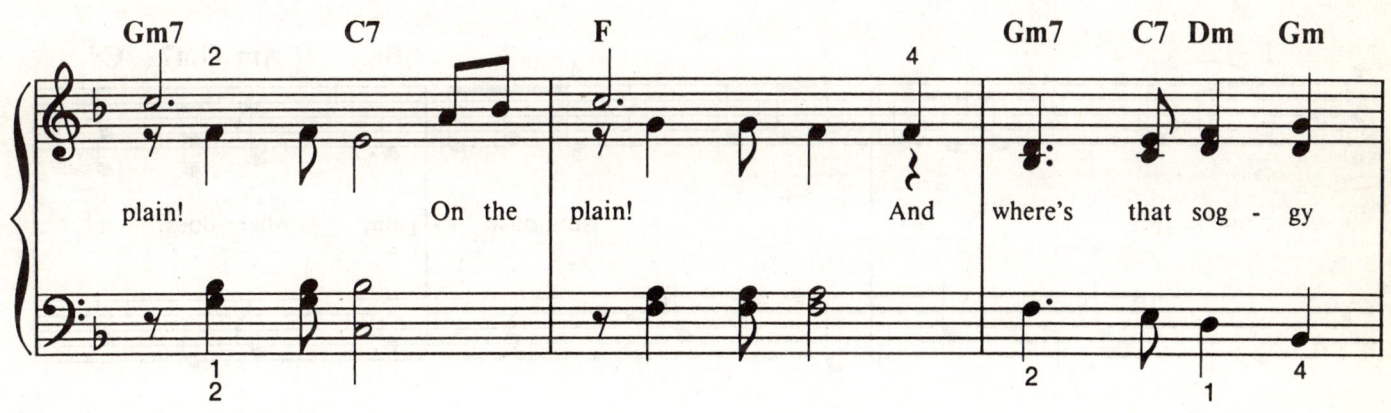

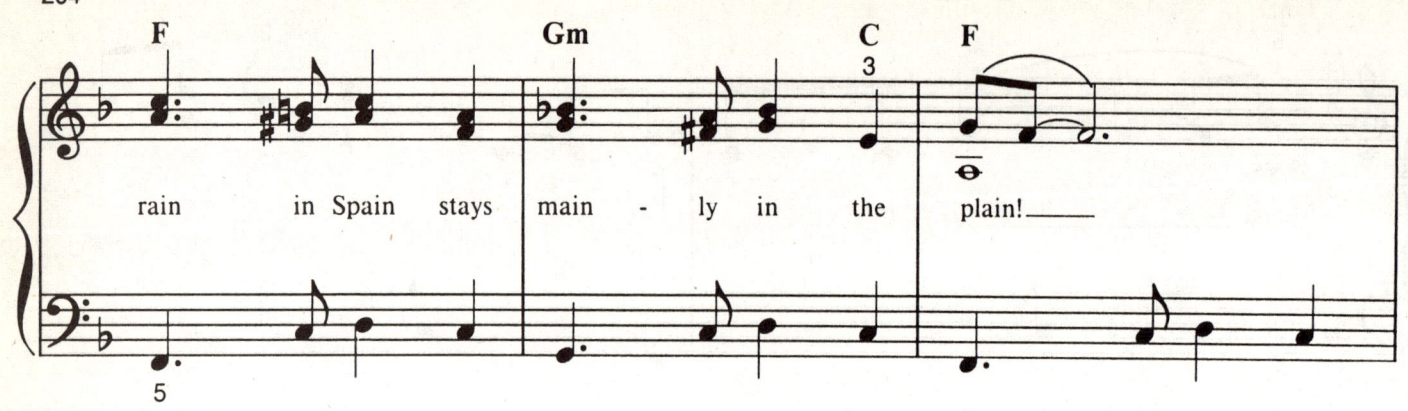

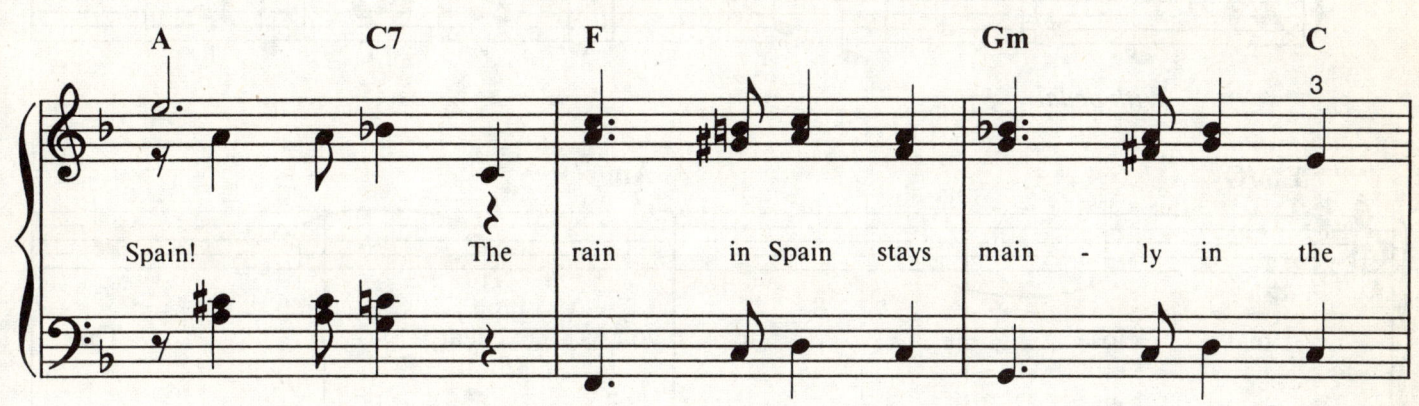

SO IN LOVE
from KISS ME, KATE

Words and Music by
COLE PORTER

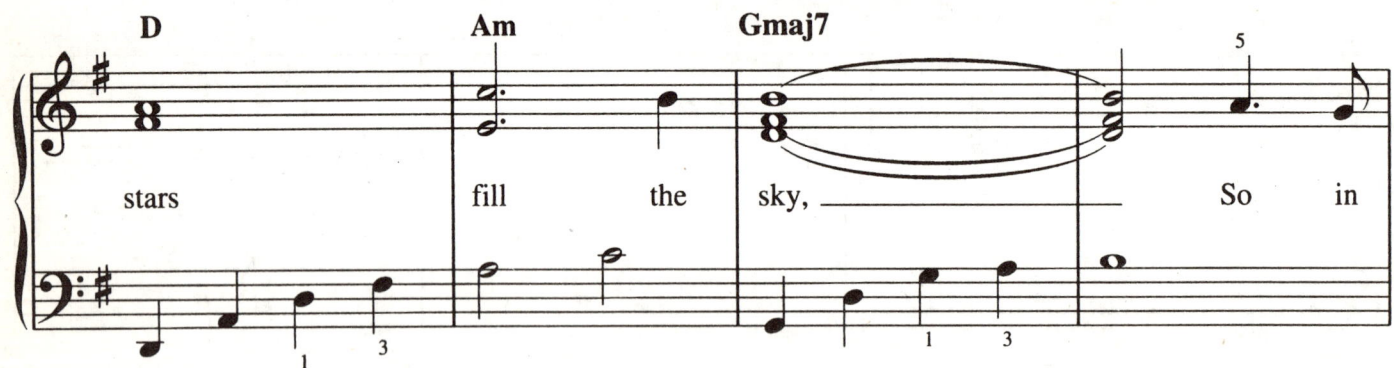
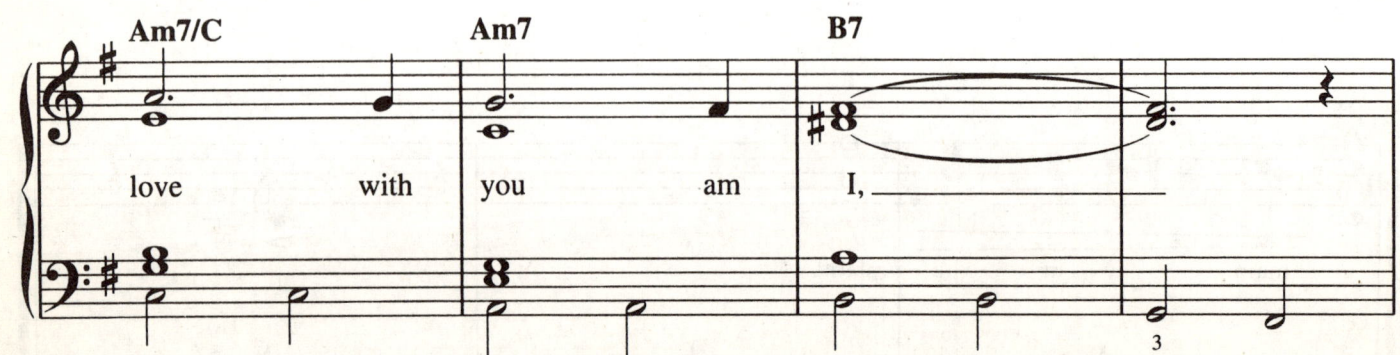

Copyright © 1948 by Cole Porter
Copyright Renewed, Assigned to John F. Wharton, Trustee of the Cole Porter Musical and Literary Property Trusts
Chappell & Co. owner of publication and allied rights throughout the world
International Copyright Secured   All Rights Reserved

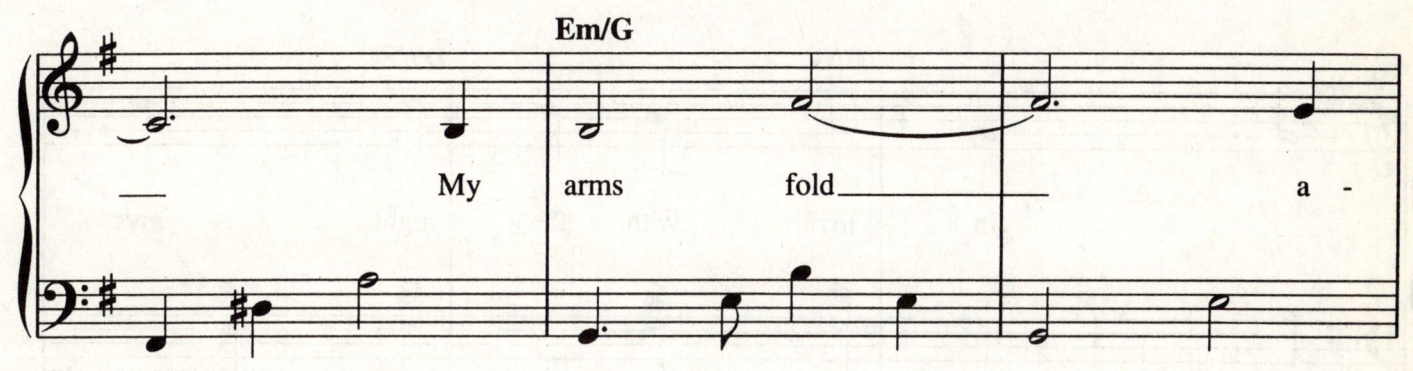

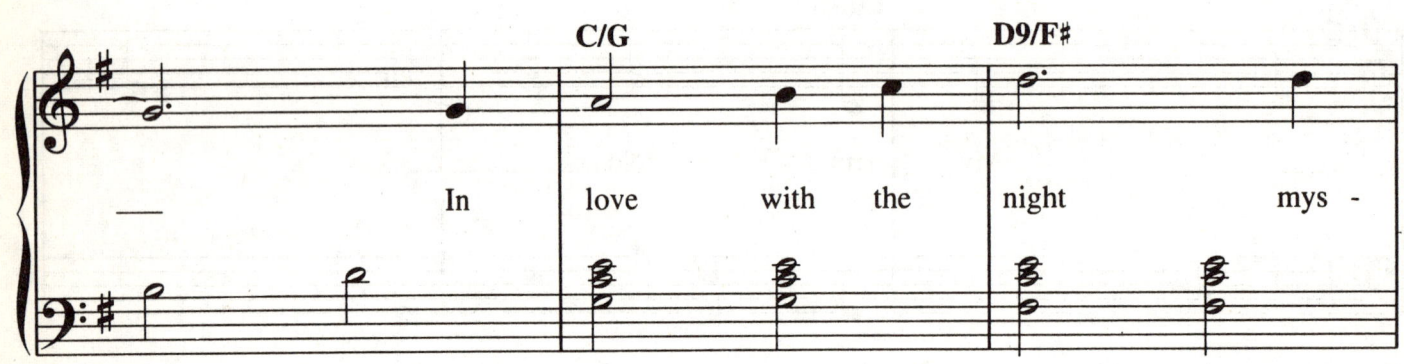

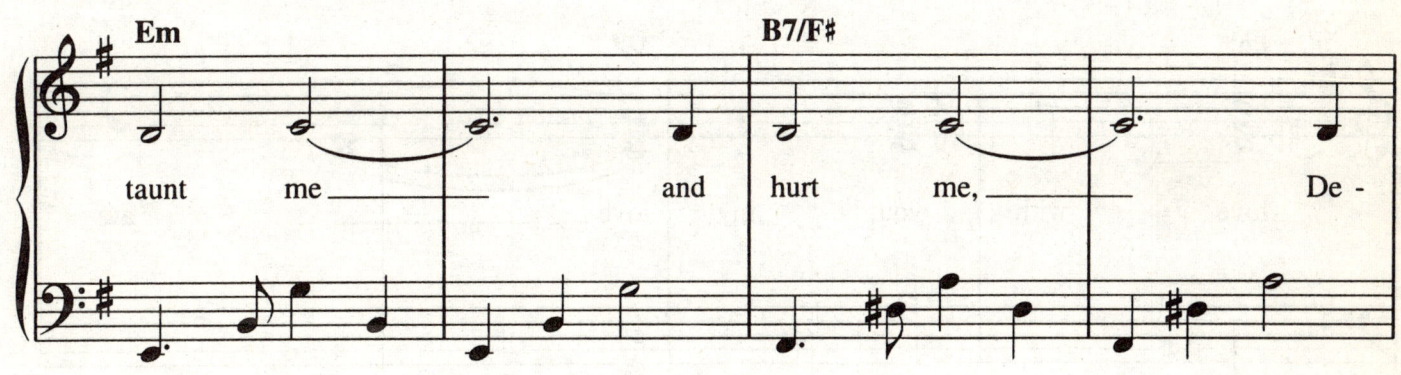

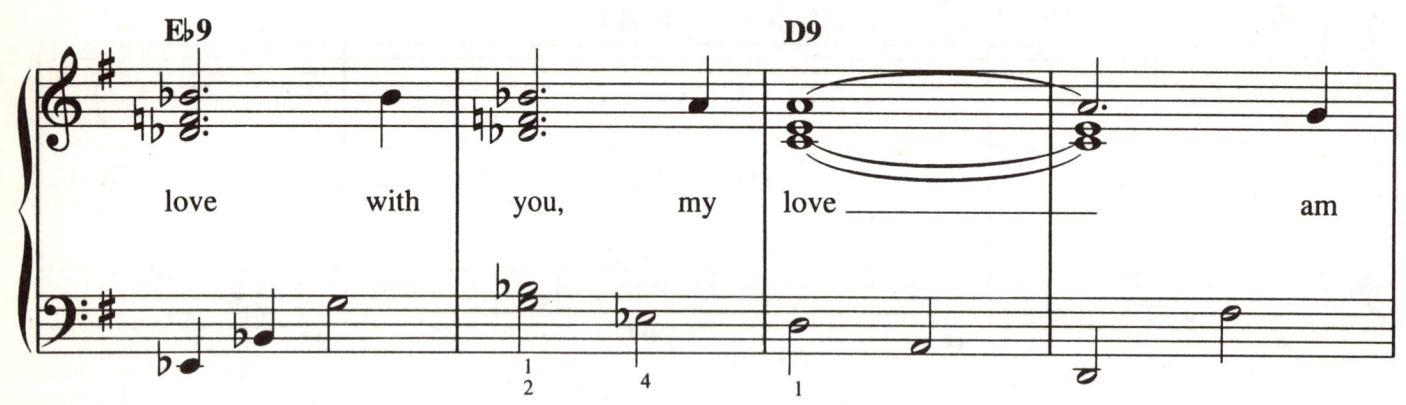

THE SOUND OF MUSIC
from THE SOUND OF MUSIC

Lyrics by OSCAR HAMMERSTEIN II
Music by RICHARD RODGERS

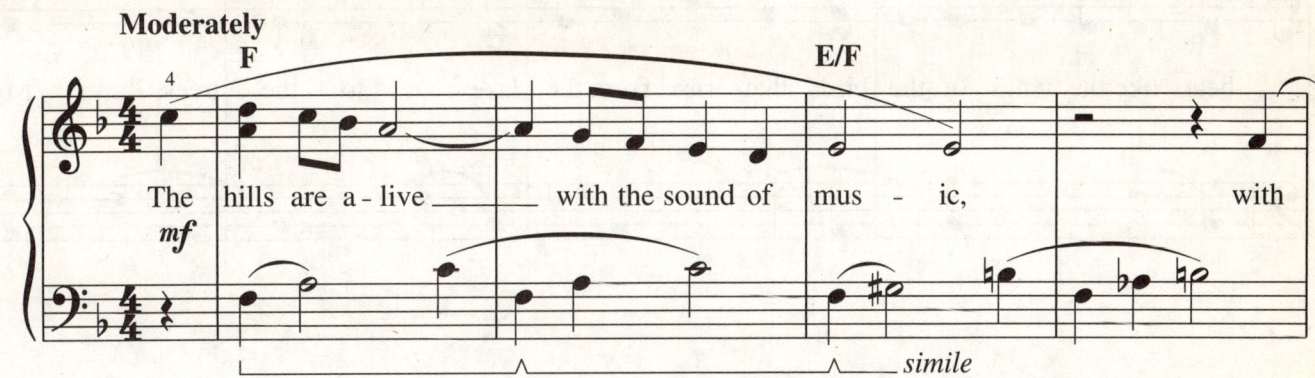

Copyright © 1959 by Richard Rodgers and Oscar Hammerstein II
Copyright Renewed
WILLIAMSON MUSIC owner of publication and allied rights throughout the world
International Copyright Secured   All Rights Reserved

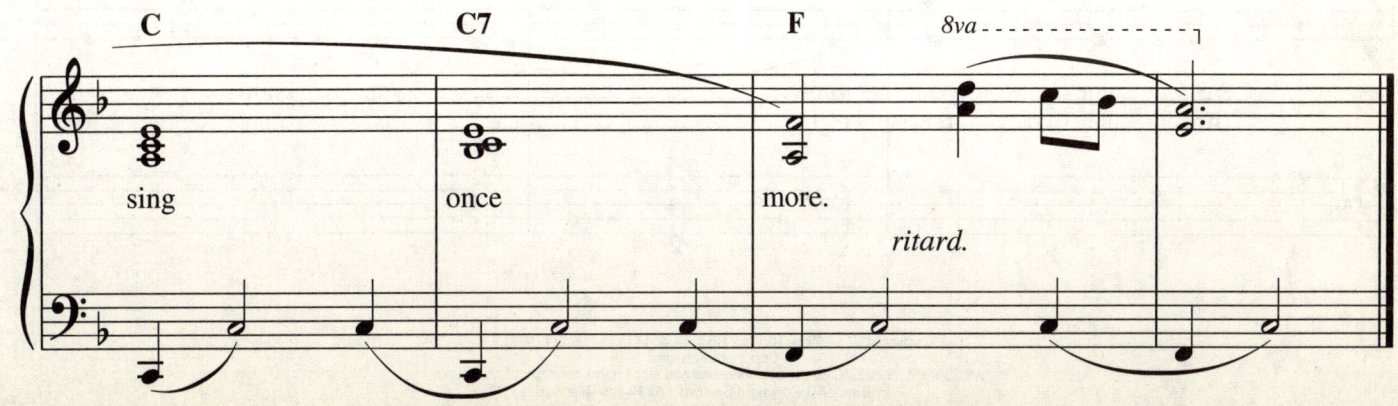

SOME ENCHANTED EVENING
from SOUTH PACIFIC

Lyrics by OSCAR HAMMERSTEIN II
Music by RICHARD RODGERS

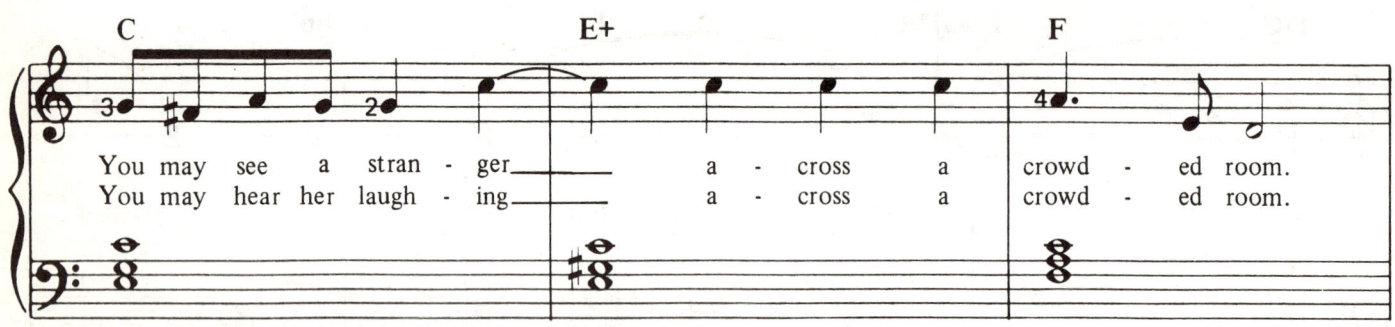
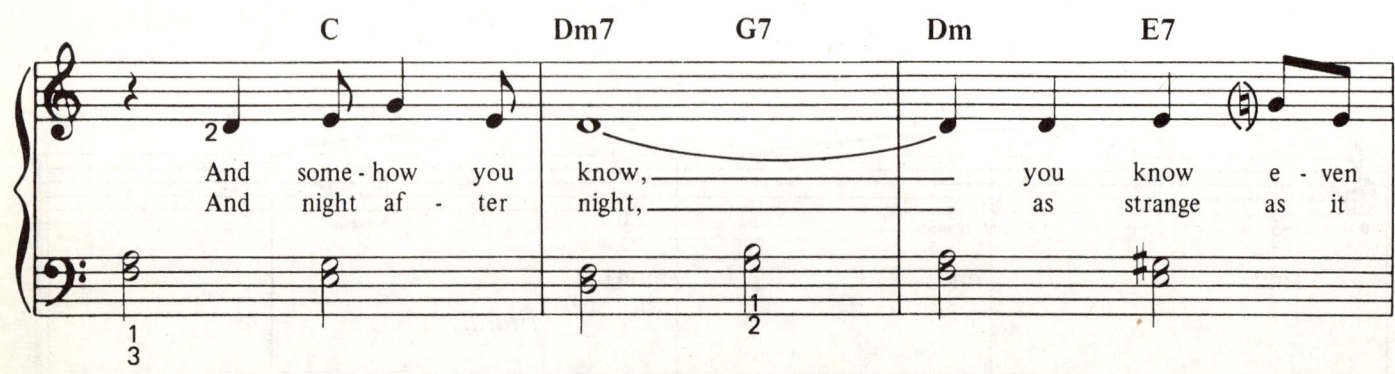

Copyright © 1949 by Richard Rodgers and Oscar Hammerstein II
Copyright Renewed
WILLIAMSON MUSIC owner of publication and allied rights throughout the world
International Copyright Secured   All Rights Reserved

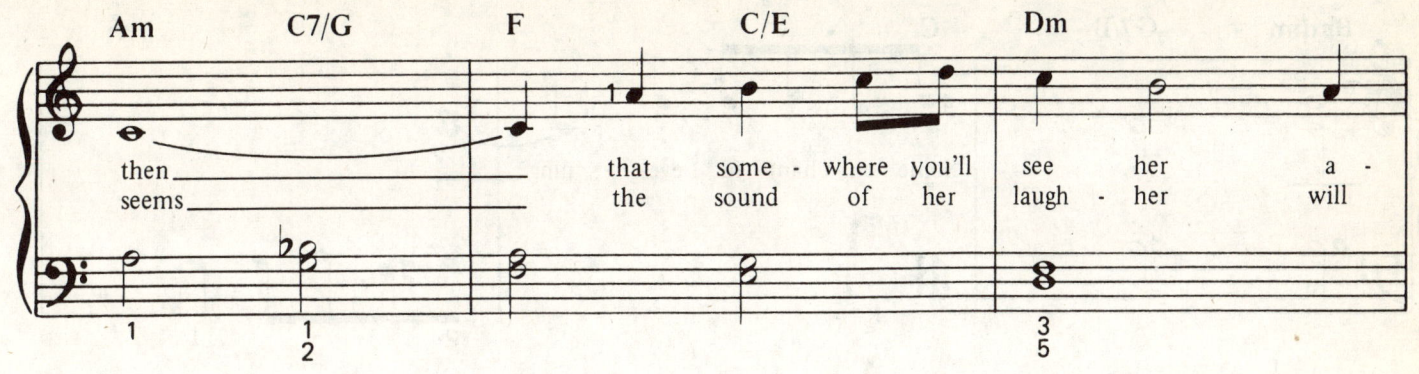

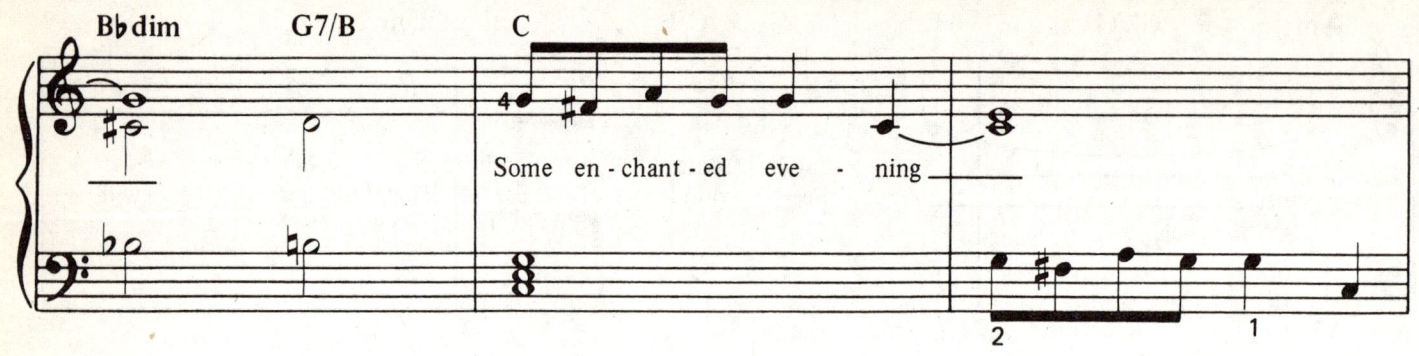

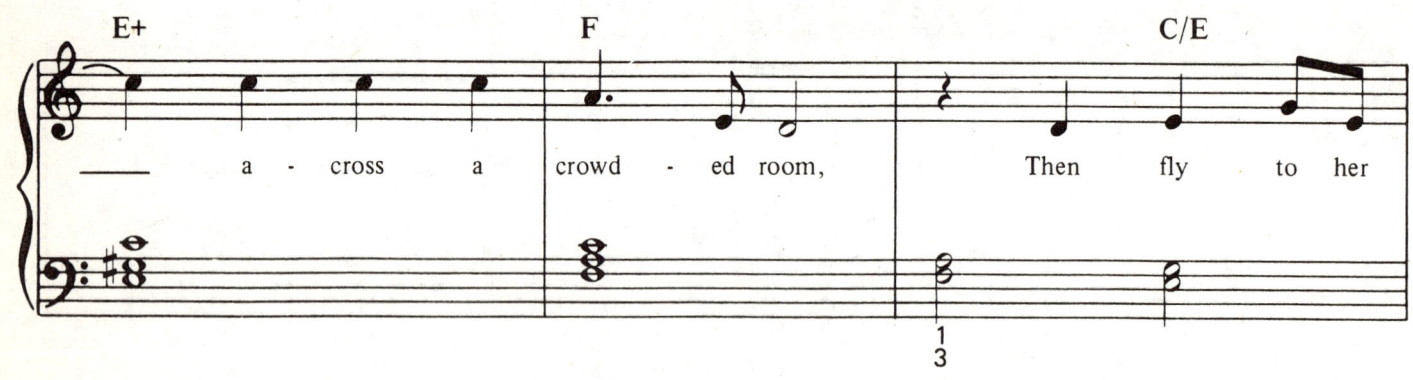
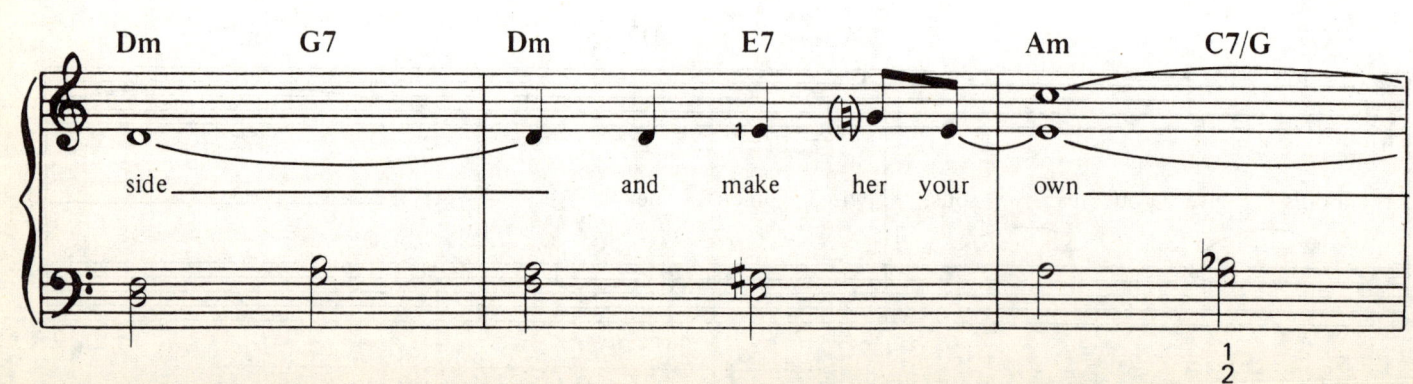

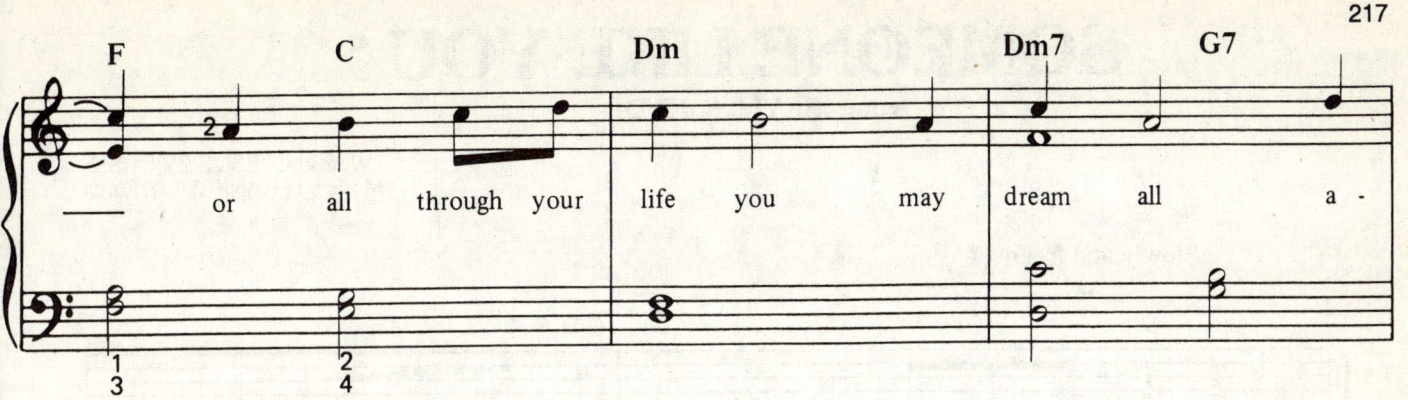

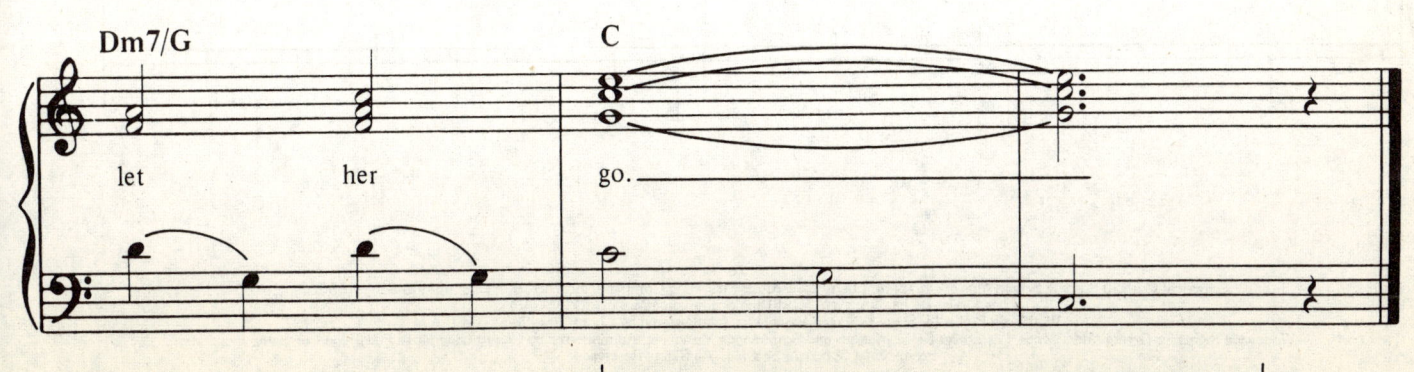

SOMEONE LIKE YOU
from JEKYLL & HYDE

Words by LESLIE BRICUSSE
Music by FRANK WILDHORN

Slowly and freely

I peer through windows, watch life go by,

dream of tomorrow, and wonder "why?"

The past is holding me, keeping life at bay.

I wander, lost in yesterday, wanting to

Copyright © 1990 Stage & Screen Music, Ltd. (BMI), Cherry Lane Music Publishing Company, Inc. (ASCAP), DreamWorks Songs (ASCAP),
Les Etoiles De La Musique (ASCAP) and Scaramanga Music, Inc. (ASCAP)
Worldwide Rights for Stage & Screen Music, Ltd. Administered by Cherry River Music Co.
Worldwide Rights for DreamWorks Songs, Les Etoiles De La Musique and Scaramanga Music, Inc. Administered by Cherry Lane Music Publishing Company, Inc.
International Copyright Secured   All Rights Reserved

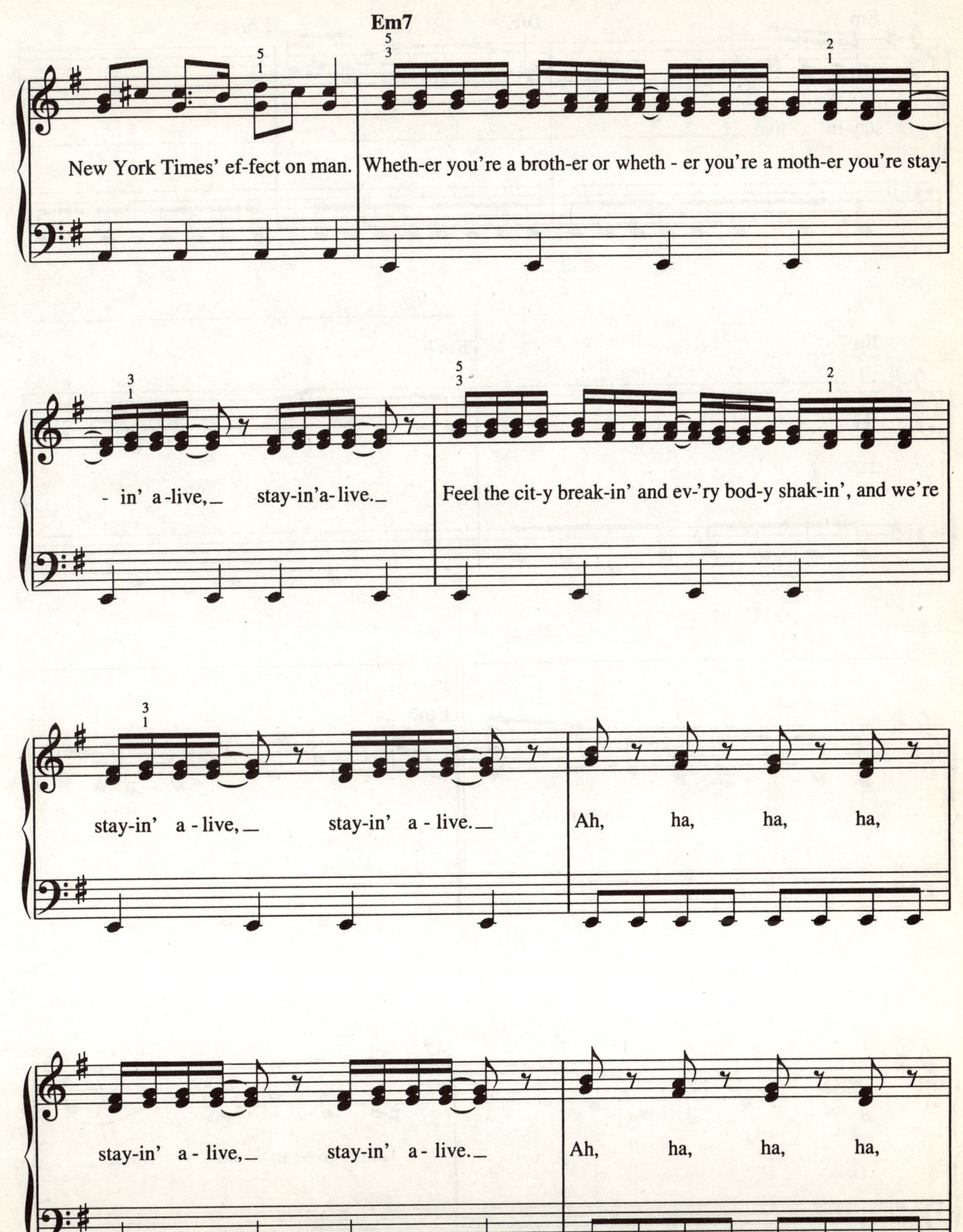

SUMMER NIGHTS
from GREASE

Lyric and Music by WARREN CASEY
and JIM JACOBS

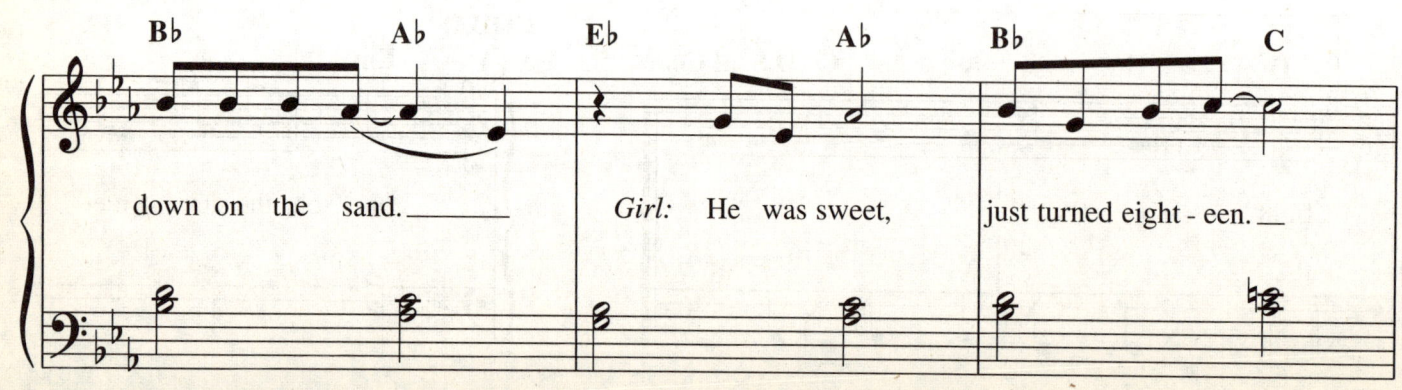

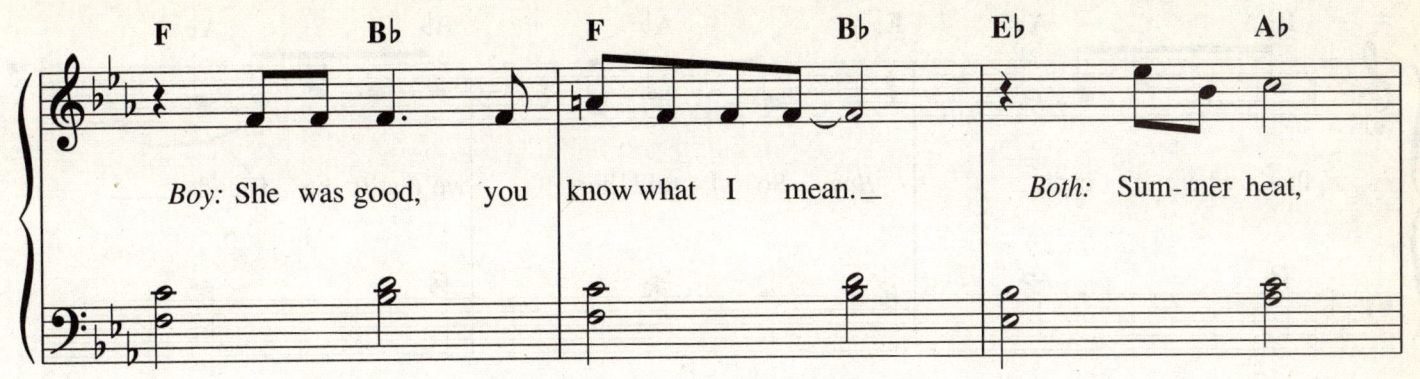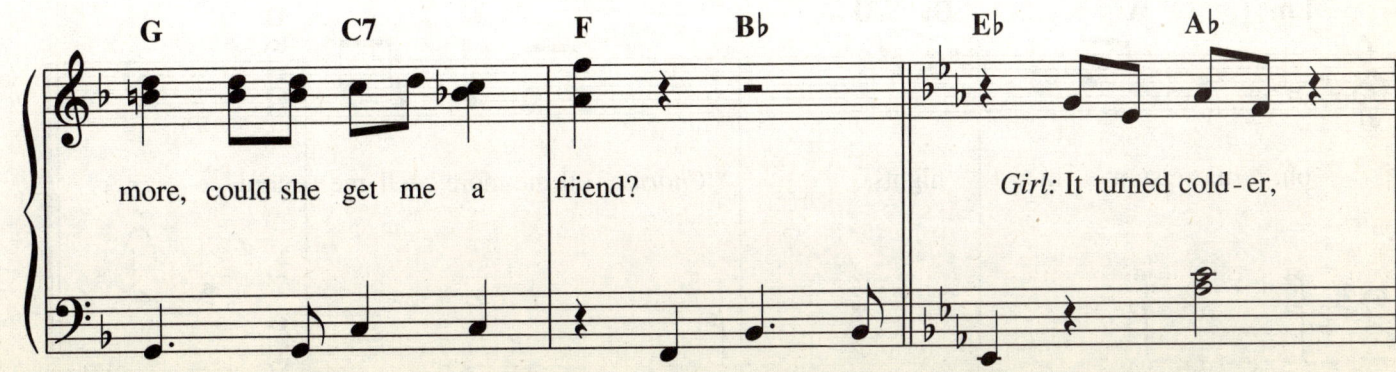

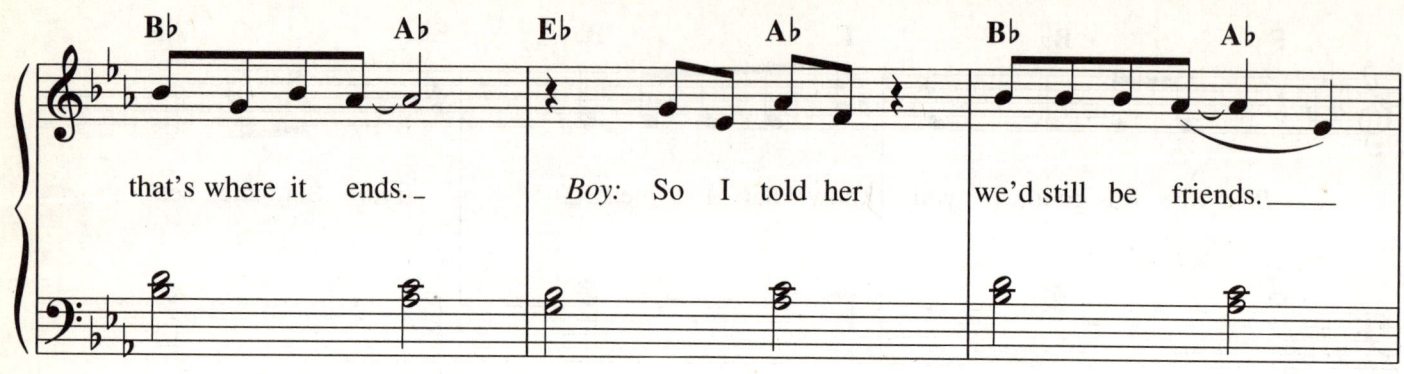

SUN AND MOON
from MISS SAIGON

Music by CLAUDE-MICHEL SCHÖNBERG
Lyrics by RICHARD MALTBY JR. and ALAIN BOUBLIL
Adapted from original French Lyrics by ALAIN BOUBLIL

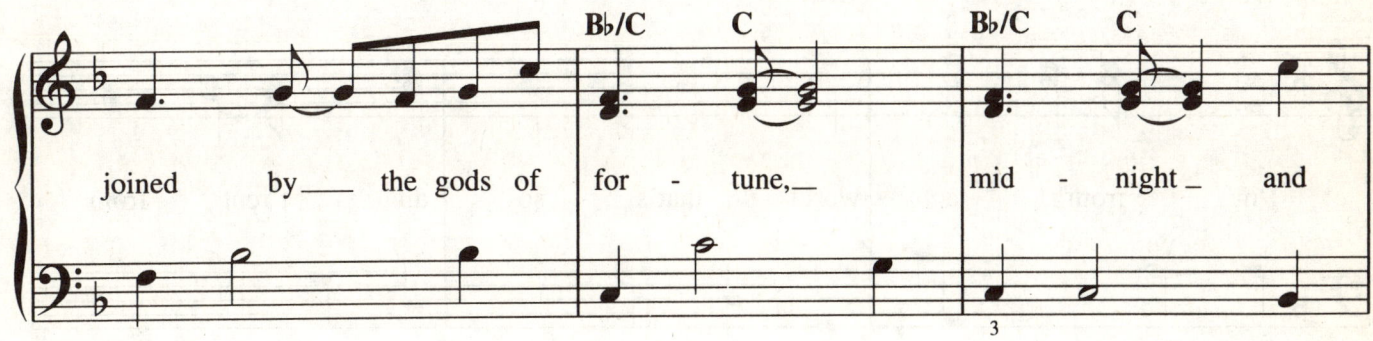

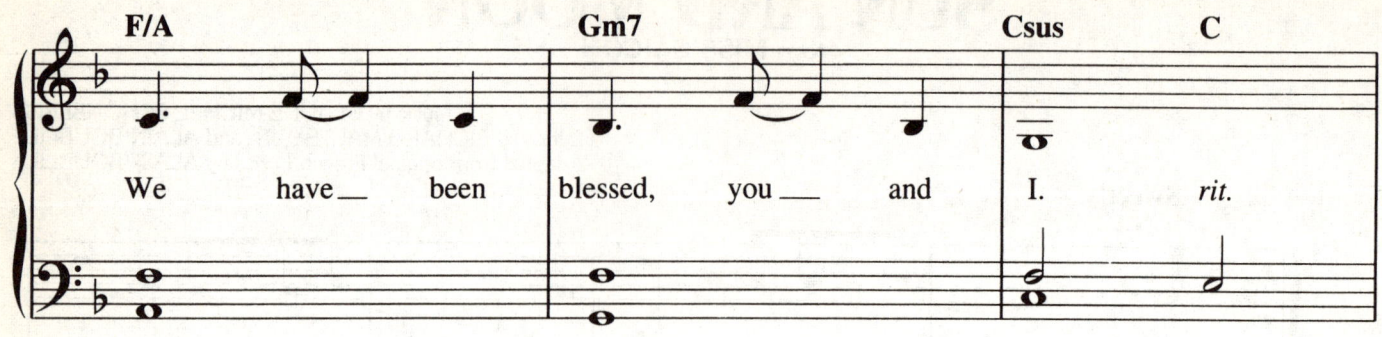

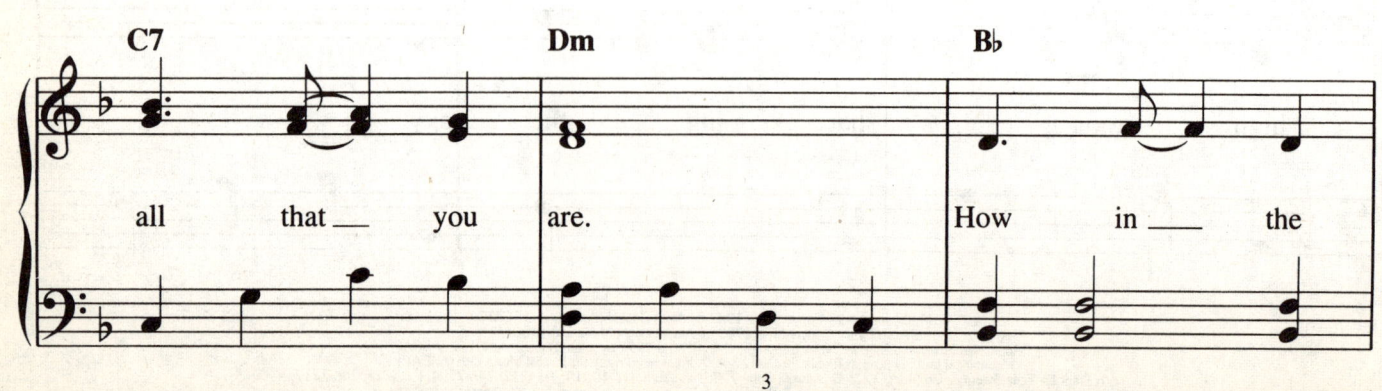

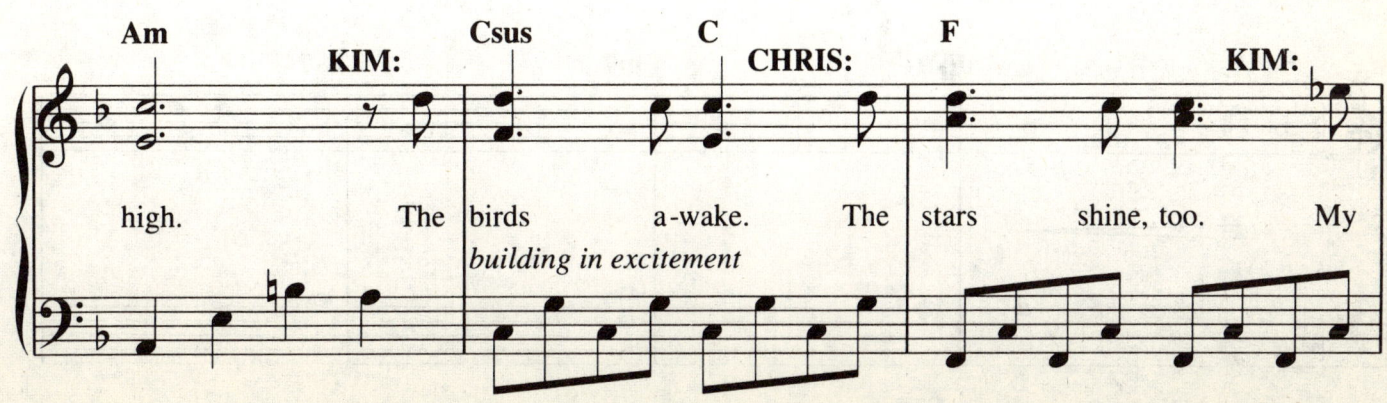

235

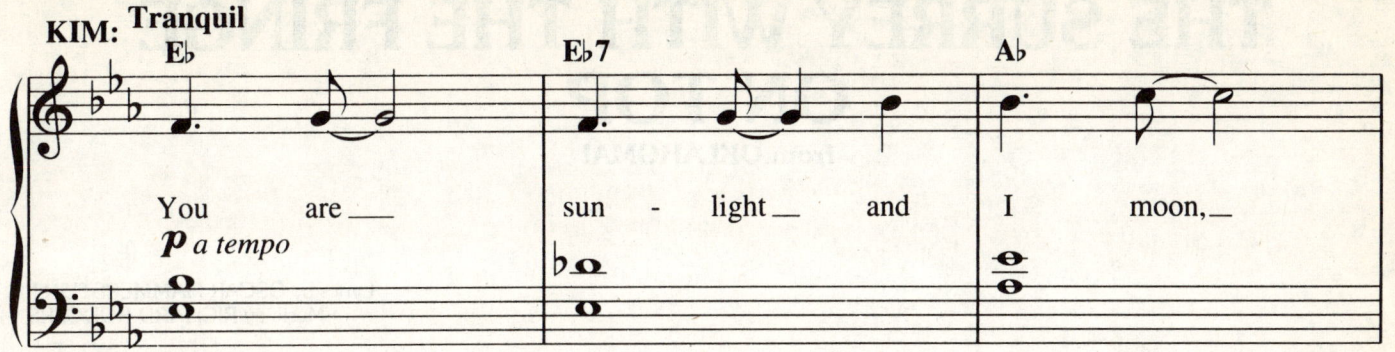

THE SURREY WITH THE FRINGE ON TOP
from OKLAHOMA!

Lyrics by OSCAR HAMMERSTEIN II
Music by RICHARD RODGERS

Easily, with a bounce

When I take you out to-night with

me _____ Hon-ey here's the

Copyright © 1943 by WILLIAMSON MUSIC
Copyright Renewed
International Copyright Secured   All Rights Reserved

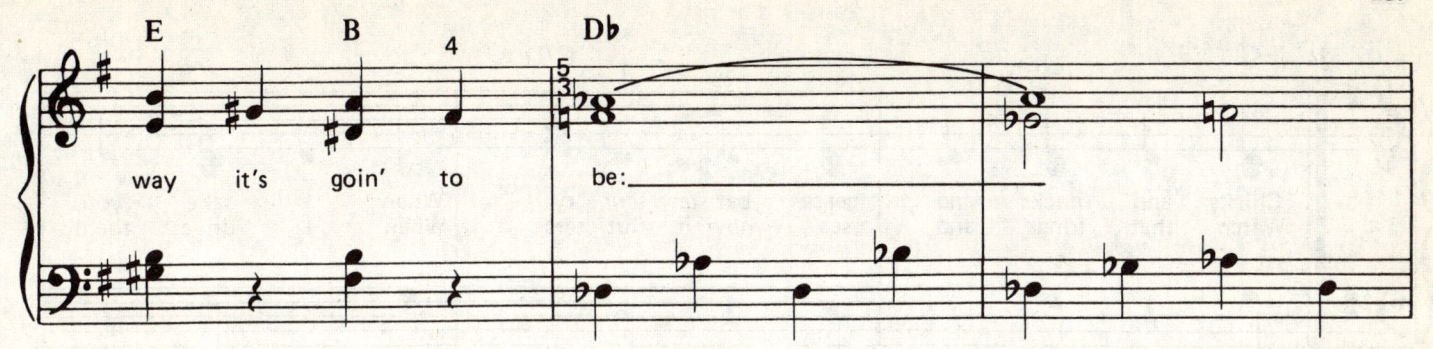

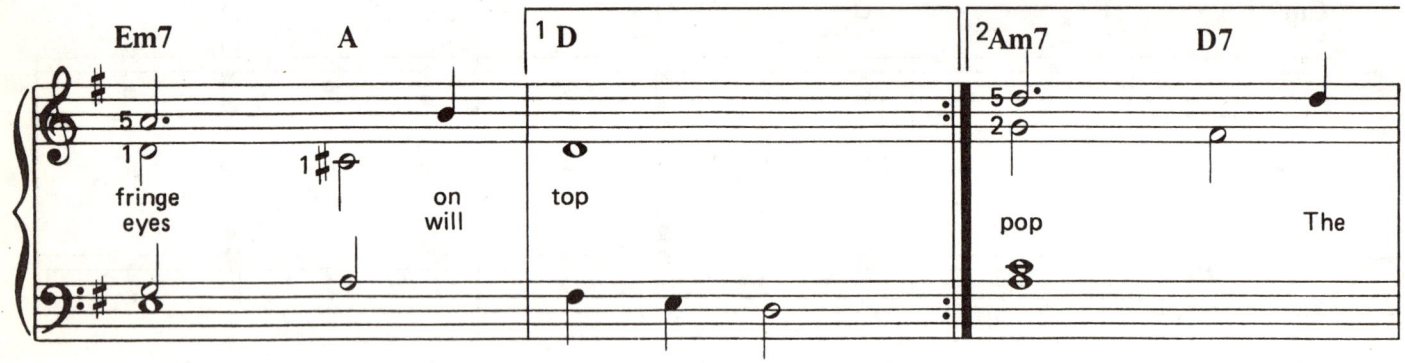

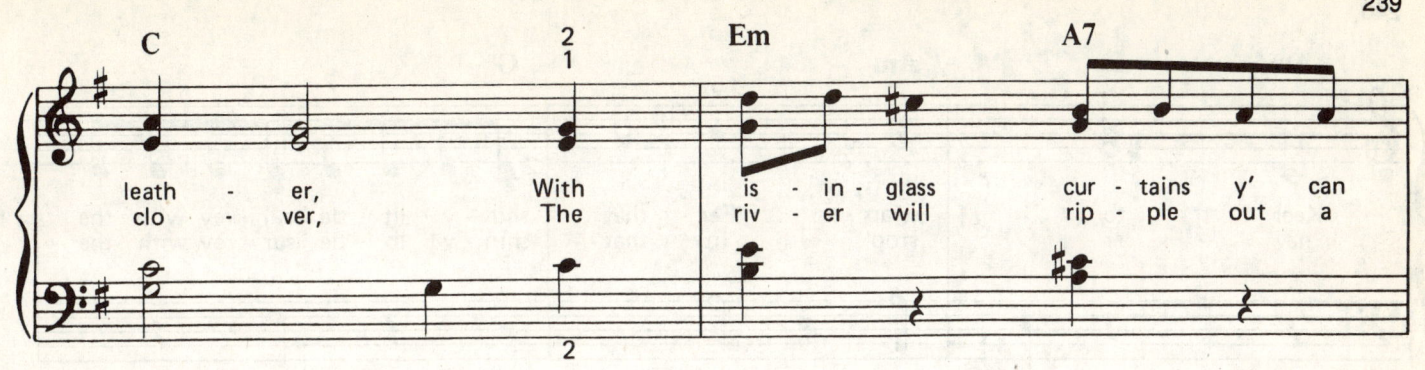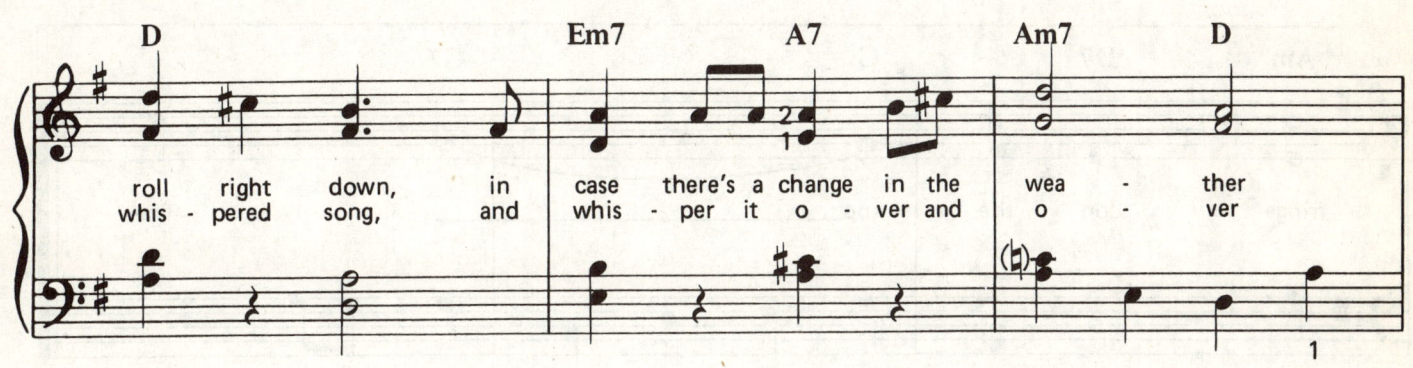

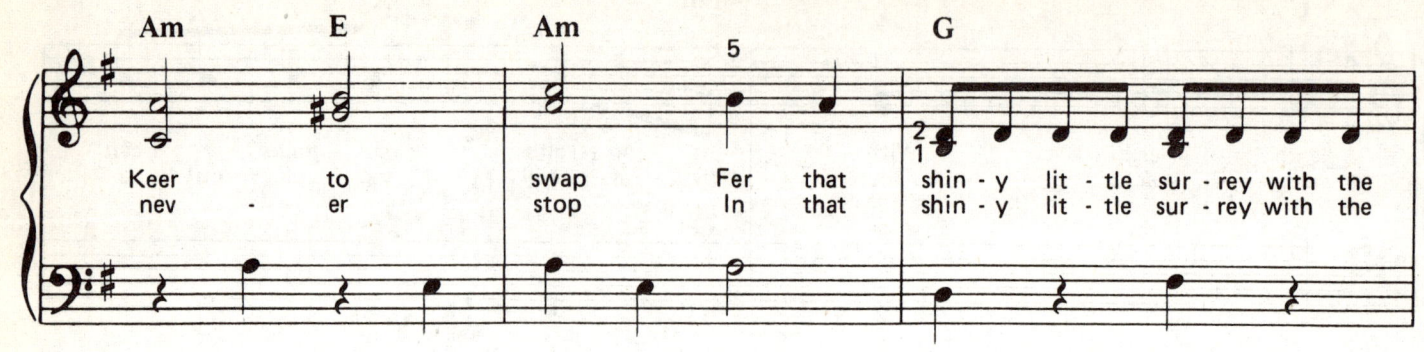
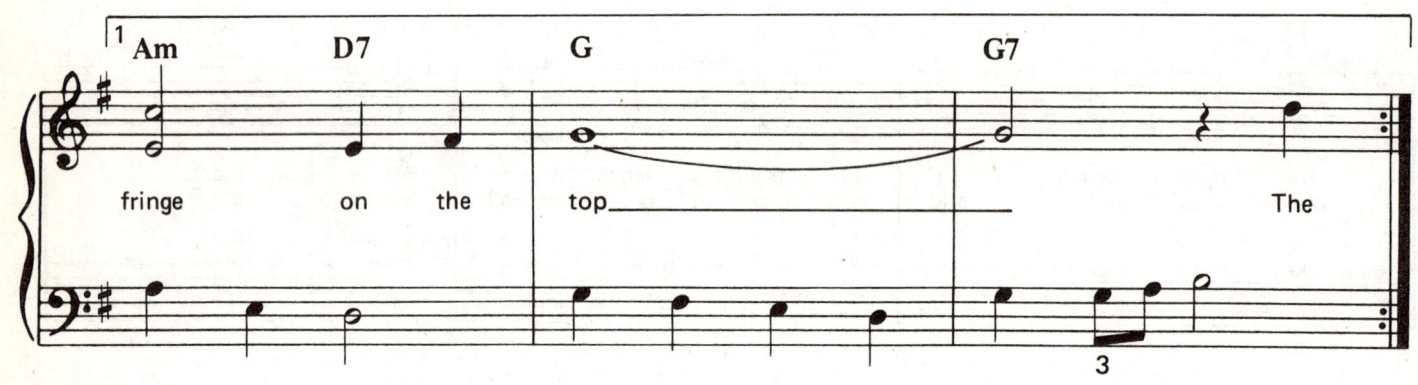

TEN CENTS A DANCE
from SIMPLE SIMON

Words by LORENZ HART
Music by RICHARD RODGERS

Slowly with a jazz feel

Ten cents a dance; That's what they pay me.

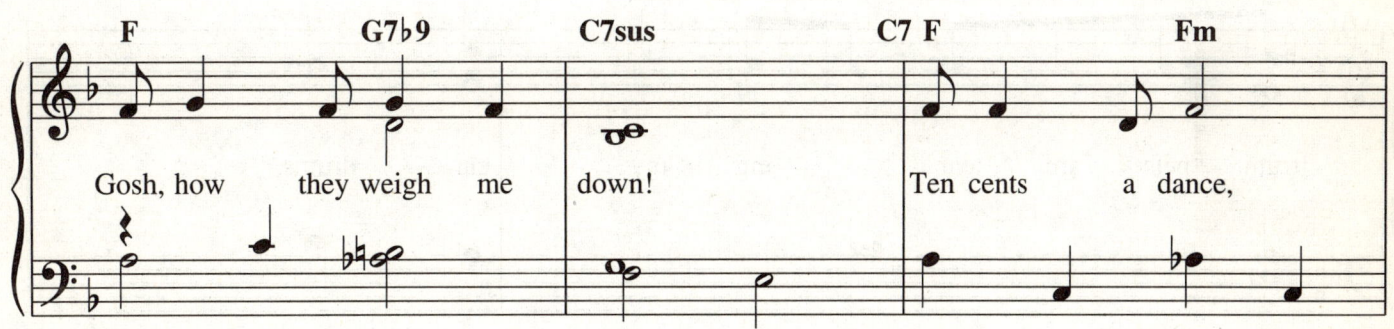

Gosh, how they weigh me down! Ten cents a dance,

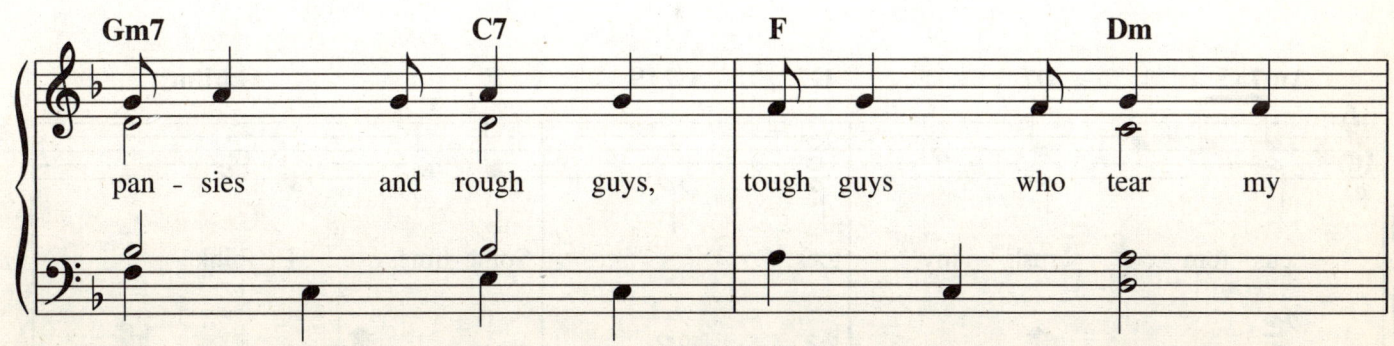

pan-sies and rough guys, tough guys who tear my

Copyright © 1930 (Renewed) by Chappell & Co.
Rights for the Extended Renewal Term in the U.S. Controlled by Williamson Music and WB Music Corp. o/b/o The Estate Of Lorenz Hart
International Copyright Secured   All Rights Reserved

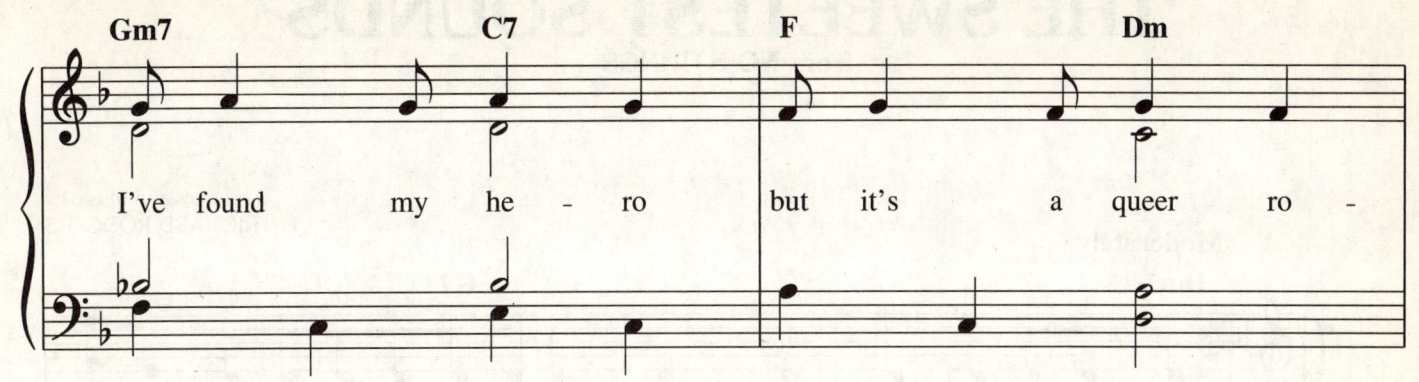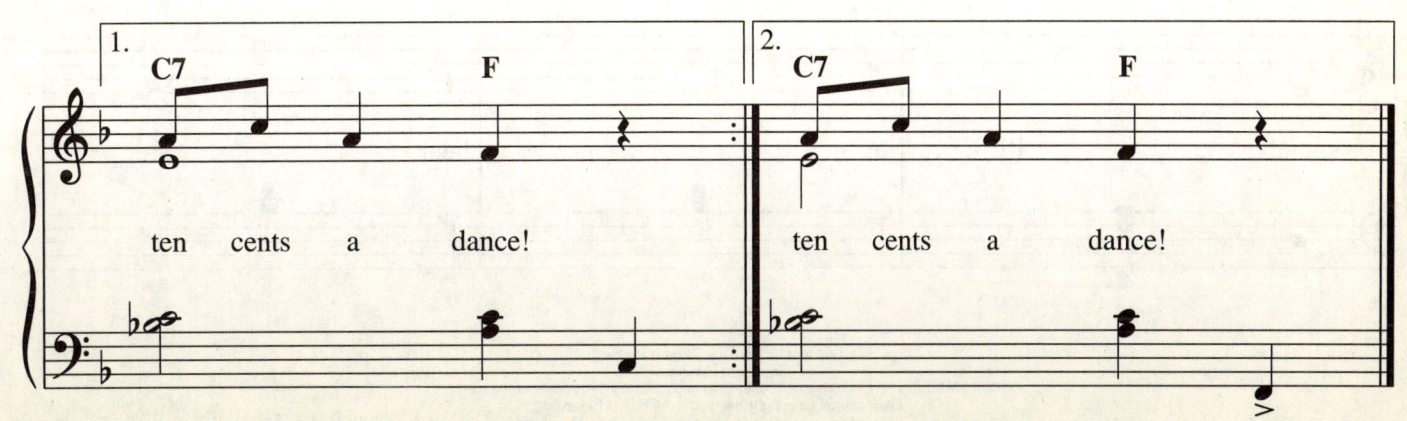

THE SWEETEST SOUNDS
from NO STRINGS

Lyrics and Music by
RICHARD RODGERS

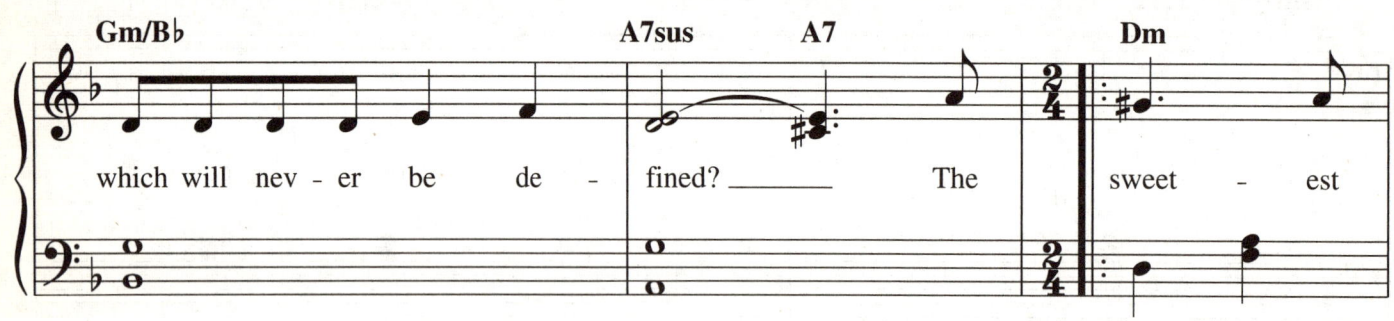
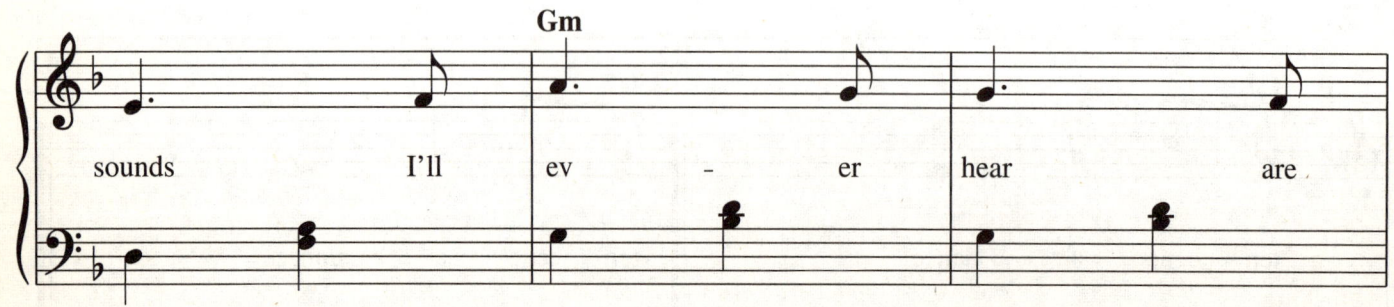

Copyright © 1962 by Richard Rodgers
Copyright Renewed
WILLIAMSON MUSIC owner of publication and allied rights throughout the world
International Copyright Secured   All Rights Reserved

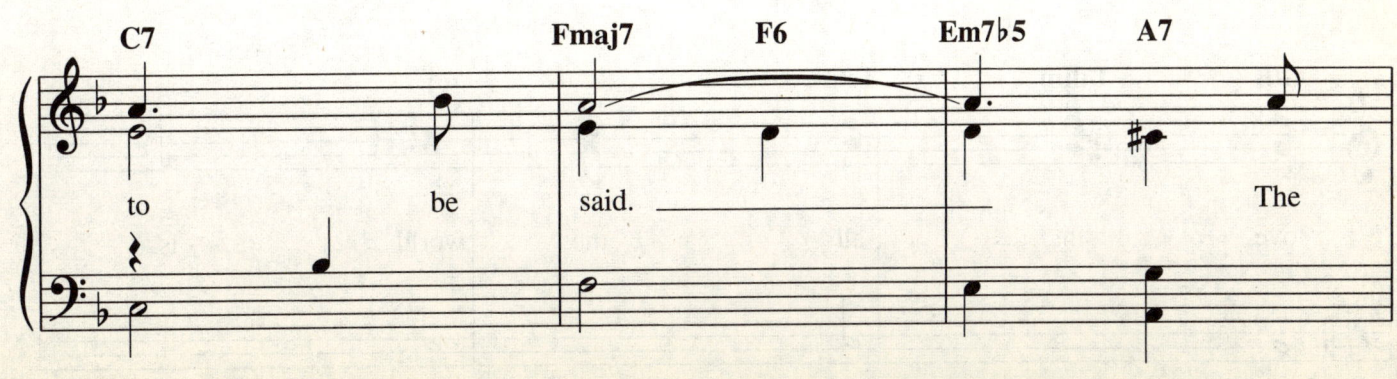

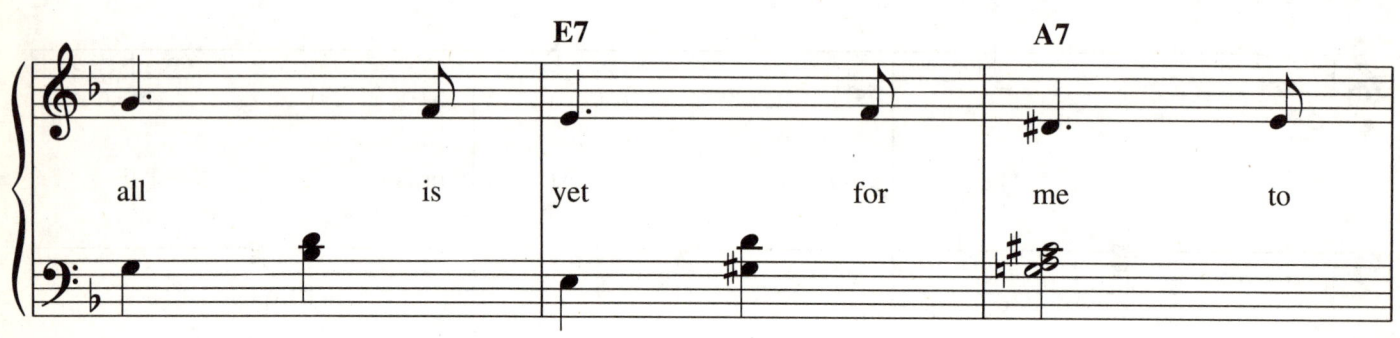

247

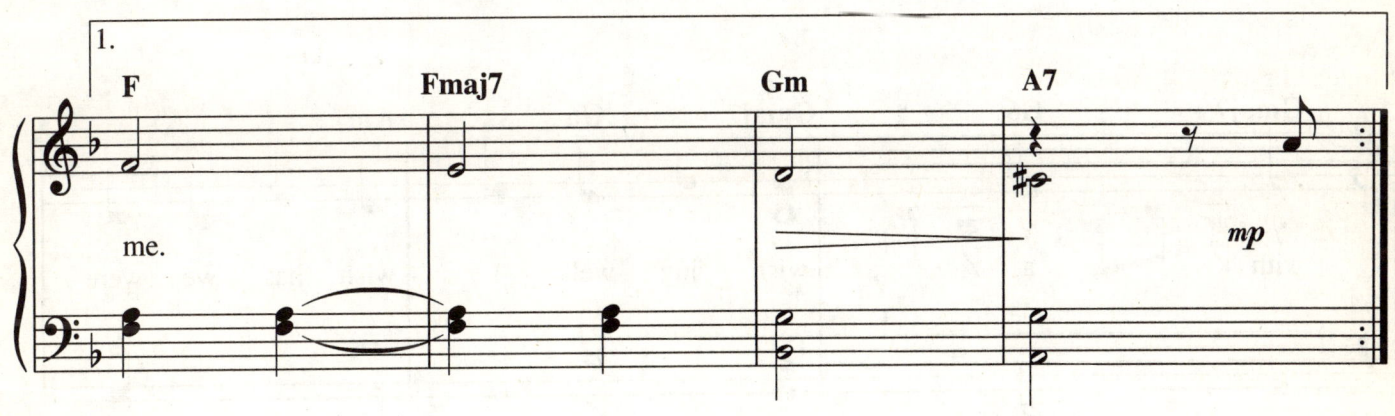

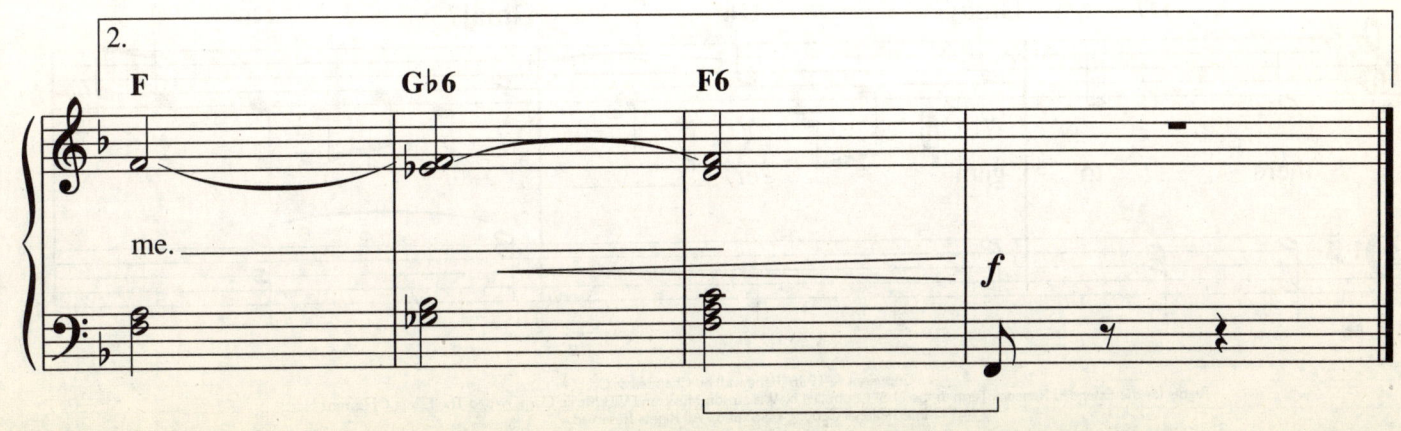

THERE'S A SMALL HOTEL
from ON YOUR TOES

Words by LORENZ HART
Music by RICHARD RODGERS

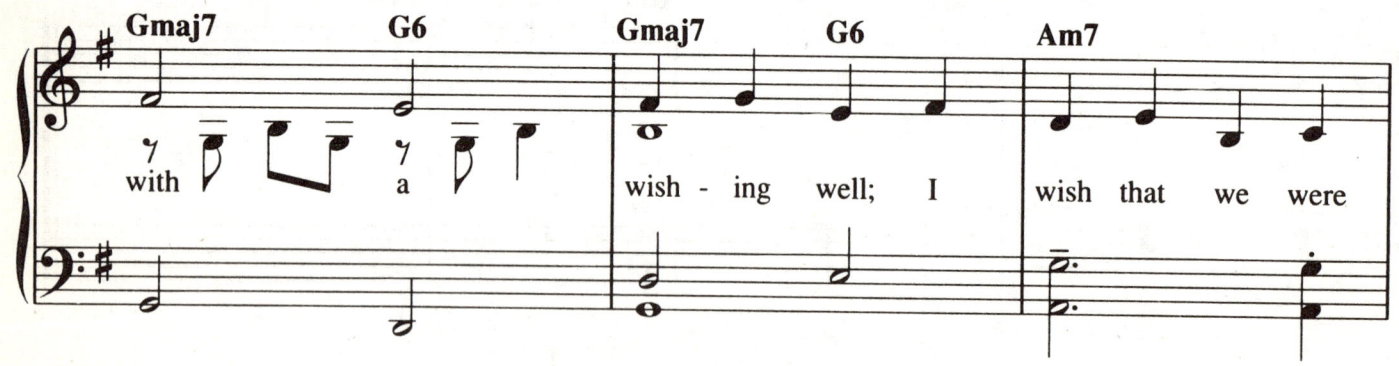

Copyright © 1936 (Renewed) by Chappell & Co.
Rights for the Extended Renewal Term in the U.S. Controlled by Williamson Music and WB Music Corp. o/b/o The Estate Of Lorenz Hart
International Copyright Secured   All Rights Reserved

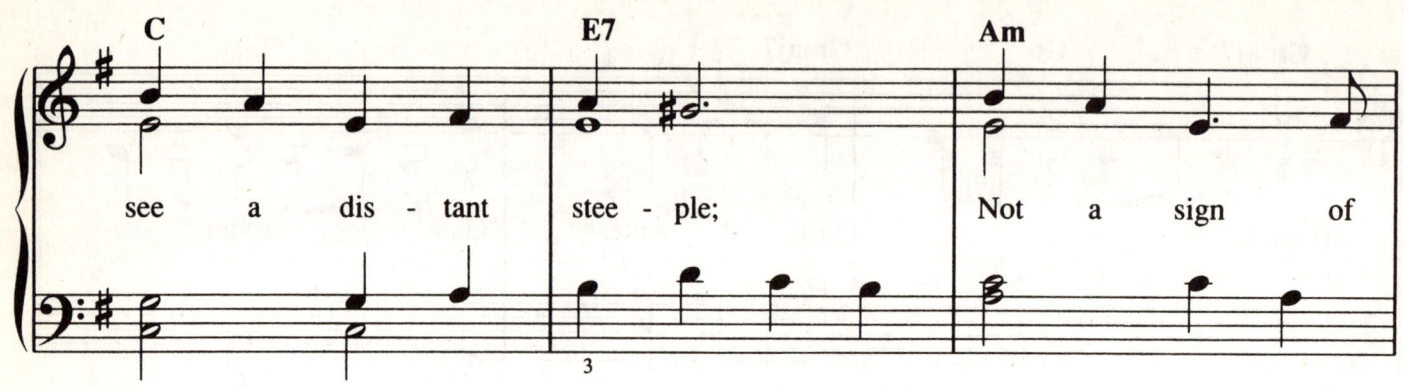

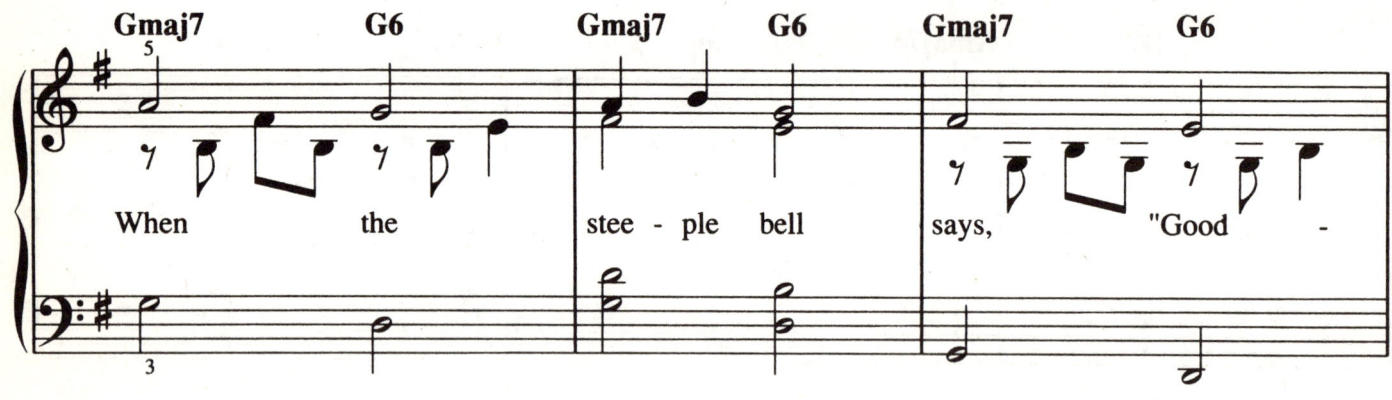
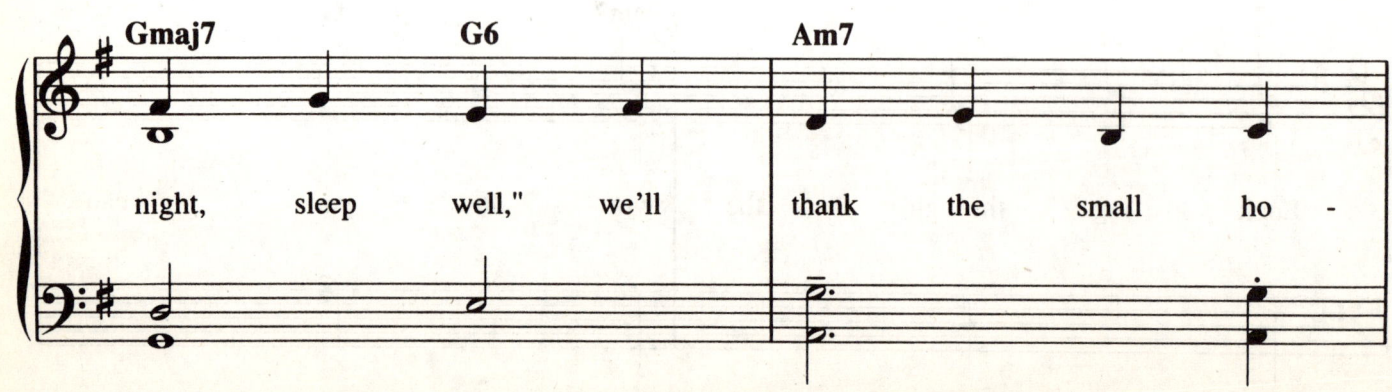

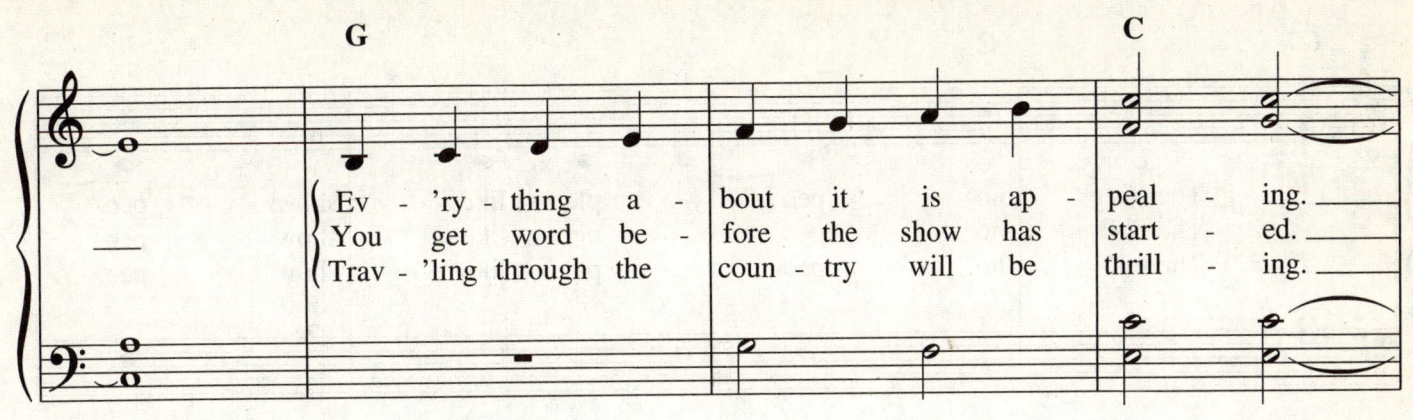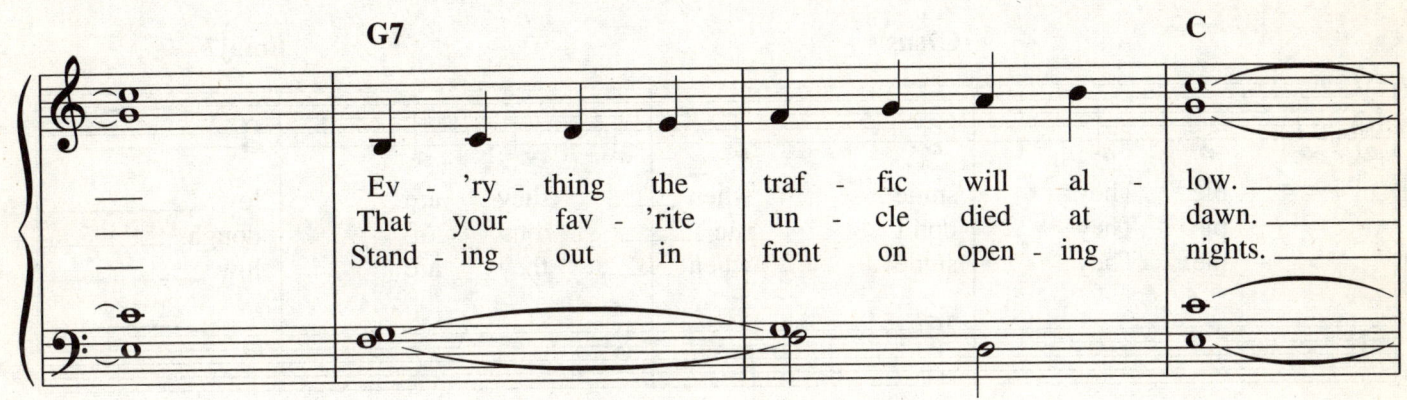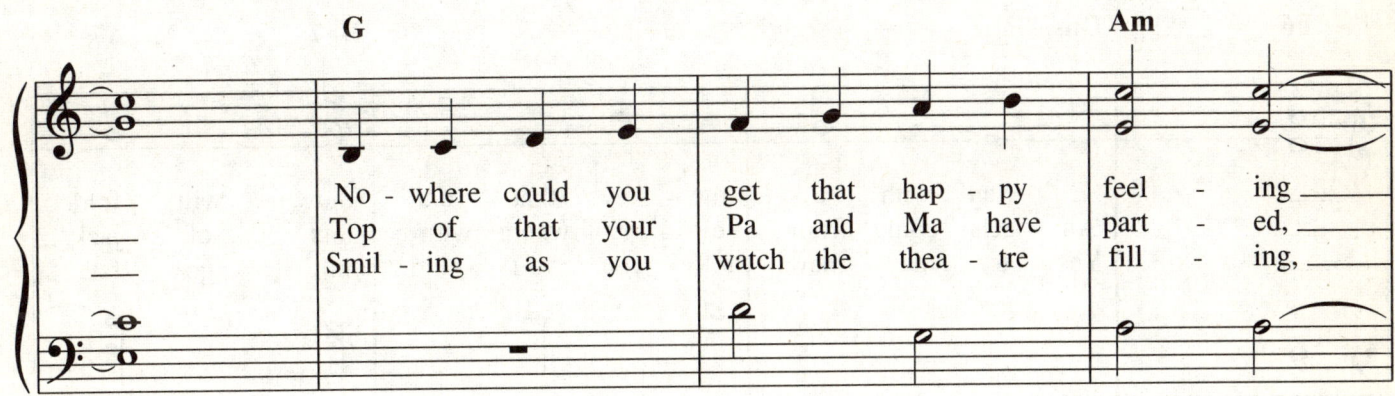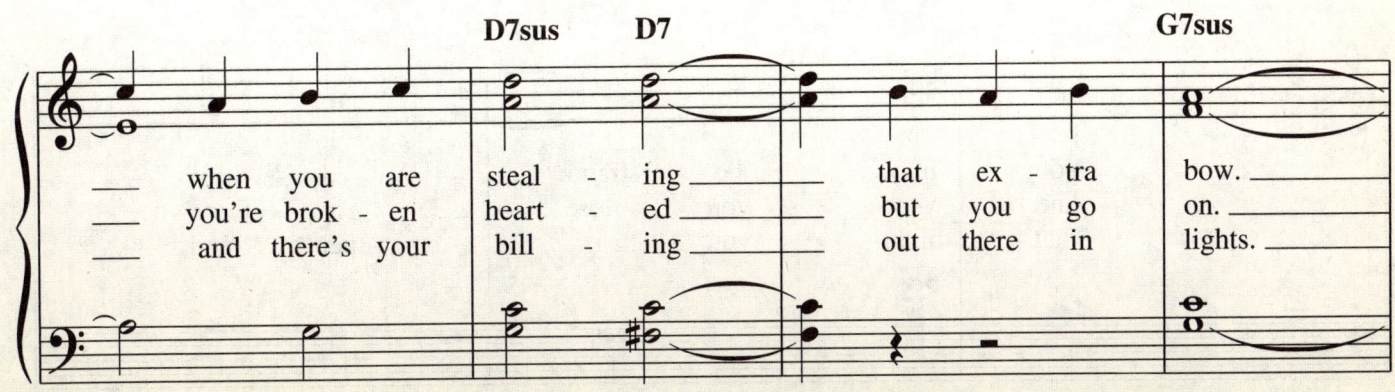

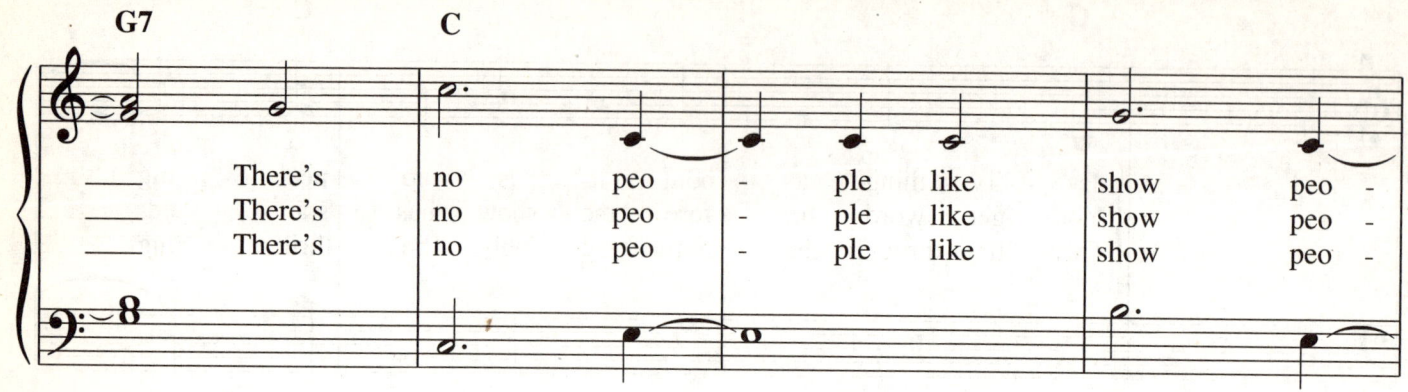
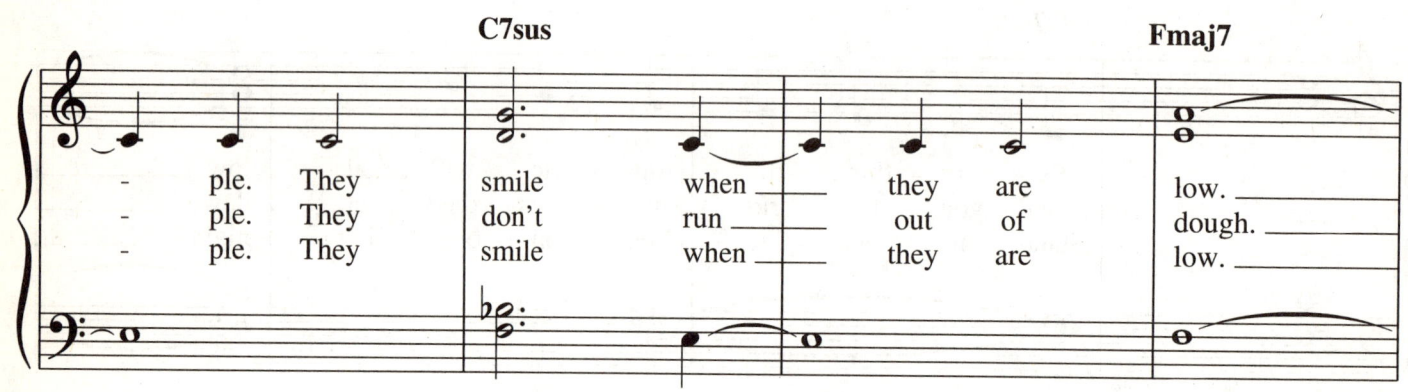
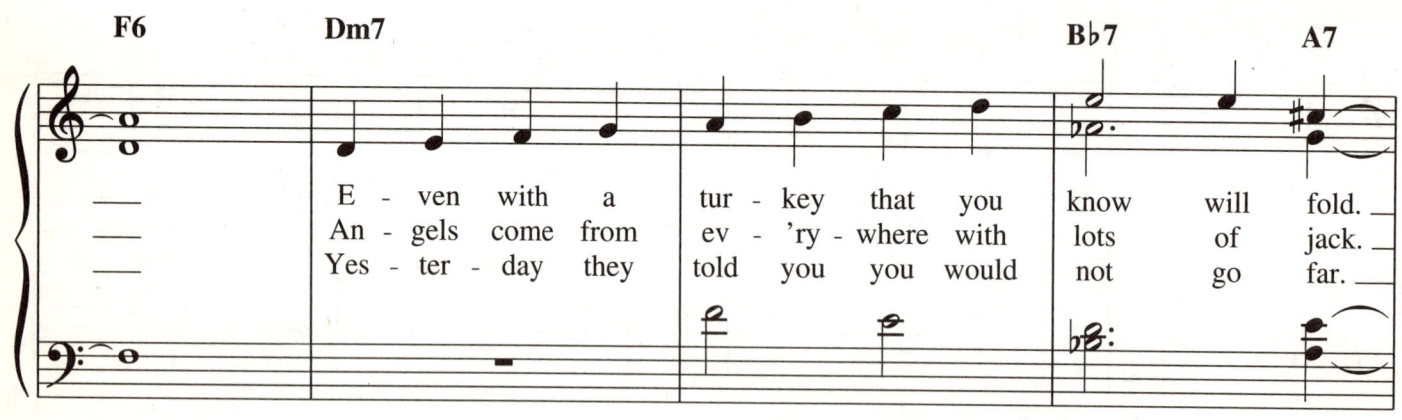

THIS IS THE MOMENT
from JEKYLL & HYDE

Words by LESLIE BRICUSSE
Music by FRANK WILDHORN

Copyright © 1990, 1995 Stage & Screen Music, Ltd. (BMI), Cherry Lane Music Publishing Company, Inc. (ASCAP), DreamWorks Songs (ASCAP),
Les Etoiles De La Musique (ASCAP) and Scaramanga Music, Inc. (ASCAP)
Worldwide Rights for Stage & Screen Music, Ltd. Administered by Cherry River Music Co.
Worldwide Rights for DreamWorks Songs, Les Etoiles De La Musique and Scaramanga Music, Inc. Administered by Cherry Lane Music Publishing Company, Inc.
International Copyright Secured   All Rights Reserved

THOROUGHLY MODERN MILLIE
from THOROUGHLY MODERN MILLIE

Words by SAMMY CAHN
Music by JAMES VAN HEUSEN

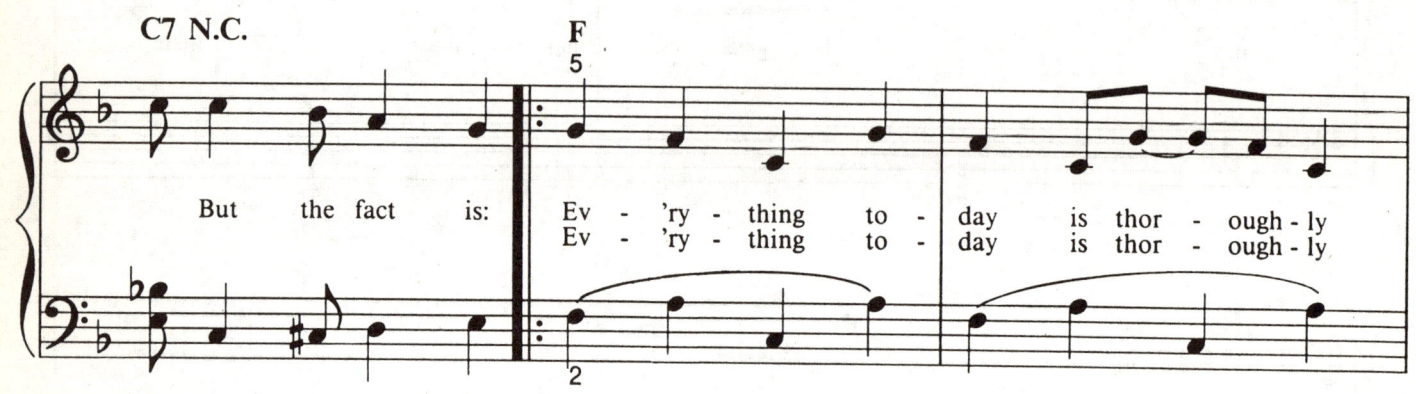

But the fact is: Ev-'ry-thing to-day is thor-ough-ly
Ev-'ry-thing to-day is thor-ough-ly

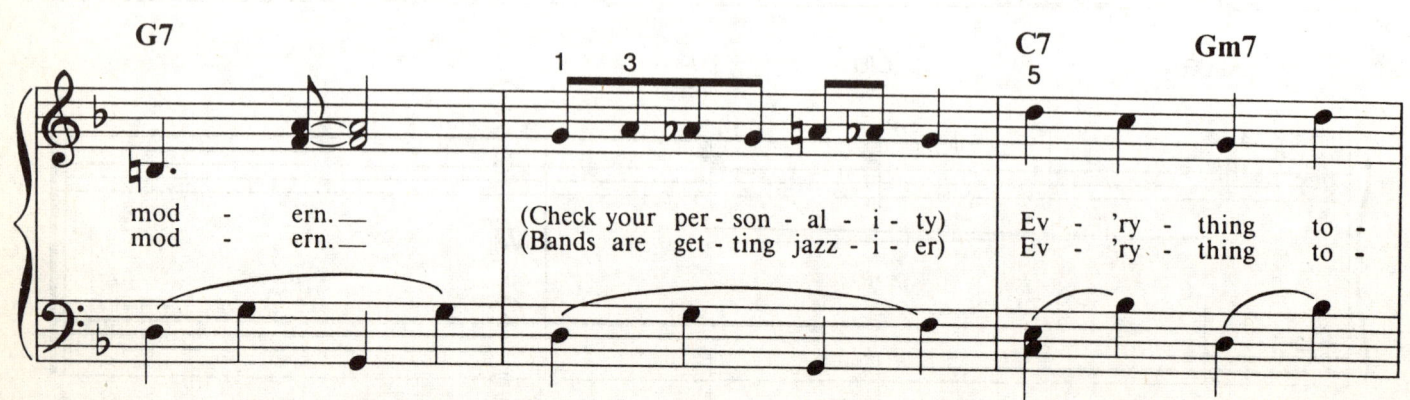

mod - ern. (Check your per-son-al-i-ty) Ev-'ry-thing to-
mod - ern. (Bands are get-ting jazz-i-er) Ev-'ry-thing to-

Copyright © 1967; Renewed 1995 Cahn Music Company (ASCAP) and Universal - Northern Music Company, Inc. (ASCAP)
All Rights for Cahn Music Company Administered by Cherry Lane Music Publishing Company, Inc. and DreamWorks Songs
International Copyright Secured   All Rights Reserved

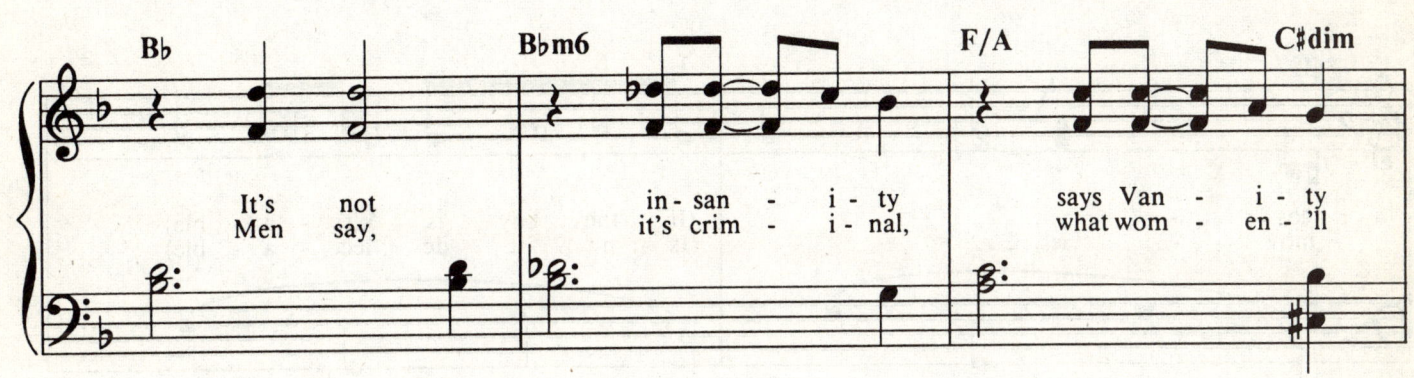
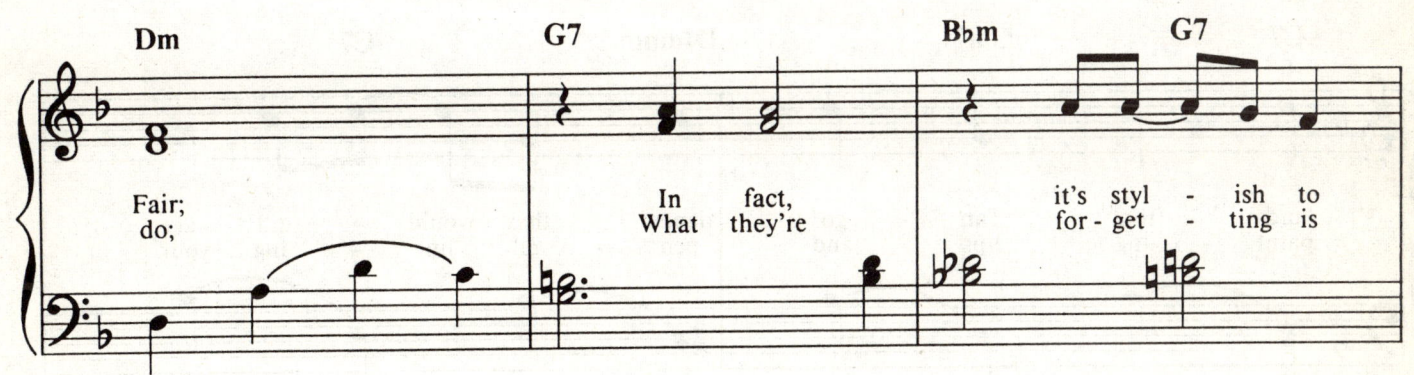
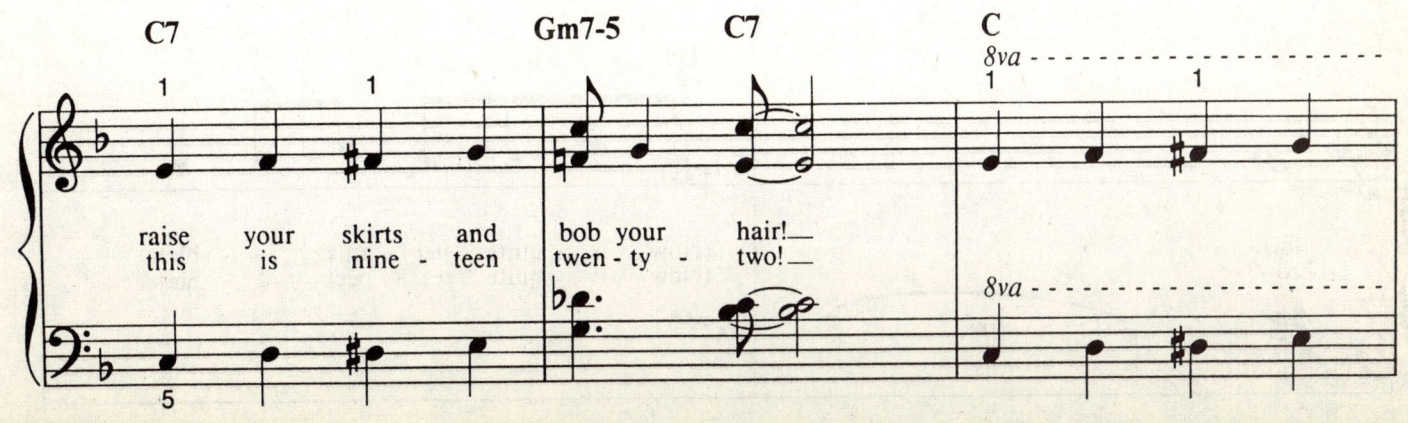

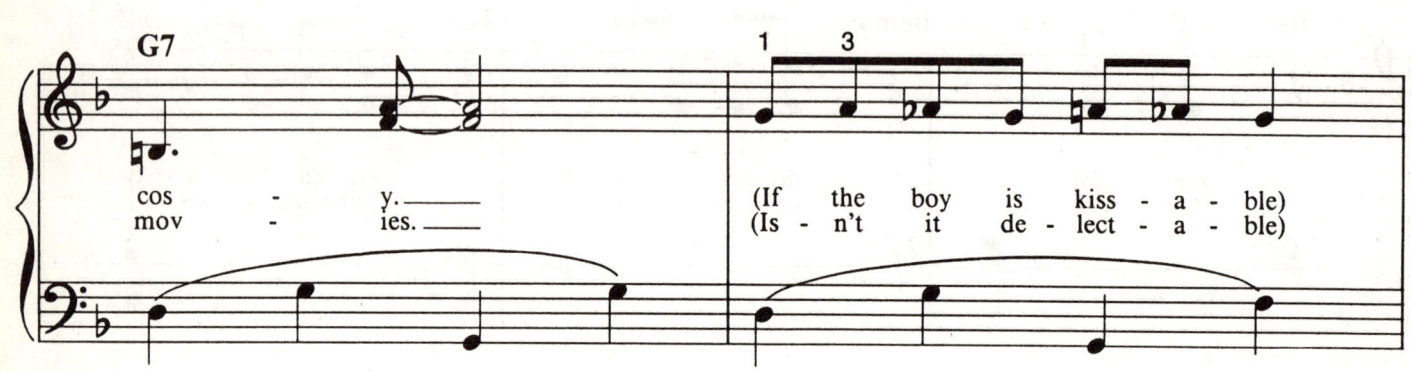

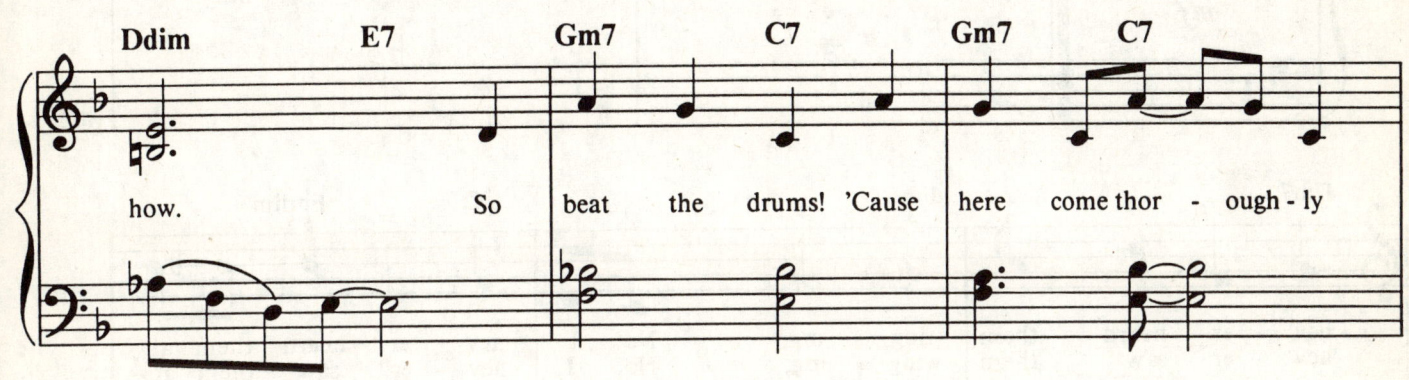

TURN BACK, O MAN
from the Musical GODSPELL

Words and Music by
STEPHEN SCHWARTZ

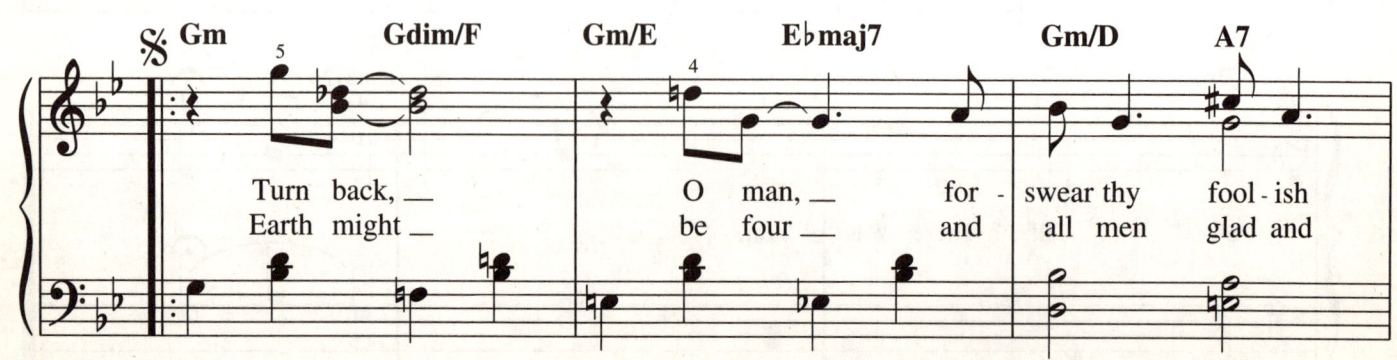

Turn back,___ O man,___ for-swear thy fool-ish
Earth might___ be four___ and all men glad and

Copyright © 1971 by Range Road Music Inc., Quartet Music, Inc. and New Cadenza Music Corporation
Copyright Renewed
International Copyright Secured All Rights Reserved
Used by Permission

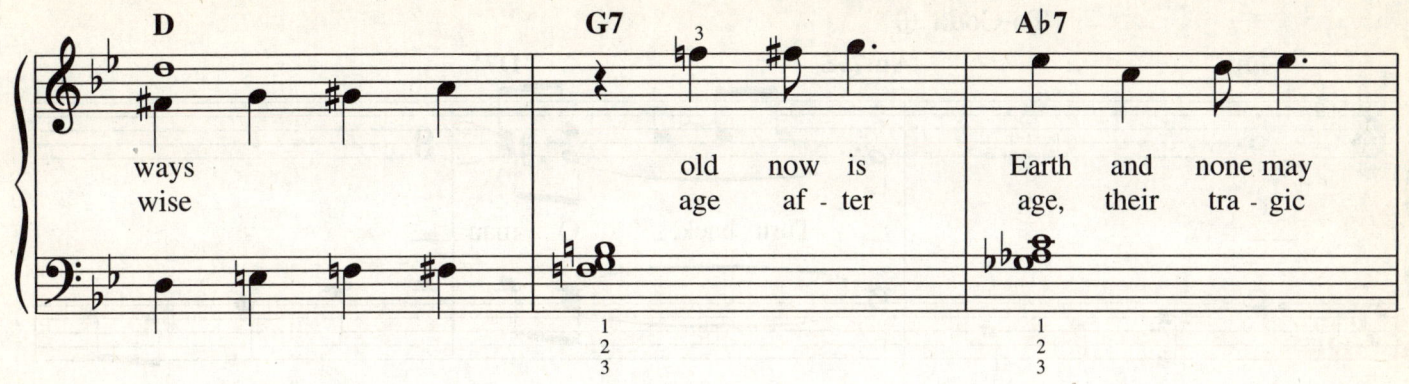

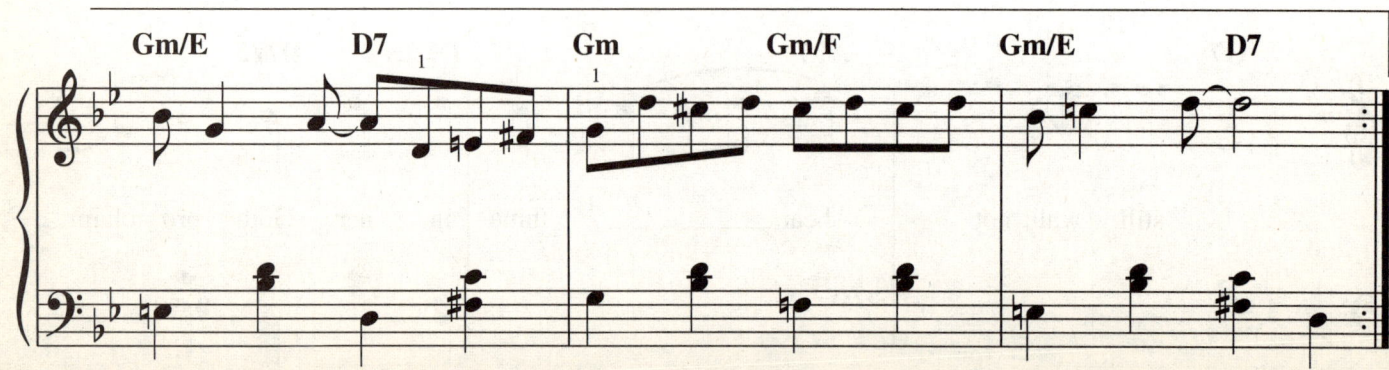

269

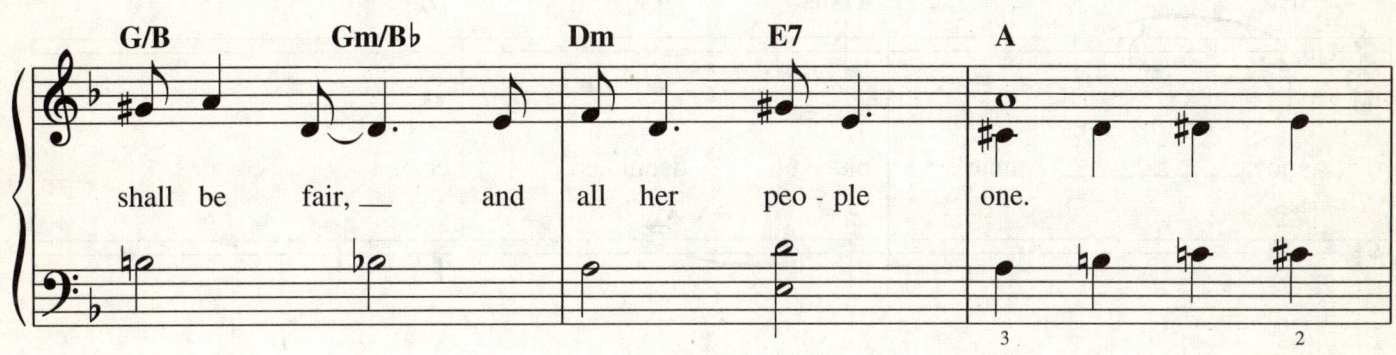

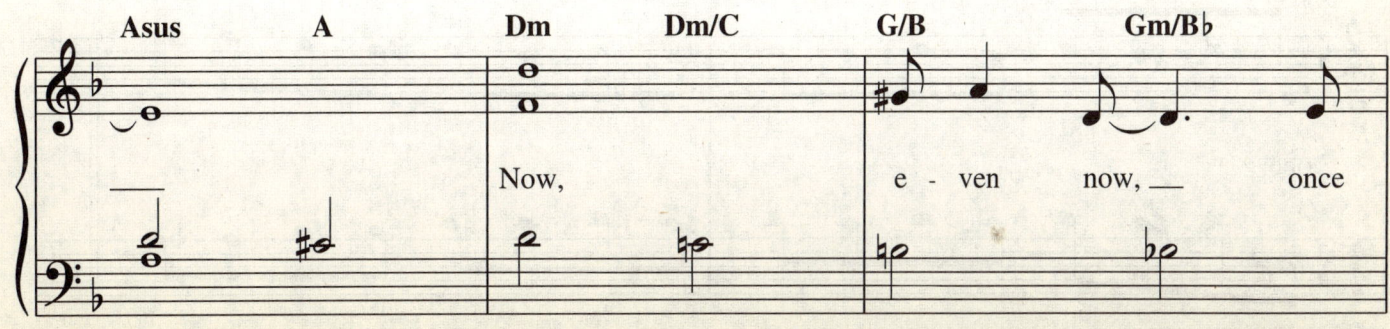

271

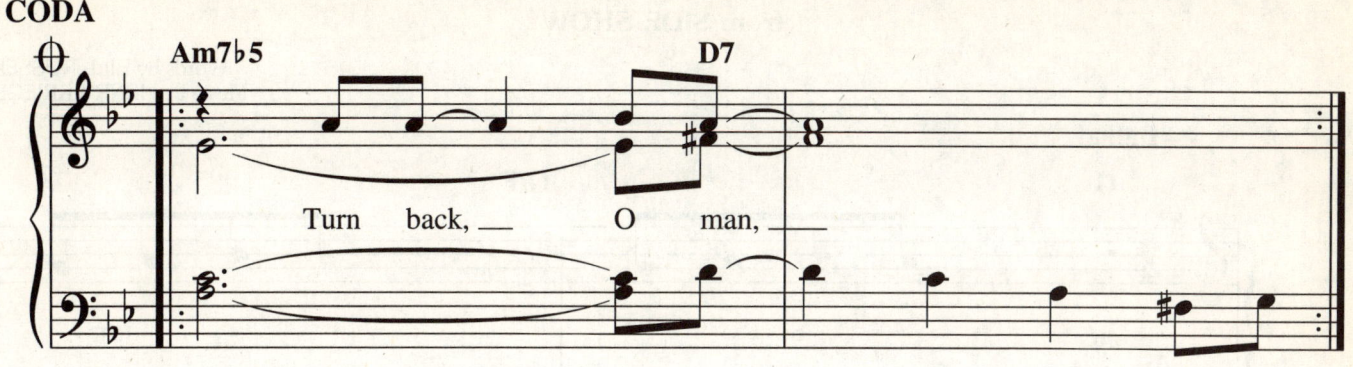
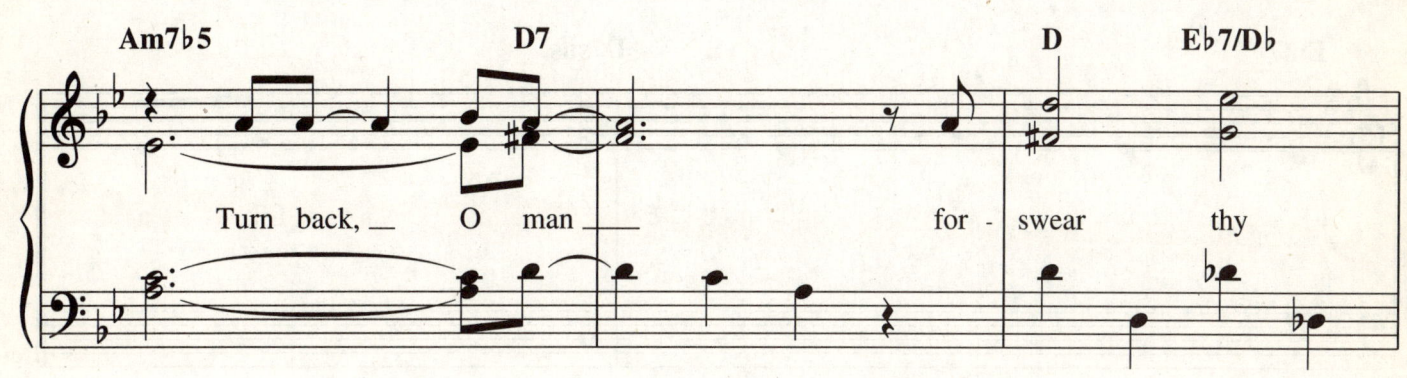

WHO WILL LOVE ME AS I AM?
from SIDE SHOW

Words by BILL RUSSELL
Music by HENRY KRIEGER

Like a

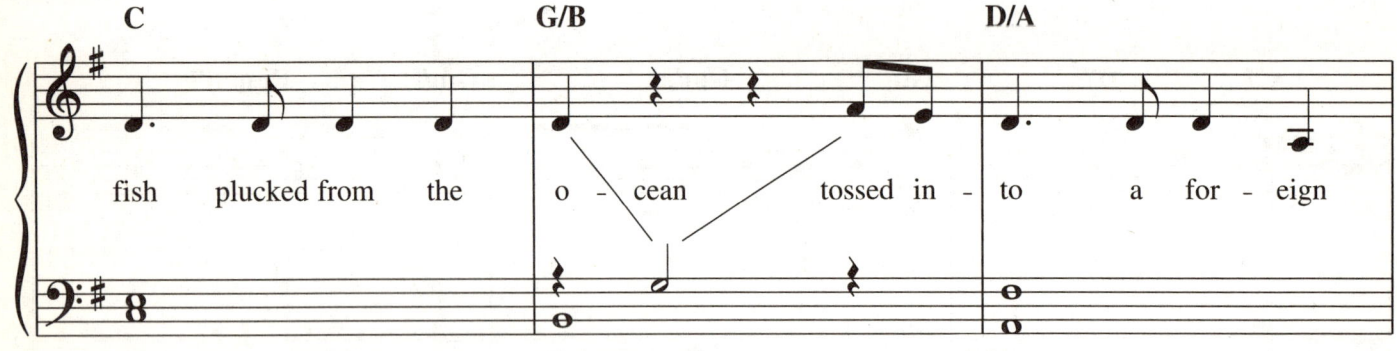
fish plucked from the o- cean tossed in- to a for- eign

stream, al- ways knew that I was dif- f'rent of- ten

© 1994 MIROKU MUSIC (ASCAP)/Administered by A. Schroeder International LLC, 200 West 51st Street, Suite 1009, New York, NY 10019
and STILLBILL MUSIC (ASCAP), 1500 Broadway, Suite 2001, New York, NY 10036
International Copyright Secured All Rights Reserved

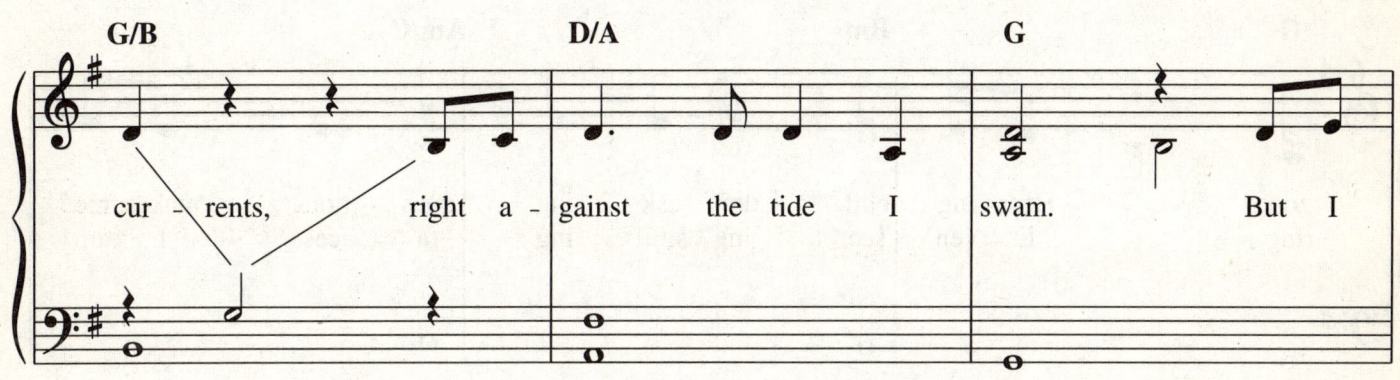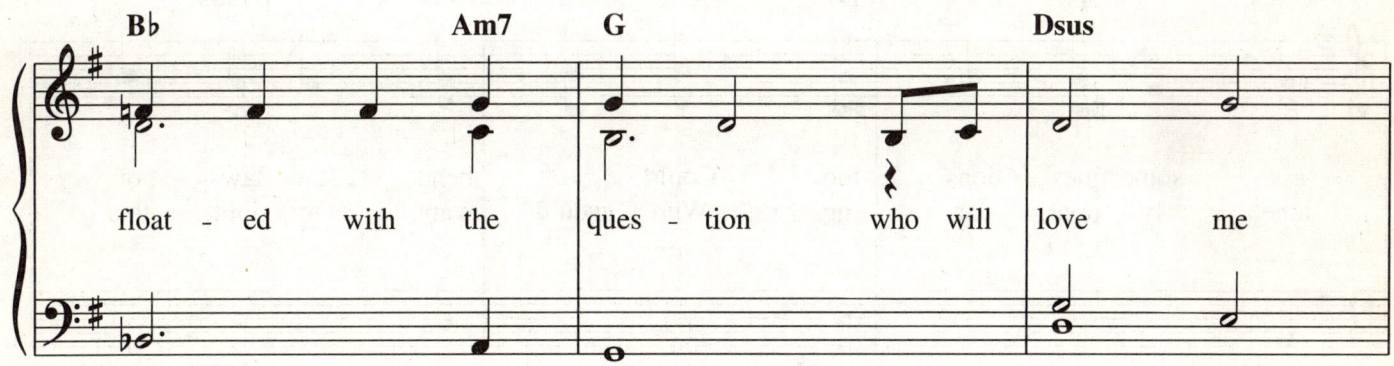

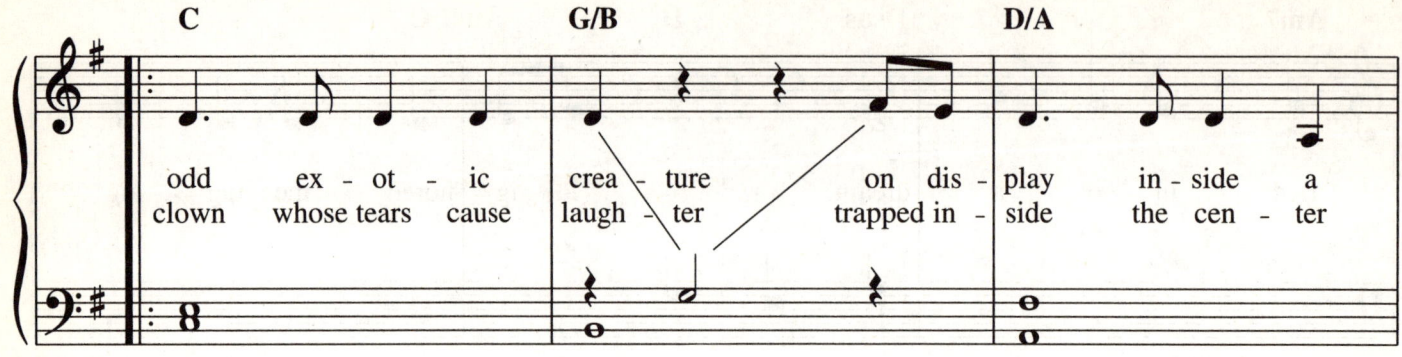
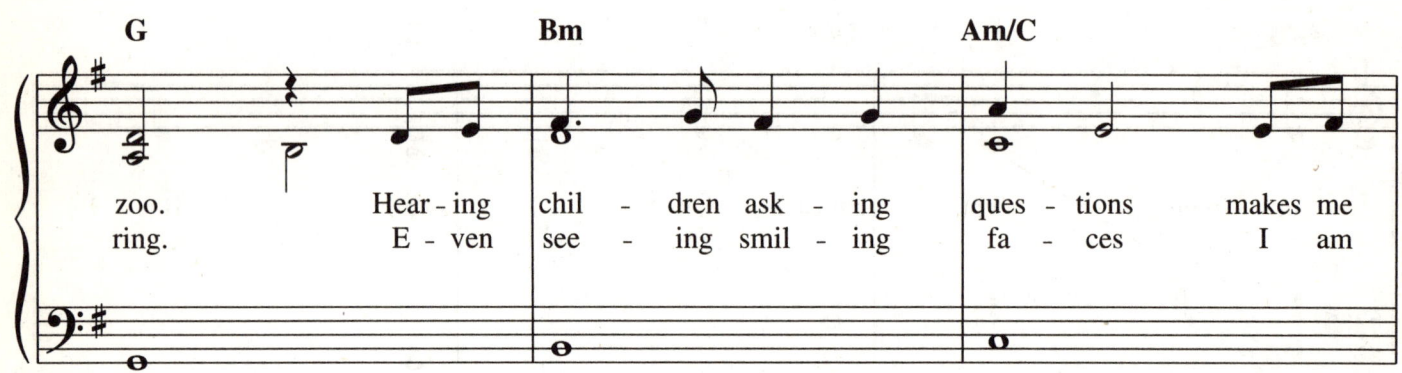

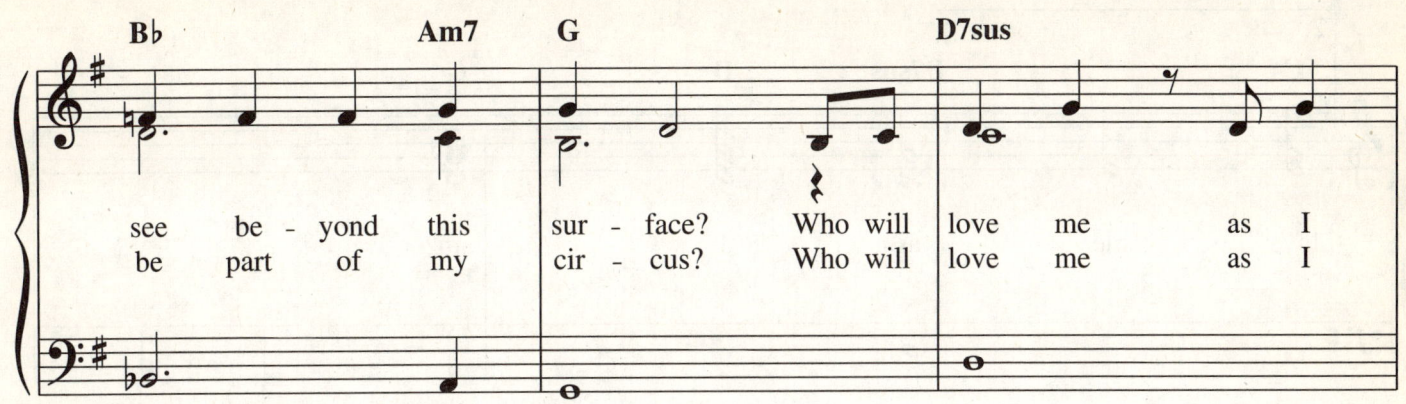

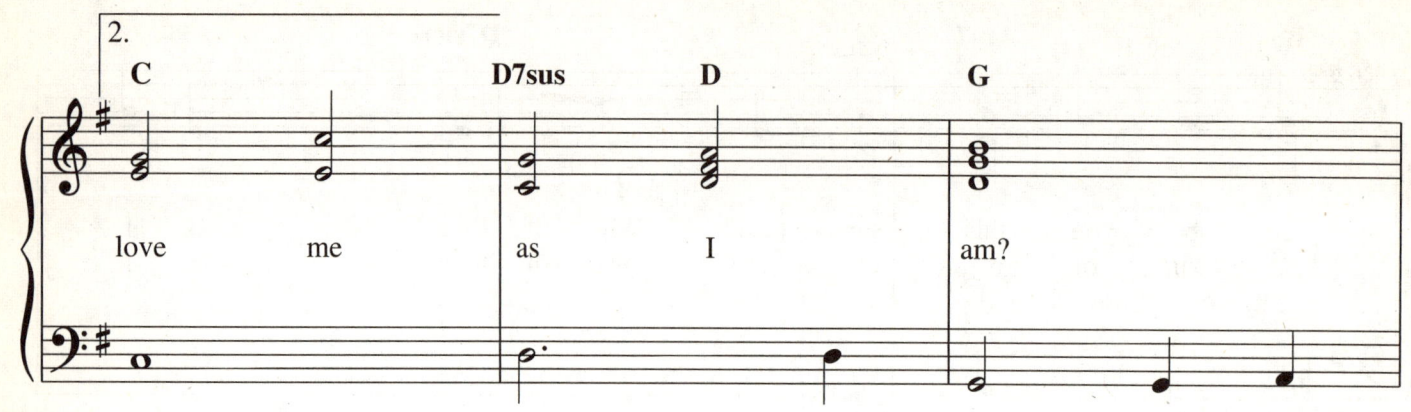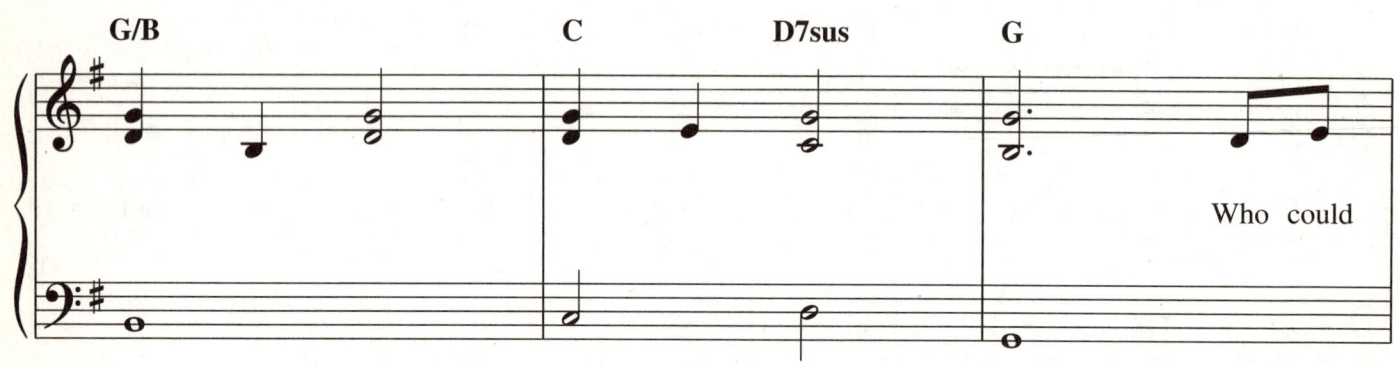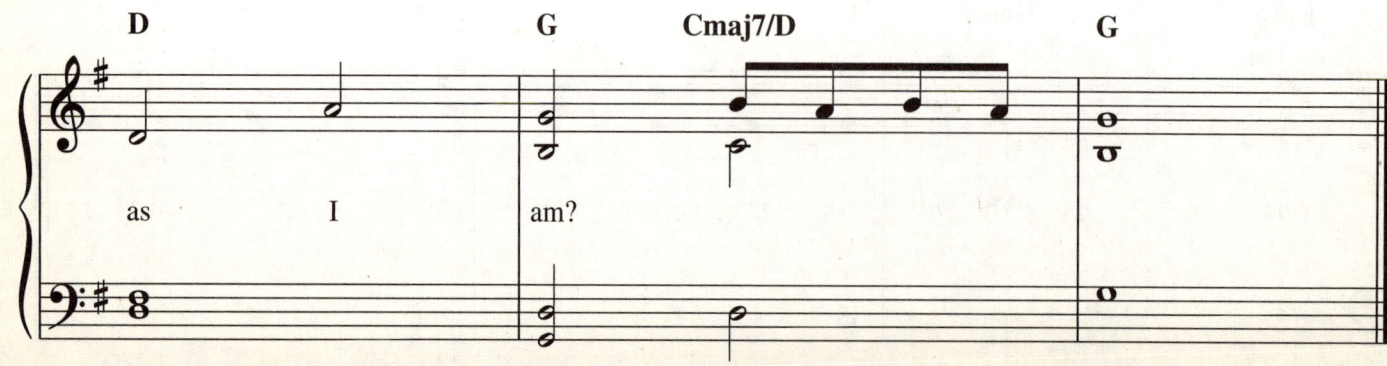

WISH YOU WERE HERE
from WISH YOU WERE HERE

Words and Music by
HAROLD ROME

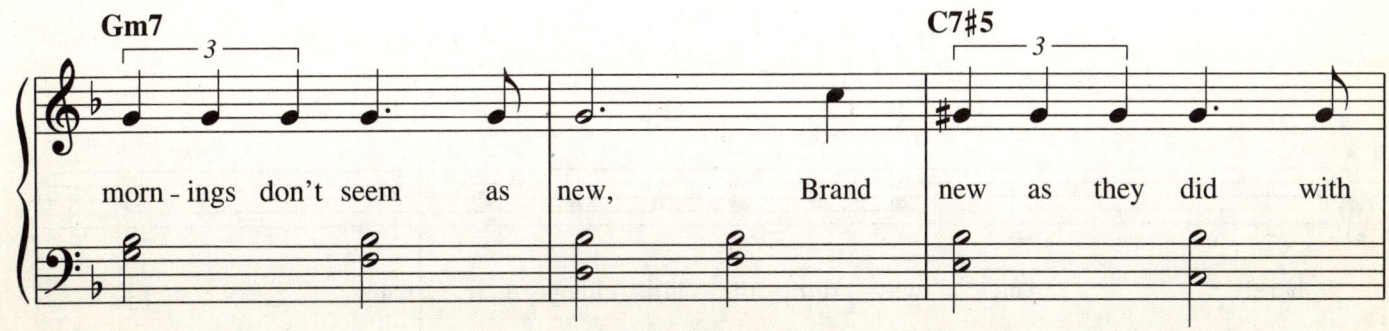

Copyright © 1952 by Harold Rome
Copyright Renewed, Assigned to Chappell & Co.
International Copyright Secured   All Rights Reserved

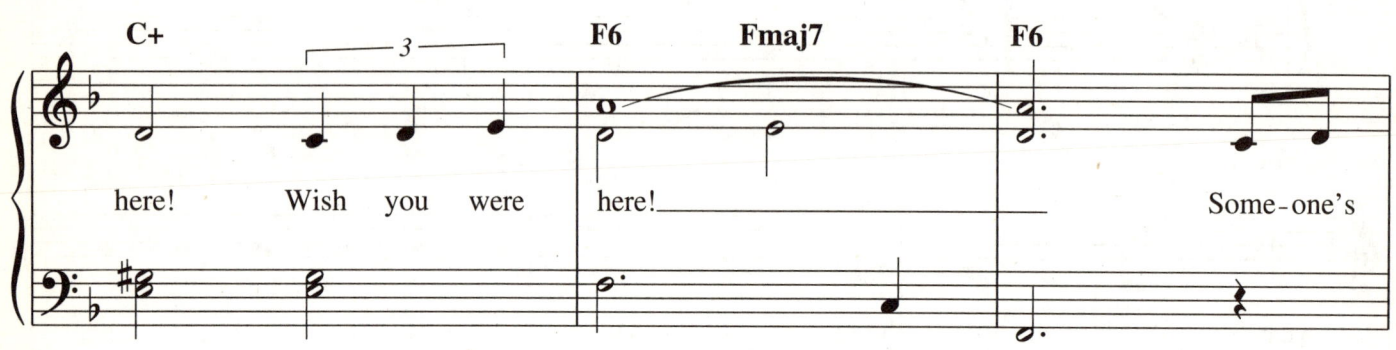

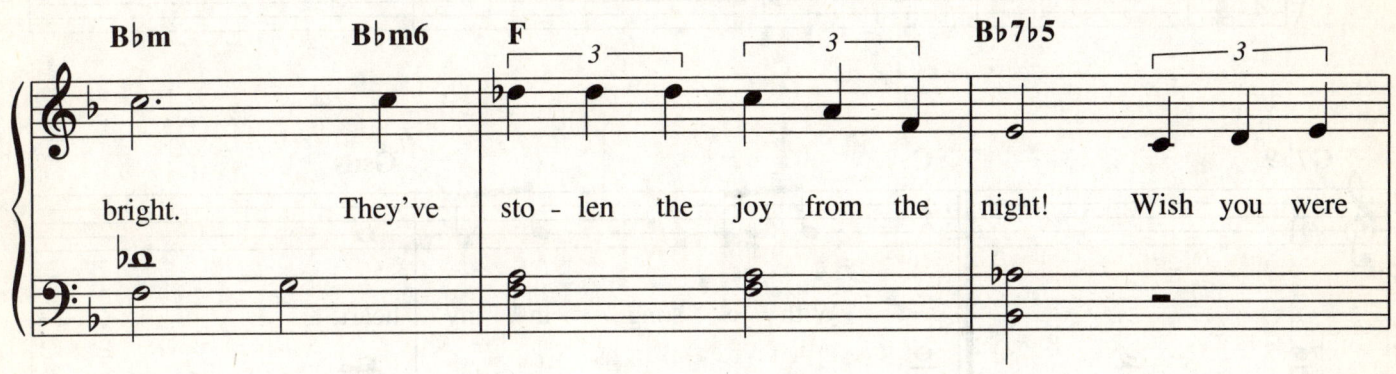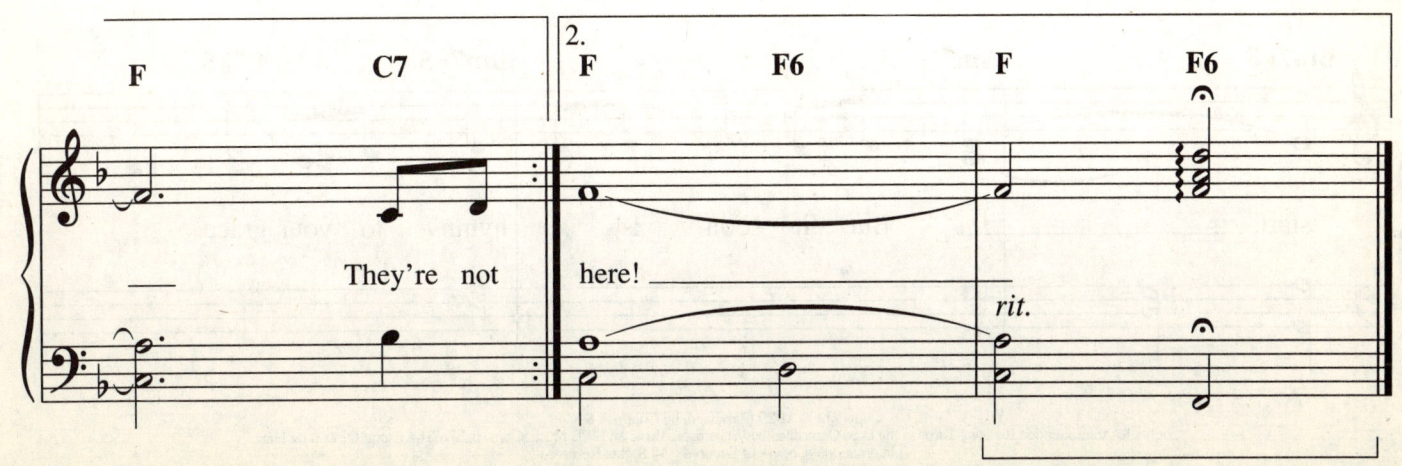

WITH A SONG IN MY HEART
from SPRING IS HERE

Words by LORENZ HART
Music by RICHARD RODGERS

Copyright © 1929 (Renewed) by Chappell & Co.
Rights for the Extended Renewal Term in the U.S. Controlled by Williamson Music and WB Music Corp. o/b/o The Estate Of Lorenz Hart
International Copyright Secured   All Rights Reserved

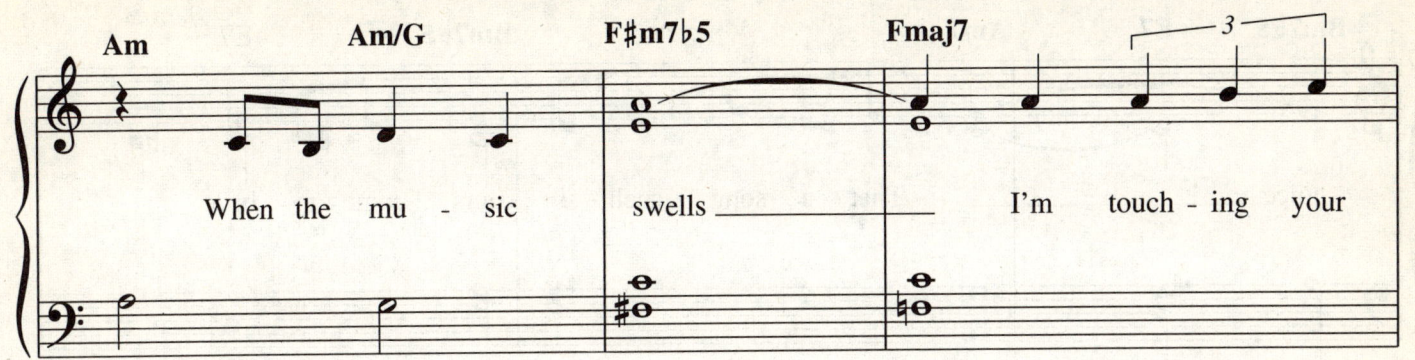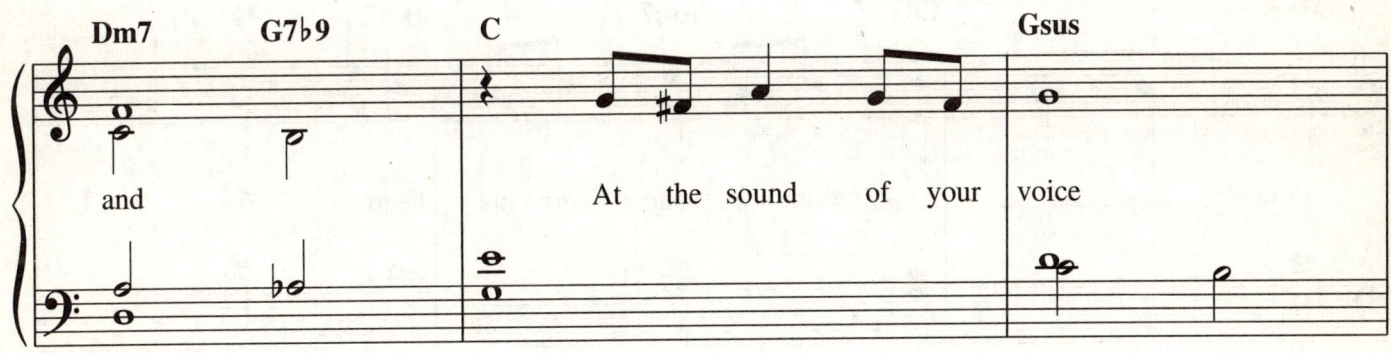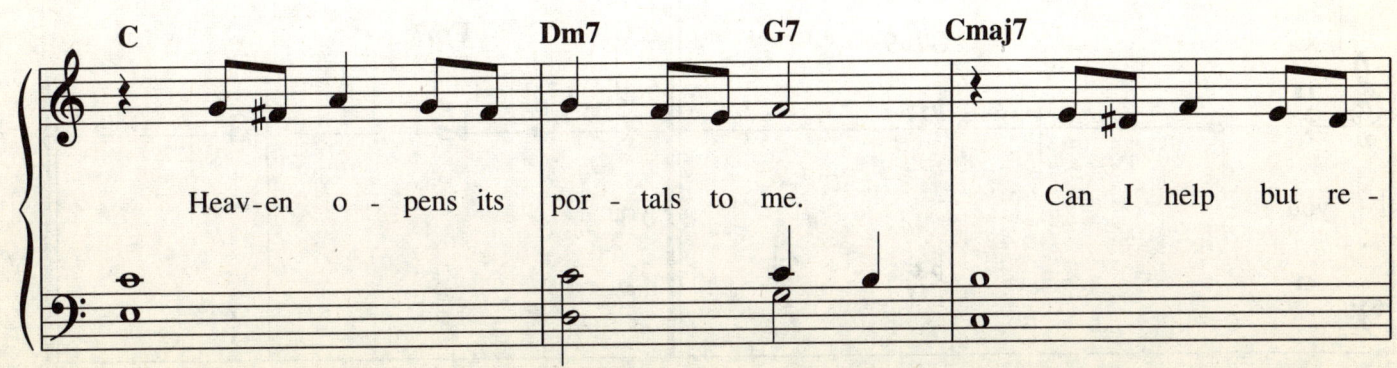

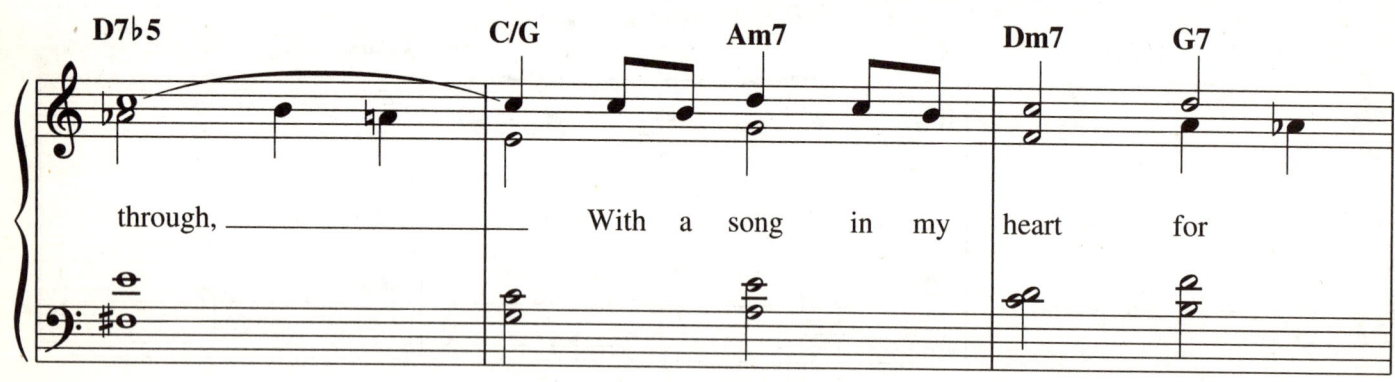
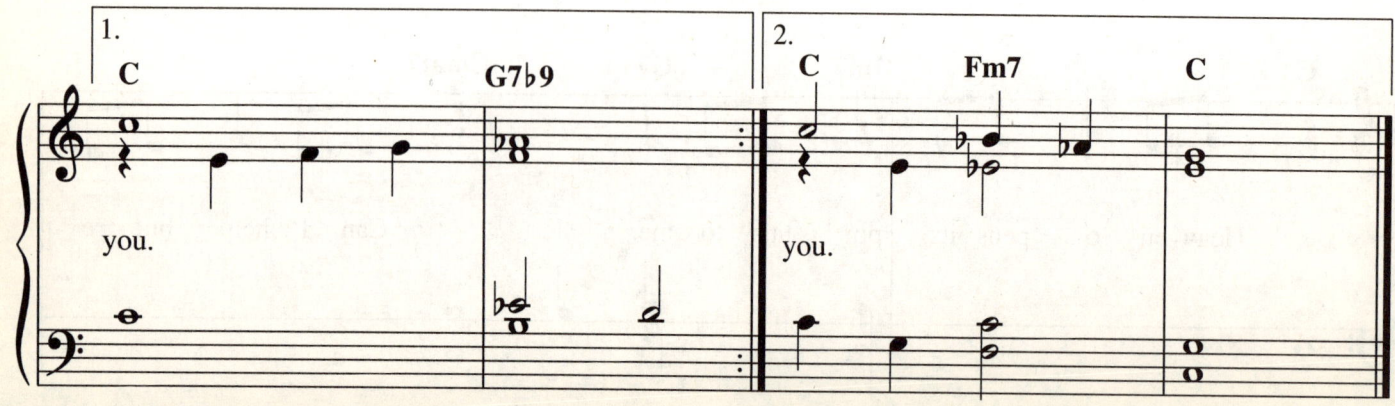

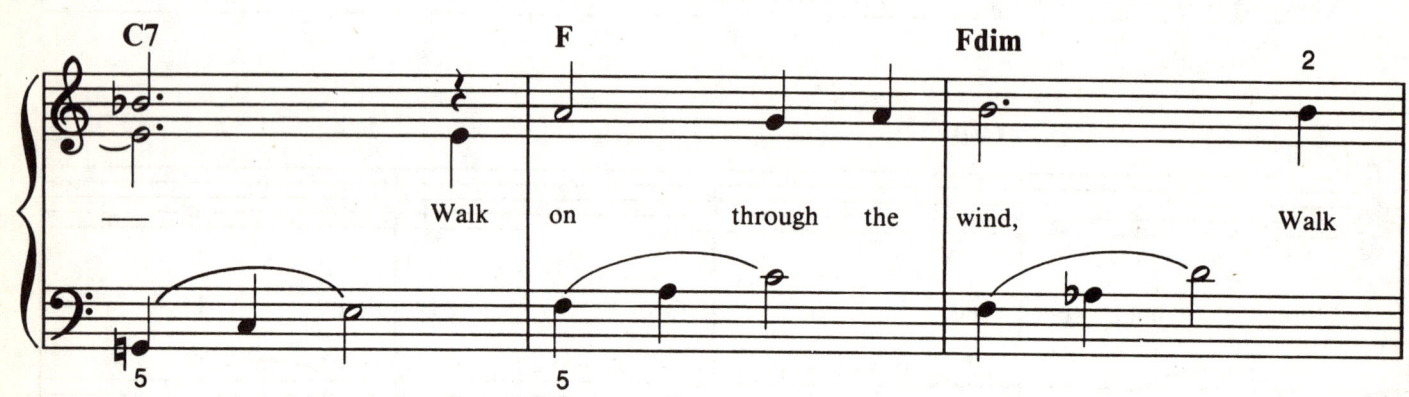
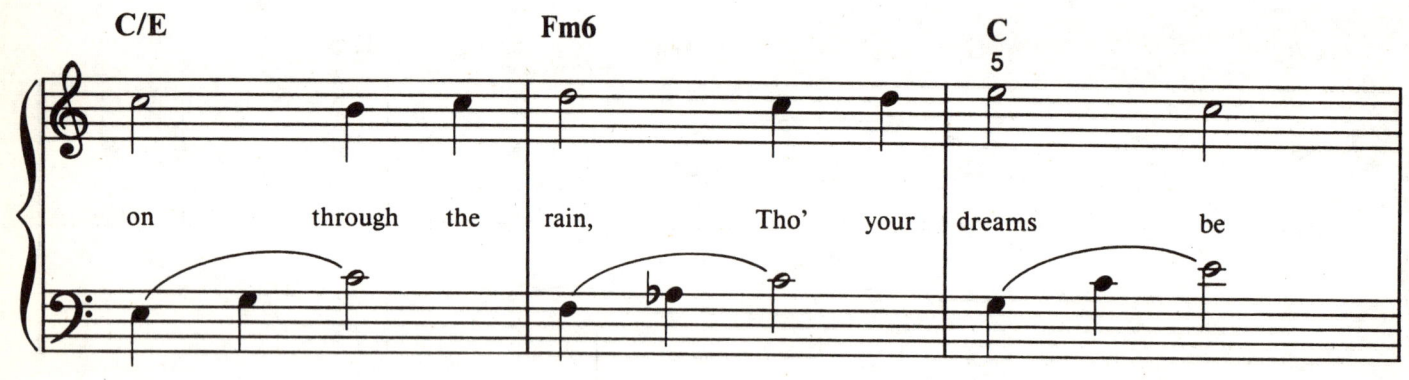
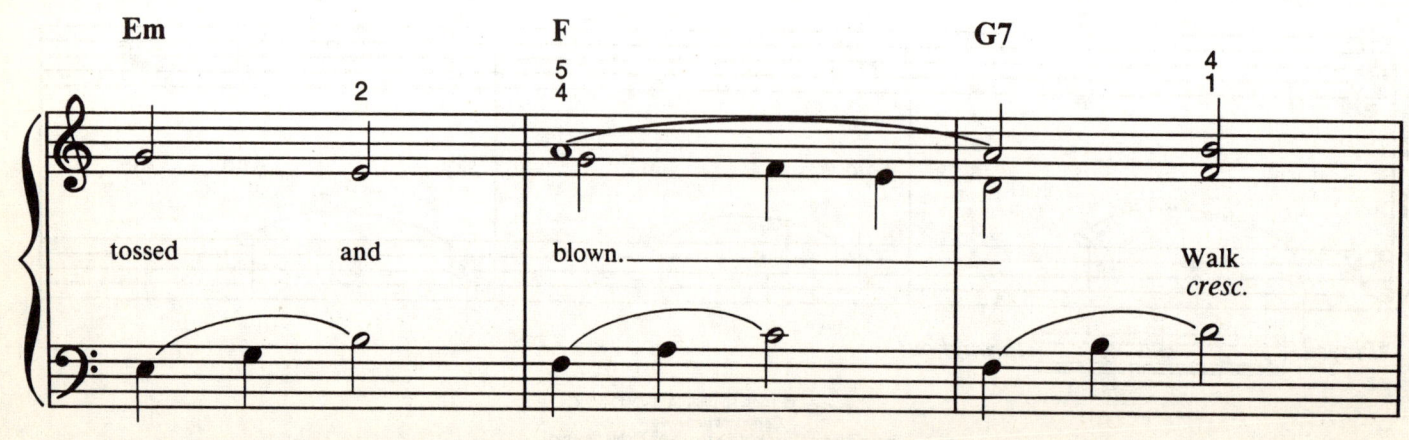

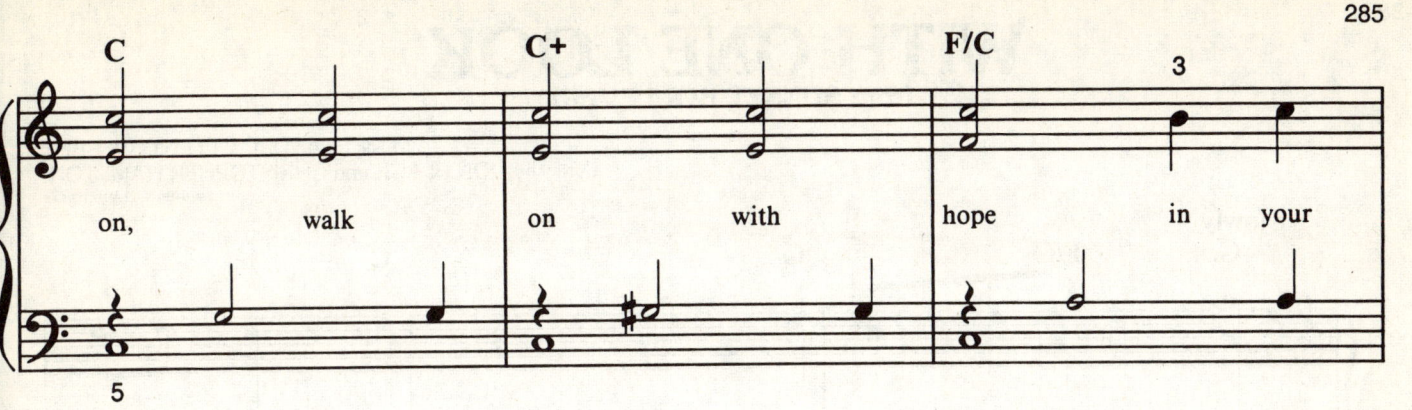
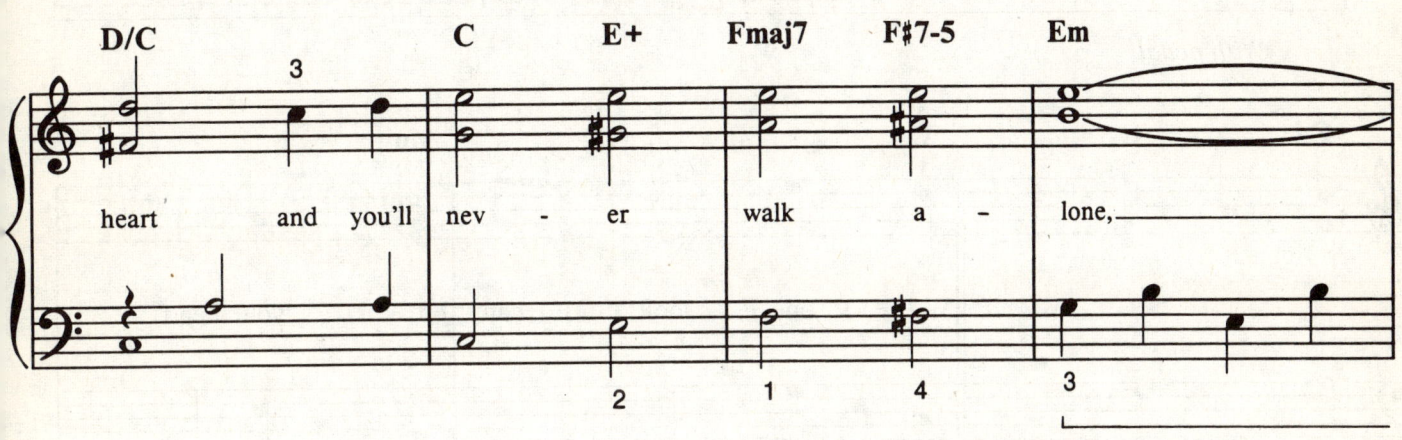
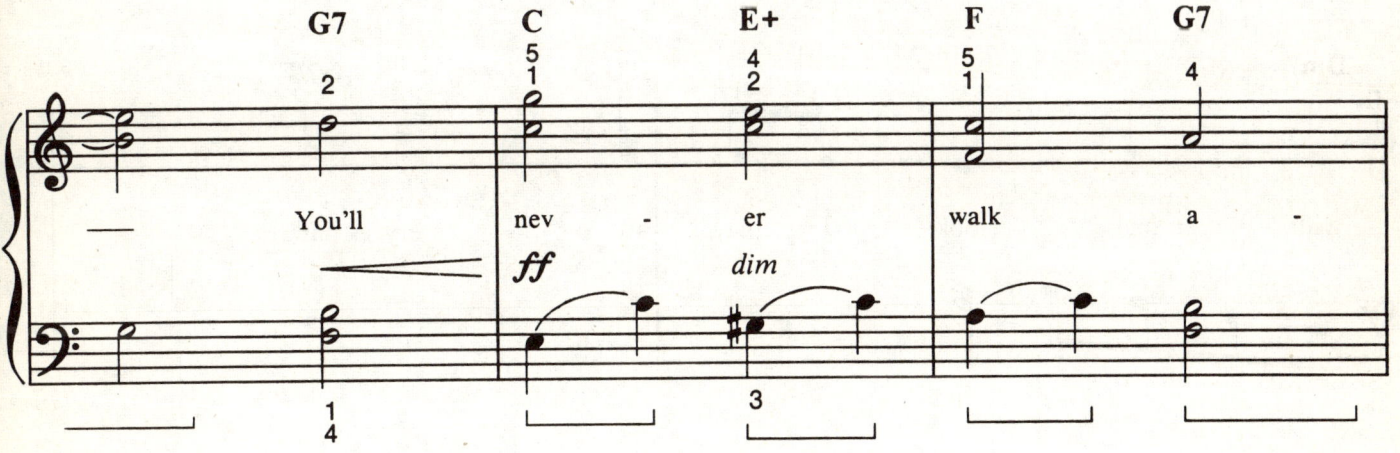

WITH ONE LOOK
from SUNSET BOULEVARD

Music by ANDREW LLOYD WEBBER
Lyrics by DON BLACK and CHRISTOPHER HAMPTON,
with contributions by AMY POWERS

Norma: With one look I can break your heart,

with one look I play ev-ery part.

I can make your sad heart sing, with one

© Copyright 1993 The Really Useful Group Ltd.
International Copyright Secured   All Rights Reserved

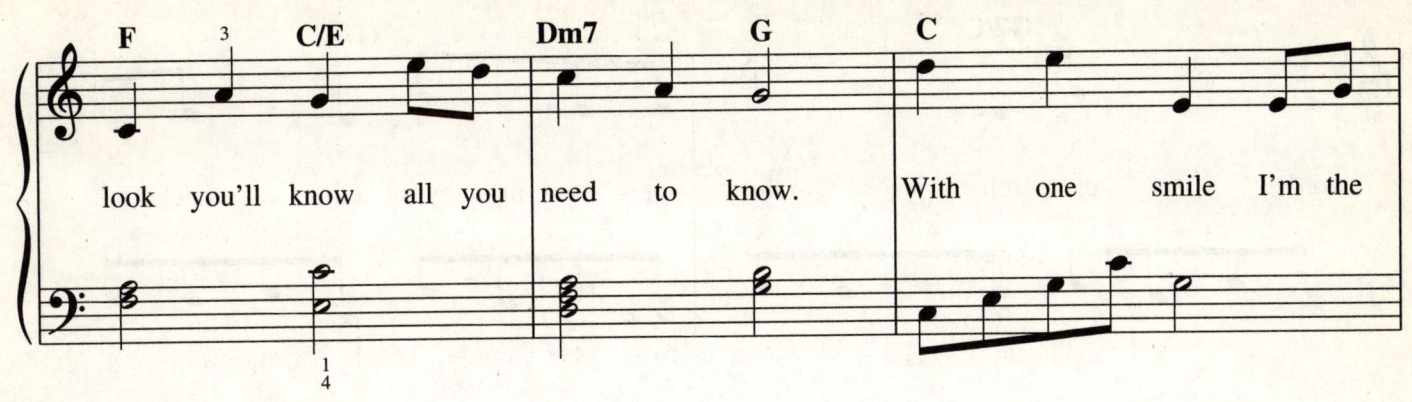
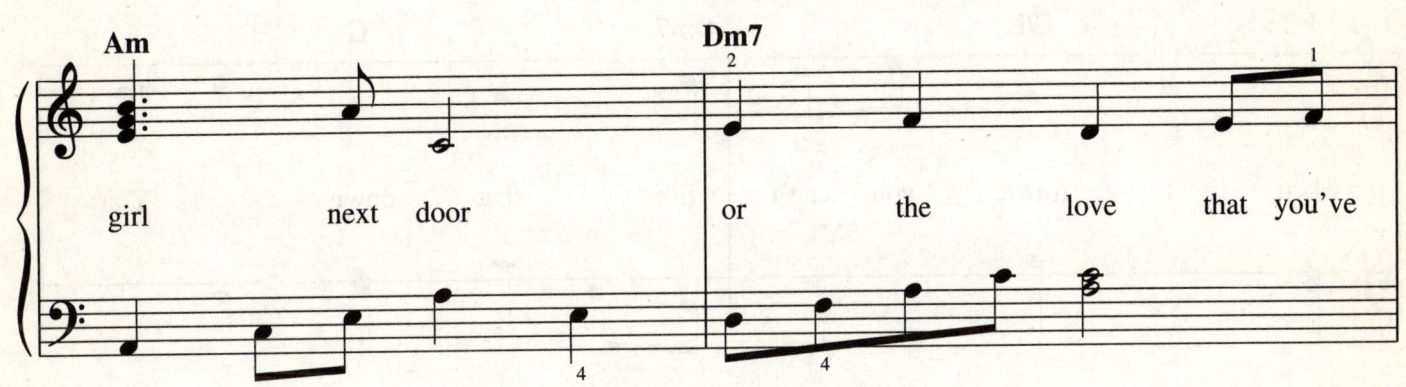
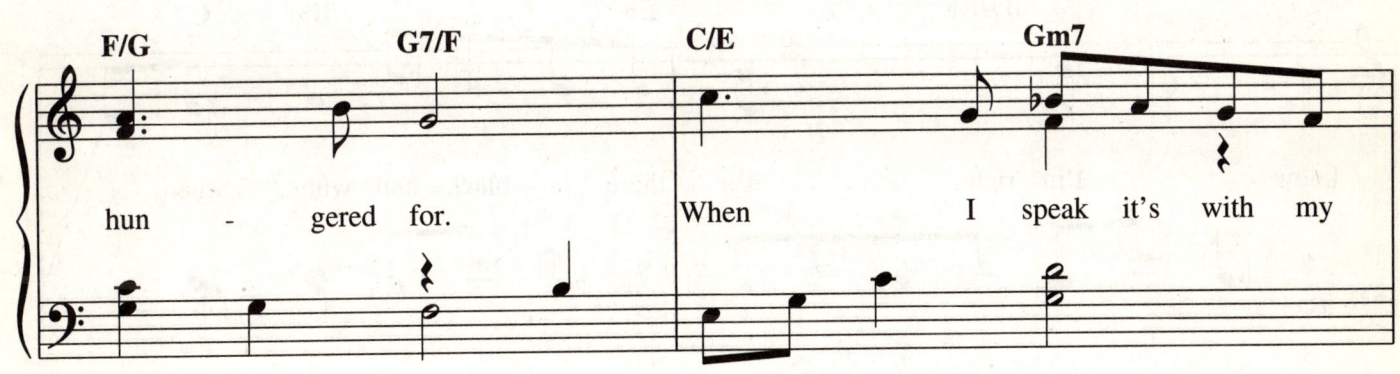

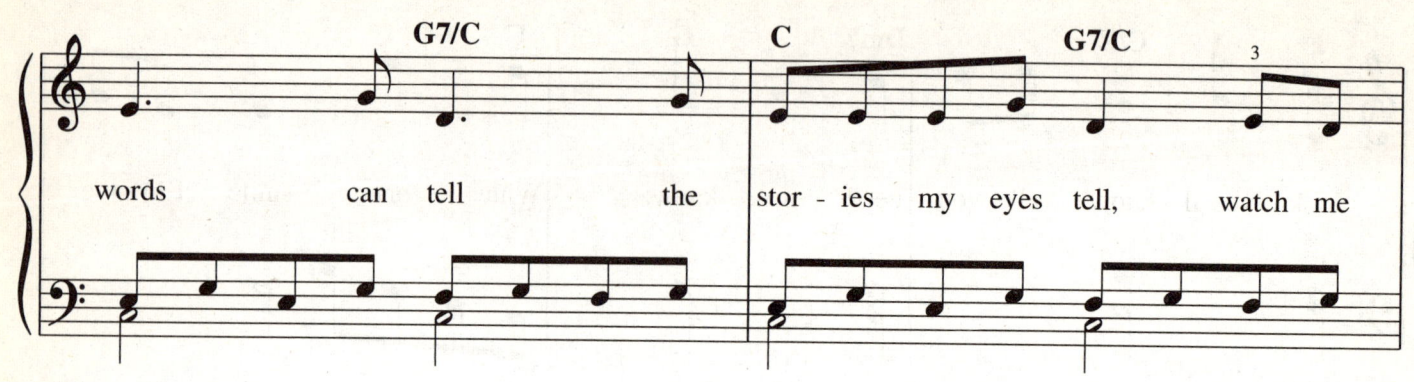

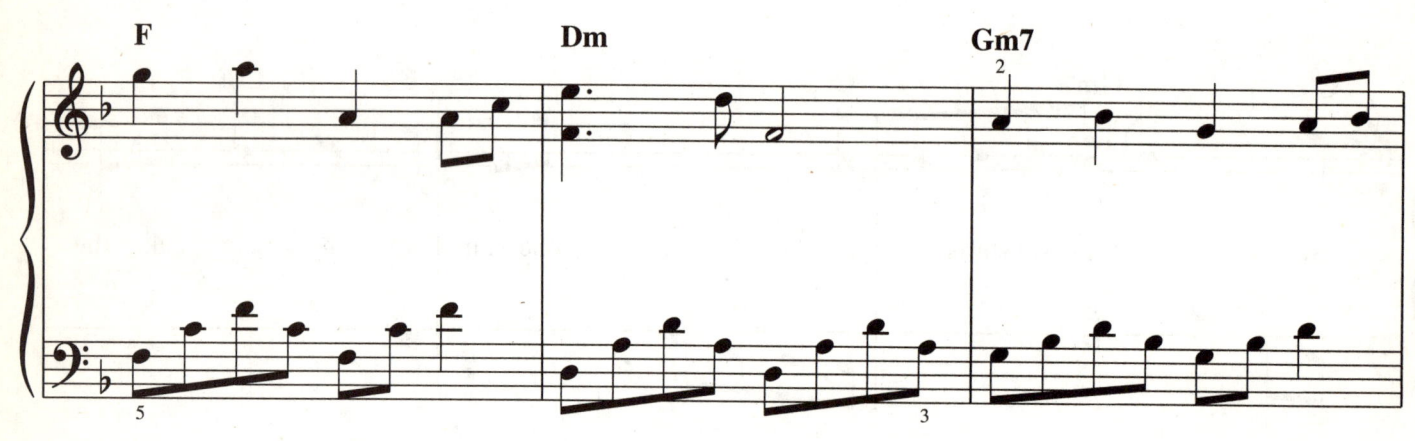
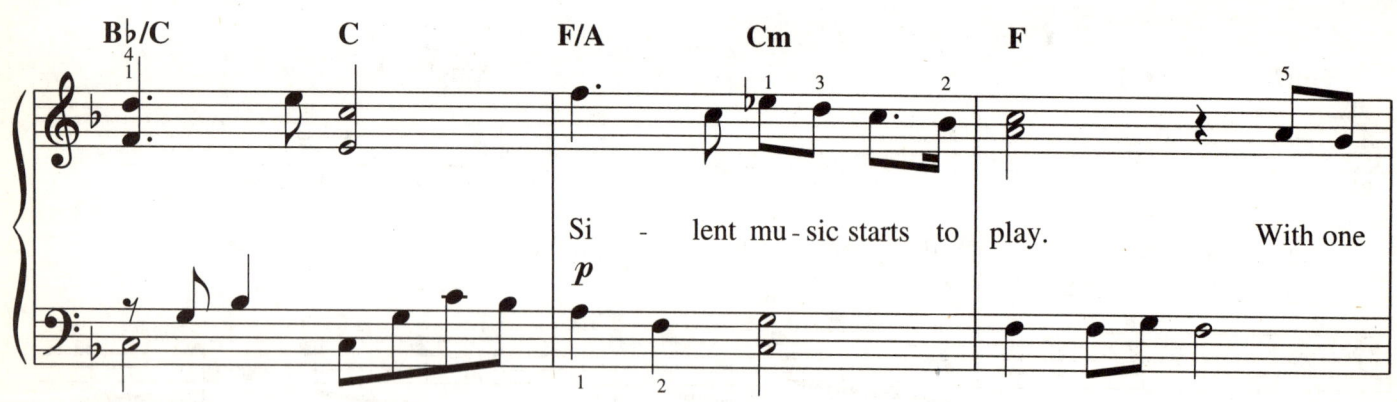
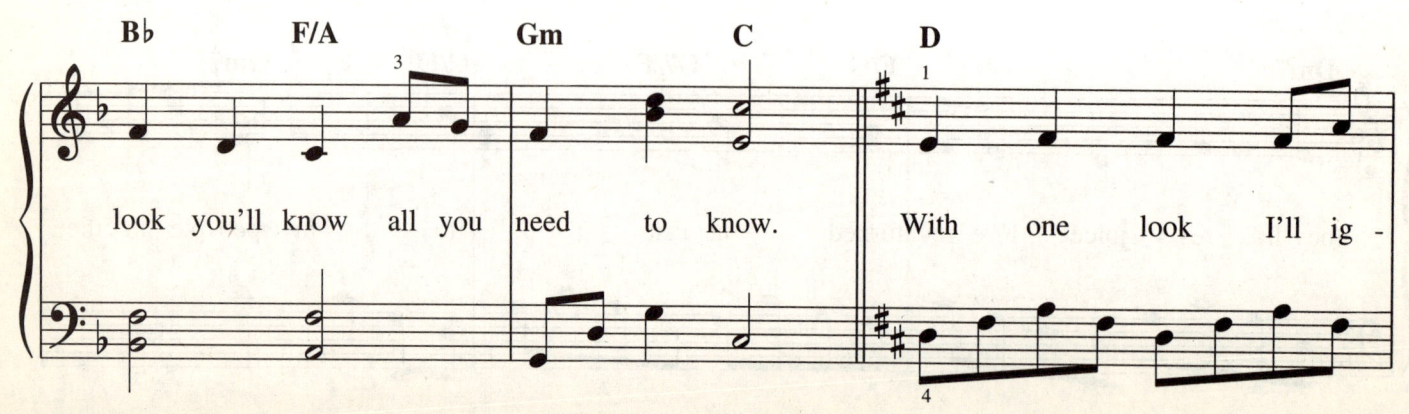

WITHOUT YOU
from RENT

Words and Music by
JONATHAN LARSON

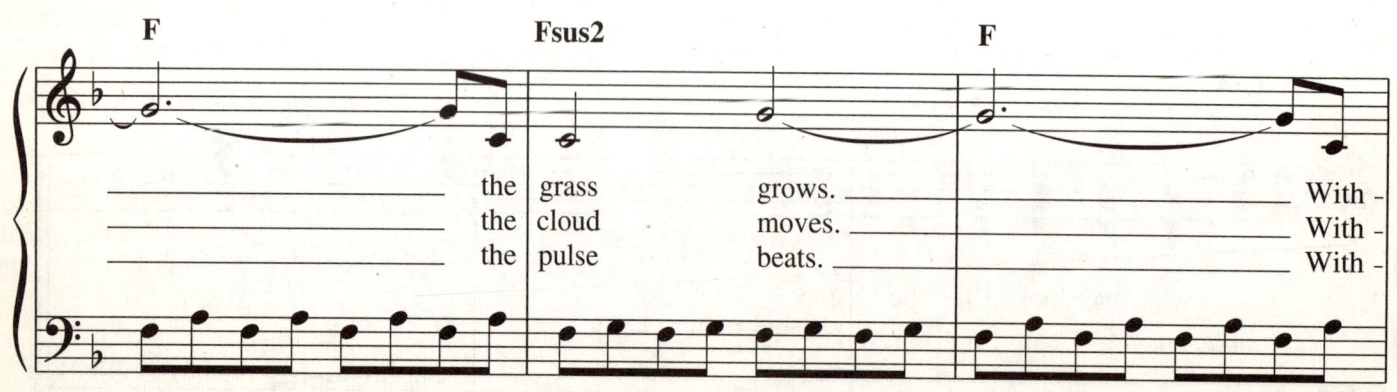

© 1996 FINSTER & LUCY MUSIC LTD. CO.
All Rights Controlled and Administered by EMI APRIL MUSIC INC.
All Rights Reserved   International Copyright Secured   Used by Permission

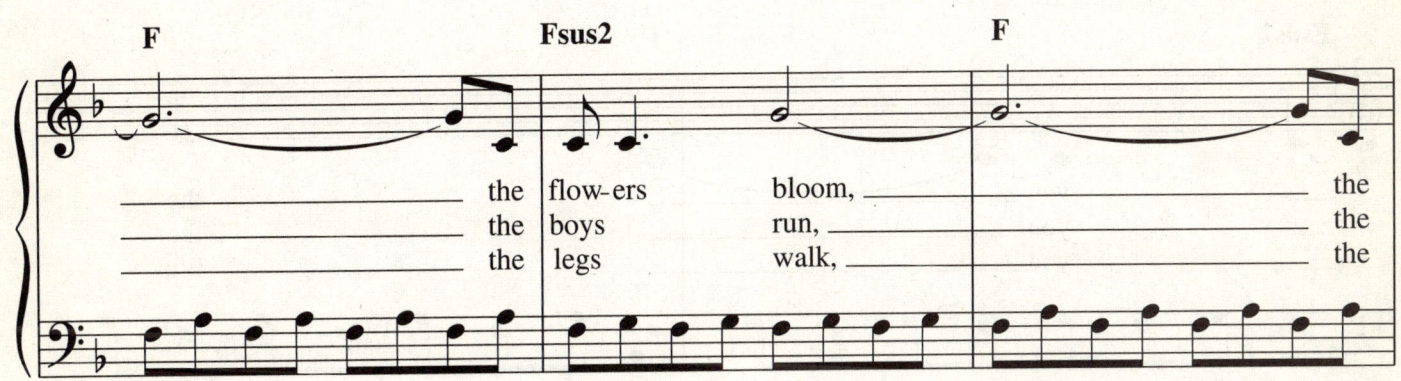

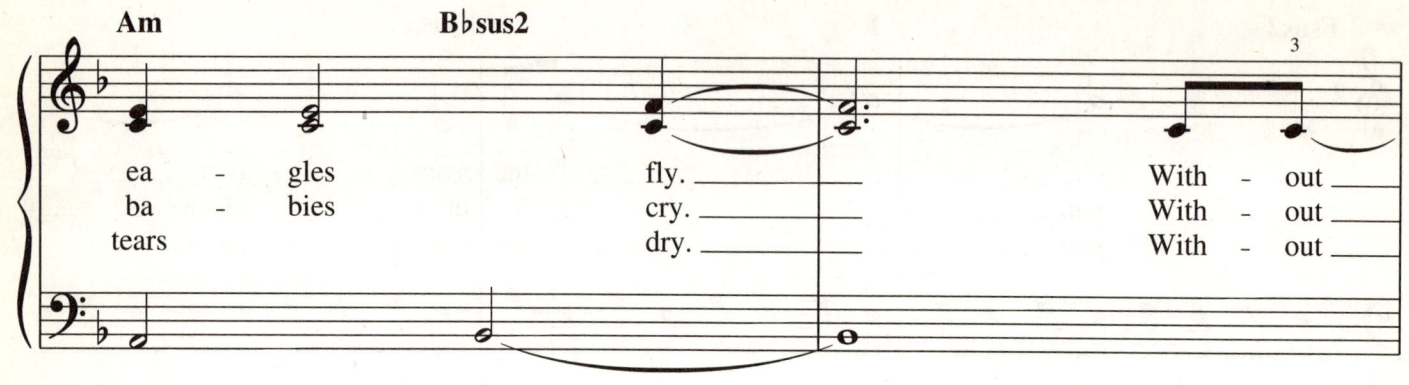

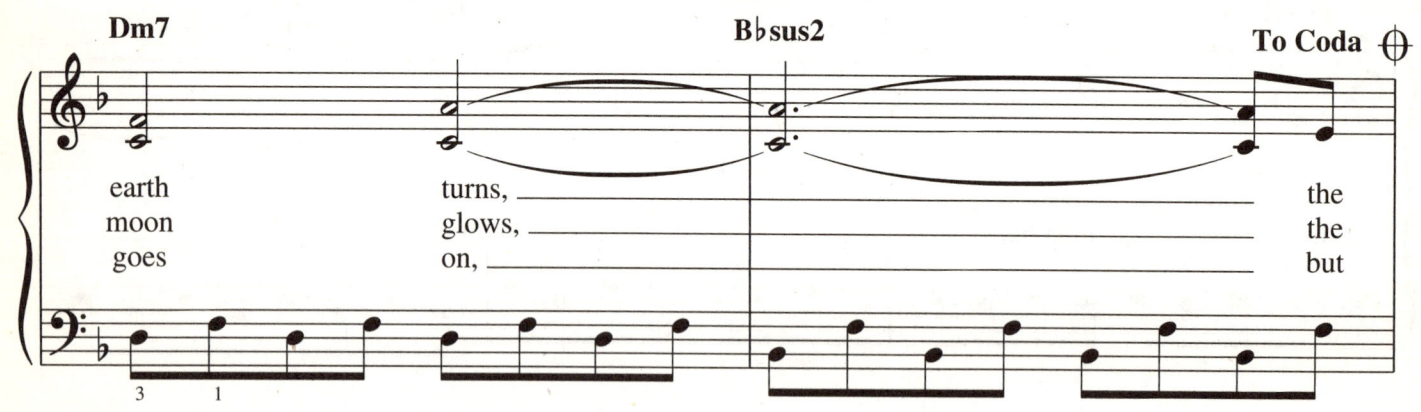
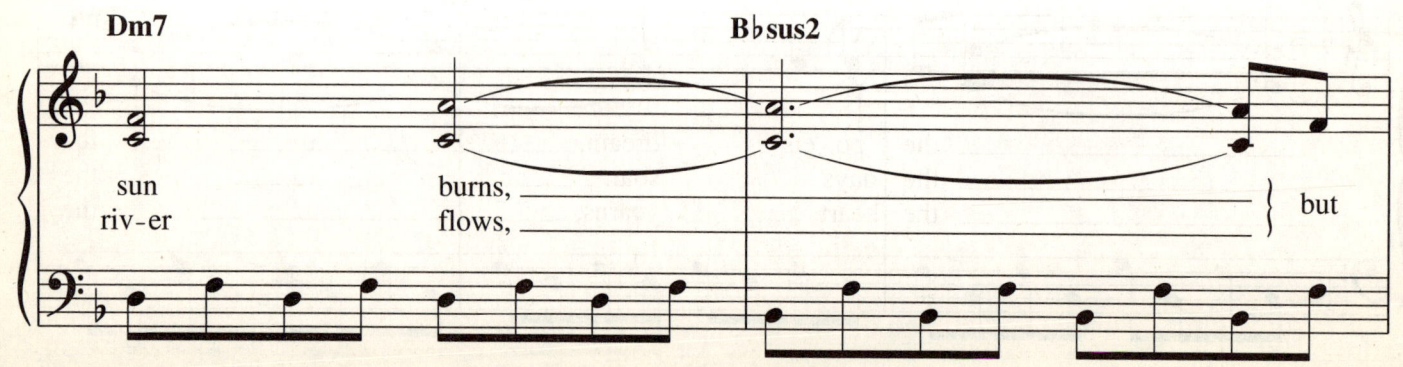

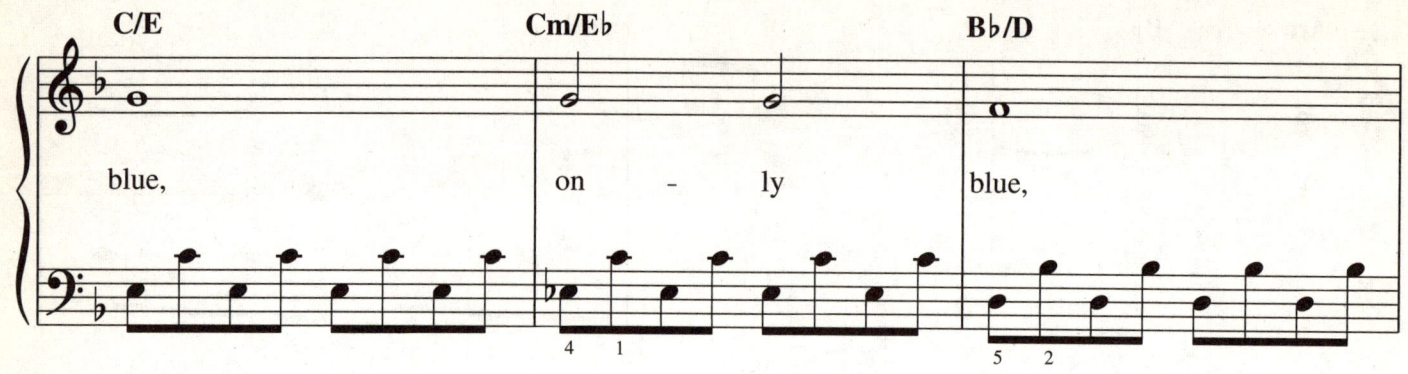

297

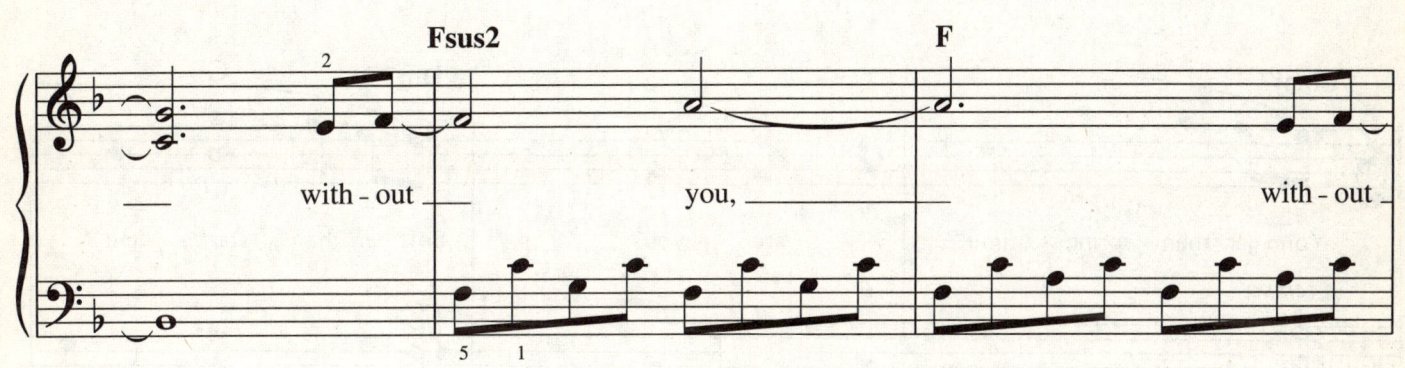

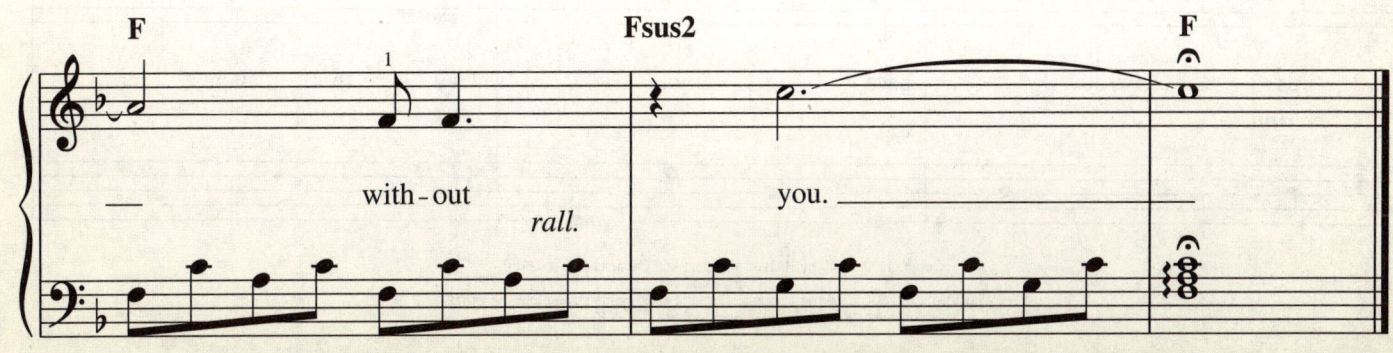

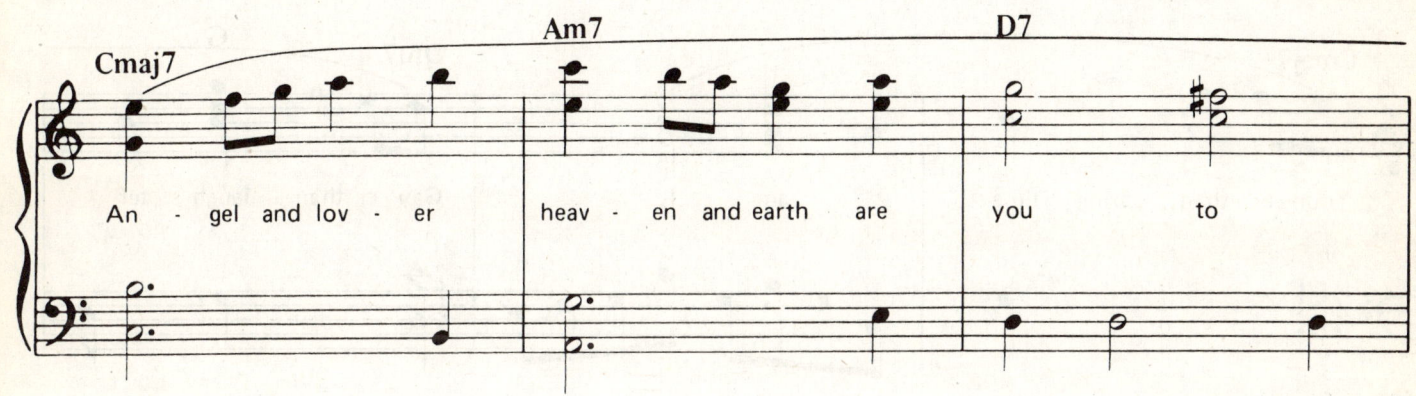
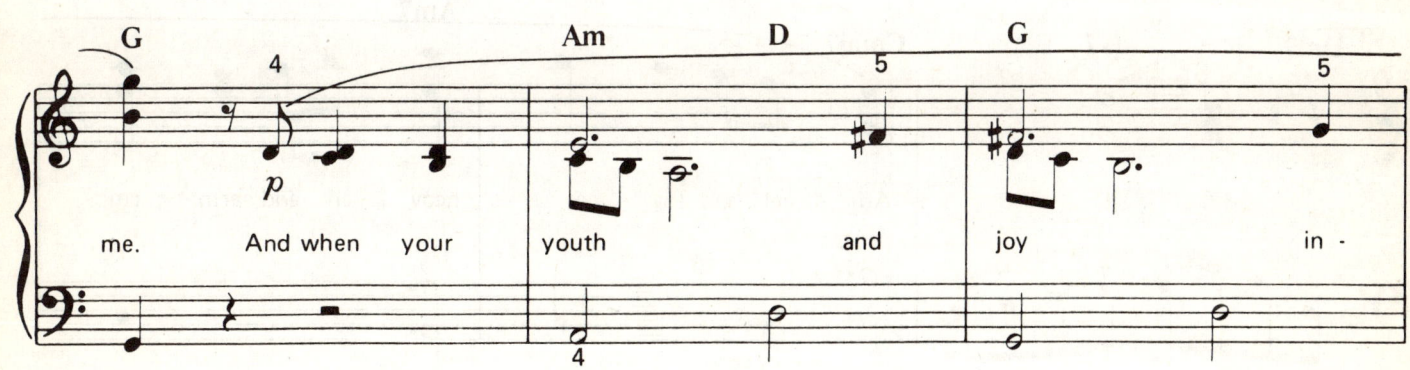

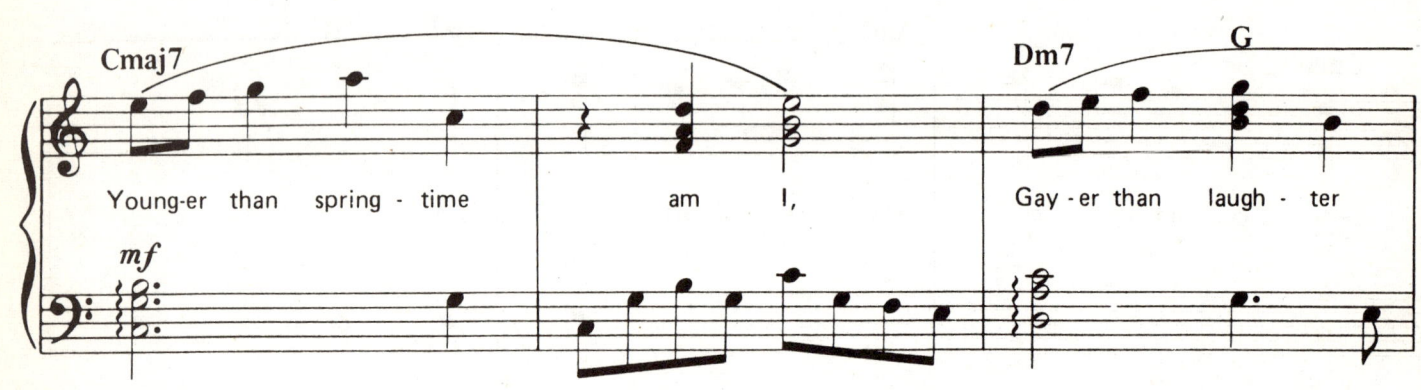
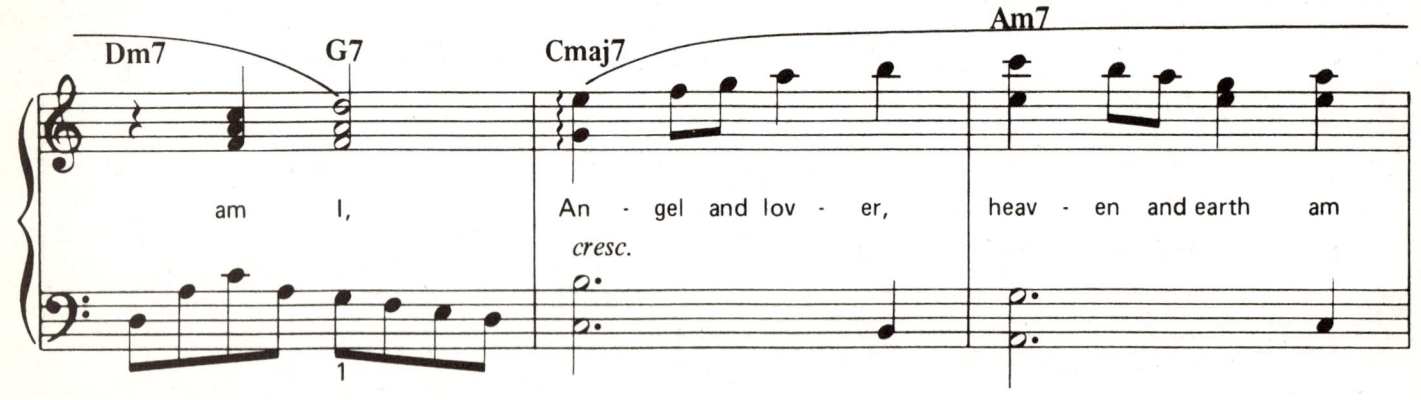

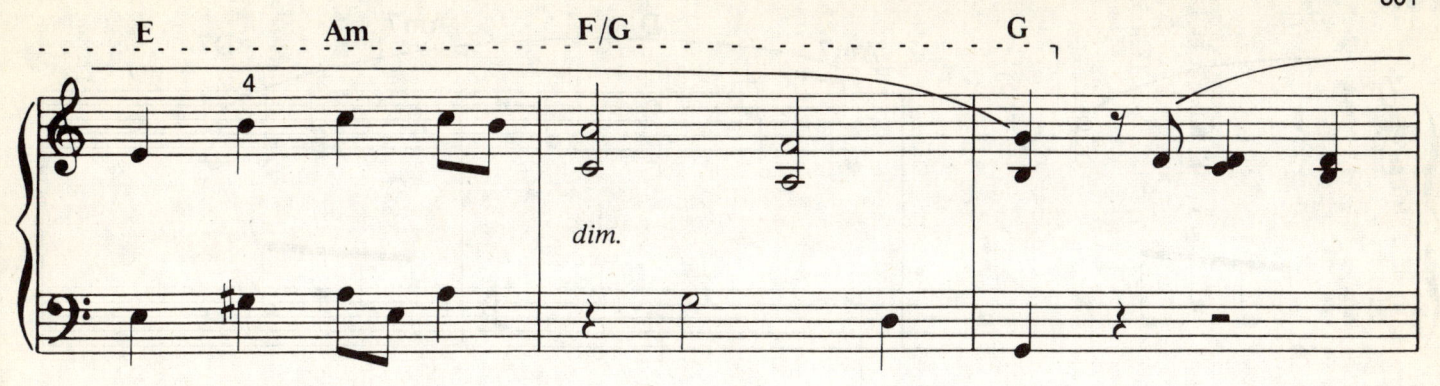

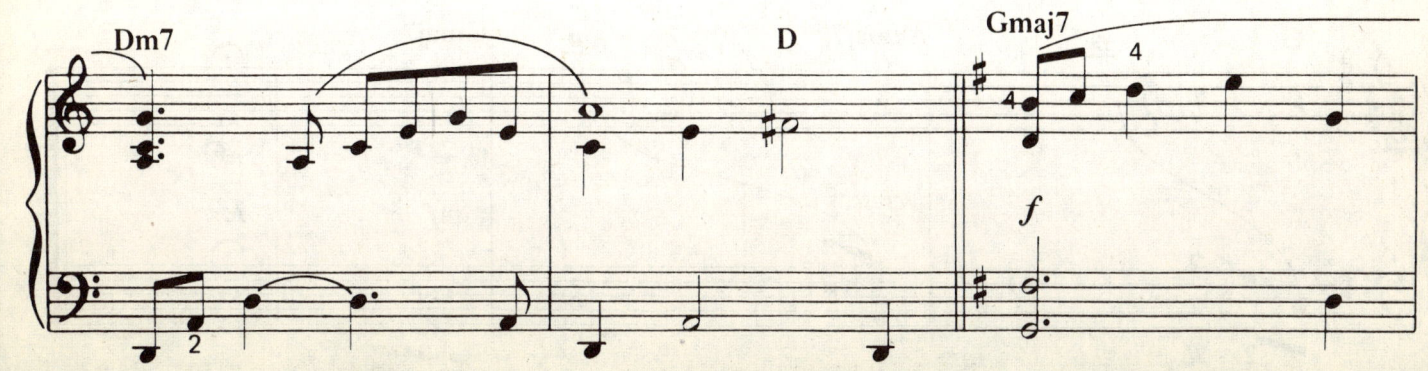

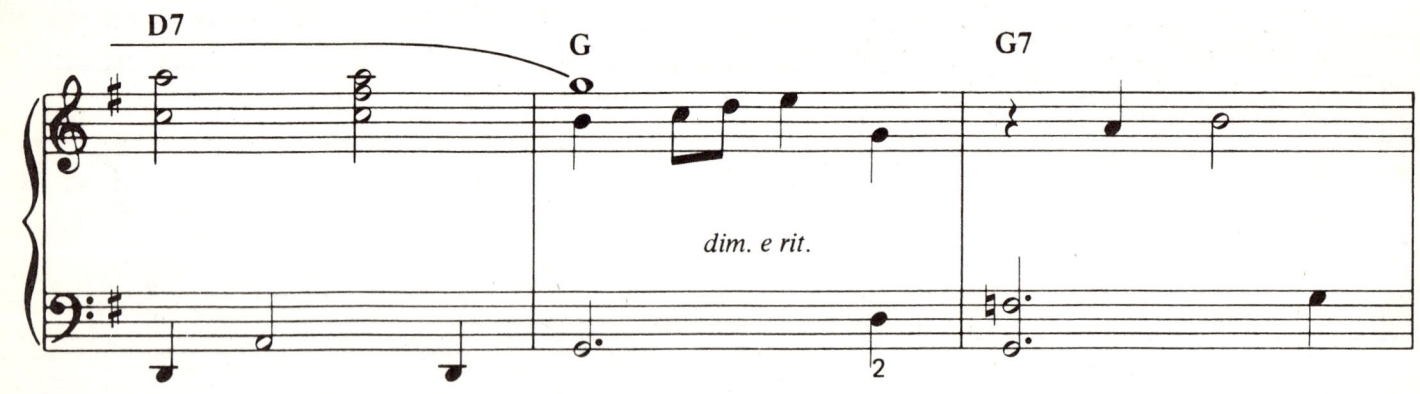